With thanks for giving me
the chance to see Tito's country.

Love,

Barbara.

Summer 1956.

By VLADIMIR DEDIJER

TITO

SIMON AND SCHUSTER, NEW YORK

1953

Contents

Contents

vii

"Serious things are involved . . ."

MY BOOK is about Tito, and about Yugoslavia. To the extent that it has been possible, I have told it in Tito's own words, for he has spoken often to me of his youth in his native village, of his years as a wandering mechanic in the workshops of Europe, of his struggles as a socialist for the rights of workers, of hunger strikes and of the many years he spent in different jails. I have filled the gaps from the words of his friends and associates, and from documents. And, of course, I have called upon my own recollections of events, for I have been, and remain, one who was a member of the movement which Tito leads.

I have known him personally for fourteen years, in some of the most crucial periods of his life and work: in the years before the Second World War, under the terror of the Karageorgevich dynasty, when he reorganized and prepared the Communist Party of Yugoslavia for the coming decisive events, I knew him those strenuous days when he used to hide for a few days in my home from the persecution of the police. I was with him all through the Second World War, when he started the war of liberation against Hitler and Mussolini.

I was with him on the most critical day of that war, in 1943, when the German High Command had decided to destroy us at any cost. An extensive plan had been drawn up, and in mid-May six German and five Italian divisions and one Bulgarian regiment surrounded our main forces. For our part, we had three divisions, including Supreme Headquarters on the border of Montenegro and Bosnia, in mountainous country carved by deep canyons.

I

Tito

The fighting was fearful. The Germans held their positions while we fought to get out, suffering incredible losses. Tito had selected the north for our break-through. Our brigades stormed through the first positions, then the enemy threw reinforcements into the threatened point. To succeed in our undertaking it was necessary to move more quickly in the mountainous country: Tito ordered all heavy armaments to be buried. Hunger was fierce. We ate our horses. The day of the decisive break-through was approaching.

In the evening of the 8th of June, 1943, Supreme Headquarters set out up Mount Milinklada with its escort battalion of only two hundred men. The German positions were only two and a half miles away. As we neared them, the Germans opened fire from their mountain artillery. One shell hit our column, killing a comrade. Night was falling; we were moving through a forest and dared not have lights because the German positions were near. It had begun to rain. I was following Moša Pijade, an old Communist who had spent fourteen years in prison, and had been released just before war broke out. It had become pitch dark. At one point we lost contact with our column. We wandered through the forest. We dared not call. The Germans were near at hand. We lay on the ground trying to find the impressions of horses' hoofs in the wet grass and mud, in the hope that thus we might find our comrades.

That night the Supreme Headquarters column split up. Tito reached the summit of Milinklada with a squad. In the early dawn the Germans began to shell our position. Stukas, Heinkels, and even Fieseler-Storch reconnaissance planes swooped down upon the mountain which is about a mile and a quarter long and about five hundred yards wide.

I was with Moša Pijade at the foot of the mountain when the German aircraft arrived. They dropped small ten- and twenty-kilogram bombs for living targets. Wave after wave came while the German infantry worked up to our positions. We were waiting for Tito to descend. But he did not come. I was waiting for my wife Olga, who had joined the Partisans and being a doctor headed the surgical team of the Second Division. She too was at the top near Tito with her unit.

About noon a courier came running to us with a letter.

Tito

"Tito is wounded. . . . The Germans are advancing. Send the escort battalion urgently."

We in the valley set off uphill. Suddenly a girl with tangled hair and flushed face shouted through the wood:

"Comrade Vlado, Olga is calling you to carry her out. She has been seriously wounded."

It was nurse Ruška from Olga's unit. In a few words she told me what had happened. A bomb had hit them and Olga's shoulder had been torn away.

I hurried uphill. The wounded were coming down the slope in masses. The bombers appeared again. The Stukas were diving almost to the very tips of the huge beech trees and dropping heavy bombs. Ruška and a Bosnian fighter and I threw ourselves to the earth just as the first bomb exploded. The stench of powder suffocated us, daylight had turned into night. When the smoke cleared a little I noticed the Bosnian, a youth with large dark eyes, lying near me. Both his legs had been cut off. A stream of blood was gushing out and carrying away young green beech leaves which the explosion had torn from the branches. We couldn't help him. He was dying; he waved to me and whispered: "Long live Stalin!"

I hurried uphill. Beneath an oak, about twenty yards uphill sat Olga. Blood was flowing through the bandages that covered her whole shoulder. She looked at me with her deep dark eyes and tried to smile.

"Don't be afraid, but the wound is serious."

A courier arrived and said that all German attacks had been repulsed and Tito was coming down. I found him down in the valley. His arm was bandaged. He stopped next to Olga and me while I was giving her spoonfuls of soup and asked:

"How are you, Olga? Are you badly hurt?"

It was getting dark. Our column fell in and we set off again. Olga was on horseback. I helped her stay erect. Hand grenades were crashing, German machine guns chattering in the growing darkness. The enemy threw reinforcements into the firing line. For nine days there was ceaseless fighting night and day. The enemy battalions and some of ours were intermingled so that the Germans occasionally opened fire on their own units. Finally we got through, but we had

3

left the flower of our army in the field. There were numberless
casualties. There was no time for operations. Tito was bandaged only
once. I found him one night dictating a radiogram to Moscow about
the fighting. He was lying near a tree in a fever. Nor could my wife
be operated upon, because of the ceaseless fighting. Through heavy
rainfall, partly on horseback, partly on foot, she endured for nine
days. On the ninth day gas gangrene set in. She had to be operated
on urgently in a hut. Her arm was amputated while German bullets
struck the wooden walls.

When she regained consciousness, she said:

"Don't worry. I can't be a surgeon any more, but I'll be a children's doctor."

Four comrades carried her on a stretcher to her Divisional Headquarters. I had gone into Headquarters for a moment when machine
guns and mortars opened up. I was rushing to the place where Olga
was lying when suddenly I felt a terrible blow. I flew through the air
and fell headlong into a brook. I tumbled down the ravine, but my
wife was nowhere to be found. The four comrades had taken her to a
mill where she lay the whole night long.

We met again the following day. My head wound was bleeding
and I was in fever. We were climbing Mount Romania. A doctor,
a friend of Olga's, wanted to give her a shot of camphor to ease her
pain.

"Stanojka, don't waste that precious drug," Olga said. "Keep it
to save comrades' lives!"

They put down the stretcher to rest awhile. Olga called me:

"Take care of Milica. See that she is brought up properly and let
her be an army doctor. . . ."

A few minutes later she breathed her last. It was dark, the wind
was soughing through the giant spruces. We dug a grave for Olga
with knives and our bare hands because we had no spades; the Germans were already in the village down below where we could have
borrowed them.

Partisan Laza, a miner, threw earth out of the grave with his hands.

"Vlado, we're down to the rock," he said.

We laid my wife in the shallow grave, covered her with turf and
then made a mound of stone. We removed our caps; a salvo of four

Tito

shots was fired and Partisan Laza exclaimed: "Long live her memory."

Then we set out through the dark forest to catch up with our units.

That was in June, 1943. I tear my mind away from the memory and it leaps four and a half years, leaps over the last days of the war, the triumph and the sadness of victory, the beginning of the struggle to win Yugoslavia's right to be independent, the right to go its own way. I recall a fateful day in mid-February of 1948.

It had been decided that I should go to Calcutta and attend the Second Congress of the Communist Party of India as the delegate of the Communist Party of Yugoslavia. I was making preparations for this long journey when two days before my departure my telephone rang and Tito's secretary asked whether I was free that evening; Tito wanted to talk to me about my journey.

I walked slowly to 15 Rumunska Street. The officer at the gate admitted me and I trod the familiar winding lane toward Tito's villa. The lane runs for thirty-odd yards through a big garden and is flanked by low, strong trees whose branches meet to make a canopy. For me it is always a pleasure to go through that lane with the creeper-covered walls behind me.

As I entered Tito was working at his desk; he raised his eyes from the report he was reading, and motioned me toward the farther end of the study. He seemed to me to be tired. That surprised me, for he does not usually look tired.

I expected we should begin our talk about my journey when Tito lit a cigarette and sticking it, as is his habit, into his silver-studded pipe-shaped holder, inhaled and crossed his legs. He appeared to be a man who wants to talk to someone about something complex and wishes to hear his reaction. I was quite familiar with his gesture.

All happened in a matter of moments. Although I had known Tito then for fully ten years and been in frequent contact with him, I could still never have guessed what he was going to tell me. I was taken aback when, instead of the expected question about my journey, he said: "Have you seen what has happened in Rumania? They have ordered all my photographs to be removed! Surely you have read it in the reports of the foreign agencies?"

Tito

I was astonished by the seriousness of his voice. I had read these reports, but I was convinced that there was no truth in them.

I have always thought myself awkward when talking to Tito, because I have hardly ever voiced the thought I have prepared in in answer to his question, but simply what first comes off my tongue. So from my lips fell the words: "How is that? Isn't it all the usual falsehood?"

Anguish suddenly overspread his face. Only at that moment did I look at him better and see clearly that his appearance had altered. His face had darkened, and deep worries had lined it. Pouches under his eyes were evidence that he had not slept.

At once it was clear to me that my first impression on entering the study had not been wrong. Tito was tired, dead tired. I immediately understood that something serious was involved, something difficult that troubled him inwardly and left such visible traces on his face.

Crossing his legs again nervously, Tito took a long pull at his cigarette and, as if he had not heard my confused question, continued: "You are a lucky man. You don't know anything yet. Those were wonderful times during the war, during the Fifth Offensive, when we were surrounded by the Germans on all sides. We knew then we had been left to fend for ourselves, and we fought our way out as best we could. But now . . . when all the conditions are there to help us, the Russians are hindering us."

I was tongue-tied. Thoughts swarmed like lightning and clashed in my brain, causing almost physical pain. I recalled a conversation I had had a few days back with Kalinin, the new VOKS (the Soviet organization for cultural relations with foreign countries) representative in Belgrade. He told me that the Yugoslavs did not love the Soviet Union, that Russian was studied little, that there were more courses in English and French, that things were quite different in Bulgaria, where the Society for Friendship with the Soviet Union had almost a million members. I had not taken Kalinin's words seriously, because it did not enter my head that this little Soviet clerk could lecture Yugoslavia. I laughed and said: "It is quite easy to understand how it is in Bulgaria. They did not manage to love the Soviet Union during the war, when it was a matter of to be or not to be, and now they want to make up for it."

6

Tito

But what Tito had just told me meant that this zealous clerk, recently come from Moscow, was speaking according to instructions received from above. I recalled his boast that Zhdanov personally had sent him to Yugoslavia. I connected all this with what Tito was telling me at this moment, so, it was not by chance. This meant a conflict with the Soviet Union, a conflict with Stalin. But surely, that was impossible! There must be some misunderstanding. Was there anyone in this country who did not love the Soviet Union? How could we possibly quarrel with Stalin? It was as if someone had said we had quarreled among ourselves. All these thoughts sped through my brain.

Tito noticed the impression his words had made on me. I was gradually realizing the import of the lines on his face and that tired expression. A fateful decision was pending, perhaps the most fateful decision in our latter-day history. It was a matter not only of individuals but of the future of Yugoslavia, of her whole people. What would happen if this country broke with the Soviet Union? Our entire foreign policy, everything was linked with the Soviet Union. All our economic plans, all our capital goods agreements, had been concluded with the Soviets. Where should we be if we had to break with them? I was roused from these thoughts by Tito's voice.

"We shall see what happens next," he said. "Kardelj, Djilas and Bakarić are in Moscow."

"Aren't they there to discuss military aid and capital goods for our industry?"

"No, not only that. Much more serious things are involved. We expect them back at any moment."

That was all. We went on to talk about India, and then I took leave of him.

Today I realize that Tito, that day, was making his decision. Before him lay two roads, and on only one of them could he travel. He had fought with Stalin, he had looked to Stalin for support, the Soviet Union had been his beacon. The lines of his face were the outward sign of a soul in torment.

And the days that followed, as I made my way to India and back, I, too, faced the same decision. In time every Yugoslav faced it. It was the most crucial decision to be made. And it was made. It did not mean only the right for Yugoslavia *to be independent*, it meant

7

also the right of every people *to go to progress in its own way*. It meant a red rag before Stalin's eyes. The heart of his fury, of his rage against Yugoslavia, is a simple fact. Tito is the conscience of Stalin, the conscience Stalin had lost.

As this momentous struggle goes on, Yugoslavia is in the center of world attention. Books are being written about it and about Tito, true and false, well-intentioned and otherwise.

I thought it only right that a Yugoslav should also present Tito to world public opinion, as a Yugoslav sees him. I do not think of this as a final biography of Tito, but only as a contribution to his biography. In fifty or a hundred years, when everything shines in all its glory, and baseness is seen in its true light; when the scales of history have weighed not what men wished to do but what they really did; when someone from a future generation undertakes to write of our times and the people who lived in them, I hope he will find here something valuable about Yugoslavia and her people, and, above all, about Tito.

It is my wish to present Tito as he is, with all his human desires and passions, as an ordinary man whose character is marked by some unusually developed features through which he plays the part he is playing today.

Some will say that I have written this biography with bias, with passion, with hatred or love. This I shall not deny: I love my country and I love Tito. I am putting forward our views. I record matters as we see them. And I think it right that the views of the people from the small land of Yugoslavia, exposed to pressure as perhaps no country of its size has ever been exposed, should be heard and made known.

CHAPTER I

1900:

"My childhood was difficult . . ."

IN THE summer of 1942, after two months of hard fighting in the rocky mountains of Montenegro, the Partisans set out on their 185-mile march through territory held by the Italians and Germans, toward western Bosnia.

Dusk was descending when we reached the foothills of Zelengora. Nature's apparel had suddenly changed. Instead of bare rock, we were now passing through meadows of narcissus and forests of beech. A Partisan rarely has time to heed the countryside through which he passes, but now the change was so abrupt and the picture so impressive that we began to chatter about our new surroundings. As his horse stepped wearily along, Tito said:

"This vegetation means life. The stony region behind us gives the impression of death. This country reminds me of Zagorje, my native land."

We halted at a clearing, where we erected our tents and made fires of beech, the fuel most precious to Partisans because it gives the hottest embers. For supper we each had a pound of meat. We cut it into small pieces, added salt and flavored it with the garlic that grew abundantly nearby, skewered the meat and held it over the hot embers. Then there was singing.

We heard machine-gun fire, so distant it sounded like the whispering of the breeze through the branches. Our shackled horses were grazing not far from the fire, neighing nervously, pricking up their ears as if fearing wolves. Someone threw a thick branch on the fire, and the flame lit Tito's face. His are regular features; his forehead is high, his jaw rather protruding, his cheeks strong, giving his whole

9

countenance a certain sharpness and determination. But his eyes and smile add a tone of tenderness. These two elements, constantly alternating, make it difficult to describe him whenever friends of mine ask me what Tito looks like.

The fire began to die down and so did the singing. Then Tito began to tell us about his Zagorje, which so greatly resembles the regions we were passing through:

I was born Josip Broz in May, 1892, in the Croatian village of Kumrovec, which lies in a district called Zagorje ("the country behind the mountain"). This is in the northwestern part of Croatia, one of the six Yugoslav republics. My village rests in a pretty valley bordered by wooded hills, where the little green Sutla River meanders through woods, past pastel-blue cottages roofed with homemade tiles or shingles green with moss.

Wherever you look in Zagorje you see on the hilltops the walls of some ancient fortress, castle or church, the relics of a history that goes back to Roman times, a history full of war and oppression. On one of the hills above Kumrovec, towering like a giant, is Cesargrad, the jagged ruins of the medieval castle of the Counts Erdödy. They were the masters of my village and the surrounding countryside until the middle of the last century, when feudalism was officially abolished in Croatia. They were cruel, and their serfs were often in revolt.

One winter morning in 1573 the serfs of Cesargrad, wearing the cock's feather as a symbol of revolt, stormed into the castle, beheaded the bailiff, burned one part of the castle, and seized several cannon and some muskets. The leader of the rebels was Matija Gubec but the main body was led by Ilija Gregorić, who crossed the Sutla from Cesargrad to rouse the Slovenian serfs to arms. The rebellion spread through the whole of Zagorje and parts of Slovenia; there were tens of thousands of rebels. But the army of the nobility, under the command of Juraj Drašković, Governor of Croatia and Bishop of Zagreb, was mounted and stronger. The poorly clad serfs suffered from the harsh winter weather. Near my home, Gregorić retreated to Zagorje, and at the crossing of the Sutla between St. Peter and Kumrovec, beneath Cesargrad, he was defeated. The following day saw the decisive battle with the main body of the rebel serfs near Donja Stubica,* where the serfs were led by Matija Gubec. He was captured. The Bishop-Governor Drašković informed the Austrian Emperor Maximilian:

"As an example to others, with Your Holy Majesty's permission, I shall crown Gubec with an iron crown, and a red-hot one at that."

And he did. Ilija Gregorić was captured and taken to Vienna, where he was interrogated and after a year returned to the Erdödys in Zagorje, who beheaded him.

The Zagorje serfs were severely punished. Historians say that the bodies of hundreds of peasants hung from the trees in the villages. It is estimated that during this rebellion between four thousand and six thousand serfs were killed in Zagorje. Baroness Barbara Erdödy, who had escaped the sack of her castle, was particularly cruel to the Cesargrad serfs. Three centuries later, whenever as children we awoke at night our mother threatened that the Black Queen of Cesargrad would take us away if we did not go back to sleep at once.

My forefathers probably were in this famous rebellion, for they had come to Kumrovec from Dalmatia in the middle of the sixteenth century, retreating before the onslaught of the Turkish invaders, and were serfs of the Erdödy family. In later generations there was always at least one of them who became a blacksmith, so that the family came to bear the nickname of Kovači, or Blacksmith. The tradition may later have influenced my own choice of a trade.

My ancestors lived in a patriarchal collective called the "zadruga." The land was tilled in common, and the whole zadruga was under the rule of the "Gospodar" (head man), who was elected. He lived in the biggest house, in which everybody ate together. When a member of the zadruga married, the zadruga would build him a special little room attached to the big house, so that the whole zadruga looked like a beehive. Twice a year the Gospodar paid the dues to the Count of Erdödy and to the Church.

Count Erdödy was required to maintain fifty horsemen and two hundred footmen for the army of the Hapsburg Emperor. Usually these soldiers were recruited from among the village idlers, for the Count wanted to keep the good workers. As far as I have heard tell

---

* In his study in Belgrade, Tito has a picture six yards wide of the battle of Donja Stubica, by the Croatian painter Krsto Hegedušić.

there were no soldiers from the Broz family except one, and he was a sentinel on the Drava bridge during the Hungarian rebellion of 1848.

This same year saw the end of the rule of the Erdödys over our village and the beginning of the decay of the zadruga. The serfs of Kumrovec received the land, but they had to pay for it, and taxes were increased, especially after the wars of 1859 and 1866 which ended to the disadvantage of Austria-Hungary, which ruled Croatia. As the number of members and the cost of maintenance increased, the zadruga began to decline.

Abruptly, the bankers of Budapest and Vienna replaced the Erdödys. The peasants needed land; the firm of Deutsch and Gruenwald bought the entire Erdödy estate, and offered it for sale to the peasants. But the peasants had no money. In a nearby town, Deutsch and Gruenwald established a bank to lend it to them. The rate of interest was nominally 8 per cent, but commissions and extras raised it to 24 per cent.

My grandfather Martin was the last Broz to live in the zadruga. In the sixties he left and began to earn his living carting merchandise from Zagreb to nearby towns. He married Ana Blažičko, a tall strong woman who was extremely proud of coming from a peasant family who had been freemen for more than two centuries. One winter, while Grandfather Martin was driving a cart of salt, a wheel broke and the load crushed the old man. He left a son and six daughters; the son, Franjo, was my father.

At that time an Austrian law was in force in Croatia, according to which the eldest son could no longer be sole heir, but had to share the inheritance equally among all members of the family. This measure was intended to accelerate the disintegration of the peasant holdings. Thus Franjo Broz, reluctant to sell his father's land, was forced into debt so that he might buy off his sisters. Soon the debt was too much for him, and he began to sell one acre after another.

My father was a wiry man with black curly hair and an aquiline nose. The peasants of Kumrovec and the whole of that part of Zagorje used to cross the River Sutla to the wooded Slovene hills where they secretly cut fuel, which they otherwise lacked. Going to the villages across the Sutla, Franjo became acquainted with a sixteen-year-old Slovene girl called Marija, the oldest of fourteen children of Martin Javeršek, who owned sixty-five acres of farm and woodland.

She was a tall, blonde woman, with an attractive face. The wedding took place in January, 1881, when my father was twenty-four. It was a very big wedding and my aunt Ana told me the guests came from Kumrovec on five sleighs.

A hard life awaited my parents. Fifteen acres of land, which dwindled as my father's debts came due, were insufficient to feed the family. When the debts became intolerable, the soft and good-natured Franjo gave it up and took to drinking, and the whole family burden fell upon my mother, an energetic woman, proud and religious.

My father and mother had fifteen children, of whom I was the seventh. In those days, about 80 per cent of the children of Zagorje died before the age of fifteen, most of them in infancy. My parents were only a little more fortunate than most. Of their fifteen children, seven survived.* When I was ten I fell ill with diphtheria, one of the commonest scourges of our countryside, which had already killed one of my sisters, but I recovered with no bad effects.

Our family lived in house No. 8 at Kumrovec, built almost a century ago, solid, with big windows. We shared the house with a cousin. The hall was used by both families; on either side of the hall were two rooms. An open-hearth kitchen, where there was always a stock of firewood, was also shared.

My childhood was difficult. There were many children in the family and it was no easy matter to look after them. Often there was not enough bread, and my mother was driven to lock the larder while we children received what she considered she could give us, and not what we could eat. In January my father had to buy corn-meal bread because we could not afford wheat. We children often

---

* One of Tito's brothers, Dragutin-Karlo, died in Kumrovec in 1932. Of Tito's five brothers and sisters still living, four are in Yugoslavia; his eldest brother, Martin, now lives in Hungary as a retired railway worker. One brother, Štefan, born in 1893, is a peasant in the village of Bratina, Croatia. A sister, Matilda, born in 1896, is married to a peasant Alojzije Oslaković and lives in the village of Kranjica in Croatia. She has eight children. One brother, Vjekoslav-Slavko, born in 1898, is a janitor in Zagreb. The younger sister, Tereza-Rezika, born in 1902, lives in the town of Samobor, Croatia, with her husband Dragutin Ferjanić, a shoemaker.

took advantage of the visit of relatives to beg a slice of bread more than the ration we had eaten. My mother, a proud woman, would not refuse us before relatives. But after they went there was scolding and even an occasional whipping.

One feast-day our parents went somewhere for a visit. We were hungry. Up in the garret hung a smoked pig's head which we were keeping for the New Year. My brothers and sisters were crying, so I brought the head down and dropped it into a pan of boiling water. I added a bit of flour and let it cook for an hour or two. What a feast we had! But the meal was so greasy that we all became sick. When my mother returned we were silent except for an occasional groan. She took pity on us, and that time we got off without a hiding.

Then came the "lukno," a feudal custom that still survived at Kumrovec in my childhood. After Christmas, for the New Year, friars from Klanjec would appear in every village carrying a cross and followed by a sexton with a sack. A friar would chalk the words "Anno Domini . . ." on the door, thus wishing us a happy New Year, and the host would have to give him a few pounds of corn, a bunch of golden flax or two forinths, which in those days meant two days' wages. You can imagine how we children felt as we stood by, hungry as usual, and watched the sexton pour our corn into his sack.

I remember very well how in my childhood the Hungarian soldiers once entered our village. In 1903 the people in Croatia revolted against the fiscal system which helped Hungary plunder Croatia, and against Hungarian control over Croatian railways. In our country there were thirty-six thousand railwaymen, all Hungarians, and if a Croat went to a station to buy a ticket, he was compelled to ask for it in Hungarian, or be refused. At a nearby village in Zagorje, peasants removed the Hungarian flag from the station. The police opened fire, killing one and wounding some ten others. Incidents followed throughout Croatia, in which three thousand people were arrested and twenty-six killed. As punishment, the people had to maintain the Hungarian troops. Four Hungarian soldiers were billeted in our house, and we had to feed them a whole month, out of supplies that were not enough for our own meager needs.

The happiest days of my childhood were spent at the house of my maternal grandfather in Slovenia. He was a small stocky man, who called me Jožek (Joey). I looked after the livestock and carried water for the household. His village was in a wood on the steep slopes above the river, and I played in the wood and carved whistles and made whips for the horses I tended.

This was the job I liked best, for as early as I can remember, one of my greatest pleasures was to be with horses. I was already riding bareback when my head barely reached the horse's belly; my father had a horse called "Putko" that I alone could bridle. I learned in those days that the better you tend a horse, the better he will serve you. During the war I made a point of dismounting from my horse, Lasta (Swallow), when climbing a hill, and I urged my men to save their horses for the plain.

My grandfather Martin was a very witty man and liked practical jokes. From him I inherited the habit which still persists. When my sister was to be married, I, unnoticed by anyone, took her wreath and put it on the chicken-coop. They looked for it all over the house and at last they found it. I no longer remember whether I laughed or not. Let me tell you how the joke was once on me, when I was six. I was on a visit to my grandfather Martin and often went to a spot where some neighbors were burning lime. One day one of them asked me: "Josip, would you like to get married?" I said I would, and he promised to find me a bride. He sent me into the hills where my uncle lived and taught me what to say. "When you get there," he told me, "you first say 'good evening—good appetite!' They will reply, 'Thank you very much, draw up a chair with us!' Then you say 'Thanks, but I've already . . .' Then they'll ask you why you came. Tell them you've heard there is a girl in the house and that you would like to get married." Now that girl was my cousin. I did as I was told. I went, and declared in all earnestness why I had come. They all burst out laughing. I felt ashamed because, being so little, I had not the faintest idea what it all meant. My uncle put me on his knees, showed me the girl, and said: "There is your bride!" Finally I had to tell who had played the joke on me.

But once I caused my grandfather great pain. He always liked to keep the tip of a head of sugar for himself because it was the sweetest. (Sugar was sold in big chunks, the size of a large grenade.) For the same reason I liked the tip too. One day I took the whole head, small as I was, and carried it off toward a copse to hide it. Un-

Tito

fortunately, as I was crossing a brook the sugar slipped from my arms and fell into the water. It was not fated that I should satisfy my sweet tooth, and Grandfather was equally distressed.

My happy days with him soon came to an end and I returned home.

It was taken for granted in my village that by the time a child was seven, he was already a productive worker. I drove the cattle and helped hoe the corn and weed the garden and, I remember so well, turned the heavy grindstone that made our grain into flour. Hundreds of times I finished, soaked with sweat, and the porridge was the sweeter for that. But the hardest task of all was not physical. It was when my father would send me round the village with his I.O.U. to ask someone to endorse it for him. The other peasants were, like my father, deep in debt, hungry, with many children. I had to listen to curses and complaints and then, at last, almost always they would endorse the I.O.U.

One terrible winter when there was no food in the house and no wood for the fire, my father decided to sell our sheepdog, Polak. He traded him with an estate keeper for two cords of wood. Welcome as the fire was, we children were inconsolable. Polak was our faithful friend who had helped us with our first steps, for when we could only crawl we would reach up to him, hold on to his thick fur and draw ourselves to our feet, and Polak would then walk slowly round the room. We cried bitterly when we watched our father take him away. Imagine how glad we were when he reappeared even before Father got home. Father took him back to the estate keeper, and again he returned. This time we hid him in a cave in the woods and fed him secretly for two weeks. By then the estate keeper had given up hope of finding him, so we brought him out of the woods and Father relented and let us keep him. He stayed with us for many years and lived to be sixteen. Polak gave me a lasting love for dogs. I had one with me whenever I could and later, during the war, a dog called Lux saved my life.

In Croatia in those years 60 per cent of the population was illiterate. There were few schools, and many peasants resented schooling, for it took their children away from the fields and cost them their labor. But in that respect I was lucky. An elementary school was opened in Kumrovec when I was seven years old and my parents, despite their poverty, agreed that I should go. I had trouble learning. The lessons were in Croatian and having spent so much time with Grandfather Martin I spoke better Slovenian; and I still had to work. I had little time for study. I would go to the meadow with a book in my hand, but reading was out of the question. The cow would drag me by the tether wherever she pleased. If I let my eye wander from her or dropped the tether, off she would go into someone else's field. I did rather badly my first year. But gradually I learned and during my fourth year, as I found when I visited my old school recently, my marks were: conduct—excellent; catechism—very good; Croatian language—good; arithmetic—fair; drawing—good; singing—good; gymnastics—very good; gardening—very good.

There were more than 350 boys and girls in our school, and only one teacher for them all. Our teacher had consumption. He would cough and spit blood into his handkerchief, which I would later take and wash in the stream. Then we used to dry it over a fire, because it was the only handkerchief he had and I would return to the schoolroom with it in half an hour. The teacher was very fond of me, and often used to give me bread. One day his mother came and took him away. We all stood at the fence as his cart drove off, and he waved to us with his handkerchief while we all wept.

Then a mistress came, a very severe person, but she married and soon left Kumrovec. Our third teacher was Stjepan Vimpulšek, a mild man, always considerate to his pupils, although he had a large family, a small salary, and many domestic worries.

It was a custom at Kumrovec for children to go to church on Sundays. Whenever the parish priest Vjekoslav Homostarić held divine service in St. Roko's Chapel at Kumrovec, he took me as an acolyte. Once after the service I could not remove the vestments from the big fat priest, who was in a hurry. He was irritated and slapped me. I never went to church again.

I had many good friends in my school. I remember a cousin called Ivan Broz, who was a bright boy but a little lazy. The teacher recorded in the school register that he was mentally deficient, but later that boy became a very good mechanic.

There are other memories: of playing under the walls of the great Cesargrad Castle, where we boys imagined that we were charging against the Black Queen; of fishing and cooking the catch by the

riverbank in a bed of charcoal; of hunting for hickory nuts and wal-
nuts and raiding the neighbor's apple orchard; of Pikuša, a game that
we played, a combination of hockey, cricket and golf, played five a
side. It involved pushing a wooden ball into a hole in the ground,
which one side defended with sticks. We made war on the boys of
nearby villages; tended the flocks in the green valley in the long hot
summer months; sat by the fire in the evening while the grownups
told stories of the old days of Matija Gubec and talked of far-off
places they had seen in their travels when they went out into the
world to look for work.

All this ended when I was twelve. At that age it was customary for
the boys of Zagorje to choose a means of livelihood, for they were
then considered capable of supporting themselves. For a while I
worked for my mother's brother tending his cattle. For this I received my food, and a promise from my uncle that he would buy me
a new pair of boots at the end of the year. But he did not keep his
word; he took my old boots, which had ornaments on them, repaired
them for his son, and gave me a pair which were far worse than my
old ones.

He was a stingy man, and I became so dissatisfied with his treat-
ment that at last he realized that we could not go on with our arrangement and he advised me to leave if I wanted to. Soon afterward
a relative called Jurica, a staff sergeant in the army, came to visit in
the village. He took an interest in me and told me I should become a
waiter; waiters, he said, are always well dressed, always among nice
people and get plenty to eat without too much hard work.

Perhaps it was the point about dressing well that interested me
most. My ambition while I was a small boy was to be a tailor, a natural result of the wish of every little peasant in Zagorje to have nice
clothes. I remember a baron who used to come to our district, an
engineer, big and strong. He had a car that looked like a carriage and
could do about fifteen miles an hour. The children would gather
around it screaming when he stopped. But he lost every bit of respect
in our eyes because the seat of his trousers was mended. We said:
"What kind of baron is he supposed to be with trousers mended like
ours?"

My father received Jurica's idea coldly at first, for he was hoping
to be able to send me to America. All Croatia was in the middle of

bad times. To protect itself against the flood of American grain, the Austro-Hungarian government set up customs tariffs on imported grain, which was of advantage chiefly to the large landowners and richer peasants; while the village poor, the greater part of the rural population, were scarcely able to survive on their own grain. Grain, and food in general, were extremely dear. Two hundred pounds of grain cost eighteen crowns ($4.50) in America and twenty-four ($6.00) in Austria. There was no work to be found in the villages. Large-scale emigration developed in Croatia, mostly to America. But such a journey could be made only by peasants who had enough money for the transatlantic journey. Perhaps 250,000 people went from Croatia to America between 1899 and 1913. Many more would have gone if they had had the money, but the journey cost about four hundred crowns ($100), which was a great deal in those times. My father tried to collect the money for my passage, but such a sum was beyond him and he finally agreed to Jurica's suggestion.

And so at fifteen I set off with my relative, Staff Sergeant Jurica Broz, for a little town about sixty miles away called Sisak. I looked with wonder at the old castle, a witness of the great history of this town, which in Roman times had some 130,000 inhabitants and was the capital of the whole province. Situated at the confluence of three rivers, it became a great stronghold against Turkish onslaughts. Its fame revived for a time during the last century when a branch of the Vienna-Trieste railway line was extended as far as Sisak, and all goods going east to Belgrade were reloaded into small vessels; but when the line was extended beyond Sisak, the little town again fell into obscurity.

For me it was a wonder after my own village. What most excited me was undoubtedly the railway engine that carried us to Sisak. How I envied the engine driver! However, I had to take a job, not with engines but in a restaurant belonging to some friends of my cousin.

It was a pleasant place, with a garden and a skittle alley where the officers and noncommissioned officers of the 27th Home Guard Regiment, whose camp was nearby, would come in the evenings and bowl under the big chestnut trees by the light of bright acetylene lamps, while a tambouritsa band played lively music. Nevertheless my new profession soon disappointed me, for I learned nothing and found that I had to do all sorts of jobs, including dishwashing. After my day's work I had to set up the skittle pins until late at night and be on my feet until the last guest had left.

Soon I met some apprentices who worked for a man called Nikola Karas, a locksmith. At that time a locksmith in my country not only made locks but was a sort of general mechanic in a town. He mended bicycles, shotguns, threshing machines, and repaired the hand rails on stairs. Locksmithing was considered a craft. My friends told me that locksmithing was a form of engineering and that engineering was the most beautiful trade in the world; that engineers built ships and railways and bridges. With my family tradition of blacksmithing, this appealed to me, and I went to see Karas, a kindly man of sixty, who told me that I must send for my father because only he could sign the contract for my apprenticeship. My father came and reached an understanding with Karas under which my master was to give me food and lodging, my father clothes. But my father had no money, so from the small amount I had saved from tips in the restaurant, I bought blue overalls and began the career I was to follow for many years. Karas' locksmithy had one or two journeymen and three or four apprentices; for those times in Croatia it was one of the larger workshops. This very vividly illustrates how the economic development of my country was impeded, being restricted to supplying the industries of Vienna and Budapest with raw material. In all Croatia the annual production of iron and steel amounted to no more than three pounds to an inhabitant.

Life as an apprentice was an improvement over life in the restaurant. Our workshop was not large, consisting of two rooms in the cellar. In the middle of the shop was the block with the anvil. In winter months the apprentices slept on a long table, and in summer they went out into the yard and slept on the hay in the stable. Work began at six o'clock in the morning and finished about six in the evening. About midday, Karas' daughter Zora would come to the shop and bring the boys food, and then the work would go straight on.

The food was not bad. In the morning we used to get a pint of milk and coffee and a three-kreutzer scone.

I recall those years with pleasure because I had a great opportunity to learn. Twice a week I went to the apprentice school from five to seven o'clock in the evening, where we were taught geography, history, languages and general subjects. There was one teacher, Feliks

Despot, whom I did not like at first. True to his name, he was very severe, and never smiled. One day I learned why. He had been married to a girl who had died in childbirth. Once as I was going past the cemetery I saw my teacher lying prostrate over his wife's grave and crying like a child. I quickly withdrew so as not to be seen and after that I had a strange respect for him. For three whole years we had never seen him smiling.

On Sunday afternoon we apprentices from different workshops would meet while our masters were having their nap after a heavy Sunday dinner. My brother Štefan was also one of Karas' apprentices, and he and I would bring our pigeons and white rabbits, like the other boys. This was actually an apprentices' pigeon and rabbit exchange. I remember a saddler apprentice called Miho Merkos, and a boy barrel-maker called Mirko Špoljar, who were my good friends. They gave me their performing pigeons and I gave them my fat white rabbits, which I had been secretly feeding with scraps of which I had deprived myself.

One day, all Sisak was excited. The riverbed near Sisak was being dredged, and the workers discovered the foundations of old Roman buildings, long submerged. Roman pots, vases, busts, and even an occasional gold piece were brought up from the riverbed. One and all rushed to the river to search in the mud, hoping to find gold pieces. We apprentices went to hunt for the Roman treasure in the river while Karas was away. We came back empty-handed and muddy and got a severe scolding from our master.

Twice I found myself in trouble during my apprenticeship. There was another teacher I did not like very much and on April Fool's Day I smeared some ink on the black chair he sat on. But instead our school director, Ferdo Kefelja, came in, and in white trousers. I was too stunned to open my mouth. I wanted to tell him what I had done and kept hoping he would not sit down. He made straight for the chair, however, and when he left it there was ink on his white trousers. Afterward I confessed and told him truthfully whom I had prepared the ink for, and being a good-natured man he forgave me.

The other episode was more serious.

Going to the apprentice school had awakened in me a passion for reading. I seized everything I could lay my hands on: histories, both classical and modern novels, travel stories, adventure serials, Sherlock Holmes. It took me forever to get money, mostly from making keys or repairing locks for neighbors, and there was not much time for reading: twelve hours in the workshop, school twice a week, and the lamp allowed only long enough to get ready for bed. So I read during working hours. Once I was working on a lathe with a new drill, reading aloud while the other apprentices listened. They usually set a guard to look out for Karas, but Sherlock Holmes' adventures were so absorbing that the sentry forgot all about his watch. Karas came into the shop and crept behind my back; and as ill luck would have it, the drill cracked just at that moment. Karas flew into a rage and slapped my face.

I felt very bad about the slap and decided to run away, although it was the last month of my three-year apprenticeship. From Sisak I fled straight to a nearby brick factory, but Karas reported my escape to the authorities, and the gendarmes came to the factory and escorted me to the prison in Sisak. Old Karas had a good heart, though. He sent dinner to me in prison, and arranged for me to be released to complete my training and to do my first job on my own: making rails for the staircase of the District Court in Sisak.

One day a journeyman called Schmidt came to Karas' workshop from Zagreb. He was a good-looking boy who wore a red scarf, and had a friendly, cheerful nature. Unlike most of the other journeymen, he never slapped or beat us. He could talk about all sorts of things, about Halley's comet, and the aviator Farman and other marvels, while we listened open-mouthed. On the eve of May Day, 1909, he told us that it was the workers' holiday and that we must bring green boughs and flowers to decorate our workshop. I had many talks afterward with Schmidt and learned more. To my regret he soon moved on, in the usual journeyman's way, but then another one came—Gasparić. He was a strong fellow and taught us wrestling in the Greco-Roman style. Gasparić was even more militant than Schmidt. He and some other workers, particularly carpenters and printers, began to meet at the Lovački Rog (Hunter's Horn) beerhouse to discuss organizing unions. Although trade unions in Croatia had been formed far back in the middle of the last century, and the Social Democratic Party was organized in 1894, they were persecuted. In one year, twenty-three out of twenty-four issues of a socialist paper were banned. In Sisak there were no trade unions, for they were forbidden by the local authorities.

We apprentices were not allowed to go to the beerhouse for ourselves, but often Karas would send us to fetch him a pail and then we used to peep inquisitively into the room where Gasparić and his friends met. They held their talks under difficult conditions. The innkeeper would not allow them to stay unless they ordered something to drink. Within an hour they would become mellow and gay, and thereafter nothing serious would be accomplished. This sort of trouble was common, and resulted in the building of workers' halls. There was already one in nearby Brod, but none in Sisak.

Gasparić did what he could, which consisted of indoctrinating us apprentices. At his suggestion I collected donations for *Free Word*, the socialist newspaper, and sold "workers' matches," 5 per cent of the proceeds going to the paper. I read the pamphlets he brought to the shop for us, especially the book *Looking Backward* by Edward Bellamy and, of course, *Free Word*, which gave us news of the workers' movements in other countries. I remember especially the stories of the persecutions in Russia, of the twelve Japanese socialists who had been sentenced to death by the Mikado, and of the "Socialist Republic" that was being formed in Milwaukee, where the socialists had won the election.

In Croatia, where because of the property qualification only 7 per cent of the people could vote, the Social-Democrats had only one deputy in Parliament. In my own village there were only three voters. I was filled with ambition to do something about these conditions and was ready to set out from Sisak into the world on my own. I was, as it will be easy to understand, an ardent sympathizer of the Social-Democratic Party and looked forward eagerly to joining a trade union.

Another important reason for leaving Sisak when I became a journeyman was my desire to perfect my trade. At that time there was no specialization, and a locksmith was obliged to know all kinds of engineering work. On the other hand, it was a custom for a master to keep all knowledge of precision work from his apprentices, to prevent competition when they in turn became masters, and Karas was no exception to this rule.

So in my eighteenth year, the world lay open before me.

CHAPTER II

1912:

"I learned many complex jobs . . . and spoke against the war."

ON THE hundred-and-sixth day of the long march of the Partisan brigades, we reached the town of Drvar in western Bosnia. There was once a big sawmill here, but when Italian tanks broke into the town the Partisans set fire to the mill lest it fall into enemy hands. Later the Partisans drove the Italians out of the town.

Supreme Headquarters had arrived in the town toward evening. Tito had ordered an officer attached to Headquarters to examine the mill to see whether it could still be used. He returned during the night and reported: "Two of the lathes can still be used."

These words angered Tito: "What do you mean, lathes in a sawmill? They're frame saws! You're supposed to be an intellectual, and you should know the difference between machines!"

Later Tito's temper cooled and in the evening, in camp on the hill overlooking Drvar, he began to tell us how he learned his trade. I asked him how he became a good craftsman and he started to tell us.

The nearest big city to Sisak was Zagreb, where there were mechanics' workshops with machinery far more up-to-date than that in Karas' establishment.

With the help of some journeymen who used to work at Sisak, I found employment in the workshop of a master called Haramina, in the main street of Zagreb. My daily wages were two crowns and thirty hellers (about 56¢). My lodging cost me twenty crowns a month and board seven. The cost of living was constantly rising. Meat cost one crown a pound.

A few days after being taken on, I went to the Union of Metal Workers in the Workers' Hall in the main street of Zagreb and became a member. In this way I also became a member of the Social-Democratic Party of Croatia and Slavonia. It was in October, 1910, that I received my membership card and badge: two hands clasping a hammer. I was eighteen, and it was one of the proudest moments of my life.

I worked in Zagreb for two months. Every day, after work, I used to go to the trade-union headquarters where I read literature and saw many of my fellow workers. One day I took part in my first political activity. The Governor of Croatia, Tomašić, known for his pro-Hungarian leanings, renewed his persecution of the Croatian population, particularly the workers. We surged into the main street, Ilica, with red banners and torches, where the police brutally attacked us as we shouted slogans for workers' rights.

In this workshop I learned many complex jobs which I had not had the opportunity to learn at Karas'. We worked ten hours a day. Here I had at last a chance to fulfill one of my long-standing wishes —to buy myself a new suit and to return well dressed to Zagorje and my own people. Although the cost of living was high, and the wages relatively low, I kept saving steadily until I had about thirty crowns.

I went to a shop and for twenty crowns chose a nice new suit. How joyful I was! I left it at home and went back to the shop to say good-by. When I returned, the door of my room was wide open, and there was no trace of my new suit. How sad and dejected I was! I had to go to a secondhand dealer to buy an old suit for four crowns, for I did not have the heart to return home to Zagorje in the same clothes I had worn when I worked as an apprentice.

At last, in December, the day arrived when I returned to my village as a self-made man. Before leaving, I went to a shop and bought gifts for my mother and relatives. I reached home in the evening and found my parents, brothers and sisters waiting for me in front of the house. Supper was served in my honor. My mother had prepared my favorite dish, chicken soup with noodles, and cheese pies called "štruklje," which no one in the whole village could make as she could.

In the morning I paid visits to all my relatives and I went to my old school, but my teacher Vimpulšek was not there. He had died the year before. I also went across the Sutla to see my mother's relatives, walking through the meadows where I had watched our horses during the warm summer nights.

So the days went by, and I put aside my plans of going away from my village to find a new job. In the evening we would sit round the warm stove until midnight with our neighbors. Old folks recounted legends of Matija Gubec and his deeds; and old women would tell the story of a wounded French soldier who remained in our village after Napoleon's retreat. Younger people talked about their summer journeys to far-off places. I spoke about my experiences in Zagreb. Although it was nothing thrilling, I was proud to tell it, and the people listened.

The little money I had brought had soon gone, especially after I had stood my former schoolmates a few drinks. Our house was poor, as always at this time of the year, because all the grain was eaten. I helped my brother Dragutin-Karlo, who was hired by a building contractor to make tiles and cement pipes for canals. Nobody was pleased about it. I could often hear my family and other villagers saying it was not necessary to waste three years learning a trade, in order to make cement pipes. I did not trouble much about gossip.

But one day I heard my mother speaking to my father about it and I was angry and grieved. I made up my mind to leave home again and try to find a job somewhere, although again there was a depression. My father had horses and he drove me to the nearest railway station, where I took the train for Ljubljana, capital of Slovenia.

I had ten crowns in my pocket, and although I lived very modestly in Ljubljana, I was soon broke. I went round to several shops in Ljubljana but there were no hands needed, so I had to go on. This time I chose Trieste for my target. I had no money for the train, so I went on foot about sixty miles across the mountains; it was still winter and I struggled through snow for three days before reaching Trieste. In a village where I slept the last night of my journey, I met with misfortune in the stable where I spent the night. A cow, looking for salt, tore my suit to bits while I slept. I was not lucky with suits.

In Trieste I was overwhelmed by the harbor and its immense transatlantic liners. Being a trade-union member, I received unemployment relief from the Trieste trade union organization, but I could not find work.

I looked for a job for about ten days, and finding nothing, I had to walk back home. Riding in a peasant's cart I fell asleep, and the peasant took me to the wrong place, where he stopped at his house and gave me food. Then I spent the night in another village and finally, after several days, got home to Kumrovec where everyone was surprised to see me again.

I could not and would not stay long with the family. I spent only a few days resting; poor as the house was, I thought it best to leave as soon as possible. In March of the same year I went to Zagreb and there started working in Master Knaus' mechanic's workshop at Prilaz. Knaus repaired cars, bicycles and similar machines. He was an elderly man, tall, always well dressed, with nice manners.

The first Saturday, upon receiving my weekly wages, I went to join my union. I had to pay all my back dues, because now I had a job. In those days trade unions were fighting against the high cost of living and ever-increasing military expenditure.

I remember a poster saying that a worker in Croatia eats five times less meat than a worker in England and Belgium. We protested also against the lack of any relief for unemployed and aged workers. These were the principal rallying cries for the May Day demonstrations of that year. The stoppage of work on May Day was absolute. Before the demonstrations began I went round to all the establishments with a group of my friends to see to it that all the workers had gone to celebrate May Day. We were so strong that the police did not dare attack us, so the demonstrations ended peacefully, after we had marched proudly through the main streets with our banners.

At that time a fearful campaign was being conducted, especially by the clergy, against the socialists and May Day. In the churches the Catholic priests said that the socialists were devils, and that anyone who took part in the May Day parade would go to hell. This propaganda had its effect even among the workers, particularly among the workers' wives. I remember marching along the main street in the parade beside one of my older friends, married, whose wife and child happened to be in the same street watching the parade. As we came up the child said: "Look, Mother, there's our father among the devils."

As a newly qualified worker, I had a wage of two crowns, sixty hellers a day (65 cents). This was sufficient for me, as a bachelor, to meet my most urgent needs. When I at last bought a new suit for Easter, my father took this to mean that I had big money. Bills kept coming in from him, and my father's desires grew bigger all the time. What I could send went not to my father but directly to my mother, and very little was left over for me. With difficulty I managed to save two crowns sixty hellers to buy Upton Sinclair's *The Jungle*, which was being widely read by Croatian workers because it described the life of European emigrants employed in the slaughter houses of Chicago.

A few weeks later our union decided by a vote of ten to one to call a strike for higher wages. After ten days of hard fighting, our demands were partially met, but although my working conditions were improved, I wasn't inclined to stay in Zagreb. Even my own master Knaus persuaded me to go into the world. "You see, when I was young, I went into the world, too, and learned German and my trade."

Before I left, Knaus paid my wages to the end of the month, although I had not earned them.

I bought a ticket to Vienna, but in the middle of the journey I changed my mind and went to Ljubljana instead for I was afraid that it would be as difficult to find work in Vienna as it had been in Trieste.

From Ljubljana I went on to Kamnik, a little town nearby, and found work in a metal-goods factory with about a hundred and fifty workers. In my free time I joined the "Soko" (Falcon), a gymnastic organization with an anti-Hapsburg platform. I liked their colored uniforms and feather-tipped caps. I bought one on installment and took part in every parade, marching at a smart gait behind the band. I did physical exercises three times a week, which were a very great help in strengthening my body, for I had been a frail boy. Across from our training ground was the playing field of a pro-Hapsburg Catholic clerical organization called "Orlovi" (Eagles). There was not a single day that we Falcons did not come to grips with the black Austrophile Eagles.

I stayed in Kamnik until 1912, when the factory I worked in, the property of a Viennese corporation which suddenly went bankrupt, had to close down. The next morning the factory manager assembled us and proposed that we go to Jiney Cenkovy in Bohemia, to a large metal works which made safes and similar things, because workers were wanted there. The manager was kind enough to offer each worker a hundred crowns for the journey, more than a whole month's pay. Suspecting nothing, I and fifty comrades accepted his suggestion with cheers. We went by way of Vienna, stopped to have a look around, and then went on to Bohemia. But at the station we were met by a crowd of workers who explained that they were on strike and that we were, in fact, to be strikebreakers.

From the station we all went to the Workers' Hall, where we found out that we had been deceived and decided not to go to work. The factory management realized that they would not get us to blackleg, and had to yield to their workers' demands. The men got a raise, and with them we who had come from Slovenia also received better wages.

The labor organization in that metal-working factory was fairly strong and had managed to win the battle. The Czech workers came to love our people very much and I had never felt more welcome abroad than in Bohemia. Among our people there were two Croatians; most of the rest were Slovenes. In Cenkovy I worked for a couple of months and then, curious as all young men are, I decided to see the biggest metal factories in that part of Europe. In a few months I traveled up and down Germany and Austria-Hungary, making short stops in every place of interest to me. I remember I was hardly impressed at all by the Skoda works in Pilsen, because in those days they were obsolescent. I liked the Ruhr much better, what with all the smokestacks sprouting like a forest on so small an area. The factories in Munich were sordid, but the beerhouses were worth seeing. All in all, my journeys were an excellent school, broadening the views of a young man. I gained much as far as my trade went; I learned German well and Czech adequately, and I began to appreciate the latent strength of the metal workers, in their huge factories where thousands of men work together on the most up-to-date machinery.

I recalled the words of my former teacher Vimpulšek from Zagorje, who used to say that the metal workers were the men of the future. Wandering around Europe in this way I had lost contact with my family. My journeys finally brought me to Vienna, and I wrote home. A few days later I received a letter from my mother saying that my eldest brother Martin, who had left Zagorje when I was a little boy, was nearby at Wiener Neustadt working at the station as a railwayman. I was eager to see someone of my folks, and I hurried to Wiener Neustadt to inquire at the station if anyone knew Martin Broz. The third man I asked replied: "I am Martin Broz."

We had not seen each other for more than ten years. How much we had to tell each other!

My brother took me to his house in the small village of Neudorf an der Leita, where he had settled down with his wife and year-old son. Shortly afterward I got a job in the Daimler factory in Wiener Neustadt. My brother asked me to stay with him and I went to the factory by train every day.

The work here interested me more than in any other factory. I even became a test driver, running the big, powerful cars with their heavy brasswork, rubber-bulb horns and outside hand-brakes, to put them through their paces. These were useful experiences. When I was off duty, there were other pleasures. On Sunday afternoons I would go to Vienna with my friends. We usually went to a place called the Orpheum, a sort of music hall with magicians, clowns, light Viennese music.

I could not afford the big Viennese coffeehouses, but I used to lean against the railings of the open-air restaurants listening to the orchestras until the headwaiter chased me away. My chief pastime in Wiener Neustadt was training twice a week, in a gymnasium, with special attention to fencing.

At one time some friends and I were seized with the desire to learn to dance, and entered a school run by an old dancing master. I quickly learned the waltz, but I had trouble with the quadrille and polonaise. The old master was extremely persistent. "You must learn all or nothing," he used to say.

But by then it was 1913, I was twenty-one, and the time had come to return to Croatia to do my two-year military service in the army of the Austro-Hungarian Empire. Service in the Austro-Hungarian army did not attract me for several reasons. It was an army of oppression, which not only held my people in subjection but served as an instrument to enslave other nations. Moreover, it was an old-fashioned and unintelligent army. It operated by rule and formula and, instead of teaching men how to fight, taught them how to drill.

I will never forget my first day in the army barracks. When I entered the army, I had a head of hair of which, like every young man, I was very proud. But my corporal was not of the same opinion: "Mister Socialist, do come here, I'll give you a nice haircut."

Then he took up a hair clipper and snipped away the hair of which I was so fond.

Then came new nuisances. We had to learn by heart all the names of the royal family. Our corporal was a despot. He slept with thirty of us in one room. When he wanted to light a cigarette, he would make a hissing sound. "Pspspspsps." And all thirty of us were obliged to jump up from our beds and hurry to him with a match.

If someone was late, he was punished. Some punishments were odd. For example, a soldier was obliged to go out and find a frog. Then the corporal would take a piece of chalk and make a circle on the floor. The frog was put inside the circle and the soldier was required to remain on guard to prevent the frog from leaping outside the circle.

I remember a friend of mine, from my village, who remained in Kumrovec after I went to the town. He was a simple peasant boy and was unable to learn quickly the long names of the royalty—cause enough for punishment. The corporal made him climb a big unheated stove made of tiles in the corner of the room. He was obliged to sit on his haunches and to keep striking himself with his finger on his forehead, repeating all the time: "I am stupid, I am stupid."

My poor countryman was tormented that way for more than an hour. When he came down, we went to a far corner of the courtyard and he wept.

In the Austro-Hungarian army, individual initiative was strongly discouraged. However, I used the opportunity to learn as much about military science as I could. I was sent to the school for non-commissioned officers and became the youngest sergeant major in the regiment. I won the regimental championship in fencing and later second prize in the all-army championship in Budapest, and became a good skier. We practiced skiing on the slopes of Sljeme Mountain just outside Zagreb, where I served my term in the barracks of the Twenty-fifth Home Guards.

Overnight my life in the army changed. War broke out in 1914.

Tito

One evening, all our companies were mustered on the barracks parade ground and our regimental commander informed us sadly that Crown Prince Francis Ferdinand had been assassinated in Sarajevo. Dismissed from ranks, we began to nudge each other. Anti-Austrian feeling had been growing in the whole of Croatia, and even in our regiment. Ever since the Turks had been driven out of the Balkan Peninsula in 1912, after five centuries of rule, our people looked forward to the day when the end of Austro-Hungarian rule would also come to an end. In my town, Zagreb, this was manifested by two attempts on the lives of two pro-Austria "bans" (the provincial governors) at Zagreb. They were wounded. One of the assassins was a Yugoslav youth who had emigrated to America to work, then had made the long journey back to Zagreb to vent his anti-Austrian feelings.

After Sarajevo, it was clear that the outbreak of war was but a matter of days. We peasants and workers in the regiment looked upon war as offering a chance to free our country from the yoke of the Hapsburg monarchy.

A month after the assassination in Sarajevo, we were lined up to hear the declaration of war. Composed of sixteen companies, each with 263 men, our regiment moved out to take its place in the line. Hungarian regiments arrived in Zagreb in order to prevent resistance, if any, against Austria-Hungary. Antiwar feelings were mounting. We all hoped for another heavy defeat like the one the Empire suffered at Koeniggraetz, and prayed the hated state would dissolve.

In the ranks, I spoke out against war. An old sergeant major, loyal to Emperor Francis Joseph, heard of this and betrayed me. I was arrested, and without formalities was thrown into jail in the fortress of Petrovaradin on the Danube.

The place was a real den, with not a single window. Left in the darkness, I began to grope on all sides. "*Komm hier, komm hier,*" I heard a voice say. (Come here.) I told my cellmate my name and that I was a worker, and learned that he was a German soldier and also a worker. He told me he had been in the cell two weeks and had not been questioned once. Profiting by his story, I began to raise a din, pounding the door with my fists and demanding to be brought at once before the commandant. After four days I succeeded. The commandant luckily believed one of the witnesses, who was my friend, rather than the sergeant major, and I was acquitted.

Shortly afterward my regiment was sent to the Carpathians, where for the first time I met the Russians. They had advanced over the Carpathians in the autumn of 1914, reaching a point 125 miles from Budapest, and preparations were being made to strengthen the defenses of Vienna. Our four regiments from Croatia, together with other divisions, raced to stop up the gap in the Austro-Hungarian front and to seal off the Russian advance. It was bitterly cold when we reached the front. A war of attrition was going on in the trenches. We were badly equipped and poorly armed. Those good uniforms and leather boots we had received when the war broke out were replaced with boots of such poor material that they virtually melted off our feet after three days. The proportion of nettle in the army greatcoats was raised at the expense of wool, and they were useless against the rain. The Russian soldiers were worse off in equipment. Moreover, their armaments were inferior to ours; there were whole Russian companies without firearms. They charged our positions repeatedly at bayonet point without any preliminary artillery barrage. It was a horrible massacre. On our own side enormous numbers of men froze to death for lack of warm clothing. I got to hate war and perceived all its senselessness. I pondered over it deeply, especially at night in the observation post.

The men in my company all came from my native Zagorje. During the two months of fighting we had received reinforcements twice to replace men who had been killed or frozen to death in that mountain range.

All of us were exhausted and had nothing to fight for. Neither the everyday words of encouragement nor the severe measures of punishment meted out by our company commander, Captain Tomaševié,* were of any avail. A close watch was kept on us; our every step and act was fixed by army rules and we were not allowed to show the least initiative.

One thing interested me in the science of warfare: that was scouting, because it required a clear head.

---

* Tito and Tomašević met again in World War II, this time as opponents. When the Partisans attacked the Bosnian town of Bihać in November, 1942, the big Ustashi garrison was commanded by Tomašević, who was a general. Bihać was taken, but Tomašević succeeded in escaping. He was responsible for mass atrocities committed against the civilian population in the vicinity of Bihać. He fought until the end of the war on the side of the Germans. He was captured in 1945 and sentenced to death.

Tito

Soon my wishes were granted and I was given command of a platoon which night after night crossed the enemy lines and operated deep in the rear. We were very successful and the reason, I believe, was that I took care of my men, saw to it that they were not cheated on their food rations, that they had shoes and the best possible sleeping accommodations. I talked with them about their homes and families and they trusted me. Once we surprised eighty Russian soldiers who had gone to sleep in a house and had left no sentinels. Some of my men proposed killing them, but I have never believed in useless bloodshed, so we brought them all back to our line.

Then came days of a lull in the fighting. I remember a rare soldier's delight. My orderly, a Tsigane, found a hen and prepared a meal in his own way. He took the hen and killed it and, after cleaning out the entrails, wrapped it up, feathers and all, in a coat of clay. Then he covered it up in hot ashes. When the clay had been baked as hard as earthenware, he withdrew it from the ashes and struck it with his rifle butt. The clay dropped off with the feathers stuck to it, and what presented itself to our eyes was chicken baked to a tender, tempting brown, the like of which I had never eaten before.

In the spring of 1915 a new Russian offensive began in the Carpathians against the sector of the front which our regiment was holding.* On March 22, on Easter Day, my regiment was in position near the small town of Okno. The Russians launched a surprise attack on us. Our officers were in the rear at Headquarters celebrating Easter. We held against the infantry advancing frontally against us, but suddenly the right flank yielded, and through the gap poured cavalry of the Tcherkezi, a tribe from Asia. Before we knew it they were thundering through our positions, leaping from their horses and throwing themselves into our trenches with lances lowered. One of

---

* After the Second World War when the Soviet Marshal Tolbukhin came to Belgrade to see Tito, they discovered that they fought against each other in the Carpathians in 1915. At that time Tolbukhin was a noncommissioned officer on the Russian side. Tolbukhin was very much surprised to hear it. He said to Tito:

"You shot at us."

"You shot at us," answered Tito.

"But you shot at us, at Russians," said Tolbukhin.

"But you were the soldiers of the Russian Tsar and we were the soldiers of the Austrian Tsar," answered Tito.

At this Tolbukhin changed the subject.

them rammed his two-meter iron-tipped double-pronged lance into my back just below the left arm. I fainted. Then, as I learned, the Tcherkezi began to butcher the wounded, even slashing them with their knives. Fortunately, Russian infantry reached the positions and put an end to the orgy.

Thus I became a prisoner of war. I was transported deep into the rear and found myself in a hospital that had been an old monastery in the little town of Sviashsk near Kazan, which lies on the banks of the River Volga. My wound was deep and troublesome, and in my weakened state I developed pneumonia. In my delirium, I learned later, I used to accuse the saint on an icon of wanting to steal my belongings. The other prisoners told me about this quarrel with the saint after I had come through the crisis.

Many of my wardmates thought I was going to die. One day when I was in a high fever and unconscious, a nurse put a red ribbon on my bed to mark a dying man who should be removed from the ward at once.

But I recovered at last and I could move round the hospital. I studied Russian, and learned it quickly because of its similarity to my native language. Across the road from the building that housed the prisoners lived some secondary-school girls: the daughter of a mechanic banished to Siberia, and the daughter of a doctor. They sent books to the prisoners, and I got Russian classical literature, Tolstoy, Turgenev and Kuprin.

Having recovered pretty well from my illness and from the effects of the wound, I was ordered to leave Sviashsk and go to Ardatov, another small town in the vicinity, where I was to work. This was my own wish; according to the Hague conventions, as a noncommissioned officer I was not obliged to work. But I was reluctant to sit idle, for there is nothing more killing for a man than a life of idleness. I was assigned to the village of Kalasiev near Ardatov in what is today the Kuibishev province, inhabited by Tartars, Mordvins and Russians. I worked in a small motor-driven mill owned by three rich Mordvin peasants, which ground grain for the village and the neighborhood.

One of the owners of the mill liked me very much, because I knew how to repair his mill. Once when we were in the village Turkish bath, beating ourselves with small branches of trees while the whole room filled with steam, the owner of the mill proposed that I marry his daughter. He said to me, "You are a skilled mechanic and my daughter could bear for me another little mechanic."

I laughed and told him that I had no intention of marrying.

I did not have much work in the mill and had plenty of time for reading. A teacher's family lived in the village and from them I got books regularly. I also became acquainted with some anti-Tsarist Russians.

But I did not stay long at Ardatov, for I was withdrawn to the prisoner-of-war transport and sent to the Urals, and thence to the small town of Kungur, near the city of Perm. There I was made commander of the prisoner-of-war camp. We were employed at various jobs: first the construction of a railway line, then repairing the St. Petersburg–Siberia railway. Then came the winter of 1916–17. We were poorly clothed, and some one of our group died every day. To be sure, we received wages for our work, but they were insufficient for nourishing food in that severe cold.

Food and clothing parcels from the International Red Cross were the greatest help to us. The parcels were distributed first by the American Red Cross, a duty later taken on by the Swedish Red Cross. Thus I came into contact with the representative of the Swedish Red Cross, whose name as far as I remember was Sarve.

I noticed, however, that the chief of the railway section where we worked was stealing our parcels. The lives of several hundred prisoners of war were at stake. One day I wrote a letter to Sarve and explained the whole affair. There was a scandal. Even the head of the Red Cross at Kungur, an old Russian countess, felt herself affronted.

The chief of the section was hauled over the coals and developed a keen hatred for me in consequence. He was a sinister figure, always full of praise for the Tsar, and displeased that I kept company with the workers, suspecting that I had political connections with them.

He seized the first opportunity to avenge himself on me. One day three prisoners of war, all Rumanians, failed to arrive at work because they were repairing their felt boots in the barracks. It was terribly cold and if the men had gone out in their unrepaired boots their feet would have frozen. They were expected on the job at any moment. Suddenly the head of the section broke into the barrack room and inquired why I had marked them as being at work while in fact they were loafing in the barracks.

I informed him that the men were repairing their boots and would be at work at any minute, but he refused to listen. Shortly afterward three Cossacks appeared and took me to jail.

That was a jail I shall remember as long as I live for the black memories it has left in my mind. No sooner had I crossed the threshold of that dank building and been flung into a cellar when the three Cossacks drew out their knouts and began to lash me across the back. I endured thirty blows that I shall remember all my life.

While I was lying in the cellar on straw that night, the door was thrown open and the jailer, an old Russian, entered. He called: "*Austrits, Austrits* [Austrian, Austrian], come with me."

He told me the Cossacks had left, and took me to his quarters in the cellar of the jail, where his three daughters were sitting. They poured out some tea from the samovar, and then played to us on the balalaika.

Restored and rested, I was taken back to my cell by the jailer, who gave me a blanket to keep me from freezing.

I spent several days in this prison. One evening I heard a noise in the courtyard and ran to the door hoping to hear what was happening. From the distance I heard cries of "Down with the Tsar." Armed workers from Kungur, hearing that the Tsar had been overthrown, had come to free the prisoners. This meant that revolution had begun in Russia.

At last I was freed and returned to the prisoner-of-war camp. The chief of the section gave me a black look but dared not do anything against me. There was no end of excitement in the camp. The Russian Tsar had been overthrown. We prisoners from Croatia asked ourselves when the day would come for the overthrow of Charles Francis Joseph, the Austro-Hungarian Emperor.

There was an engineer in the railway workshop, a rather elderly Pole. He had a son in the Putilovski factories at St. Petersburg, who was also an engineer. The father took me one day to his home, where there was a group of workers, Bolsheviks. There we read some of Lenin's writings.

The situation changed. The provisional government wanted to

prolong war by all means and intensified the struggle against the workers. The men refused to go to the front. I was seized again one day and thrown into jail, where I remained for a long time. I don't know what fate would have befallen me had it not been for the engineer in the workshop. At his intervention I was released and in May, 1917, transferred to a small railway station near the town of Perm. A group of thirty Rumanian prisoners of war were there, and we worked on repairing the line.

However, danger continued to stalk me, because the workers with which I had contacts had been arrested, and I had to flee. It was already late June. The old engineer gave me some civilian clothes and I went on foot the distance of two stations, and climbed into a train loaded with grain going from Siberia to St. Petersburg. Lying between sacks of wheat, I arrived in the Russian capital several days later.

I went directly to the old engineer's son, who was employed in the Putilovski factory. I brought him greetings from his father and he took me to his flat.

Several days later big demonstrations took place against the provisional government, known as the July Demonstrations. I was in the procession of workers. Arriving near a big railway station, we became the target of heavy machine guns from the roof of the station buildings and many people were killed. Large-scale arrests of workers began. My friend the engineer was one of those arrested, and I had to hide near the bridges of St. Petersburg. Finally, I decided to flee to Finland. I reached the border, but the Imperial police, with an eye open for all suspects, took me into custody. At the interrogation I stated that I was an Austrian prisoner of war. I was returned to St. Petersburg, where I was arrested and imprisoned.

At St. Petersburg I was kept in the jails of the Petropavlovsk Citadel. The River Neva rose to the very windowpanes. The cell was all stone, and running with rats. Three weeks later I was banished back to Kungur, to the Urals. I was extremely reluctant to return to this place, knowing well that nothing good awaited me there, and I watched for an opportunity to escape from the train. We were traveling slowly. The days passed. Arriving at Yekaterinburg (today Sverdlovsk), I asked one of the guards to allow me to fetch some water for tea. I had already emerged from the station when I came face to face with our second guard, who had also left the train. He recognized me and said: "*Zdrastvuy*, Yoshka!" (Hello, Yoshka).

Then suddenly he shouted, because he had realized my attempt to escape. He was removing his rifle as I lost myself in the crowd. Making my way back to the station platform, I jumped into a passenger train already moving off.

I was in civilian clothes and had an excellent command of Russian and no one would have guessed I was a prisoner of war. The Yekaterinburg station notified all other stations that a prisoner of war had escaped. When we arrived at the Tumen station, a gendarme entered my carriage and, seeing me sitting on the nearest bench, came straight up to me and asked: "Is there a fugitive Austrian among you?"

I answered: "*Nyet*" (No).

The train proceeded on its way. The conductor was a good man and let me go on without a ticket. My fellow passengers gave me food. We crossed the Urals and entered Siberia. One evening the train stopped at the Atamansky Hutor station, near Omsk.

A group of armed workers surrounded the train. We all inquired what was happening.

"This is Soviet government!" exclaimed a worker.

The October Revolution had started that day, and the armed workers were Bolsheviks from Omsk. They had been dispatched to the station to catch fugitive members of the bourgeoisie. They interrogated one passenger after another, until my turn came. I told them I was an Austrian prisoner of war, a worker like themselves. They told me everything was in order, that I should go to the prisoner-of-war camp, where the prisoners had already joined the Bolsheviks and formed the Red International Guard.

Arriving at the camp, I immediately applied to join the Red Guard. There I found many Czechs, Hungarians and Rumanians, all prisoners of war. It has been written on many occasions that I took considerable part in the October Revolution and civil war in Russia. Unfortunately, that is not so. I served several months in the Red International Guard, but I never fought at the front, because I was still weak from my wound and from illness, especially after having wandered from Kungur * to St. Petersburg and back on a meager

* In 1945 Tito received a special message of greetings from the local Soviet at Kungur.

diet. Our unit asked constantly to be sent to the front, but Headquarters held us back to do sentry duty at Omsk and to work at the Marianovka railway station.

In the International Guard we read Bolshevik papers and Lenin's pamphlets. Of all the leaders of the October Revolution we heard most about Lenin. Trotsky was also mentioned. Less was known about the others. As for Stalin, during the time I stayed in Russia I never once heard his name.

One day in 1918 the Czech Corps, presumably on its way to the western front, staged a coup in favor of the Whites and attacked and broke up our Guard. Admiral Kolchak entered Omsk and proclaimed himself "the ruler of Russia." A White terror followed in Omsk. I managed to escape and took refuge in a village about thirty-five miles away.

The village was one of those inhabited by the Moslem Kirghizi, a people who lived a primitive, half-nomadic life. In the autumn and winter they lived in dugouts and in summer they moved to tents. However, their chief, Isaiah, had acquired a motorized mill and he needed a mechanic to operate it. He took a liking to me. He was a powerful friend to have, for he was the supreme judge of the Kirghizi and personally owned more than twenty-five hundred horses in the steppes. My own knowledge of horses came in handy almost at once. A few days after I arrived in the village a festival began, and tribal members rode in from remote regions to attend. At one point a horse was led from a dark tent. He was well fed, but had never been saddle-broken. My hosts suggested that I try to ride him. The horse reared and pawed the air furiously but I finally managed to get him saddled and bridled. He rode off with me like the wind straight into a small wood, and as we crashed through it the branches lashed me, leaving bloody streaks across my face. Nevertheless, after half an hour's mad race, I calmed him down and rode back among the Kirghizi. From that moment our relations were good.

Isaiah helped me buy a fine mare called Mercedes. I also acquired a dog, but wolves accounted for it. Later I found another dog, a young wolfhound, which grew to be strong and fought well against the wolves. I caught two wolf cubs and tried raising them, but when they became big enough they escaped to the woods.

While in Kirghizia I once had a toothache. Seeing how I suffered, an old woman offered to help me and I consented to try out her cure.

She placed three tubes in a pan of water. Then she made three candles and lit them, sticking them into pyramids made of dough. While she did this her daughters-in-law brought blankets and covered me with them, head to foot; the old woman told me to open my mouth over the pan, and then she covered me with some more blankets, the candles burned, and I kept my mouth open. The dough caught fire from the candles and my tooth began to ache unbearably. The air under the blankets was so suffocating that I nearly fainted and I forgot the pain. But the woman from the beginning had been clapping her hands around me and screaming: *"Karan, Karan—kout, kout"* (devil, devil—out, out). Finally they uncovered me. The old woman began to remove maggots from the water which had supposedly come out of my tooth. Actually she had dropped them into the pan. Wet with perspiration, and almost suffocated, I gasped for breath. My tooth had stopped aching and I gave the old woman her fee.

I remained quite a long time among the Kirghizi, and even learned their language. I was unable to leave Isaiah's settlement because the whole region was under the rule of the Whites. During the whole of 1919 fighting raged along the Siberian railway between the Reds and the Whites. At last in the late autumn of 1919 Omsk and its surroundings were freed from Admiral Kolchak. I took leave of Isaiah, who tried his best to hold me back, and left for Omsk by sleigh. On the way I was met by a gang of mounted bandits. The chief aimed a rifle at my breast, and just as he was about to pull the trigger I told him that I was a prisoner of war. The bandits satisfied themselves with my belongings and allowed me to proceed to Omsk.

A few days later while walking through the market-place, I noticed a vendor in tatters with a very familiar face. Taking a better look at him, I recognized the chief of the bandits who had robbed me a few days before. I called a militiaman and the bandit was arrested. He had come secretly to Omsk to learn when a transport of goods was due to leave. This band had been plundering and killing in the neighborhood of Omsk for several months.

I stayed only a short time in Omsk. Before leaving I married Pelaghia Belousnova, a Russian girl of sixteen, whom I had met for the first time before the coup staged by the Czech Corps. I had been seeing her for some time. She lived with her parents, who were workers in this town. After the wedding we set off by the first train to St. Petersburg.

I was eager to be home after six years' absence. I remained in the Russian capital a few weeks, then with a group of released prisoners of war set out for home. The first sizable station was Narva. There we were quartered in a fortress and kept in quarantine for several weeks. The Bolsheviks were not in power here. Every night someone was taken away from the fortress and shot on suspicion of being a Bolshevik. This was the work of fugitive White Guards. Jaroslav Hašek, the famous Czech writer, author of the celebrated antiwar satire *The Good Soldier Schweik*, was also in this fortress with me. He was, however, an extremely retiring man, who never smiled. Finally we left Narva on board the *Lili Feuermann*. She was a beautiful vessel, but the Baltic Sea was so foggy that the voyage was very unpleasant. We docked at Stettin, where the former prisoners of war were sorted into nationalities, and from Stettin I went on by train to Yugoslavia. There were two of my countrymen in our group who pretended to be Bolsheviks. But when we arrived at the Yugoslav border they suddenly leapt on me and began to curse me, asking the Yugoslav border authorities to arrest me as a Bolshevik.

So, upon arrival in my country after six long years of war, I landed in jail with my wife, who was on the eve of childbirth.

We were released after a few days, and at last I came home to Zagorje in September, 1920. It was six years since I had left and I hurried to Kumrovec to see my family. They were not there, except one brother, but I learned that my father had moved to another village not far away. I arrived there one night and found my father and one of my brothers at supper. They told me my mother had died in 1918.

A few hours later my wife gave birth to my first child, a boy who died after two days.

In sadness we went to Zagreb, where I found work in a machine shop.

CHAPTER III

1923:

"I was elected a member of the District Party Committee . . ."

PROFOUND changes took place during the six years of the war while Tito was away from his country. The cock's feather reappeared in the hats of the Zagorje peasants; the Austro-Hungarian monarchy was rocking on its foundations. Defeats at the front depleted the Austrian regiments and the Zagorje peasants refused to fill the ranks. Once armed, they fled to the woods, where they organized the "green corps."

The rule of the Hapsburgs came to an end in Croatia in October, 1918, after more than four centuries. With the cock's feather in his hat, the Zagorje peasant had been stolidly chalking his account with the nobility ever since the time of Matija Gubec.

Now the time had come for a settlement: every night a castle went up in flames, and the next morning saw the distribution of the landlord's estate among the peasants. The time had come at last when the Zagorje serf was to receive his own land in his own free country. As they had once marched on Cesargrad, the property of the Erdödys, the men of Zagorje now stormed Banja Castle, which also belonged to the Erdödys. Joined by the workers from the neighboring coal mine, the peasants from the surrounding villages, including Kumrovec, broke into the castle, took whatever was of value in it, set it on fire and finally blew it up with dynamite.

In Zagorje, as in other parts of Croatia, there was a strong desire to create a united state of all the South Slav peoples, of the Serbs, Croats, Slovenes, Montenegrins, Macedonians, and Bulgarians. Through their long dismal history, the idea of union had fired the

43

South Slavs. Now, with the collapse of Austria-Hungary, it seemed within their grasp. But the first hopes were attended by the first disappointments. In place of Budapest and Vienna, the peasants of Kumrovec, Zagorje and the whole of Croatia were confronted with a new enemy. What were known as National Councils were quickly organized in the towns, especially in Zagreb; they were composed of representatives of the bourgeois parties and were intended to preserve the social order as it had been in Austria-Hungary.

The National Councils put their hopes in Belgrade, in the Regent Alexander and his circle. They asked for immediate help, begging that the Serbian army, which had at such cost defended its own country during the war, be sent to Croatia to suppress the movement of the Croatian peasants. Alexander promptly ordered the Serbian regiments to Croatia; with them went French colonial troops, several regiments of Annamites.

The National Council, composed of politicians of various parties, sent a delegation to Belgrade to pay homage to Alexander, and proclaimed the creation of the united State of Serbs, Croats and Slovenes.

The only man in the National Council who opposed this act was the leader of the Croatian Republican Peasant Party, Stjepan Radić, who cried to the deputation as it prepared to leave for Belgrade: "Look before you leap. . . . It is a political error to confront your own people with a *fait accompli* of your own fancy."

Thus the new state was created without reference to the people, who were never asked what kind of state it should be, how relationships among the different nationalities should be settled, whether it should be a republic or a kingdom, or what social organization should be adopted.

Only a few days after the proclamation of the united state a mutiny broke out in Zagreb involving the Twenty-fifth Domobrani (the regiment Tito had served in, most of whose men were from Zagreb) and the Fifty-third Infantry Regiment. An armed skirmish took place in the main square in Zagreb, and the mutiny was bloodily suppressed. There were thirteen dead and seventeen wounded. Similar revolts took place in other parts of the country. Terror stalked in Montenegro, where unification had also been proclaimed without the people being consulted.

Conditions were bad; the war had brought great losses. In Serbia, for instance, casualties had amounted to 21 per cent of the population. The peasants, who made up over 85 per cent of the whole nation, were poorer than ever and in many regions were in rebellion. Industrial workers were even worse off. There were few factories, and even these were shut or working only part time, with consequent widespread unemployment. Prices had increased four times as fast as wages.

Alexander had been educated at the Court of St. Petersburg in the Cadet Corps, and soon displayed his intention to run Yugoslavia on the principles he had learned there. He even had dreams of seating the Karageorgević dynasty upon the throne of the Romanovs. In 1919 an item appeared in a leading Belgrade paper that Alexander intended to appoint as his heir the son of his sister Yelena, who was the wife of a Russian Grand Duke (it was thought at the time that Alexander would not have children). In this way the dynasties of Romanov, Karageorgevich and Njegoš would be united.

From Alexander and his circle waves of corruption spread over the country; one of the first questions he raised after the death of his father King Peter in 1921 was the increase of his civil list. The verbatim records of the Assembly reveal that the Nikola Pašić government submitted a special bill in the National Assembly requesting that the civil list be raised to twenty-four million dinars a year. Presenting the bill, the government pointed out that King Alexander had great merits, that "since the day when the civil list of twelve hundred thousand dinars had been voted forty years ago the Kingdom had increased almost sevenfold," that "the salary of William of Germany was seventeen million marks, and that of Francis Joseph of Austria forty-two million crowns a year."

The government demanded that the civil list be paid on the basis of the French franc. The opposition (Agrarians, Socialists and Republicans) pointed out that the civil list actually amounted to sixty million dinars a year, not twenty-four. In the end the Assembly passed the bill but allowed the King to receive only a quarter of his civil list in francs. This he disregarded and in the course of ten years he cashed over one hundred and seventy-three million dinars in francs.

Alexander also became in 1921 one of the chief shareholders of the

National Bank, forcing the representatives of the Export Bank, Belgrade Co-operative and the Adriatic Bank to cede to him part of their shares in the National Bank. He paid up these shares from dividends in the course of four years, while their value was increasing from five hundred to six thousand dinars. Nor did King Alexander shrink from the smallest business affairs. He took over the former state farm at Topčider and sold vegetables and eggs on the Belgrade market in competition with the peasants. Soldiers of the Royal Guard labored for him without pay, and sold King's vegetables in the market in military trousers and civilian overcoats. The huckster King also opened enterprises for the production of wine and Šljivovica (plum brandy) at Topola and Demir Kapija. All these properties were free from taxes because they were the King's personal possessions!

Through agents the King established connections with foreign capital, especially French, which began to make ever-increasing profits in the new state.

Despite weak leadership, the working class at first drove ahead. An eight-hour day was accepted, the trade unions numbered about two hundred and fifty thousand organized workers, the new Workers' Party had sixty thousand members and was reckoned to be the third or fourth Party in the Communist International. The situation that prevailed in Yugoslavia at the time is best demonstrated by the case of an army unit of the Belgrade garrison, which placed itself with its entire staff at the disposal of the Party.

When the Hungarian Commune broke out, Yugoslavia was the only neighboring country which failed to dispatch armed troops. No doubt the government wanted to do so, but the idea was given up after a general strike on June 21 and 22, 1919. Protest strikes were called jointly in Great Britain, France, Italy, and other European countries to prevent intervention in Hungary and Russia. The life of the whole country came to a standstill. In Zagorje, peasants and soldiers together attacked the neighboring prison of Varaždin, freeing three hundred peasants who were there for having burned down the property of the big landowners and redistributed the land. After these events, Alexander did not dare send Yugoslav troops to Hungary.

But the leadership of the new Socialist Workers' Party, under its Secretary General, Professor Sima Marković, was so hesitant that

Alexander succeeded in regaining the initiative in 1920. First a great strike of railwaymen and seamen failed a few days before May Day. The strike broke out because the Minister of Transport, the Catholic priest Anton Korošec, violated the formal agreement on workers' representatives and workers' control. He had first cunningly accepted the seamen's demands in order to break up the union; then he struck with force against the railwaymen. In Ljubljana he ordered police to open fire on a group of strikers who were going to a meeting. Ten persons were killed and twenty-one severely wounded. Sima Marković immediately withdrew and issued a slogan: "Let us not be provoked." The strike failed. Two days later, during the May Day celebration, the Central Committee of the Socialist Workers' Party under the influence of Sima Marković prohibited the workers from celebrating their holiday: *"On May Day stay at home."*

The working masses wanted to fight, as they showed during the municipal elections held the same year. The Communists were victorious in Belgrade and the five largest towns in Serbia, in Zagreb and in many other towns. When the newly elected town council of Zagreb met in the City Hall, police broke in and while the Communist mayor Delić was speaking from the rostrum carried him out bodily. Similar events took place in Belgrade.

In such an atmosphere Josip Broz arrived in Zagreb in September, 1920. He found a job in the mechanics' workshop of Filip Baum at 3 Petrinjska Street, immediately applied for trade-union membership and joined the Communist Party of Yugoslavia. On his head was the fur cap that he had worn in Russia, still bearing the mark of the five-pointed star.

One evening in the winter of 1942 when the headquarters of our Supreme Command were in the town of Bihać in western Bosnia, this is how Tito recalled those days:

For almost six years I had not seen my native land. My early life in my own country and my travels and jobs in Europe had already made me a socialist, but I still had much to learn. The years as a soldier, a prisoner of war, a witness of the Russian October Revolution, a refugee among the nomadic Kirghizi people, had matured me and enabled me to understand better what I now saw.

I took part in several strikes, especially in the successful waiters' strike in Zagreb. During the celebration of the October Revolution,

I gave a lecture in the headquarters of the Zagreb trade unions, and ended with the cry: "The workers can conquer only with the help of arms!"

This was on the eve of the general elections to choose delegates who would write the country's Constitution. The Party put up a list of workers, peasants and intellectuals, long active in the workers' movement. I took part in the campaign in Zagreb. We had a great success, winning fifty-nine seats; we were third among the dozen parties that contested the elections.

Alexander's reply a few weeks later was the "Obznana" (Proclamation), outlawing the Party and the trade unions, and confiscating all their property. In Zagreb we organized a protest strike, but elsewhere in the country the leaders were intimidated and passive.

Thousands of workers were arrested. Wages dropped. Extreme confusion dominated among our rank and file. The following summer a group of young Communists from the Vojvodina, led by a mason called Baćo Stejić, threw a bomb from an unfinished building while the King was passing by in his carriage on the way back from Parliament. The bomb struck telephone wires and dropped behind the King, wounding some soldiers but leaving Alexander unscathed. Baćo Stejić was arrested on the spot and sentenced to life imprisonment.*

A month later, at a summer mountain resort in Croatia, a group

---

* When war broke out in 1941 Baćo Stejić was in Mitrovica Prison, which Germans and Ustashis (Croatian Fascists) took over. They were planning to shoot all the Communists in jail. But Baćo Stejić and his cellmates managed to dig a tunnel, escape from prison and join a Partisan detachment. When Baćo Stejić threw the bomb in 1921, Dr. Ivan Ribar, at that time the speaker in the Constitutional Assembly, was in the carriage with the King. He later dissociated himself from the King and joined the opposition. When the country was attacked by the Germans in 1941, he joined the Partisan movement, and subsequently became speaker in the AVNOJ (Anti-Fascist Assembly of the National Liberation of Yugoslavia). At Bihać, in western Bosnia, where the AVNOJ held its first meeting, Ribar met Baćo Stejić. In his book My Political Papers, published after World War II, Ribar mentions this meeting: "When I met Baćo Stejić, it was the first meeting in our lives. We embraced and kissed cordially. I thanked him that the bomb had not hit me when I was in the carriage with Alexander." Six months after this meeting, Baćo Stejić was killed by the Germans during the Fifth Offensive. Ivan Ribar came safely through the war, but his two sons were killed and his wife was executed by the Germans. Dr. Ivan Ribar became Chairman of the Presidium of the Yugoslav Parliament after the war.

of young Communists from Zagreb assassinated Milorad Drašković, the author of the "Obznana" and Minister of Interior. These were private acts not authorized by the Party leadership. However, the government immediately expelled all the Communist members from Parliament, and began mass arrests of workers and persecution of anyone suspected of radical beliefs. The worker Alija Alijagić, who had taken part in the assassination of the Minister of the Interior, was sentenced to death. When the President of the Tribunal asked him whether he felt guilty, Alijagić replied: "I feel guilty of having deprived a wife of her husband and children of their father. I feel guilty of having as a man taken another man's life, but I do not feel guilty of having as a Communist killed the Minister who was the persecutor of Communists. I did my duty."

There was a great public campaign for a pardon for him, but he was executed. On the anniversary of his death there was such a pilgrimage to his grave in Zagreb that the police one night dug up his coffin and buried him secretly in the nearest Moslem cemetery in Bosnia, and to this day no one knows exactly where he is buried.

I worked at Filip Baum's shop. A locksmith's wages were as low as three crowns an hour, but the rent of a small room was up to six hundred crowns a month. Soon I was dismissed. There was little to be gained by staying in Zagreb, where the trade unions were disbanded and mass arrests of the workers continued. I read in a newspaper advertisement that the owner of a flour mill in the village of Veliko Trojstvo (Holy Trinity), some sixty miles away, required a mechanic.

I went to this village early in 1921. Veliko Trojstvo, which lies on a railway line with very fertile surroundings, had about three hundred and thirty well-built houses. The mill owner was a goodhearted Jew with a large family; his mill was a medium-sized affair with five workers, which could grind ten tons of grain a day. I was in charge of a fifty-horsepower charcoal-burning engine.

Rebellion was stirring among the peasants in the village. A year before I arrived there had been a big uprising in the whole area and three people were killed in village skirmishes.

My duty in the mill was to look after the engine; otherwise I sat in the yard talking to the peasants who were waiting for their grain to be ground. We talked about everything: about the harvest prospects, about the high cost of industrial goods, about taxes. The peasants heard that I had been in Russia during the revolution, and asked curiously about many things.

I told them how much the White Guard relied on the backwardness and religious superstition of the people, how they spread the news that Christ would come to fight against the Bolsheviks.

On one sector of the front, the White Guards, helped by priests, put up large tents and lit them from inside. Then the figure of Christ with the Cross appeared. All this was to show the Red Army men that the White Guards were led by Christ himself. The Bolsheviks immediately guessed that it was a well-staged hoax and organized a flanking attack. "Christ" was surrounded; the priests and their false "Christ" were exposed in the tent and the whole front discovered the ill-advised deception.

One day a tall, quiet and friendly young man called Stevo Šabić* came to the mill. He became my best friend. He too had been in Russia during the war, having been an officer in the Austro-Hungarian army, and was taken prisoner in 1915 in the Carpathians. When the revolution broke out, Šabić joined the Red Army and advanced rapidly, becoming chief of staff of an army corps under the command of the former Tsarist General Muravyev. When Muravyev was preparing to open the whole of the front to the Whites and betray the Red Army, Šabić took part in his unmasking and arrest. Returning to Yugoslavia, he was refused admission into the Royal Yugoslav Army, and pensioned as a lieutenant. With Šabić and some other workers and peasants in the neighborhood who had been active before the "Obznana" we secretly started our political work again.

At first we had no contact with the underground cells of the Communist Party of Yugoslavia which were formed in 1923 in the nearby towns of Bjelovar and Križevci. But during the general elections of 1923 we read in a local paper that a group of workers had tried to put up their candidates for the elections, but were arrested by the

---

* Stevo Šabić was one of Tito's personal friends. When Tito left the village of Veliko Trojstvo in 1925, Stevo remained in his village, actively working in the labor movement until 1941, when Yugoslavia was occupied by the Germans and the Quisling Pavelić was put in power in Croatia. Stevo was arrested, immediately sent to the Jasenovac concentration camp, murdered there with a hammer blow on the back of the head and thrown in the River Sava.

police when they went to the president of the law court to file the names of their candidates.

My friend Stevo and I went immediately to the editors of this paper, asking for more details about the arrested workers, and when they were released a few weeks later we met them and established Party contact. At first they were reticent, and gave me a bagful of leaflets to test me. I distributed the leaflets and won their confidence. We maintained contact, and extended our work among the peasants. Sometime later I was elected a member of the District Party Committee.

On the same committee there was a carpenter called Josip Valenta, a man with a great reputation in the town of Bjelovar, where he worked in an agricultural implements factory and had successfully organized four strikes. Valenta was consumptive and died in 1924. The Regional Committee decided to bury him in a worthy manner. He had been a distinguished working-class fighter and the Social Democrats considered that he belonged to them, as he had been a member of the Social-Democratic Party since 1910. Both Communists and Socialists attended Valenta's funeral. For the first time in this region a wreath with a hammer and sickle was placed on a worker's bier. The wreath was carried in front of the funeral procession and made a great impression on the workers. When the coffin was taken out of the house one of the Social Democrats was to have made a speech, but the Catholic priest, a certain Ricko, objected. In this he was supported by Valenta's parents, who were extremely conservative, so the Social Democrat withdrew.

When the procession arrived at the cemetery it was the turn of a Communist to make a speech. I went to the coffin and said farewell to the dead comrade. My speech ended with these words:

"Comrade, we swear to fight to the end of our lives for the ideas to which you were so devoted."

At that moment a red flag was unfurled above Valenta's grave.

With this the funeral ended, but the Catholic priest promptly went to the police station and reported that a Communist funeral had been held and that he could not carry out his church ritual properly. The police started an investigation and found out that a friend of mine, a locksmith called Djuro Šegović, had taken part in the funeral. They arrested him and asked who had delivered the oration, but he refused to tell. Somehow the police found out that the speaker was a miller. So they went around to all the mills in the neighborhood of Bjelovar with the arrested Šegović. They arrived at Veliko Trojstvo and when they asked me if I had spoken at the funeral, I said I had. They arrested me and chained me to Šegović. We had to walk from our village to the town of Bjelovar. Šegović was constantly falling because he was weak and each time he fell the chain tore at me. We arrived at Bjelovar with our hands bleeding. The police marched us through the street, so that the population would think we were criminals, and then to jail, where we were kept eight days. We were sent to the law court, but the investigating counsel who prepared the trial was Orthodox and very antagonistic to the Catholic priest. He advised us what to say to the judges, and we were soon released. The court decision read that we were acquitted, having been taken into custody for insufficient reason and without evidence.

The political situation in Croatia at that time was very tense. Stjepan Radić, leader of the Croatian Republican Peasant Party, visited Moscow, where he arranged to affiliate with the Red Peasant League. On his return to Yugoslavia his party was banned and he had to go underground. In Croatia, especially in the villages, people reacted with fury. Organizations of the Croatian Republican Party in the countryside took the initiative and began to collect weapons, intending an armed rebellion. In our own region, Šabić and I received instructions to collect weapons and did the work well, making a secret dump in a hill near the village, where we had a few rifles, pistols and hand grenades stored.*

I visited Zagreb often on behalf of the Regional Committee, and maintained contact with the Provincial Committee of the Communist Party of Croatia. There on one occasion I met Ljubo Radovanović, who was at that time Secretary of the Provincial Committee of the Communist Party of Yugoslavia for Croatia. I reported to Radovanović on the local situation, the disposition of the masses, the activities of the Croatian Republican Peasant Party and the contacts that the Križevci Regional Committee had established with them,

---

* These hoarded weapons remained in the dump till 1941, when the war broke out. At the time of the uprising the Partisans made use of them against the Germans and the Ustashis.

and on the fact that a considerable quantity of weapons had been collected on the initiative of the Regional Committee. Finally I openly declared that the Party would have to make a decision on this question.

But Radovanović rejected all our proposals and when I returned to Trojstvo I said to Stevo Šabić and other comrades: "Under such leadership the Communist Party of Yugoslavia will never be able to come to power."

Ljubo Radovanović did not like what I said. The Secretary of the Union of Woodworkers, Predojević, told me at a meeting that Ljubo Radovanović * was frightened of me after our conversation and considered me a *provocateur!*

In the meantime, at the beginning of 1925, there were important changes in the political life of the country. All the leaders of the Croatian Republican Peasant Party were arrested. Radić remained for some time in a hide-out in his house in Zagreb, but later gave himself up to the authorities. The whole country was excited. The terror against the working class and peasantry was intensified. The Central Committee of the Communist Party of Yugoslavia decided to publish an illegal newspaper, and named as editor and publisher Moša Pijade, an intellectual and painter from an old Jewish family in Belgrade, a slightly built man with very quick movements, known for his excellent articles in various newspapers of the Party before "Obznana" in 1921. He assembled a printing plant in an apartment in a suburb of Belgrade and published three numbers of *Communist*. But an *agent provocateur*, Vlada Mitić, who was also the Secretary of the Union of Woodworkers, discovered where Moša Pijade printed *Communist* and reported everything to the police.

Moša Pijade's trial began in the middle of the struggle against the Croatian Republican Peasant Party. Several judges who enjoyed the confidence of the regime were transferred to the Belgrade Court in order to sentence Moša Pijade according to the wishes of the Royal Court. One of the judges, Kostić, from Priština, even demanded the death sentence; Judge Marinković proposed twenty years hard labor; and Judge Vukajlović, a Republican by conviction, fifteen years.

---

* When the war broke out in 1941 Ljubo Radovanović did not want to fight against the Germans. He remained in Belgrade and was arrested for a while but later was released. In 1948 he was among the first to join Stalin against Tito.

Agreement was reached on a twenty-year sentence. When Pijade's brother went to the Court of Appeal to inquire why so drastic a sentence had been passed, he was told, through a friend, that the Royal Court had demanded it, to terrify the leaders of the Croatian Peasant Republican Party.

In February, 1925, parliamentary elections were held. The Croatian Republican Party won 67 seats, giving them an absolute majority in Croatia. But Radić was soon to betray the cause of the Croatian peasantry. On March 27, 1925, Pavle Radić, with the authorization of Stjepan Radić, who was in jail, made a statement in Parliament recognizing the monarchy and King Alexander's constitution of 1921! Very soon all the leaders of Radić's party were set free, and in the summer of 1925 he entered the so-called R.R. Government (Radical Radichite Government) headed by Nikola Pašić.

The Croatian peasants were astounded and discouraged. The man who had led them had now betrayed their interests. The fighting spirit of the peasants decreased and none of the local leaders offered serious resistance to Radić's action. The same feeling prevailed in the neighborhood of Bjelovar. The peasants were disappointed, subdued and frustrated.

There was a change in the mill too. Old Samuel Polak, the mill owner, did not want to interfere with my political activities. He said: "You are a good mechanic and it is not my concern what you do outside the mill."

However, very soon Polak fell sick and died. His son-in-law, Oskar Rosenberg,* a shop assistant from Bjelovar, became the owner of the mill. He was an arrogant man who liked to live lavishly. He soon found his expenses mounting, and sought to cover them by reducing the wages of the mill workers. This brought him into conflict with me and one day he sent for me and said: "Either you go in for politics or you work." At that time the gendarmes visited my room almost every Saturday and searched my things, and this, too, had its effect on Rosenberg.

---

* Rosenberg soon sold his mill and the new owner set fire to it to get the insurance money. So the building was destroyed. In the room occupied for a time by Josip Broz, a mill with one pair of stones is working again. The fate of Oskar Rosenberg is unknown. Some peasants say that he was deported to Poland and killed in a camp in 1942.

Upon advice of some comrades on the Provincial Committee I left the village and went to Kraljevica, a town on the northern Adriatic, to organize shipyard workers. After four and a half years, I left the village of Veliko Trojstvo with mixed feelings. I was given a send-off by all my comrades and friends. During our stay at Veliko Trojstvo, my wife had borne three more children, a girl called Zlatica and two boys Hinko and Žarko. But the first boy died after seven days of dysentery, and little Zlatica, a beautiful child with golden hair, died of diphtheria when she was two. I carried her coffin to the cemetery and buried her myself. As soon as I had the money to do so, I built a headstone over their graves.* My son Žarko lived and is the father of my grandchildren Josip and Zlatica, who are among the great pleasures of my life.

---

* The headstone of Zlatica and Hinko Broz is well preserved. Until 1941, Elsa Polak, a cousin of the mill owner, took special care of the grave. She was the illegitimate child of one of Polak's sisters and lived with her uncle as a housemaid. As a young girl she read Marxist literature. When little Hinko was born she offered to become the child's godmother, but as she was a Jewess the church beadle was entered in the register as the godfather. From the time Tito left Veliko Trojstvo until the war Elsa Polak looked after the grave. Just before the war she married, but it is unknown today what happened to her.

The coffin for Tito's children who had died was made by a cabinetmaker by the name of Franjo Podupski, who is still living in the village. He remembers this tragic event. He says: "I remember that Joska was deeply moved, especially after the death of little Zlatica. It was very hard on him to be childless. It was the third child that had died. Such was the life of a worker. . . . He took the coffin to the small village cemetery, which is situated on a small hill. I never charged anything for the coffin. . . . After the war, I wrote a letter to Joska telling him I was alive. He invited me to Belgrade, and I was a guest in his house. He gave me many gifts, among others a pair of boots. I write to him occasionally. Once I asked for some special medicine for a friend of mine in a nearby village, and he sent it to me."

CHAPTER IV

1925:

"I decided to begin a hunger strike . . ."

LATE in the autumn of 1942, when Supreme Headquarters was in an old Moslem house just outside the small Bosnian town of Petrovac, we were sitting around a warm stove of crudely made tiles. Outside it was snowing; night was falling. That day we had received a report on the successes of Dalmatian Partisans who had organized the first Partisan navy by arming an ordinary fishing smack with a machine gun, and had challenged a big Italian five-thousand-ton vessel. The machine gun was aimed at the captain's bridge, and the crew surrendered their vessel.

We laughed with pride over this odd triumph, Tito with the rest of us. But for Tito it recalled old memories, and he began to tell us about his life at the Kraljevica shipyards, where he had worked in 1925.

I moved from the village of Veliko Trojstvo to the shipyards of Kraljevica, the excellent natural harbor on the northern Adriatic, in the autumn of 1925. The shipyards were founded more than two hundred years ago and in their time built many famous ships, including the frigate *Austria*, which the Vienna government presented to the Duke of Tuscany. Toward the end of the last century they began to build modern vessels. In 1908 the shipyards were taken over by the big Hungarian firm of Ganz-Danubius and later Armstrong-Vickers and a French company had interests in the enterprise.

When I started work at Kraljevica there were less than two hundred workers in the shipyards. At first I was in the workshop doing repairs and making parts for steam engines and motors. On one occasion I took part in building a large motor launch for the then Minister of Finance, Milan Stojadinović. The little vessel was equipped with a seaplane engine, which we had a great deal of trouble in building into the little craft. We made trial runs, trying to force the motor exhaust directly into the water, thus giving more driving power to the little vessel.

We had even more trouble repairing the torpedo boats which Yugoslavia inherited from Austria-Hungary. From 1918, when the Austro-Hungarians capitulated, until 1923 these ships were in the hands of the Italians, who stripped them thoroughly before they handed them over to Yugoslavia. They even poured acids into the most sensitive part of the machinery, giving us a hell of a lot of work. We were all excited when the first torpedo boat started on its trial journey. The pistons squeaked and we were terrified that the old iron would fail under full pressure. But all went well.

From the first day of my arrival, I assumed the task of organizing a trade-union branch. A few weeks later the elections for shop stewards were called, and I was among those elected. After getting to know the shipyard workers, I restored a Party organization which police terror had disbanded for many years. We organized a workers' sports association, and I remember a trip to Zagreb to buy some guitars for our culture group. I had brought my library from Trojstvo, consisting of some fifty books including the *Iron Heel* by Jack London, *Women and Socialism* by Bebel, and *Mother* by Gorky. My new friends used to come and borrow them. My home became a sort of workers' library.

The little free time I had I spent with a fisherman friend. Once while we were out in our boat we saw a shark's fin. It cut the water with such speed that we made haste toward land. A few days later the shark rushed straight into the nets of a fishing boat and was caught. It was twenty-one feet long, and somebody's boots and quite a collection of other things were found in it. From then on I never swam far from the shore.

The shipyard management was slowly becoming late with its wages, and when we completed repair work on the torpedo boat, our pay was seven weeks in arrears. Our Party cell organized a work stoppage for two hours. The sirens announced the strike, the workers gathered, and I made a speech.

"They are holding back our wages. They keep our money and in the meantime use it as capital, which is just robbing us. On the other hand the shopkeeper sells us our food on credit at much higher price than if we paid in cash, so that we are in fact paying the shopkeeper interest on credit, while the management does not pay us anything for using our money as capital."

To prevent a strike the management paid us several days' wages, but they were still in arrears. The director protested that the Navy Department had not paid for the torpedo-boat repairs.

On behalf of the trade-union branch I immediately sent a letter to the General Council of the Metal Workers' Union in Belgrade, requesting that through the Labor Inspectorate the Council should demand the payment of the workers from the Navy Department of the War Office. A few days later a reply came that the Navy Department had fulfilled all its obligations. We had been cheated and the management had lied to us. Our trade-union branch immediately decided to call a strike. The wailing of the sirens again announced that the workers had struck. The strike lasted nine days and the management was compelled to yield. We got all our overdue wages; but a few days later the management tacked up a list of workers "no longer required." I was one of them.

In October, 1926, I returned to Zagreb and went on to Belgrade. I heard that workers were wanted in the railway-carriage factory at Smederevska Palanka, forty miles from the capital. The factory had been opened in 1923 with mixed French-Yugoslav capital, and when I came it was employing nine hundred workers.

Conditions were very hard. I was elected shop steward, and wrote an article in a Zagreb trade-union paper about the hardships in this enterprise. Incidentally, this was one of the first newspaper articles I had written in my life. I shall quote a few paragraphs from it.

"Lately workers have begun to pour into Palanka in large numbers to look for work in the Railway Wagon Works despite repeated warnings in the Belgrade *Organized Worker* that comrade workers should not go to Palanka, because they only helped to make matters worse in this penitentiary.

"The workers do not seem to heed these warnings, and are simply fooled by the factory management's announcements. This management, which is in Belgrade, advertises regularly throughout the year for fifty or more workers at a time, and to make matters still more attractive they even ask for fifty highly qualified workers. What do these highly qualified workers do there? They straighten out old iron and repair the wagons. Pay is only three to five and a half dinars an hour, although the management promises eight and a half dinars to ten dinars. In most cases the management in Belgrade interviews workers and sends them to Palanka, and when they arrive the director tells them that they cannot start yet, but must wait a couple of days. Then the workers start turning up at the factory every day, waiting to be taken on until they finally realize that they have been deceived, so that nothing is left to them but to sell their last shirt to get back to Belgrade. Every workingman here should be aware that the management does this merely to have as many unemployed workers as possible at the factory gates, to frighten the others.

"Working hours here are as much as sixteen a day. Hygienic conditions are truly horrible. Half the workers had pneumonia this winter. Because there is a terrific draft and it is bitterly cold inside the workshop, the men were allowed to make fires out of old greasy wagon boards which make such an awful smoke that everybody chokes.

"Workers are fined every day for no reason, except that the manager wants it. The provincial labor inspector turns a deaf ear to all our complaints.

"A month ago an election for shop stewards was held. The management did all they possibly could to prevent it, and succeeded to the extent that only 94 out of 300 workers voted.

"In such a situation, comrades, there is nothing to do but to rely on our own forces. Nobody takes care of us, all the social institutions are mere words and paper. We, comrades, must all join our militant trade-union organization and then carry out an energetic struggle against the cruel exploitation of the insatiable bourgeoisie."

This article was published on March 17, and ten days later I was sacked. As shop steward I had intervened and defended a young worker from Croatia, against whom an unreasonable fine had been imposed. That afternoon I was fired.

I returned directly to Zagreb and found work in a large engineering workshop. There was no trade union and I tried to organize one, but the manager got furious. He badgered me the whole day long, trying to prove that I was a poor mechanic, which caused me deep distress. On one occasion he even tried to be rough with me in the presence of all the workers, which he had no right to do. I threw my hammer in front of him, telling him that he had no right to shout, and asked for my worker's registration book at once. The manager became frightened and gave way, and our trade-union branch was organized. Naturally, I soon left this workshop because I could not endure the manager's behavior.

Since my duties in trade unions and in the Party organizations demanded more and more of my time, our Party decided that I should take over the job of secretary of the Metal Workers' Union for Zagreb, and later for the whole of Croatia. I was then thirty-five and the event was a decisive point in my life for it made me a full-time executive of the workers' movement. A few weeks after I took over my new duties, the offices of the Metal Workers' Union were invaded by the police, while I was alone there. One of the plain-clothes men informed me that I was arrested. I asked:

"Will you kindly tell me why I am being arrested?"

"Broz, you have got into trouble for so much that we could arrest you at any time, and choose among a dozen charges," he replied.

So I locked the office and went to jail. At first my comrades were very much annoyed because they did not know where the police had taken me. For a while I did not know why I had been arrested, and where I should be taken. To Veliko Trojstvo? To Belgrade? To Smederevska Palanka? The Kraljevica shipyards never occurred to me.

But that is just where I was taken. Some of the friends to whom I used to lend my books had been arrested, and one of them, a young fellow of eighteen, admitted that I had given him a book. The local police exaggerated the whole matter, sending to the Ministry of the Interior in Belgrade an impressive report about the discovery of a Communist plot for the overthrow of the government. The Ministry accepted the information and ordered a thorough investigation.

So with chained hands, accompanied by two gendarmes, I was escorted one hot day in June, 1927, to the town of Bakar, a few miles from Kraljevica, where I found six of my comrades from the shipyards. We spent nine days in prison and were then transferred to the County Jail of Ogulin for trial. The gendarmes took all seven of us from Bakar in chains, with a lame comrade called Rade Celer bringing up the rear. It was impossible for him to keep pace with us. We were taken out in the evening when the quay of Bakar was solid with people. As soon as we stepped up our pace to pass quickly away from the crowds, our lame friend stumbled and fell, bringing down the other six after him. It was a humiliating scene, and we were relieved to be put in the train for Ogulin.

The jail at the Courthouse of Ogulin was in the Frankopan Tower, dating back to the fifteenth century, on the market square in the center of the city. It was a two-story building with a few windows covered by boards. I was put into number 6 cell on the second floor. None of my comrades were in the same cell, and I found myself among criminals, mostly local thieves.

Days passed but the County Court took no steps and the defendants were not questioned. The food in the prison was very bad and I ate almost nothing. I protested from the outset but the guards would not pass my messages to the judges.

I spent my time talking to the men in the cell with me, explaining to them why the working class must fight against such a state of affairs in the country. My words were received with interest, particularly by some young men. One Sunday afternoon there was a meeting in the square in front of the jail, at which the leading citizens of Ogulin gathered, headed by the County Court Judge and the District Prefect.

The Prefect opened the meeting with a speech which ended with: "Long live His Majesty King Alexander!" At that very moment a young man from Lika, who was in the cell with me, well worked up by my words against the existing order and annoyed with the Prefect's speech, jumped to the window and shouted at the top of his raucous voice: "May the King go to the devil!"

The ceremonial stand was only ten yards from the window, and the embarrassing shout from the young man struck the Prefect dumb. Dead silence fell upon the public while the Prefect and several gendarmes rushed into the prison to find out who had spoken so rudely about the King.

As soon as I heard what our young friend had done, I advised everybody in the room to lie down and pretend to be asleep. The Prefect and his followers found it difficult to establish which window the shout had come from. An investigation was ordered but no one from my cell would give the young man away, and it was quietly abandoned.

After this lively incident, life in prison became tedious again. It became terrifically hot and the atmosphere in the prison was unbearable, yet the County Court would not consider our case. So I decided to begin a hunger strike.

Through the hunger strike I wanted to protest against the system prevailing in the jail. I had been thrown from one jail to another under most difficult conditions. Instead of food I was given just ordinary slops, and on top of everything the Court would not even question me. The strike was my protest. The first day the guards paid no attention to it, but on the second day the commotion began. It is on the second day that the crisis comes in a hunger strike. The organism ceases to feed itself from the stomach and begins to consume energy from the body itself. You feel overwhelming hunger, but if you can get through this crucial period your mind falls into a state of light unconsciousness and you cease to feel the hunger so much. Naturally, you need fairly strong will power. The organism consumes the bodily resources systematically, first exhausting the accumulated fat around the waist and other parts and then starting on the muscles; later it begins on the marrow in the bones and finally on the heart and the brain. That is when the agony starts. A hunger strike may last up to twenty days, when death usually occurs. When the striker refuses to accept water he is a strong man if he lasts as long as seven days.

In the Yugoslav penitentiaries and prisons we are used to hunger strikes, sometimes with an entire group joining in the struggle. At Ogulin I was on strike alone. On the third day, when I had begun to lose consciousness, not only did the guards grow alarmed but I was in great difficulties with the convicts who were in my cell. They began to offer me their food to try to persuade me "not to die, for God's sake." I tried to explain to them what I wanted to achieve through my strike, what we Communists are, and what kind of fight we are waging.

I remained on strike for five days, lying still all the time since I was already much weakened from the time spent in the Bakar jail. At noon, on the fifth day, Stjepan Bakarić, the Chairman of the County Court of Ogulin, came into my cell.

I said to him: "Either take me to the Court or release me, but as a Communist I cannot allow myself to live in these inhuman conditions any longer." The judge tried to persuade me to end my hunger strike as my life was precious to the Communist Party, but I kept repeating: "Either take me to Court or release me." Finally he accepted my conditions and gave me his word of honor that the investigation would be completed soon. So ended my strike.

"I'll send you a drop of nice soup from my home, that will be best for your exhausted body after this strike," said old Bakarić. He really kept his word. The investigations were completed immediately afterward and Judge Bakarić * even took me to his own home a few days later and showed me into his library: "I have here a few Marxist books too! I know as a Communist you will be interested!"

The independent left newspaper *Borba* † commented on the trial:

". . . Throughout the trial it was evident that the entire indictment was based on the Law for the Protection of the State, and had no real foundation at all. It relied only on confidential reports and police agents' old *corpus delicti*, a few scientific books which to this day can be bought in the bookshops, such as: *The Morale and the Class Norms, Trade Unionism Theory and Practice, Unemployment* by P. (Pavlović).

"At the request of the Public Prosecutor the trial was secret. The State Prosecutor tried to present the work of our accused comrades in their trade-union organizations as forbidden Communist agitation. In the view of the State Prosecutor from Ogulin all those in trade-union organizations are Communist anti-state elements. Karl Marx is the father of Communism, and therefore all Marxist literature comes under the attack of the Law for the Protection of the State! It is

---

* Judge Bakarić had a son who, at that time, was a boy of fifteen. The youngster later joined the Communist movement and became one of the leaders of the Communist Party of Yugoslavia. Now the son of Judge Bakarić is the Prime Minister of Croatia, Vladimir Bakarić.

† *Borba* was always under the influence of the Communist Party of Yugoslavia. It was banned in 1929, but during the war, in 1941, when a part of Yugoslavia was liberated from the Germans, *Borba* appeared again, as the official organ of the Communist Party of Yugoslavia.

quite a different matter when such literature is read by a capitalist or an intellectual who reads it for scientific purposes, but when such literature is read by the workers it is Communism, which undermines the state. Even the judge remarked: 'What do the workers need to read scientific books for, when their job is merely to chop things with an axe or hit them with a hammer, why should they get interested in politics?' "

And so I returned to Zagreb. The year 1928 began in Yugoslavia with an ever-worsening situation as far as the workers' living conditions were concerned. There were more than 200,000 unemployed and wages fell to the lowest level in Europe. Agricultural products were sold for next to nothing. A kilogram of wheat cost exactly one dinar (two cents). Three peasant households would buy one box of matches among them. The indebtedness of the peasants mounted rapidly, while the terrible drought of that year brought real starvation in several parts of the country, especially in Herzegovina. The only response of the Alexander regime was preparations for open dictatorship. The working class was the first target: wages sank still lower, strikes were suppressed pitilessly, the workers' press was confiscated. During 1928, 52 out of 86 issues of *Borba* were suppressed. Terror increased, especially in Macedonia and Croatia, and some petit-bourgeois politicians lost their heads completely.

The police were particularly active in suppressing the trade unions, whose officials were constantly harassed with arrest. Because of this, on my return from the trial at Ogulin I had to take on the duties not only of Secretary of the Metal Workers' Union but of the Leather and Processing Workers' Union as well.

I had plenty of work to do: a strike in a shoe factory, a strike in a metal workshop, signing contracts with the employers in the name of the trade unions, organizing help for arrested trade-union members, plus my Party work. In the meantime I was elected a member of the local Committee of the Communist Party of Yugoslavia for Zagreb. The leadership of the Communist Party at that time, instead of concentrating all its powers in the struggle for a better life for the workers and peasants, was sunk in a struggle between the right and left factions, a conflict not of principle but merely a careerist struggle for Party positions. Many workers in Zagreb were deeply concerned about the damage done by factional strife, not only to the Communist Party but to the entire working class of the country. It hampered the trade-union movement in the direct struggle of the working class for better living and working conditions.

In the local Party organization at Zagreb there was a strong group of workers who were against both these factions. It was clear that without unity in the Party there could be no future for our work.

I remember how we used to walk all night until dawn deep in discussion, seeking a means to save the Party from the Party plague. We inevitably came to the conclusion that the healing of the Party organism could only come from below, from the Party members themselves, and with great zeal we set to work in that direction. We considered it our most important task to save the Zagreb Party organization from factional pestilence, to strengthen it as much as we could on organizational as well as political lines, and then to launch a campaign against both right and left factions.

Our first big opportunity came when the eighth Party conference for the city of Zagreb was convened for February, 1928. It was clandestine, of course, for the Communist Party was outlawed and the police continually persecuted us. A small house was found in one of the hilly suburbs of Zagreb and delegates for the conference were elected at five district meetings. I was delegate of the metal workers.

On the evening of February 25, we gathered one after the other, moving stealthily for fear police agents were shadowing us. At last all thirty-two elected delegates assembled in the little house, heavily guarded against a surprise descent of the police upon us.

At 9 P.M. the proceedings began. Both factions were represented by members of the Central Committee. The conference was also attended throughout by a delegate of the Comintern, a Ukrainian called Milković. He was especially assigned by the Comintern to investigate the situation in the Yugoslav Communist Party and to devise means of putting an end to the factional struggle.

When the Secretary of the Committee submitted an extensive report full of flowery words, trying to justify the absence of any work by the local committee and excusing it by references to the great activities of the police, complete silence reigned in the room. It was occasionally interrupted by the stealthy steps of the comrade on guard who, from time to time, entered the house to be replaced by another. But it was only the calm before the storm.

The discussion that followed was bitter. Delegate after delegate sharply criticized the Secretary's report.

"We cannot accept the report, which does not correspond to the real state of affairs. The real position is that we have left-wingers on one hand and right-wingers on the other, while in the middle, outside both camps, stand the workers. We do not want either of the two sides, we want a strong Party organization purged of all factions," said a worker named Kraš. Other speakers confirmed his words. The Central Committee was infuriated.

I took the floor and criticized the report and the work of the local committee. I said that several activities of the workers could not be carried out because factionalism, the worst of all evils, prevailed in the Party. It formed no Party cells, it neither improved nor distributed the Party press, nor did it create new Party cadres. The local committee were occupied only with jockeying for position. Finally, I demanded that a letter be sent to the Comintern against both factions, and that the Zagreb Party conference should take a determined stand against factionalism.

At the end the conference rejected the Secretary's report and accepted the stand of the workers. A new local committee was elected and I was chosen as Secretary.

It was 5 A.M. when the conference ended. Outside it was still dark and snowing. One by one we left the house unnoticed.

The new committee started work immediately. At that time, Zagreb had more industries than any other city in the country, with about four thousand metal workers alone, but living conditions were deteriorating from day to day. In the leather works half the workers were dismissed, the rest working only four days a week. Thirty per cent of the metal workers were unemployed. Wages sank so low that they were less than the dole in Germany or England. The lack of integration in the trade unions made our struggle extremely difficult; there were three different trade-union organizations, and we fought hard to unite them. Very quickly we formed new Party cells, even in some military factories. The influence of the Party was felt in the workers' cultural and sports associations. Our committee did a lot to raise new cadres, which is a slow and painful process. One had to be very patient, to go deep into a man's being, to help him, to look at the good in him instead of the bad, to encourage his positive features, to help him to get rid of his shortcomings, to make allowances for his background, his educational handicaps, his personal life. Only in this way could cadres be built.

We made ambitious preparations for the May Day demonstrations. I worked out a plan for the demonstrations to begin simultaneously at four or five different places in the city so that the police could not concentrate on one spot. This proved effective. These demonstrations were a great working-class success and a display of real strength in Zagreb. As for me, I was arrested and sentenced to two weeks' imprisonment.*

The situation in Yugoslavia in the middle of 1928 was very grim. King Alexander and the Serbian bourgeoisie around him were thinking of proclaiming an open dictatorship, dissolving Parliament and applying drastic measures against all liberal and workers' movements.

Even in Parliament, from which the Communist deputies had been ejected in 1921, he had strong opposition, headed by Stjepan Radić, the leader of the Croatian Peasant Party. Shoulder to shoulder with Radić was Svetozar Pribičević, a Serb from Croatia, after the war one of Alexander's most ardent supporters and one of his ablest Ministers of the Interior. But even he could not accept the despotic methods of the King, and those of the Greater-Serb circles round him.

King Alexander awaited the opportunity to establish the dictatorship. In Parliament on June 20, 1928, a member called Puniša Račić, a Palace hireling, drew his pistol during a heated debate with Radić, and opened fire. He wounded Radić seriously and killed two of his followers. Radić died two days later.

The events in the Belgrade Parliament caused a tremendous commotion in Croatia, but the leaders of the Croatian Peasant Party did not move. The independent trade unions, under Communist influence, proposed joint action to the Croatian Workers' Council, which

---

* A metal worker from Zagreb, Blaž Pavošev, remembers these demonstrations: "The directives issued by the local committee were that not a single worker must be allowed to be arrested during the May Day demonstration, and that all those held up by the police must be freed by the demonstrators. When struggling to free one of the workers from the police, Josip Broz himself was arrested. He managed to free a man from the hands of the plain-clothes man, but while he was moving toward another group he found himself alone for a minute, and the plain-clothes man followed him and dragged him off. The police gave him two weeks for 'disorderly behavior.' "

was in the hands of Radić's men. They were bewildered and after some hesitation rejected this proposal. Then our local committee, acting through the independent trade unions, took the initiative. We went so far as to issue a proclamation calling upon the people to reply with arms to the murder of Radić. The demonstrations lasted three days and were the most violent in the postwar history of Zagreb.

Thereafter the police were constantly after me. I was nearly nabbed when one day I had slipped into the headquarters of the Metal Workers' Union. The police arrived while I was still there. One of them, who did not know me, saluted and asked: "Is Josip Broz here?" I spread my arms in surprise and replied: "Don't you see he isn't here?" They looked round at all those present, turned toward me, saluted again, thanked me and went away.

I wore black glasses and changed my clothes so that the police would not know me. Once when I had chanced a visit to Headquarters, I found the police there and this time they recognized me. I jumped from a window to the roof of an adjoining building, ran down the stairs and managed to lose myself in the crowd.

I was obliged to change my flat. In a workers' suburb in Zagreb, at 46 Vinogradska Street, I rented a room where I used to spend the night from time to time. It was also used by some other comrades who were wanted by the police. I always had a revolver with me. At 11 P.M. on August 4, 1928, I was entering my room in Vinogradska Street when suddenly two men jumped on me. They were plainclothes policemen. They tied my hands so tightly that they turned blue, searched my room and took me to jail the same night. There I was chained and questioned. My manner irritated a detective and he struck me such a blow across the face that I went dizzy. When I refused to sign any statement, he grabbed an office chair and hit me twice across the chest. I looked at him with contempt and said: "What a strong fellow you are who can beat a chained man." I asked for medical help, but it was refused. I spat blood for a long time after that.

I remained in the police prison for more than three months. In all, the police arrested fifteen people, among them a worker called Franjo Novoselić who from time to time used to come to sleep in my room. Once again torture in jail and the manner in which the police investigation was delayed led me to try a hunger strike. Immediately after this strike I was transferred to the Court Jail, and my trial was announced. The State Prosecutor accused five other persons besides me: the worker Novoselić, a student called Pavle Brajer, who had also come to my room one day, and the three people who lived in the house.

CHAPTER V

1928:

"I consider myself responsible only to my Communist Party . . ."

UNITS of the Ninth Yugoslav Army liberated Zagreb, the capital of Croatia, by the end of April, 1945. In the archives of the Royal Court of Justice files were found of the trial of Josip Broz and his five codefendants in the week beginning November 6, 1928, at eight-thirty in the morning. The files contained the complete minutes of the trial taken down in small, almost illegible longhand, by the Court clerk Zvonko Turina, along with press cuttings.

The minutes first state that the Court was composed of five judges: Svetozar Tomić, Dr. Ivo Pack, Janko Nežić, Julijan Mician, Dr. Djuro Kosijer.*

A local right-wing paper, *Novosti*, wrote about the beginning of the trial: "The small hall of the Zagreb Court of Justice was packed to capacity yesterday. On the one hand, the defense seeks to present the whole thing as a police fabrication. The chief actors tell the Court that they haven't the foggiest idea what the Central Committee of the Communist Party is, what the Executive Committee of the Communist International is, what the Association of the Communist Youth of Yugoslavia is and so forth. On the other hand, the younger workers and students have taken an extraordinary interest in this trial, squeezing themselves into the courtroom until there is no room to move! They are young men with long curly hair, or young girls with bobbed hair, perhaps followers of the new gospel, perhaps acquaintances of the six defendants, who never come to

---

* Of these five judges who presided at the trial of Tito, three are still alive and receiving state pensions.

'bourgeois' trials but only attend such propaganda, militant, international-messiah cases.

"All this strange audience listens attentively, stands patiently and eats every word, bursting out laughing at every joke made by the defendants and during the breaks whispering to each other or exchanging significant glances."

On the first day three of the accused were heard. On the second day at eleven o'clock in the morning, Josip Broz was brought before the judges. He was the principal defendant.

This is how *Novosti* of November 8 reported his hearing:

"The Communist trial in the big hall of the Zagreb Court was continued yesterday. After the hearing of the defendant Franjo Novoselić, Josip Broz was ushered into the hall. He is undoubtedly the most interesting person in the trial; his face makes one think of steel. His shining eyes look over his spectacles in a cool but energetic way. In his case, perhaps, his attitude before the Court will not merely be a display of arrogance, for he is a man who has already been prosecuted, and who has several times been sentenced for his political views. A large number of spectators no doubt knew the stubbornness with which he maintains his beliefs, for a silent attention reigned in the Court throughout his hearing."

When the Presiding Judge asked Josip Broz whether he considered himself guilty, he replied, according to the report in *Novosti:*

"I am guilty according to the indictment, but in fact I am not guilty."

Presiding Judge: "Then tell me of what you do consider yourself guilty."

Defendant Broz: "I admit that I am a member of the illegal Communist Party of Yugoslavia and I admit that I have propagated Communism. I tried to point out to the proletariat all the injustices done to them. But I do not recognize the bourgeois Court of Justice because I consider myself responsible only to my Communist Party."

Presiding Judge: "Are you acquainted with the Law for the Protection of the State?"

Josip Broz: "Yes, I have heard of that law but I have not read it because it really does not interest me."

Presiding Judge: "That law, however, forbids every kind of Communist propaganda; are you aware of that?"

Tito

Josip Broz: "Yes, I am, but that is only a temporary law."

Presiding Judge: "It is, however, still in force like any other law. That law takes you, and everyone who breaks it, to Lepoglava Prison. The law has been passed by the nation against you Communists, who, according to the people's view, are trying to corrupt them, and who want to defend themselves against your destructive activity."

Josip Broz: "I know, but that law was not passed by the people. I am not afraid of it at all. It would be a bad thing if the Communist Party were to be frightened by a temporary act of legislation."

Presiding Judge: "You are only pigheadedly sacrificing your young lives without being of any help at all."

Josip Broz: "Yes, I am quite prepared to suffer."

The second question which the Presiding Judge asked Josip Broz related to bombs and Communist literature allegedly found in his flat.

According to the minutes Josip Broz answered:

". . . In June, 1928, I rented a room with Božičković, partly for my own use and partly for my comrades who were coming to Zagreb and who were sought by the police. I paid him three hundred dinars in June and July. I have slept in that room three or four times. I have also sent various men to spend the night there, but I will not tell their names. I knew about the Communist literature that was found, I knew that it was brought there by my comrades whose names I shall not disclose. I didn't know that this literature was actually taken into Božičković's flat but I am ready to admit that, although it may have been taken to another place. I only learned that this literature was stored in Božičković's flat when the police search discovered it there. I do not believe that bombs were found in the same room. I didn't take them and don't know about them. They were probably put there by the police themselves. My comrades and I did not do any work in Božičković's flat and therefore Božičković has nothing at all to do with us. It is true that I sent Franjo Novoselić to Božičković a few days before his arrest. I met him by chance and he told me that he had just come from Germany so I sent him to Božičković. I admit that my comrades used to send

Communist literature by reliable agents and through reliable men, and I have been in charge of the distribution of that material."

Presiding Judge: "What is the meaning of these notes in your notebook, such as R 1 25 B?"

Josip Broz: "Those are signs for the dispatch of Communist literature, and I admit that the literature which was discovered was only a part of what my comrades and I sent for the purpose of Communist propaganda, which we distributed and are distributing wrapped in paper such as the police found."

State Prosecutor: "What is the meaning of 26.1.80.1?"

Josip Broz: "These are the signs for the book *The Foundations of Leninism*, which was very widely distributed, but I don't know where the book was sent from."

State Prosecutor: "What is the meaning of R.I.R.II.B.?"

Josip Broz: "I cannot say."

During the hearings of Josip Broz, he disclosed that he had been mistreated by the police. This is how the *Jutarnji List*, a local morning paper, reported the event:

Presiding Judge: "Is it a mere coincidence that the bombs were found in your room?"

Josip Broz: "After the events of June 20, it was necessary to find a scapegoat, and it is my opinion that the police planted these bombs. I have had sufficient experience of police methods. They shot down three workers, and then had to throw the blame upon the workers themselves, so the bombs and weapons were planted."

"Did you perhaps yourselves kill them so that you could fish in troubled waters?" asked the State Prosecutor. "Do you know anything about the leaflets which called a strike after the events of June 20?"

"Yes, I do."

"Did you write them?"

"No, I did not."

"They were found in your room. Even the ink for the mimeograph machine was there."

"I don't know who wrote the leaflets or who mimeographed them. At the police station they treated me in a bestial and inhuman way."

"But the others all say that they were well treated."

"Yes, they expect to be let out of this place, and they are afraid that the police will terrorize them afterward. When I was arrested they tied my hands and took me to the police station at Ilica Street, and in a room packed with six guards I was questioned by the detective Anžulović. They tied my hands so hard that they went blue. When I was brought face to face with Eva Koprivnjak and she said she didn't know me, the Detective Supervisor swore at me in such words that I cannot repeat them here.

"Then he called me to come closer to his desk. Not suspecting anything wrong I did so, whereupon he struck me a blow in the face with his hand so that I went dizzy. Then he called me to his desk again, but I refused because I expected him to strike me again; then he struck me twice with a chair on my chest and the injuries I got lasted quite a long time.

"I asked for medical assistance but they refused it and for that reason I went on a seven days' hunger strike. Many times during the night I heard the terrible cries of those who were being questioned by the police. But these people here do not dare to say so."

The State Prosecutor interrupted him:

"You are telling these stories to make a martyr of yourself and to get money from Moscow."

"I have admitted many things and I have no reason to fear. I know in any case that whatever I say I shall not get out of this place soon. All the others will, and that is why they say that they were well treated at the Police Court."

The trial was continued on November 7, with the evidence of witnesses including police agents Julije Rimaj, Milan Rakić and Anton Štefuj.

According to the minutes Štefuj said:

"When arrested, Broz declared that if he had had a hundred-to-one chance he would have tried either to get away or shoot."

Josip Broz: "That is not true."

The State Prosecutor began his speech on November 9. In his final plea he indicted Josip Broz and Franjo Novoselić. This is what the minutes record:

"That Josip Broz did throughout the years of 1921 to 1928 in Zagreb and other places, as a member of the illegal Communist

Party of Yugoslavia, carry out Communist propaganda in so far as he organized members of that Party, held regional and local conferences on the subjects 'The Attitude of the Party Leadership on the Events and Political Attitude of S.D.K.,' 'Reorganization of Cells and Regions,' 'Strengthening of the Communist Party in England, Germany and so on,' 'The New Line of the Party Policy and Strengthening of the Party,' and thus spread Communist ideas with the aim of the first stated above under paragraph III in the indictment, therefore that he organized and became a member of an association which has as its declared purpose the propagating of Communism and illegal, forcible seizure of power."

When the State Prosecutor concluded his speech, the Presiding Judge gave the floor to the counsel for defense, Dr. Ivo Politeo, who objected to the indictment since additions had been made to it after the evidence was concluded, and therefore asked the release of his clients, or in the case of an unfavorable verdict as mild a sentence as possible. During his speech the defense counsel was twice called to order by the Presiding Judge.

At the end of the trial Josip Broz and his defense counsel challenged the Presiding Judge, Tomić, because he refused Broz a rebuttal.

This is what is entered in the minutes:

"After the defense counsel concluded his hour-long speech, the Presiding Judge asked the defendants whether they had anything to add in their defense. All the defendants declined except Broz, who began to make a statement about his background and to explain how it happened that he became a Communist. The Presiding Judge remarked that the defendant Josip Broz had been quite sufficiently questioned about his earlier background, and that the point was now rather out of order.

"Josip Broz and his counsel protested and since both of them began to talk rather heatedly the words of Broz became inaudible, but he was heard to say that he must be permitted to defend his own Communist ideas.

"The Presiding Judge then withdrew Broz' right to speak on the subject, halted any further discussion, declared the trial concluded and ruled that the sentence would be pronounced on Wednesday, November 14, 1928, at ten o'clock in the morning. The counsel for defense lodged a plea that the ruling of the Court be annulled. The State Prosecutor demanded the right to speak but was refused by the Presiding Judge since the trial was already concluded.

"When the Presiding Judge ordered the guards to remove the defendants Josip Broz began to protest. He turned toward the citizens who filled the hall and shouted, 'Long live the Communist Party of Yugoslavia,' 'Police spirit prevails in this place' and several other words which in the general confusion could not be understood."

Sentence was pronounced on November 14. Josip Broz was sentenced to five years' hard labor, Franjo Novoselić to three and Andrija Božićković to two. Eva Koprivnjak and Pavle Brajer were found not guilty.

After this when the Presiding Judge ordered the defendants to be taken away and chained, Josip Broz while leaving the courtroom shouted: "Long live the Communist Party of Yugoslavia! Long live the International!"

Commenting on the end of the trial, *Novosti* of November 15 wrote sarcastically:

"The Communist trial which has become known as the bomb throwers' trial was concluded yesterday, with its dominant tone struck once more at the end by Josip Broz. After the sentence was read, he rose and, turning to the large audience which was already rising to leave the courtroom, shouted three times "Long live the Communist Party!,' 'Long live the Third International!' But his comrades, who certainly must have been in the courtroom in force, did not respond to his cry, although under their breath they were probably shouting with him. Thus it was that this unyielding Communist disappeared behind prison walls, for all the world like the captain of a ship who shouts when his ship is sinking."

Two days later *Borba* also commented on the trial. At that time this paper was not the official organ of the banned Communist Party but *Borba* represented the views of the Party:

"The trial of Josip Broz and his comrades has shown the bourgeois character of our judicial system, and the sinking of the courts to the level of mere tools of the police.

"The bourgeoisie is wrong if it hopes that by this judiciary practice it will defeat the struggle of the working people. Out of the blood of the innocent victims thousands of new fighters are rising, while years of hard labor meted out by the class courts of justice are only an incentive for an intensified class struggle."

On January 6, 1929, while Josip Broz was waiting to be taken to prison to serve his sentence, King Alexander introduced his full dictatorship.

All political parties were banned, Parliament was dissolved, the Constitution of 1921 abrogated. A rigid preventive censorship was introduced for all newspapers and publications, under which proofs of the daily press had first to be taken to the police buildings where they were censored by semiliterate police clerks. These "censors" had a list of forbidden words which were meticulously struck out wherever they were found.

The last issue of *Borba* appeared on January 12, 1929. Every article that had been submitted was forbidden by the police, and instead the editors of *Borba* wrote: "Since for certain reasons we are no longer in a position to publish many things about our internal problems and economic situation, we shall confine ourselves to the publication of some better-known works of our own and foreign literature. In the present issue we shall give a number of poems by the old liberal Serbian poet Zmaj Jovanović and a passage from the Old Testament."

Displayed most prominently was Zmaj's famous poem "The National Anthem of the State of Jutunin." A rough translation would read:

> O thou Holy God, keep our King alive
> In good health, strong, proud and glorious,
> Since this earth has never seen, nor shall
> Ever see a King equal to him.
> Give him, O Lord, the holiest gifts from heaven:
> Police, gendarmeries and spies,
> If he doesn't fight the foe,
> Let him keep his own people under his heel.

The dictatorship was introduced in the midst of an economic crisis. The industrial firms were running into heavy weather and the number of employed decreased steadily. Foreign capital took advantage of the free currency exchange introduced by the Finance Minister and one billion dinars' worth of foreign exchange fled the country. This worsened the already hard economic situation in the country, and made foreign payment particularly difficult.

The exports of agricultural products fell in both quality and quantity, prices frequently approaching zero. For ten dinars (twenty cents) you could get thirty-three eggs. A liter of milk cost half a dinar (one cent), a liter of wine one dinar. In several parts of Croatia peasants had to leave cattle at the market because they could neither sell them nor feed them.

Living conditions of the workers deteriorated rapidly. Wages went down, all trade unions were banned and factory owners took this opportunity for further measures against the men. Unemployment was widespread and there was no state assistance.

The Communist Party of Yugoslavia was not ready to meet the attack of the dictatorship. Only a few months before, at a Party congress held illegally in Dresden, new Party leadership was elected with the sheet-metal worker Djuro Djaković at its head. But with so little time he was unable to introduce order into a Party divided by factions, or to prepare it to fight a dictatorship which was eager to settle accounts with the Communists.

The first reply to the 6th of January dictatorship was given by the Regional Committee for Serbia. On the night of January 12, a leaflet was distributed which was issued jointly by the Regional Committee of the Party and the SKOY (Young Communist League of Yugoslavia).

The leaflet was printed on an illegal press by the Secretary of the Provincial Committee of SKOY for Serbia, Aleksandar Ranković, aged nineteen, who came from a peasant family in Šumadija, near Belgrade. In the course of its distribution, on the very eve of the Orthodox New Year, a Communist was arrested and the organization was breached. He gave the names of other members of the Provincial Committee of SKOY, who were also arrested. Aleksandar Ranković succeeded in evading the police agents for a few days but was finally arrested on January 20. He was taken to the notorious police prison Glavnjača, where torture began immediately. He was beaten the whole night on the soles of his feet with a wooden truncheon. Then he was thrown into a cell with a cement floor over which water had been thrown. Winter that year was so hard that the Danube was frozen. Ranković even put his loaf of bread under his spine to avoid lying directly on the cement, while under his head he kept an empty tin. But he admitted nothing. His entire deposition consisted of two sentences: "I don't know anything. I am a member of my trade union and nothing else." At the trial he was sentenced to six years at hard labor.

During the trial he tore off his clothes to show the judges the open wounds inflicted upon him in prison. The President of the Court sent for the doctor, who declared that this was tuberculosis of the skin. At that moment the police agents Vujković and Kosmajac entered the courtroom, and the defendants demonstrated so violently that the President had to remove the agents.

When the sentence was passed the whole group of convicts began to shout, "Long live the Communist Party!" Even on the way to prison through the main streets of Belgrade, they shouted slogans from the police wagon.

This was only the first of many Communist groups to be tried before the Court for the Protection of the State. The police shattered the local Party organization in many places. A group of SKOY members was brought from Ljubljana to Belgrade for trial, headed by the Secretary of the Regional Committee, Edvard Kardelj, a twenty-year-old teacher.

By the end of 1930 Moscow sent a member of the Central Committee of SKOY, a Slovene intellectual named Kocmur, and he too was arrested in Belgrade. Under beating in jail he named Edvard Kardelj as Secretary of the Regional Committee of SKOY, who was in touch with a member of the Central Committee of the Communist Party of Yugoslavia, Krka Dimitrijević. Kocmur gave to the chief of the police agents in Belgrade, Svetozar Vujković, Kardelj's password. On February 17, 1930, Vujković arrived in Ljubljana and went to the meeting place in a street near the theater. He gave the password and immediately asked where he could meet Krka Dimitrijević, for whom he pretended to have messages. Suspecting nothing, Edvard Kardelj told him he was to meet Krka Dimitrijević the same day at seven-thirty in the evening in Tivoli Park.

At this Vujković shouted and drew his pistol, while from surrounding streets police agents rushed out, pushed Edvard Kardelj into a courtyard and immediately began to beat him. They punched him in the stomach, hit him with a revolver over the head and then threw him into a motorcar and drove him to the police station, where

Vujković continued to beat him, horse-whipping him over the face and back. It was then about five o'clock in the afternoon, and at seven-thirty Krka Dimitrijević was to be at Tivoli. It was therefore necessary somehow to outmaneuver Vujković and make it impossible for him to catch Dimitrijević. Finally Edvard Kardelj begged Vujković to stop beating him while he told him something: "When I said 'seven-thirty at Tivoli' that in fact was the password," Kardelj said. "You were to answer that 'it is cold there,' another password in reply to mine, and when you did not answer with the proper password I knew immediately that you were a police agent."

Vujković was thoroughly deceived. He resumed the beating, demanding that Kardelj tell him "the truth." After some time Kardelj pretended to break down, and told Vujković that a meeting had been fixed for eight o'clock in the evening at Smartinska Street, far away from Tivoli Park.

Some ten minutes before eight o'clock, Edvard Kardelj, beaten up as he was, was taken to Smartinska Street. Agents blocked all the surrounding streets. Eight o'clock struck but Krka Dimitrijević did not appear. Edvard stood alone in the street while Vujković kept cursing him from the entrance of a house. At eight-thirty it was evident that Krka Dimitrijević was not going to appear. Edvard Kardelj had cheated Vujković of his victim. Krka Dimitrijević had really turned up at seven-thirty at Tivoli and waited an hour, furious at not seeing Edvard Kardelj. Next morning he learned of the arrest and left Ljubljana quickly for the Soviet Union.

When Vujković realized that he had been victimized, he began to whip Kardelj again, and continued the night through at the police station. He got nothing more from Kardelj. After two successive nights of beating, Vujković left for Belgrade and issued orders that Kardelj was to be brought to the Belgrade police station. On his way Kardelj was kept for two days at the Zagreb police station, where he was questioned and beaten again. Once in Belgrade, Kardelj was taken to the new buildings of the police, where he was tortured. Throughout the night the beating went on, while during the day Edvard Kardelj, with fifteen of his comrades, was kept in a small room on the roof. Among them sat police, who for the smallest fancied offense continued to beat Kardelj and his other comrades.

On the third night Vujković seized Kardelj, opened the window and thrust him out head down, while two police held him suspended by one leg. Kardelj remained hanging from the sixth floor while Vujković repeated: "Confess, you son of a bitch, since otherwise we will throw you down on the pavement, just as we did to Nešić."

On the fourth night of the beating Vujković ordered a big sack to be brought, and threatening Kardelj: "You will be thrown into the Danube."

Some ten days later Kardelj and the other comrades who were given away by Kocmur were finally transferred to another building, where the beatings diminished.

"How did I feel while I was being tortured?" says Kardelj. "I scarcely felt the blows. It is difficult to try to explain it, but one thing of which I was certain was that not for a single moment did I think that I would not be able to stand it."

In September a trial was held in Belgrade before the Court for the Protection of the State. Edvard Kardelj was sentenced to two years at hard labor. After his own sentence Josip Broz spent some time in the court jail in Zagreb waiting to be transferred to the Lepoglava prison. One day a guard slipped him a message from the Party organization, telling him that his escape was being organized. The guard was a locksmith who had joined the prison service because he was unemployed, but he sympathized with the Communist Party and did great services for many imprisoned Communists. This man brought Josip Broz a loaf of bread in which a file was hidden. This is how Tito remembers these days:

There were six bars on the small window of my cell. On the first morning I began to cut through the first one, between five and six when the prisoners were getting up, because the doors were open, cans and dirt were being taken out and there was plenty of noise. In five nights I sawed through five bars. One to go, and I would be free. In front of the jail my friends waited with a bicycle. Everything was ready, and I started to saw the last bar. To deaden the noise I put moist bread round the bar and the file, but suddenly I heard the key being turned in the lock of my door. I jumped from the window and sat on my bed. The guards came in and one of them shouted to me: "Get out, you are going to be transferred to another cell."

Tito

Bad luck! I was moved out of that wing with all the prisoners because gallows were being erected in the court yard for an execution. I had no opportunity to escape from the new cell, for a few days later I was sent to Lepoglava Prison to serve my term.

Lepoglava is a lovely little town sheltered under the mountain of Ivančica, on the border of my own Zagorje. In earlier days it was famous as a center of science and arts, for in the seventeenth century it was the seat of the first university in Croatia, which occupied the buildings of the great Pavlin Monastery built by the White Friars in 1300. But at the end of the eighteenth century the Emperor Francis Joseph II dissolved the Pavlin order and they were obliged to close their academy, which by then had the rank of a university. The buildings were left unoccupied until the Austro-Hungarian government converted this ancient building into Lepoglava Prison, the synonym for oppression and forced labor. Here I arrived on a gray January afternoon in 1929. The other new prisoners and I were first taken to the prison governor, who told us how to behave and what the routine was. As he talked I began to think that I had known him somewhere before. Then I recognized him; he was Bohaček, who was in my regiment in the Carpathians and who for a time had been prisoner of war in Russia. He recognized me. There was no conversation between us.

From his spacious room we were taken to a compartment which they called a "bath." Here began one of the most degrading experiences any human being could endure. Our hair was cut to the scalp and then we were told to undress and enter a big tub of dirty water with a scum of mud and human hair. Twenty of us had to use it one after another shivering with cold. Then we were given convict uniforms—bundles of holes hung together, worn out through many years by other convicts. Then the medical examination, and then through a maze of corridors and many iron gates, and we reached the cells. Each cell contained a folding cot with a thin, dirty mattress and two blankets. In the corner were a small stool and a can. The floor was cement and the cells were freezing; the cold made sleep impossible. In the evening we got some thin soup. Every fifteen minutes throughout the night you heard the voice of a guard in the prison yard: "Guard beware!" This was to frighten those who might be thinking of escape. At about six in the morning the keys opened doors along the line of cells and the guards yelled: "Cans and dirt out!" Our breakfast was a small loaf of bread. Soon I would be brought a basketful of goose feathers which were to be cleaned by the evening. I was allowed no books. So I spent my first three months in prison as Number 483.

But again my knowledge of machinery proved valuable. The prison contained a small electric power plant which supplied current to the prison and the village. I was put in charge of it and in keeping with my responsibilities was allowed to have books and other amenities. I also had an assistant, Comrade Moša Pijade. He had been scooped up in the first wave of persecutions, as I have already said, and sentenced to fourteen years. We lost no time in creating a Party cell; and since there were many comrades in the prison, we soon had a large and thriving organization inside Lepoglava's gray walls.

Outside, the oppressions of the regime had practically destroyed our Party organization. It was all the more necessary for us in prison to use our time to advantage; it was particularly necessary that the young men, who had joined the Party in its illegal days and thus lacked experience and knowledge of Marxism, should be trained for the future. With the few books and little means at our disposal, we organized courses of studies and lectures. I was able to keep fairly close contact with my comrades because, in my role of electrical engineer, I could move all over the prison with my test bulb in one hand and a screw driver in the other.

Moša Pijade was an ardent painter. He managed somehow to get some paints and canvas and began to make portraits, first of all his cellmates, then of the scenery visible through the little window in our cell. One day he had nothing more to paint, so he decided to make a portrait of a prison guard, who was an interesting subject. A round nose, heavy hanging lips, a greasy old cap. It was in the afternoon, and the guard was sleeping. Pijade worked fast, and in half an hour his portrait was ready. He was just putting down his palette when the guard suddenly jumped up. "You made a portrait of me!" he shouted at Pijade. Pijade said he had. The guard was furious: "You did it while I was sleeping. . . ." Pijade explained to him that this was a work of art, that it was one of the best portraits he had ever made. But the guard was inflexible. He seized the canvas and, with his thick fingers, smeared the fresh paint. Pijade was very sad the whole day.

I was also sent into the village sometimes to do repairs. A guard always accompanied me, but even so I was able to meet and talk with comrades coming from Zagreb.

Opposite the prison was a café and above it were flats. The owner * was quite a religious and kindhearted woman and did what she could to help prisoners. So every two or three months, by arrangement, there would be trouble with the electricity in her flat. When I came with my guard she would offer him a drink and while he enjoyed himself in the café I was upstairs talking with the comrades.

This tolerable life was ended when I was unjustly accused of conspiring to escape and transferred to Maribor, the worst prison in Yugoslavia. The warden was nicknamed Rabelj (Executioner). I was kept in solitary confinement in a stinking cell. There were a number of other comrades in this prison and we managed to communicate and organize, and by threats of a hunger strike finally got some concessions, such as the right to have one light on in our cells until midnight and to walk in the prison courtyard once a day and twice on Sundays. We were not allowed to speak to one another, but we got round that by finger signals: a man would seem to be scratching his head, but his index finger was spelling out a message in Morse.

We were allowed to write to our relatives and friends, but the letters were severely censored. One of the first to reply to my letters was Stevo Šabić, my friend from Veliko Trojstvo.

We were permitted to receive occasional food parcels, books and periodicals. Naturally the latter were limited to what the authorities considered safe, such things as the *London Economist*. I read a good deal of psychology then and was also interested in philosophy. I asked the warden once for a book on Greek philosophy. He answered: "What do you need a book on philosophy for? Look around you—you'll see all the philosophy you want." We succeeded in

---

* The owner of the café, a certain Madame Fidlerica, still ran her café after the liberation and still helped the prisoners. As these now included many of our enemies, our authorities arrested her and wanted to bring her to trial. Tito intervened when he heard of it: "Let the old woman alone," he said. "She is a churchgoer. She used to help us and now she is helping the reactionaries. She sees no difference at all and believes she is doing a good thing."

smuggling in some Marxist literature, especially *Anti-Dühring*. We used to tear off the covers and rebind them in the covers of permitted books. A classical Marxist book was once bound in the covers of *The Arabian Nights*. While we were out walking in the prison yard, the prison guards glanced through our books, but they were so ignorant that they never realized the nature of the literature we read.

But apart from these meager comforts, life at Maribor was very hard. The warden suddenly issued new orders prohibiting all parcels and books, as well as all exercise in the prison yard. We were half starved. The beds were simply old boards with straw mattresses, and the straw was changed about every three years. There were no sheets or pillows, but only a light blanket in summer and a heavier one in winter. The only heat came from a little stove that one of our cell-mates had bought with money his relatives had sent. The place crawled with bedbugs. They hid in the cracks of the bedboards, and we spent long hours trying to find a way to destroy them. We managed to get some gasoline, but that didn't help. Finally we found that by taking the boards apart and poking into the holes with white-hot wire, we could burn the bugs.

There were eight men in the room I had, and we shared everything. When one of us got a cigarette we would mark it with a pencil into four parts—fortunately, four of our cellmates were nonsmokers. Each would smoke his share right to the line. But the strongest and sweetest was the butt end, and we solved that fairly by taking turns. We also worked out a co-operative scheme of work. During the day the eight of us were supposed to make eighteen hundred paper bags. So one of us would cut the paper, another would spread the glue, a third would stick the two parts together, and so on, and we finished the whole job in two hours. That gave us time for reading, talking and educating ourselves for the future. We were paid three and a half dinars (seven cents) a month in order, as the warden said, "to give you a start on a decent life." Cigarettes at that time cost five dinars a packet.

In such conditions, little things become big in one's mind. I remember being in solitary and hearing the puffing of a steam engine on the tracks outside. It must have been switching cars onto the sidings, because the busy puffing went on for some time. The engineer was inexperienced: he started each time with a roar and stopped with a screeching of brakes. All my mechanic's instincts rose in me, and I found myself wanting to yell, "Man, don't torture that engine!"

They tried in many ways to break me. Once Warden Rabelj had me brought before him and asked why I had not asked for a parole. I answered: "The idea of release on parole is for the prisoner to correct himself, or at least show a desire to do so. But I do not want to renounce my political beliefs, so I do not ask to be released."

So passed the years, one after the other, until five had elapsed. One month before the end of my term I reported to the warden to ask permission to have a suit of clothes made and to let my hair grow, for we prisoners had to have our hair shaved.

Escorted by a guard, I went out into town to a tailor, where I was measured for a new suit. My friend Stevo Šabić sent me the money for it.

At last on a November morning in 1933 I was summoned by the prison guard to the attic, where I changed into civilian clothes, casting off the convict's uniform after five years. I took leave of my friends, went to the warden for his final sermon and turned my back on the gates accompanied by a policeman, my hands chained.

Before I left, the warden informed me that I had to serve the remainder of the sentence I had received at my first trial at Ogulin in 1927. There was a further three and a half months to do.

Yet it was a comfort to think that this was considerably less than the time I had already done. In a dimly lit third-class carriage, where I was alone with my escort, on my way again to the medieval Frankopan Tower at Ogulin, I asked the policeman to loosen the chains on my wrists. After hesitating a moment he did me the favor.

CHAPTER VI

1934:

"I could no longer go under my own name . . ."

*J*OSIP BROZ served the remaining three months of his sentence in the Frankopan Tower at Ogulin. In March, 1934, the guards of the court jail escorted him to the police station, and he was informed that the authorities now required him to remain permanently in Kumrovec, his native village of Zagorje, and to report daily to authorities. This control was frequently applied not only to Communists but also to the representatives of the bourgeois parties who opposed King Alexander's regime.

Josip Broz reached Kumrovec toward the end of March and went directly home. His brother Dragutin-Karlo had died a short time before. In his parents' home he found his brother's wife and children. That same day he reported to Josip Jurak, President of the municipality, which consisted of Kumrovec and several neighboring villages.

When I entered his office, the President, whom I had known since we were children, quickly closed the door. He came up to me, patted me on the shoulder and said: "You put up a fine show!" Although I knew that King Alexander's regime had no support among the people, I was taken aback by the President's attitude. He had been appointed by the authorities and should have been the fundamental support of the regime in the whole district. However, what did he do? He congratulated a Communist, who had just done five years, on his behavior before the court and in prison.

The President then told me that according to the law I had to report every day, but he winked as he spoke. He obviously knew I was not going to stop long in my own village. I visited all my friends and relatives in the village, and called on my aunt across the Sutla. There was only one person in the district who was displeased at my return. One Sunday, after service in St. Roko's Chapel, the priest declared in a sermon that the Anti-Christ had appeared in the village. Several days later I decided to stop reporting to the authorities and to leave Kumrovec.

I went first to Samobor, a small town twenty miles from Zagreb, where I stayed for a time with my sister, who was married to a shoemaker there.

Noticing my disappearance from Kumrovec, the police issued a warrant for my arrest. I could no longer go under my own name; I had to alter my appearance as well. First I let my mustache grow, which rather changed my features. Then I dyed my hair reddish and took to spectacles.

Meanwhile, I had established personal contact with the Party organization at Zagreb. I first did so through a writer called Stevo Galogaža, a lean, lanky man of forty. During World War I he had been a volunteer in the Serbian army, and later became intimate with the Communists. He was specially engaged in Red Assistance, which meant that he organized the collection and delivery of parcels and money for imprisoned comrades and help for their families. He had sent me Red Assistance. Through Galogaža I got in touch with other comrades who were in Zagreb at the time, and thus established connection with the Provincial Committee for Croatia. It was a rule in the Party in those times not to use one's real name, in order to reduce the chances of exposure. For instance, if someone working with me was arrested, and flogged into revealing my real name, the police would easily trace me. But the police never knew the real person hiding behind an assumed name, such as I had in the Party. Naturally, even the assumed names often had to be changed. Even before going to prison I had taken the name of Gligorijević, and of Zagorac, meaning the "man from Zagorje." I even signed a few newspaper articles with the second.

Now I had to take a new name. I adopted first the name of Rudi, but another comrade had the same name and so I was obliged to change it, adopting the name Tito. I hardly ever used Tito at first; I assumed it exclusively in 1937, when I began to sign articles with it.

Why did I take this name "Tito" and has it special significance? I took it as I would have any other, because it occurred to me at the moment. Apart from that, this name is quite frequent in my native district. The best-known Zagorje writer of the late eighteenth century was called Tito Brezovački; his witty comedies are still given in the Croatian theater after more than a hundred years. The father of Ksaver Šandor Gjalski, one of the greatest Croatian writers, was also called Tito. Later, while in Moscow, I worked in the Comintern as "Walter."

When I arrived in Zagreb and set to work, my comrades elected me to membership of the Provincial Committee, the Party leadership for Croatia. I gained an insight into the state of affairs of the Party organization in a very short time. What I learned completed the picture we had formed in prison. Conditions in the Party in those days were extremely hard; but favorable signs were already appearing.

Up to 1933 there had been only shattered groups here and there. Almost the whole of the leading Party staff were either killed, imprisoned or in exile. But in 1933 underground cells had already begun to revive on a large scale and local committees were formed. Provincial committees had been set up by the time I was released from prison in 1934.

The basic weakness in the work of the Party was that the leadership was not in the country, among the people. When, in 1929, the Zagreb police killed the Secretary of the Central Committee, Djuro Djaković, those who remained of the Committee fled across the border and established themselves permanently in Vienna. The Comintern then appointed Jovan Mališić-Martinović, an intellectual from Montenegro, to head the Party in Vienna. Far from its own country, from the living conditions of the people of Yugoslavia, this Central Committee attempted to establish some connection with the organizations at home. It sent various Party members to Yugoslavia, but they invariably fell into the hands of the police, betraying not only individuals but whole organizations.

Hundreds of Party members were caught by the police, and as a result Party organizations at home lost all confidence in the leadership abroad, many of them refusing to maintain contact. On the other hand, the police terror did not abate. It is estimated that between 1929, when King Alexander proclaimed his dictatorship, and

1934, about thirty-five thousand political prisoners passed through the jails of Yugoslavia. Almost all were beaten, and only a small number were tried before the special Court for the Protection of the State. In my opinion the method of leadership was also responsible for the state of affairs in the Party; members were simply compelled to await instructions from abroad instead of thinking for themselves. The people at home who were directly involved in the struggle were allowed to take no political action not approved by the Central Committee. But this Committee was in Vienna. On the other hand, the Central Committee itself had no freedom of action, but had to send its every resolution to the Comintern in Moscow before it could act. In Moscow the resolutions were first delivered to subordinates and gradually climbed to higher quarters. Finally they were laid before the forum, where they were first analyzed, then pertinent decisions were taken. At long last instructions were sent to the Central Committee in Vienna and relayed to the Party organizations in Yugoslavia. Not only was this a long journey, but the decisions, when they at last arrived, were often either inappropriate or out of date. They had been made by people far from home and the direct struggle, often without any insight into conditions in the country. One of the consequences was a constant reshuffling of leaders. Whenever a line of action proved unsuitable, the Comintern would nominate someone new. As a rule the Comintern made its choice among persons who lived in Moscow, and were part of its machinery; it never trusted comrades who had steeled themselves in the struggle at home. Clearly, no remarkable results could be expected in the Party's work in Yugoslavia.

The first task facing the Provincial Committee in Zagreb was to establish connections with the Central Committee in Vienna. The members said openly that something was wrong, that the police caught everybody the Central Committee sent, the result being general exposure. There were even some who suggested cutting off connections. The leadership in Zagreb decided that I should go to Vienna to consider ways of establishing a meaningful contact.

Early in July I completed a lengthy report on Fascism for the Party organization at Zagreb University, and then left for Vienna. I had two alternative ways of traveling. One was to find a forged passport, in someone else's name; the other was to cross the border at a weakly guarded spot. Time was too short to forge a passport, and I decided to smuggle myself across the frontier. I chose the small town of Tržič, in Slovenia, as the place to cross. There the Karavanke hills separate Yugoslavia from Austria, and tourists with membership cards of the Slovene Mountaineering Society were allowed to go about eight miles into Austrian territory. I availed myself of this arrangement, got a forged mountaineer's card and in mountaineering boots and rucksack set out for Tržič. There I found a guide who was ready to see me over the border by a short route, avoiding the frontier posts where the cards of all mountaineers going to Austria were examined. The guide did this sort of thing for money and also smuggled flints, which were unavailable in Yugoslavia and therefore precious; he asked for three hundred dinars.

At dusk we left Tržič, going uphill. From time to time my guide took a pull from one of the three flasks of wine in his rucksack. We went slowly and we had not reached the border by midnight. We neared it at dawn; the guide pointed the observation post out to me and said, "Now you go ahead alone because you've only paid me up to here!"

But this was the most dangerous part of the route, and I asked to be guided farther to the part of the border easiest to cross, because the one he had shown me was near an observation post, through a clearing.

"Certainly," said the guide, "if you give me three hundred dinars more."

I had to agree. He had already drunk so much wine that he was reeling. At last we arrived about a hundred yards from the frontier, where the guide began to blackmail me again. I lost my temper and dismissed him, setting out alone toward the border and crossing into Austrian territory near a signpost. Instead of following the path, I took a short cut, came out on a dangerously steep ravine and tumbled down the slope, tearing my coat in the descent.

Dead tired, I reached a house on the Austrian side at six in the morning. The inhabitants were Slovenes. I told them I was a tourist. An old woman with a big goiter who was alone in the house took me to a hayloft to sleep. I awoke about noon and I watched life in the house from my loft. The old woman was calling her chicks: "Chick, chick, chick . . ."

Tito

The chicks gathered but the old woman could no longer call "chick, chick, chick," for air escaped from the swelling on her throat with a rasping sound, scaring the chicks away. When the scene was repeated I crawled out of the hayloft and helped her to collect her chicks. I had dinner and then set out for the nearest large village. Reaching the outlying houses, I heard gunshots, not continuously but every few minutes. At the entrance to the village, three youths suddenly jumped out wearing civilian clothes and carrying rifles.

"Halt!" one of them commanded.

I had no idea what he wanted until I looked at his sleeves, whereupon I was no longer in doubt. They wore red armlets with the swastika. Chancellor Dollfuss had been assassinated in Vienna that day, and the Austrian Hitlerites were attempting to seize power in the whole country. There had been fighting in this village, where Hitlerites had been forced to the upper end and the government troops held the rest.

I looked at the symbol on the sleeves of these youths. Several years later when Germany attacked my country, this sign was to become the symbol of oppression and slavery. I told them I was a Yugoslav tourist. They ordered me to return and with no alternative left, I turned on my heel and went uphill again.

However, I was reluctant to retrace my steps. Nearing the border, I took a roundabout way toward Klagenfurt. Fighting had been going on there too and members of the Heimwehr stopped me on the way. I had already passed the eight-mile zone where tourists were allowed without passports. I explained that I was heading for Jesenice in Yugoslavia, and had had to make this detour because of the Hitlerites.

In this way I got to the Celovec railway station and caught a train for the capital.

And so I found myself in Vienna again after thirteen years; I had seen it last on my way from captivity in Russia. My business now was to establish contact. In Zagreb my comrades had told me that I could get into touch with the Central Committee through a Yugoslav girl, the daughter of a Zagreb doctor, who was studying ballet in Vienna. I looked her up, and she told me she would let me have an answer the next day. Meanwhile she found me a room in the home of a Jew in the Nineteenth District, in Döblingerstrasse.

Naturally, I did not notify the police of my presence for after the events in Austria of the last few days the regime had become excessively severe.

The next day I met the members of the Central Committee. Milan Gorkić, the Secretary, was present along with Vladimir Čopić and some others. Milan Gorkić was a huge, stout man of about thirty, redheaded and freckled. He had been appointed Secretary in 1932 and had not lived in Yugoslavia for many years. His real name was Josip Cizinski. His father had been born in the Sub-Carpathian Ukraine and as a civil servant had been transferred to Sarajevo, in Bosnia. There Gorkić had attended commercial school, and belonged to a youth group in 1918. Afterward, he took part in some kind of conference in Vienna in 1922, and since then had been in Moscow, in the Comintern. He was engaged in youth matters, writing articles and booklets. During his stay in Moscow he was long unable to decide between Yugoslavia and Czechoslovakia, because the Sub-Carpathian Ukraine was Czechoslovak territory at the time, but finally decided for Yugoslavia. He had earned a good reputation in the Comintern.

Gorkić and the other members of the Central Committee fell on me like bees on honey. They wanted to learn all they could about Yugoslavia, about conditions in the Party. I explained everything in detail, not hesitating to tell them how the rank and file felt about the fact that the Central Committee was abroad or about the unceasing arrests and exposures of the men the Central Committee sent to Yugoslavia.

I had been in Vienna several weeks taking part in the work of the Central Committee when I was told I had been appointed to a role in the supreme Party leadership. That was late in August, 1934. I was assigned to organizing Party conferences for Croatia and Slovenia, and preparing a conference for the whole of Yugoslavia. Then I returned home by the route I had come, with no special difficulties. As soon as I arrived in Zagreb, I began to do the work I had been entrusted with.

During his work in 1934, Tito sent several reports to the Central Committee in Vienna. They were taken by special couriers, mostly students, who were studying in the Austrian capital. Several of the reports have been preserved. In that of September 3, 1934, Tito speaks about the organization of provincial conferences. "Wedding" was a code word for "conference." Here are some extracts from the report:

"A particularly deep impression was made by the wedding on the youth representative who was attending such an event for the first time. The outside delegates were no less impressed. This is sufficient indication of the immense significance attached to the big wedding. A weakness of the preparations was that material and resolutions [for the wedding] had not been prepared; the provincial delegates came unprepared so that they couldn't follow the course of the wedding critically or advance their views. Moreover the delegates from Vukovar, Osijek and Karlovac, extremely important industrial centers, were absent. This, in my opinion, was because there was too little time for preparation. But I am convinced this will be corrected with more active work by the new Provincial Committee, and the delegates will come to the big wedding fully prepared.

"The reports of several delegates from the provinces, such as Sisak, showed that the Party organization has taken strong roots. It has about sixty members there and as many in the surrounding villages, which means that there is good revolutionary material among the workers and peasants, and conditions for work are very good. All depends now on the energy and skill of the new Provincial Committee in continuing the work and expanding it over the whole province. In my opinion the Party will be able to take strongest roots in this province among the peasants, and for this reason the Central Committee will have to give Zagreb all the help possible.

"In Zagreb the organization is making very good headway. Young men have succeeded in penetrating into some of the most important enterprises, such as the railway workshops. The Party has also succeeded in activating the old members in the same enterprise, who have now agreed to get down to work. The comrades there have already pretty well freed themselves of the fear of enrolling new members and activating the old ones. But they are still overcautious in making selections, because as far as I have been able to see there are still many men outside the organization who could be attracted to work."

Tito then refers to the work in the trade unions and to the ap-

proaching municipal elections. He finally observes that county conferences have been held everywhere with very good results.

After a short stay in Zagreb, Tito went to Ljubljana to prepare the
Party conference for Slovenia. He stayed with Bojan Stupica, a
theatrical producer, and his wife Sava Severova, one of the best
actresses in Yugoslavia. At the same time he reorganized the Slovene
Provincial Committee.

The Party conference in Slovenia, held in the latter half of September, 1934, met in the summer mansion of the Slovene Bishop
Rožman, at Medvode, eight miles or so north of Ljubljana! It was
a big, lonely house outside the town. We were able to hold the conference in it through the courtesy of Bishop Rožman's half-brother,
whose relations with the Bishop had been rather strained, with the
fortunate consequence that His Grace had him removed to his summer estate to get him out of the way. Several of the gardeners on the
estate were Party members and the Party organization got in touch
with Rožman's brother through them.

About thirty delegates, including Tito, attended the conference,
which lasted two days and nights. All the delegates slept and ate in
the mansion. The Bishop's brother had the meals served in the big
dining hall in style. The tablecloths were white, the glasses were
crystal, the plates bore the Bishop's coat-of-arms. He personally
waited on table, constantly cursing his brother, the Bishop.

The conference was held despite the wave of terror throughout
Slovenia. The police not only shadowed known or suspected Communists but systematically kept a strict eye on workers in all factories.

The conference was of special significance for the development of
the struggle in Slovenia. It was decided that the Party must engage
in large-scale activity for the unity of the working class, and promote
a united struggle of the masses against the dictatorship and for democratic and national rights.

It was at this conference that Tito first met Edvard Kardelj, who
had come out of prison early in 1932 and had since been active in the
Party. Tito recalls this meeting:

"I hold that one of the main things in getting to know a man is his
behavior at work. The main thing in summing up a man is to find
out whether he is a good revolutionary, whether he exhausts all his

energy in his task or works systematically. I decide what a man is worth by the way he speaks: whether he is a phrasemonger, or whether every inaccuracy, great or small, pains him, because there are people who are great revolutionaries—in words. That is why I have always taken account of a man's conscientiousness at work.

"Comrade Kardelj was a calm, quiet man, and it was just his equanimity that impressed me most. He was an honest revolutionary at a time when many were corrupted by factionalism."

After the conference, Tito was summoned to Vienna to report to the Central Committee. His earlier experience discouraged the idea of another surreptitious crossing. Instead, he managed to get a Czechoslovak passport, to which he affixed his photograph. He forged visa seals and set off as an ordinary traveler. He thus arrived in Vienna without any great difficulties and the Yugoslav ballerina again put him in touch with the Central Committee. In Vienna a great deal of work awaited Tito. In addition to joining in the work of the Central Committee he was told to write on various problems, especially military matters, a task he was given because all the members of the Central Committee considered he had the best experience in these matters.

The minutes of the meetings of the Central Committee show that Tito attended them on September 23 and 25 and October 1 and 4, 1934. During the first of these it was decided that Tito was to write a report on the Party conference in Slovenia, to be discussed at the next meeting, and that Gorkić and Tito were to prepare a draft for a national conference. Tito was given the special task of preparing a report on workers' defense companies.

At the meeting of September 25, Tito was told to write an article on "The Duties of Communists in Prison." Gorkić and Tito were also told to prepare a letter to the Provincial Committee for Slovenia in connection with the preparations for a new strike in the big coal mine at Trbovlje, not far from Ljubljana, which employed several thousand workers.

At the meeting of October 1, Tito was told to make a draft on antimilitaristic work in Yugoslavia. The meeting also discussed work in the trade unions.

The last meeting, held three days later, was devoted exclusively to Tito's report on the Slovene conference. The minutes state:

"Approve Tito's activity in accordance with the report of the Central Committee representative on the Slovene provincial conference."

This work completed, Tito prepared to return to Yugoslavia. Before leaving, he discussed with Gorkić the organization of the Fourth Party Conference for the whole of Yugoslavia. Tito was charged with making detailed preparations for the conference at home.

On his way back he stopped in Ljubljana and had a meeting with the Provincial Committee, sending a report to Vienna on October 9. In it Tito charged that Party members had been irresolute after the big coal-mine strike at Trbovlje, and added:

"The influence of the conference yielded good results. At Jesenice the men have since stopped work twice on the initiative of our comrades, and won both times. A strike at Novo Mesto, in a textile mill employing from seventy to eighty workers, was organized and led by our comrades. It was a complete success. The workers demanded better wages and the payment of arrears for overtime, and got them. When I get detailed information, I shall write more extensively. There is great admiration for us over there and everyone says the strike was organized by the Communists and a very good thing. It is interesting that the petite bourgeoisie sympathized with the strikers. At Ruše the workers have canceled the collective contract and are also preparing to fight."

In this letter Tito speaks of the "channel" for crossing the frontier. It indicates that after his experiences he had taken steps to organize a more reliable method and instructed Yugoslavs to get in touch with members of the Communist Party of Austria who were doing their military service. He says:

"The man who had been sent to organize the channel returned after more than a month. He was arrested in Austria, but released after a short time. He went to the border, where he got in touch with members of the Heimwehr and succeeded in forming several groups to be linked with the Austrian Party. They smuggled him back. I shall give you the connections when I get there. He says the soldiers complain they cannot get in touch with the Party and that no one is working with them."

In the evening of the day Tito wrote this letter, a report arrived that King Alexander had been assassinated at Marseilles. He was killed by the Ustashi, a terrorist organization commanded by Ante Pavelic, under the patronage of Mussolini. In Yugoslavia the police took emergency measures. Houses were searched and anti-Communist measures were sharpened.

Being thoroughly compromised, Tito immediately received orders from the Central Committee to go to Vienna, and thence to the Soviet Union. It was perilous to cross the frontier in the old way, because control had been intensified. Tito resorted again to a forged passport made out in the name of a Czechoslovak engineer, with Tito's photograph added and forged visas. The forgery was not very good and he traveled with misgivings. The atmosphere in the train was depressing. The passports were examined at the border not only by the police but by Chetniks, a semi-Fascist Yugoslav organization. Tito was in a compartment with an Austrian woman with a child, six months old. This is what Tito has to say about the crossing:

"The police entered the train at the Jesenice frontier station and asked for our passports. The Austrian woman got up and asked me to hold the child for a moment. I put him on my knees, and handed my passport to the policeman with my free hand. At that moment the child responded to the urge of nature. Startled, I lifted him from my knee, and the policeman noticed what had happened and began to laugh. The incident distracted their attention, and they were not very strict with their examination. They stamped my passport and went on.

"I arrived in Vienna without mishap, and on November 19 attended a meeting of the Central Committee. At that time measures had been intensified in Vienna and the Central Committee was unable to meet there. It was therefore decided to assemble at Brno, in Czechoslovakia. I obtained a forged Austrian passport made out in the name of Jirechek, a barber. The Central Committee had decided I was to go to the Soviet Union for a long stay. The first proposal was that I should be the Yugoslav delegate in Moscow to the Trade Union International (Profintern). This proposal was dropped, because it was suggested that I should work in the Comintern on Yugoslav affairs.

"In the meantime the Fourth Party Conference for the whole of Yugoslavia, whose organization I had worked on, was held in a flat in Ljubljana. Eleven delegates took part in it. A new Central Committee headed by Gorkić was elected at this conference on December 25. I was also elected to it, and also entered the Politburo of the Central Committee.

"Shortly afterward I left for Moscow, but before that I nearly fell into the hands of the police. I was living in the flat of an old Jewess with four grown-up children. One of her daughters worked in a factory, another in a big fashion shop. The flat was on the fourth floor of a building in the Nineteenth District. I hadn't notified the police of my presence, so I had to pay more than I otherwise should have. One day I was sitting in my room, the floor littered with material, when I was disturbed by knocking at the door. I went out into the corridor and found a neighbor who told me that a smell of gas was coming from the flat. Other tenants came out, and we all went to the kitchen where the smell was coming from. There we found my landlady's daughter, who had attempted suicide.

"She was unconscious. I picked her up at once and took her to my room, where I gave her artificial respiration. But she showed no sign of life. The room filled with people. Various documents and materials I had wanted to send to Yugoslavia lay scattered on the floor and table. The situation was dangerous, especially when the police arrived. They asked me who I was and what I did. I explained I was a lodger and that no one but myself was at home, and that I had tried to help the girl. A doctor then came in from the first-aid station and began to attend to the girl, asking us all to leave.

"I went with the rest, having first somehow contrived to collect the documents and material. I went straight to the Schweden Café, where I found the old Jewess, and told her what had happened to her daughter. I asked her to pack my things and bring them to a certain place. She promised and brought me my bag in the evening, apologizing for all the unpleasantness. Her daughter had soon revived and the woman explained why the girl had tried to kill herself: she had been caught stealing money from her employer to go to the cinema.

"Several days later I set out on my journey to Moscow."

CHAPTER VII

1936:

"My whole being rebelled against what I saw in Moscow . . . I thought this was a temporary internal matter."

AFTER fourteen years Tito once more set foot on Soviet soil. In the fifteen years between his first sojourn in Russia during the war and revolution, and his present arrival, he had gained the experience that only a man can gain who is firmly resolved to devote his whole life to the purpose for which he fights. Tito returned to Russia as a mature man of forty-two. Behind him he had years of steadfast work among the rebellious peasants of northern Croatia, days of strikes in the Kraljevica shipyards and in factories in Zagreb and Palanka; arrests and hunger strikes, five years of imprisonment at Lepoglava and Maribor; all this had left its mark and affected the formation of his character.

How did Tito feel when his train came to a halt on the Polish-Soviet border before the Nagoreloye station in the winter of 1934–35? Many years later he evoked his memories:

"What did this mean for a revolutionary? In the most trying hours through dismal nights of endless interrogation and maltreatment, during days of killing solitude in cells and close confinement, we were always sustained by the hope that all these agonies were not in vain, that there was a strong mighty country, however far away, in which had been fulfilled all the dreams for which we were fighting. For us it was the homeland of the workers, in which labor was honored, in which love, comradeship and sincerity prevailed. With what joy I had felt the strength of that country as, emerging from prison in 1934, I listened in the dead of each night to Radio Moscow and heard the clock of the Kremlin tower striking the hours, and the stirring strains of the 'International'! These were not my thoughts alone; they were the thoughts of thousands of comrades I had met during my years of work.

"While our train was passing through a huge triumphal wooden arch, with 'Greetings to the workers of Europe' written on the side facing Europe, and 'Workers of the world unite' on the Soviet side, a young frontier guard in uniform came up to me, saluted and asked for my passport. Several moments later we entered the station. I walked up and down the platform, the length of the rather attractive building, decorated with portraits of Marx, Engels, Lenin and Stalin and with photographs of the gigantic plants in the Urals, of the Red Square in Moscow, of the collective farms in the Ukraine. The frontier formalities completed, we resumed our journey to Moscow."

This was Tito's first visit to the Soviet capital. During the war and revolution his route had never taken him there. He went to the Hotel Lux in Gorki Street, and reported to the representative of the Communist Party of Yugoslavia in the Comintern, Vladimir Čopić, alias Senko, whom he had known in Vienna. Tito was given a room in the Lux, where most of the functionaries lived, and that evening many Yugoslavs who lived in Moscow came to hear fresh news from the man who had just arrived from Yugoslavia. Tito lived in the Lux while he remained in Moscow. It was an old hotel of many small rooms distributed in the main building and several annexes. There was a restaurant on the ground floor, where the guests took their meals, and everyone had a primus stove or an electric cooker for preparing tea or a snack. On the right in the lobby was the "pass table" where all arrivals applied for passes, without which no one was allowed to enter the hotel, not even its permanent guests. Once a Yugoslav living at the hotel forgot to take his permanent pass with him when seeing a guest off. He saw his guest out into the street and was not allowed to re-enter the hotel although the guards at the door knew him well. He had to telephone to his floor to ask a tenant to bring him his pass.

After a short time in Moscow, which he spent touring the huge city, Tito received his assignment. At a meeting in Vienna on January 16, 1935, the Central Committee had decided that Tito was to be one of the candidates for membership in the Balkan Secretariat of the Comintern. A written report to this effect was sent to Čopić and read in part:

"We agree that Tito can take over this work. We leave the final decision with you. If he is appointed *rapporteur* see to it that people are courteous to him. Tell Valija and the others that he is a worker who spent six years in prison, and that perhaps at first he will not be as skillful as some of the intellectuals who appear more knowing. But he knows the Party, he represents the best part of our active workers and after six or eight months we shall recall him for leading work in the Central Committee. Therefore, no one should treat him as a petty official; he is a Party member who in the near future will be one of the actual and, we hope, good leaders of the Party."

The proposal of the Central Committee was adopted and Tito took up his new duties as a member of the Balkan Secretariat and *rapporteur* for Yugoslavia. All work in the Comintern was distributed through secretariats for different parts of the world, called Länder-Secretariat, each of which was headed by a member of the Comintern Presidium. (In those days the German language was used in the Comintern as well as the Russian, and all documents bore a file stamp in both Russian and German.) The Balkan Secretariat comprised Yugoslavia, Bulgaria, Greece and Rumania. At that time the Balkan Secretariat was headed by German Wilhelm Pieck. Bela Kun, the leader of the Hungarian Commune of 1919, had preceded him, but was arrested by Stalin shortly afterward.

Tito's duties in the Balkan Secretariat were varied. All reports from Yugoslavia came to him and he prepared the reports when Yugoslav affairs were discussed at meetings, as well as special reports whenever the necessity arose. When he arrived in the Comintern to work Tito was given a new name, Walter, by which he was known to everybody in the Comintern and in Moscow.

While working in the Balkan Secretariat, Tito often met Palmiro Togliatti-Ercoli, Georgi Dimitrov and Otto Kuusinen of Finland as well as Wilhelm Pieck. The representatives of the Soviet Communist Party in the Comintern were Manuilski and Knorin. After a time Knorin, who was said to have been a police agent in Tsarist times, was arrested. Tito also met there Communist leaders from other countries. He met Earl Browder, the Secretary of the Communist Party of America, for the first time in his life in front of the door to the cold showers in the Lux. Another acquaintance was José Diaz, the Secretary of the Communist Party of Spain.

Tito's office in Moscow was in the Comintern building in Mukhovaya Street, not far from the Red Square opposite what is now the Lenin Library. Later the Comintern moved somewhere on the outskirts of Moscow.

"Accustomed in prison to solitude, I went about Moscow little enough," says Tito. "I would leave my office and go to my room at the Lux. I was resolved to make the best use of my stay. All those books I had not been able to obtain in prison I now had at my disposal. Some comrades suggested it would be better if I attended a course in theory, but I thought I should learn much more if I worked alone. Every man knows best what he most needs; I chose the literature that would most suitably amplify my education. I devoted most of my attention to economics and philosophy, but I also made a serious study of military literature, first of all Frunze, works by Russian writers and then especially the German classics, Clausewitz and others, and during my stay in Moscow I greatly expanded my knowledge of military problems. Otherwise, outside my office and my room I saw little of Moscow. The Bolshoi Theater, where I went to see the wonderful ballet and to hear good operas, was an exception, but that was not often, only now and then."

Immediately on his arrival in Moscow, Tito went to a meeting of all the Yugoslav Communists there. The subject was the political situation in Yugoslavia; Tito delivered a report on the latest events in the country, being presented to the assembly as "the comrade from home."

During his spare time he also delivered lectures at the International Leninist School and the Communist University of the National Minorities in the West (KUNMZ). The Leninist School was set up for the higher Party cadre from foreign countries. It had three courses, of one, two and three years. The listeners from each country were classified in separate groups denoted by letters of the alphabet. The Yugoslavs belonged to Class S, and Tito gave them lectures on trade-union matters, being paid a fee of twenty roubles a lecture. Yugoslavs also studied at the KUNMZ, which had first been set up for Ukrainians and Byelorussians living outside the Soviet Union, but was later used by other nationalities. Edvard Kardelj, known as Birc, was also in Moscow at that time, attending the Leninist School, and he frequently called to see Tito. In his free time Kardelj gave lectures at the KUNMZ on the history of the Comintern.

Large-scale preparations were being made in Moscow for the Seventh Congress of the Comintern, which was to have been a turning point in the work of the Communist parties of the world. The fundamental question at the Congress was the formation of the National Front in the struggle against Fascism. A report on this matter was delivered by Dimitrov, while Palmiro Togliatti-Ercoli presented a report titled "The Tasks of the Comintern in Connection with the Preparations of the Imperialists for a New World War." The Congress opened in the Colonnade Hall of the Profsoyuz Palace. Stalin attended only the formal opening accompanied by Yezhov, who afterward disappeared. Tito was one of the seven members of the Yugoslav delegation, and saw Stalin then for the first time. The minutes show that Gorkić was elected head of the delegation at the meeting of July 27, Tito being elected Secretary. The question of a candidate * for the Executive Committee of the Communist International was raised at the meeting of August 14. Point six of the minutes shows that the delegation had decided at the request of the delegates from Yugoslavia to propose Tito as member in the Executive Committee of the International and Gorkić as candidate member.

This, however, was not to the liking of the Comintern officials, who wanted Milan Gorkić to be a member of the Executive Committee, so the Yugoslav delegation had to amend its decision. This came as a heavy disappointment to them. It was obvious that the Comintern was not keeping to democratic principles. The minutes of the delegation's meeting of August 19, 1935, say:

"1. Proposal for the amendment of the decision on leading offices in the E.C.C.I.

"Senko informs the comrades of talks with leading comrades in the Balkan Secretariat. These comrades consider our decision wrong and interpret it as a sign of distrust of Comrade Gorkić. Comrade Senko proposes that our decision should be amended to put up Gorkić as candidate for membership to the E.C.C.I. He explains that in putting

---

* In Communist organizations, a "candidate" is a lesser member of a committee or group, whose functions are partly those of a deputy and partly those of an alternate.

up Comrade Walter as candidate there was no intention of showing distrust of Gorkić, nor of opposing Walter to him. It is important for us to show the leading comrades in the Comintern by altering our decision that there is no friction in the Party leadership."

However, the Comintern turned down this proposal, too. Manuilski decided that no Yugoslav should be elected to membership in the E.C.C.I. and that only Milan Gorkić should be elected candidate to membership.

After the Congress Tito and the delegation toured the Soviet Union, visiting collective farms and factories.

What were his impressions of the Soviet Union? Did he then see what he knows today about the Soviet Union? I talked to Tito once about this in the autumn of 1951, while he was on his way to Zagreb to speak at the Congress of the Yugoslav Trade Unions.

"I stayed there long enough to get a definite picture. I was there during the revolution; I saw what the peasants and workers were like under the Tsarist government. I was there in 1935 and a few months in 1936. After the Congress of the Comintern, I toured the Soviet Union with the Yugoslav delegation. I visited big factories and collective farms. I revisited the places in the Urals where I had been during my captivity and the revolution. I also saw many things in Moscow.

"I knew that many things were wrong while I was working there; I witnessed a lot of careerism and elbow-pushing; I talked with collective farms members and noticed them nudging each other when they wanted to say something. People in Moscow somehow avoided each other, hesitated to speak. I was not in Moscow when the big purges occurred. But even in 1935 there were no end of arrests, and those who made the arrests were later themselves arrested. Men vanished overnight, and no one dared ask where they had been taken.

"I witnessed a great many injustices. One morning the militia summoned a Yugoslav worker, who had been living in the Soviet Union and working in a factory for many years, with his wife. They informed him he was sentenced to eight years' exile in northern Siberia, and his wife to five years in southern Siberia. They were not even allowed to return to their flat to take their things but were sent to Siberia directly. No one dared ask how they had offended.

"Arrests even reached Dimitrov, whose brother-in-law Vlko

Chervenkov (Dimitrov's sister was married to Chervenkov) was hiding from the N.K.V.D. in his flat fearing arrest. I saw all those things then, but the causes were not so clear as they are today, because things have gone much further. But it was my revolutionary duty at the time not to criticize and not to help alien propaganda against that country, for at that time it was the only country where a revolution had been carried out and where socialism had to be built. I considered propaganda should not be made against that country; that my duty was to make propaganda in my own country for socialism.

"It might be charged that I was lacking in courage. No, I think no one can say we lack courage; many of us had but one thought at that time: to do nothing to harm the further development of the international movement. I, like many others, thought this was only a temporary internal matter which would be gradually cleared up. Then, too, I had been in Russia during Tsarism, and saw how terrible and wretched things had been. My whole being rebelled against what I saw in Moscow. I told myself they had not been able to accomplish everything in spite of the long time, more than eighteen years, that had passed. . . ."

Tito left the Soviet Union before big purges took place in that country. An authoritative Yugoslav opinion of what happened these years in the Soviet Union was given by Moša Pijade, one of the leading members of the Yugoslav Communist Party, in his speech on August 6, 1951:

"In 1936, 1937 and 1938, in the Soviet Union there were killed over three million people. They didn't belong to the bourgeoisie, because it had long ago been liquidated in that country. They were Communists, from Russia and other republics in the Soviet Union. All those who refused to bow their heads to Stalin were murdered under the names of spies, Fascists and Hitlerite agents. When Stalin rid himself of all these people, he signed a pact with Hitler, a trade agreement with him—they became bosom friends."

Speaking further about the role of Molotov in these purges, Moša Pijade said:

"Molotov is known among the non-Russian people in the Soviet Union as a Stalinite fist who hammers down every movement toward freedom and independence, toward the cultural development of the non-Russian peoples. In 1937, he went with two members of the

Soviet Politburo to the Ukraine and called the whole Central Committee of the Ukrainian Communist Party to a meeting. Molotov asked that the Secretary of the Communist Party of the Ukraine, Kosjur, and two other members of the Ukrainian Politburo be ejected from the Party. The whole Central Committee unanimously rejected the demand of Molotov, expressing their confidence in the comrades whose liquidation Moscow desired. Then Molotov changed his tune. He dissolved the meeting of the Central Committee and called a meeting of the Politburo. But again all members of the Politburo declared that they trusted Comrade Kosjur and they also rejected the demands of Molotov. Then Molotov left Kiev. A few days later Kosjur and other members of the Ukrainian Politburo got an invitation to come to Moscow 'for consultations.' But instead, they went straight to prison."

Returning from the Soviet Union at the beginning of 1935, Tito was confronted with strenuous work. Conditions in the Yugoslav Central Committee had not improved. Factional strife continued and the Party suffered. Instructions were slow in coming, and when they came they were often contradictory. For example, the first elections after the death of King Alexander were held in May, 1935, and the Party favored independent participation. Instructions to this effect had originally come from the Central Committee in Vienna. Since the Party was outlawed, it could not put up its candidates openly but was already preparing to take part in the elections through its substitute, which was called the Party of the Working People. However, Gorkić sent new instructions from Vienna, disapproving of independent participation and advising Communists to vote for the candidates of the united opposition, which consisted of all the bourgeois parties opposing the dictatorship, now headed by Prince Paul. The Party representatives who approached the leaders of the united opposition to make an arrangement for joint participation were refused negotiations on an equal footing. All this provoked deep dissatisfaction with Gorkić among the members. Although voting was not secret, the government was defeated with the help of the Communists, despite its official majority. Prime Minister Jevtić resigned, and was replaced by Milan Stojadinović.

This intensified factional strife in the Central Committee. One group, headed by Čopić, held a secret plenary meeting begun in

Vienna and continued in Prague. The many absent members included Gorkić, who was on his way to Moscow, as well as those who were in the Soviet Union, Tito among them.

The Comintern reacted sharply to this plenary meeting, which was held early in 1936. It dismissed the whole Central Committee and nominated a new one whose Politburo appointed Gorkić Secretary General and Tito Organizing Secretary.

At the time Tito advanced his proposals as to how the Communist Party should work.

"I called on Dimitrov," says Tito, "and put forward my view that the basic prerequisite for the successful work of a party is that its leadership be at home, among the people, to share the rough and the smooth with them. A heated discussion developed over my proposal, Gorkić in particular opposing it. Finally it was decided that the Central Committee should split. One part, headed by me, would go home to work while Gorkić, as Political Secretary, would stay abroad. He was also given the right to veto all political resolutions and decisions adopted in Yugoslavia.

"I consented to this decision. Besides, I wanted to establish a principle concerning subsidies from the Comintern which in my opinion greatly hampered the Party in its work. The members of the Central Committee, living abroad, were relatively well paid. For instance, when the Central Committee moved to France, a member's salary was two thousand francs—a considerable sum at that time. Discussions arose every year over the Comintern subsidies when the budget was being drawn up. But if the Party were to meet its expenses out of its own funds collected at home, directly from the workers, far more attention would be paid to every dinar. Nothing can demoralize a movement more than getting money from outside. The strength of a movement and its financial resources depend on the support it enjoys among the people, on the help it receives from them."

Finally, Tito left Moscow definitely for Yugoslavia in 1936. He was on his guard against Gorkić, who did not like his views. He said: "Gorkić told me to leave for Yugoslavia immediately. He got a passport for me and told me to cross into Yugoslavia, but I obtained another passport and went quite a different way, because other comrades who got passports through Gorkić were arrested at the Yugoslav frontier. . . .

"From Moscow I went to Prague and on to Vienna. At that time the Central Committee was moving from Vienna to Paris, where the new center was to be. This resulted from the changed political situation in France, where the Popular Front was in power, and conditions for work were much more favorable there than in Vienna, where clerical-fascist police terror had gradually increased.

"On leaving Moscow, I was given the special task of organizing the mobilization of volunteers for Spain."

After spending some time in Austria and France, Tito arrived in Yugoslavia toward the end of 1936. The situation in the Party was still difficult. There were frequent police exposures. Hardly were Party committees formed and work begun when the police hounded and arrested all the members. This situation played into the hands of old liquidators, who said there was no sense in working if imprisonment was the only result. Before Tito's arrival in Yugoslavia an entire provincial committee and more than a hundred and fifty members had been arrested. Tito sent a message from Zagreb calling for consultation with a comrade from Belgrade, and Milovan Djilas, who had just been released from prison, was dispatched to Zagreb.

"Early in 1937," Djilas now recalls, "a message arrived from Zagreb that a member of the Central Committee had sent for one of the comrades to come from Belgrade. The big exposure that winter had wiped out almost the whole Party organization in Belgrade. The University alone had been spared, no one having been arrested because a comrade behaved heroically before the police and refused to reveal his connections at the University. Only a few of us remained, among them myself, because I had been in prison during the roundup.

"I took the train for Zagreb, on the watch in case I was followed by a police agent. I reached the place agreed upon—the room of a comrade of ours, Pavle Markovac, a musician. There I found the member of the Central Committee waiting. He was a man of medium height, very strong, lean. His features were firm and calm, with something tender in them; his eyes were blue and gentle. I did not know his name, because in the underground it was not customary to ask for names. He asked me about the situation in Belgrade; I told him what the police had done. He listened to me quietly and then began to advise me.

"To tell the truth, the advice he gave was something new for us Communists in Yugoslavia. We had felt that we were living in a dreary, inexplicable situation. You worked indefatigably, got some men together, founded an organization, and suddenly an exposure swept it all away. Our comrades were tortured by the police and then imprisoned. The few who survived were again organized, and then there were the same difficulties again. Despite our experiences, we were loath to get out of the rut.

"This member of the Central Committee explained the new program, never mentioning the old patterns which he was quietly smashing to smithereens. He told me how to select men for the Party according to new criteria, people from factories, workshops, schools where they were trusted. For our personal security we should no longer cultivate a narrow circle of men already generally known. The tasks this member laid before us were not difficult, and with some effort could be carried out. Before leaving he told me the General Committee would move to the homeland to be in direct contact with the people. He also told me that a youth leadership should be formed and asked me to send an uncompromised, clear-headed lad from the University—the best I could find.

"We parted with the understanding that I should return to Zagreb after a short time with this youth. In the train I racked my brains trying to remember where I had met this man before. I had an idea I must have seen him somewhere. But where? As the train was passing Sremska Mitrovica, where there was a penitentiary, it flashed through my mind. Moša Pijade had painted a portrait of this man while they were in prison together. I vaguely recalled that Pijade had told me he was a worker called Broz.

"Arriving in Belgrade, I found Aleksandar Ranković-Marko, who had spent six years in prison. I discussed with my comrades which youth to send to Broz; and we decided it should be Ivan-Lola Ribar, a law student and an unusually intelligent young man with a fine reputation among the Communists at the University.

"Several days later I returned to Zagreb and I met Broz again. Before we began to talk, I said to him:

" 'Comrade, I know you. While I was in prison Moša Pijade showed me the portrait of you he painted at Lepoglava. He told me your name was Broz. I recognize you now.'

"Tito waved his hand and laughed."

One of the first tasks Tito gave Djilas was to organize the dispatch of volunteers from Serbia to Spain. The struggle against Franco had excited the workers throughout Yugoslavia. Danger from Hitler and Mussolini was looming on Yugoslavia's frontiers, and the people regarded Spain as the area of the struggle against Fascism. Thousands were ready to go to Spain if only there was any possibility, if only the authorities would give passports and there was money for the journey. How much feeling there was in Yugoslavia for Republican Spain can best be seen from the fact that *Politika*, the biggest daily in Yugoslavia, wrote in favor of the Republicans during the first year of the war in Spain despite the severe censorship imposed by the government of Milan Stojadinović, who was steadily inclining toward the Axis powers. The owners of *Politika* actually tolerated such writing because it suited them; the people were for Republican Spain and the paper's circulation grew.

There were different channels from Yugoslavia to Spain. Whoever managed to get a passport went to Paris, and thence to Spain. The exposition in Paris which was opened in the spring of 1937 was of great help. The intellectuals in particular took this route. Most had no money for the journey, so the Party began to collect for them.

People who had been arrested and compromised as leftists went by underground channels to Austria, and then on without passports to Switzerland, from there to France and then to Spain. This was an extremely dangerous route, and when finally the police in Austria discovered the channel, many Yugoslavs on their way to Spain were arrested and delivered to the Yugoslav police, who flogged and imprisoned them.

Because of his connections with the Central Committee, and in order to improve the organization of sending Yugoslav volunteers to Spain, Tito went to Paris several times during 1937. He lived first at a hotel in the Latin Quarter. He had little time to tour Paris but often visited the Père Lachaise Cemetery, where Communards of 1871 were executed. He began to study French by reading *L'Humanité* and mastered the language enough to read political articles in the papers. He was in touch with the Legation of Republican Spain, and once traveled as far as Brest in connection with the sending of volunteers. Once Tito was almost caught by the French police. The English King paid a visit to Paris and the police took all precautions, searching for all suspicious persons and people who did not have proper passports, so Tito was obliged to leave his hotel in a great hurry. But the trouble did not end with this incident.

While returning to Yugoslavia via Strasbourg and Munich, he almost fell into the hands of Hitler's police. Before leaving Paris he had obtained a new passport and failed to take a good look at the name under which he was traveling. Being very tired, he fell into a deep sleep. Hilter's frontier officials entered the compartment after the train left Strasbourg and one of them demanded his passport. Tito gave it to him, and the policeman asked him in German for his name.

Drowsy, Tito could not remember the name on his passport. The German was persistent, and repeated his question angrily:

"Ihr Name?"

But the name still eluded Tito.

In this predicament, he pretended not to know German and turning to a fellow traveler asked in Czech what the policeman wanted. The delay served its purpose. The Czech name on his passport at last flashed into his mind.

"Oh, my name," he said, and answered at last.

The policeman angrily stamped the passport and handed it back.

Meanwhile, the number of volunteers for Spain from Yugoslavia had so increased that Gorkić decided to send a special ship from Marseilles to Yugoslav territorial waters to take on the thousand or so men, mostly from Montenegro and Dalmatia, who were waiting to be sent to fight in Spain. By Gorkić's orders the organization of this work was in the hands of a member of the Central Committee called Adolf Muk, a waiter from Dalmatia. The whole job was faultily organized and it was an open secret at Marseilles that such a ship was going to Yugoslavia.

Several days later the vessel approached Yugoslav territorial waters in the Montenegrin littoral, not far from the King's summer residence at Miločer. Preparations in Yugoslavia had already been completed. About a thousand students, workers and peasants from

Montenegro and Dalmatia had gathered on the mountains overlooking the shore, waiting to board the ship. At dusk the vessel gave the agreed signals and attempted to work in toward the open shore, from which the volunteers would be brought by small boats. But that night there was a swell and the ship could not get in. All this unusual activity could hardly escape notice by the authorities.

She was attempting to approach the spot the next night when police patrol boats appeared. Under threat of fire the French vessel had to halt. Adolf Muk and a young comrade were on board. Muk's courage failed. The young comrade suggested diving into the sea and swimming to the shore, which was several kilometers away. Muk refused and was arrested by the police. He later betrayed the whole organization of this abortive undertaking.

At the same time the police had thrown a strong ring around the beach where the volunteers were waiting. Hundreds of them were captured and taken to jail.

The organization, directed by Tito, however, continued to send volunteers through Austria and Switzerland. About one thousand five hundred Yugoslavs, including many intellectuals, were sent. The losses suffered by the Yugoslavs in Spain were extremely heavy: almost half of them were killed, three hundred were wounded, and three hundred and fifty interned in concentration camps near the French frontier after the collapse in Spain. Of these, about three hundred managed to escape and get to Yugoslavia, where they later fought in the war. These men who had been fighting for the freedom of Spain gained precious military experience which stood them in good stead in their own country. Today twenty-four "Spaniards," as they are called, are generals in the Yugoslav army and a number of others are highly placed officials.

While in Yugoslavia in the summer of 1937, Tito received a short report from Paris that Gorkić had urgently been summoned to Moscow. Before leaving, Gorkić told Rodoljub Čolaković that he did not know why he was going to the Soviet Union, probably for a "golovomoyka" (Russian for "washing" or "head rubbing"). A short time afterward a telegram arrived in Paris from Moscow ordering a brochure written by Gorkić to be immediately withdrawn from the press. This meant things were not well with him. His Polish wife, who was employed in Moscow, had been arrested on the charge of being an Intelligence Service spy. After a time Tito received a letter from the head of the Balkan Secretariat informing him of Gorkić's dismissal, and authorizing Tito to take over responsibility for the work of the Central Committee.

Tito remained briefly in Paris, settling matters as far as he could, and wrote several articles for the *Europäische Stimme* and *Imprecor*, political reviews which printed contributions from prominent European Communists and left-wingers. Toward the end of the year 1937 Tito was in Yugoslavia again, having traveled through Austria with two Yugoslav girls who were studying in Paris. Being uncompromised, they carried material, brochures and the Party paper *Proleter*, which was printed in Belgium. On his arrival, Tito found a new summons to Moscow.

"I left immediately. In Moscow I spoke with Dimitrov. I was informed that Gorkić had been dismissed from the office of Secretary General and later arrested. Many things became clear to me. Gorkić, who had been living fourteen years in Moscow, who had earned the full confidence of the Comintern, who had been imposed upon our delegation at the Seventh Congress of the Comintern as candidate for membership in the E.C.C.I., had actually always and systematically been working against the Party. As a factionalist he hampered the development of new cadres, especially among the workers. Moreover, he was in the habit of deceiving the Comintern, of sending false reports on conditions in Yugoslavia. The Comintern regarded leaflets or brochures secretly printed as proof of work in the country. Gorkić usually found an intellectual in Belgrade who hastily scribbled such a report to be sent to the Comintern.

"Besides this, Gorkić had maintained direct connections with a section of the Belgrade bourgeoisie which during World War II actually became the leading force of reaction, and in particular with Draža Mihailović. Gorkić had connections with Slobodan Jovanović, a professor of Belgrade University, later Prime Minister in the exile government in London, and with the writer Dragiša Vasić, who was chief political adviser in Draža Mihailović's headquarters during the war. The third person Gorkić was in touch with was Mladen Žujović, a Belgrade lawyer whom Draža Mihailović appointed commander of western Yugoslavia during the war.

"During my talk with Dimitrov, he informed me that I was appointed caretaker Secretary General of the Central Committee, which was to be entirely changed.

"How did I take this offer? I had no ambition to take over the leadership of the Party, and never had. But I did want the leadership to be strong, firm and revolutionary. I had never thought of becoming the head, but I did want the head to be a man who could work. What was important to me was that the collective should be strong, that the leadership should be strong: not one man, but a whole collective.

"During these talks with Dimitrov, I noticed a tendency to dissolve the Communist Party of Yugoslavia, as had been done in Poland and Korea.

"I accepted Dimitrov's offer and said: 'We will wash away the stain!'

" 'Get to work!' he answered.

"I remained in Moscow several months. The *History of the Bolshevik Party* had just come off the press, and I was told to translate it and have it ready for printing. This job tied me down for several weeks. We first printed this book abroad and smuggled it into our country. Later we printed three editions in Yugoslavia, but under very difficult conditions.

"After that I left for France through Finland and Denmark. I had a Canadian passport in the name of Spiridon Mekas. Arriving at Copenhagen, a policeman, who as I learned later was a Social-Democrat, asked me something in English. My English was very bad; I had just begun to study the language and I mumbled something. He noticed that the passport was not mine and said, laughing: 'Next time, comrade, learn better English before you use a Canadian passport!'

"I arrived in Paris early in 1938.

"Several days later I left for Yugoslavia to reorganize the Party. This reorganization ran along the following principles:

"First, the Central Committee should be located inside Yugoslavia, working among the people. It is impossible to expect a workers' democratic movement to succeed if its leadership is far from the arena of struggle. That is the elementary condition for the successful work of such a movement. To await instructions from outside, to use someone else's head instead of one's own, is deadly danger for every such movement. Moreover, life outside the country, in exile, leads men toward decay, much as they must be politically enlightened otherwise. Political exile spells ruin for a political worker. It is better if he is in his own country, among his own people, where he can fight together with them, where he can share good and evil together with them, even if his life is in the balance, rather than to roam about, far from the movement, far from the people. Hence, upon becoming Secretary General of the Central Committee of the Communist Party of Yugoslavia, I returned the headquarters of the Central Committee to Yugoslavia after six years of wandering from country to country. At the same time I did all I could to persuade our men abroad to return, in particular the comrades who had been in Spain and were interned in French camps. In Paris we set up a special organization charged with their return to the country. Naturally, we were concerned only for upright comrades. In Paris the organization forged passports in order to help them to get back as early as possible, for their experience was only too welcome.

"Second, it was necessary to secure unity in the Party. The leadership of the Communist Party of Yugoslavia had for fifteen years been suffering from factional strife. Immeasurable energy was wasted in altercations, in bickering; little was devoted to real work among the masses. Accordingly, the struggle for Party unity was of huge, decisive significance. What proportions factionalism had assumed among the leading Yugoslav Communist figures of that time is best demonstrated by the fact that there was a saying in the Comintern: 'Two Yugoslavs—three factions.'

"Consequently we created a leadership of new men, of young revolutionaries hardened directly in the field in the process of the struggle, men like Edvard Kardelj, Aleksandar Ranković, Milovan Djilas, Rade Končar, Ivo-Lola Ribar.

"Third, it was necessary to make the Party independent of foreign financial assistance. That is one of the basic conditions for success. If assistance is expected only from abroad, a man gets into the habit of never trying to find support in the surroundings in which he lives and works. During the whole period of the Communist Party's work from 1919 to 1937 the receipt of money from Moscow had had only a harmful effect. From the moment I headed the Party, we discontinued the receipt of subsidies from abroad. We then had to rely on our own resources, because the financial problem had become a political one. The support we received depended on the influence we had among the people. Furthermore, when our own money was money the workers had contributed from their salaries and the peasants from their small earnings, then the attention given to that money was much greater. Each dinar was spent with the utmost circumspection, the more so when the money was being spent not only for the purchase of printing presses, paper and printer's ink, but in order to maintain our members who were being persecuted by the police or were unable to earn a living because of the undivided devotion with which they served the Party. There were comrades who lived on three hundred dinars (six dollars) a month. We immediately strengthened an organization called National Aid, which collected donations for comrades who were in jail, for their families. The organization expended its funds exclusively for this purpose, and we made it a rule to use the money for nothing else. With the mounting influence of our Party, National Aid soon became a mighty organization, both in the number of people who contributed to it and in the amount of money it collected.

"Fourth, it was necessary to expand the Party among the workers and peasants, especially among young militants. Many mistakes had been made in this respect in the past. There had been no standard according to which to admit men to the Party. Our basic standard, however, was the respect a man enjoyed in his circle; if he was a worker, what his attitude was toward the struggle for better wages, what his attitude was toward other workers, whether he enjoyed their confidence, whether he was a good companion, whether he was unselfish, whether he was courageous, what his character was like, what respect he enjoyed with regard to his personal life: whether he was a drunkard, a gambler, what he was like at his trade. Starting with this standard, it was not difficult to select the best and most militant men in the factories, offices and villages for the Party.

"Fifth, it was necessary to devote attention to the ideological training of the men. It was necessary to help them to master the basic laws of social development so as to arm them against all forms of backwardness, against all manner of prejudices to which all of us without exception were exposed, and which we had not been able to suppress.

"Sixth, it was necessary to found Party organizations throughout Yugoslavia. There were whole regions with no Party organization.

The Communist Party of Yugoslavia had to be a nation-wide Yugoslav organization; it had to operate on the whole territory of Yugoslavia, among all its inhabitants.

"Seventh, it was necessary to introduce a new relationship toward Party members. The practice of abusing a man because he had made a mistake was abandoned; he was told why he had made his mistake, he was helped, and given the opportunity to correct it unless he himself was loath to do so or had been sent into our ranks by the enemy. This principle actually meant to find the job that best suited the man. Men are complex beings; one job suits one man better than another. This principle has never failed us. Out of a hundred cases, the method has yielded good results in ninety. How many men have we saved in this way! In the few cases where this principle failed us, the loss was insignificant, for ninety others had been saved.

"Eighth, we clarified the attitude of the Party members toward the class enemy. The conditions of the dictatorship and terror as instituted under King Alexander had not altered in the Yugoslavia of Prince Paul between 1937 and 1941. The Party organization sought to expand its activity far and wide, but the police had a sharp eye, arresting men and subjecting them to torture in order to force them to betray their comrades. Upon every member depended not only his own life but the lives of hundreds of other Communists, and, more than that, the very work of the Party. Consequently, we had to work out special instructions as to the attitude to take toward the class enemy.

"Ninth, from 1937 to 1941 the Soviet Union was the only socialist country in which the working class had taken over power. The Soviet Union was a beacon for all us Communists, our main pillar of support, proof that what we were working for was no utopia, because we believed that the Soviet Union was already realizing what we were fighting for. That is why we had issued special instructions to popularize the Soviet Union in our country. We had prepared special brochures, books, lectures: it was the bulk of our activity, it commanded the bulk of our funds.

"Such were the principles along which the Communist Party of Yugoslavia began to work when I came to head it toward the end of 1937, on the eve of the fateful events awaiting my country."

CHAPTER VIII

1939:

"As our political influence increased, our underground work grew easier . . ."

IN HIS forty-fifth year, after twenty-seven years of work in the labor movement, after the tribulations of the First World War and the October Revolution; after working with the peasants at Trojstvo, taking part in strikes in almost all the industrial towns in Yugoslavia; after his arrests and his five and a half years in prison; after his experiences in Russia, spanning eighteen years, Josip Broz Tito embarked on what was the most responsible task of his life, a task at which so many before him had failed. He became Secretary General of the Central Committee of the Communist Party of Yugoslavia.

This was in 1937, in the fateful days preceding the Second World War. What does Tito say today about the urgent duties that faced him during those years?

The basic problem in these times was to prepare my country to meet the difficult days looming on the horizon. Germany and Italy were making feverish preparations for war. The Balkan Peninsula, particularly Yugoslavia, the largest of the Balkan countries, was of the utmost strategic importance to them. Hitler's Germany was striving to grasp my country economically and soon was able to set up a system by which more than half of Yugoslavia's exports went to Germany. German capital ousted French capital and seriously threatened the position of British investments in Yugoslavia.

The situation made things easy for the Axis powers. In place of King Alexander, who had been assassinated at Marseilles in 1934, his cousin Prince Paul ruled in the name of the boy King Peter. The country's policy did not change. The rights of some nationalities were never recognized; people like the Macedonians, who live in the South of Yugoslavia, were still forcibly prevented from using their native language. Citizens were deprived of their elementary rights. Every workers' demand for better conditions was suppressed in blood. Under the influence of Rome and Berlin, with the blessings of the Cliveden Set in England, Prince Paul appointed as Prime Minister Milan Stojadinović, the Belgrade banker of whom I have already spoken. An open pro-Nazi trend followed his advent.

First he wrecked the Little Entente, that last remaining thread that still held the countries of the Danube Basin and the Balkan Peninsula together against Hitler's threats. In January, 1937, without the approval or knowledge of Czechoslovakia and Rumania, the other members of the Entente, Stojadinović concluded a pact of "eternal friendship" with King Boris of Bulgaria. During the Sinaia Conference in Rumania in the same year the members of the Little Entente could do nothing but recognize that the Little Entente was no more, that the members had been betrayed and deceived by Stojadinović, who was firmly embraced in the arms of Hitler and Mussolini. Count Ciano visited Belgrade for the first time, to meet a people who expressed their disgust in widespread demonstrations. On the other hand, President Beneš's visit to Belgrade later was the cause of enthusiastic manifestations.

Having destroyed the Little Entente, Stojadinović also broke off the alliance with Czechoslovakia and Rumania. Thus Czechoslovakia lost her ally Yugoslavia on the eve of Munich. Instead of delaying the danger to Yugoslavia by consolidating allied relationships from the past war, Prince Paul's regime betrayed all Yugoslavia's allies, and by leaning toward the Rome-Berlin Axis altered the whole foreign policy of Yugoslavia. The danger threatening Yugoslavia was countenanced and the attack of the Axis powers accelerated.

Yugoslavia was now completely alone, without allies. Hitler and Mussolini had succeeded in isolating Yugoslavia from outside and weakening her internally. Hitler was planning his first leap in the "Drive to the East," the well-known pattern of German imperialism. He completed his plans for the "Anschluss" of Austria. Milan Stojadinović visited Berlin and Hitler staged a military parade in his honor. Tanks bearing the swastika thundered past the guests, and Hitler made a statement for the Yugoslav press:

"It is our wish that Yugoslavia should be strong, mighty and free."

Five weeks later those very tanks entered Vienna. It was March, 1938. The ominous swastika flag had been unfurled on the frontiers of Yugoslavia. The day this occurred, several members of the Central Committee of the Communist Party of Yugoslavia met in Zagreb to examine the situation. Milan Stojadinović at least did not attempt to deceive the public, or to pretend that Yugoslavia was not threatened. That evening we read his statement, which said:

"After the Anschluss, official representatives of the German Reich assured us of the absolute inviolability of Yugoslavia's frontiers with Germany."

But this was only dust in the eyes of the people. That same night we released a proclamation of the Central Committee which a few days later was secretly duplicated on printing presses, on mimeographs, and often by hand in all parts of Yugoslavia. In this proclamation we drew the attention of the Yugoslav peoples to the state of affairs:

"Hitler's Fascist motorized hordes have overrun little Austria and with their bayonets torn up all the international agreements assuring this country's independence. . . . Thus Hitler is reviving the old German empire and Wilhelm's 'Drive to the East.' This road runs to the Aegean Sea through Yugoslavia. He is being aided by Mussolini, who wants Dalmatia and Bosnia for Italy. . . . With the occupation of Austria, Hitler has gripped our brother Czechoslovakia in his pincers. It is only a matter of days before the Fascist planes drone above her peaceful population.

"German Fascism is gradually and steadily pursuing its infernal plan of turning the nations of Central and Southeastern Europe into its slaves and cannon fodder for its final reckoning with democracy, and above all with the bastion of democracy—the Soviet Union. . . . Hitlerism is neither friend nor good neighbor, but an avowed enemy of the freedom and independence of the peoples of Yugoslavia. . . . Yesterday the Hitlerite soldiery trampled underfoot the freedom of the Austrian people, today it prepares its blow against Czechoslovakia, and tomorrow its companies will pour across the Karawanken into Yugoslavia. . . . Hitler's agent Stojadinović has betrayed the interests of the people. The antinational and hegemonic regime of Stojadinović is a threat to the people of Yugoslavia and to the independence of the country. He is sowing discord and preventing brotherly agreement among the peoples of Yugoslavia in these fateful hours.

"With his traitorous foreign policy he is separating Yugoslavia from her allies and selling her to Hitler and Mussolini, thus opening her doors to the Fascist invaders."

The proclamation of our Central Committee was well received among the broadest sections of people in Yugoslavia. Anyone who was caught with it was arrested and flogged. Only the small Trotskyist groups and some old factionalists received the proclamation with indignation, accustomed as they were to narrow sectarian work, ignoring the feelings of the people or the fundamental interests of the country.

Prince Paul and Milan Stojadinović continued their pro-Nazi and pro-Fascist policy. The visits of German and Italian ministers to Belgrade went on. An exhibition of Italian portrait painting through the centuries was opened by Mussolini's Minister of Culture Dino Alficri and included, besides portraits by Raphael and Titian, a large bust of Mussolini. Unable to bear this, a student overturned Mussolini's bust, to show what the people in our country thought of the abuse of the wonderful achievements of Italian art as propaganda for Italian imperialism. Several weeks later a group of German bombers roared over Belgrade, invited by Milan Stojadinović in connection with an aircraft exhibition in Belgrade. Led by General Forster, and with their own military band, Hitler's fliers marched along the main streets of our capital, where only three years later they were to rain their bombs.

Mussolini followed Hitler by sending one of his fighter squadrons to Belgrade to an air meeting. On this occasion the crowds broke through the police cordon, and fierce demonstrations against Fascism and the government took place. Stojadinović and Prince Paul continued their visits to Italy and Germany. At a meeting with Ciano, Stojadinović raised his hand in the Fascist salute. Mussolini arrived at the Yugoslav frontier and there, on September 20, declared:

"I am a friend of the Yugoslav people. I shall always be your friend. That is my wish. Once I give my word, I always keep it, as a matter of ordinary morality."

Then came the October days of 1938. Czechoslovakia was threatened. Would she resist Hitler or not? We rallied the people to her defense. Thousands of youths volunteered at the Czechoslovak Legation in Belgrade to defend the threatened country. Demonstrations were held in Yugoslav towns. Then came those terrible days of Godesberg and Munich, when Chamberlain and Daladier paid tribute to Hitler and Mussolini. Prince Paul and Stojadinović were maliciously jubilant.

Our Central Committee issued a new proclamation to the people drawing their attention to the mounting danger to Yugoslavia's independence.

"With its traitorous policy toward Yugoslavia's allies, the Stojadinović government has committed a serious crime against the peoples of Yugoslavia. It has helped the German imperialist criminals open a way to the Southeast and prepared for the people of Yugoslavia a fate like Czechoslovakia's. Stojadinović's policy has not removed the danger of Yugoslavia's dismemberment, but has on the contrary heightened that danger and brought it closer. The peoples of Yugoslavia are to become small coins in the bargaining between Germany and Italy. Hitler and Mussolini are already inciting reactionary elements in Bulgaria, Albania and Hungary against Yugoslavia, to make her easier game for the German and Italian Fascists.

"At this moment of imminent danger to Yugoslavia, the basic task of the Communist Party of Yugoslavia is to mobilize and organize all the peoples of Yugoslavia in the struggle to defend the inviolability of their country and their independence against the German and Italian Fascist aggressors and their collaborators.

"The prerequisite for the fulfillment of this duty is the overthrow of the antinational government of Stojadinović and the formation of a government capable of organizing the country's defense and confronting the Fascist aggressors with unflinching resistance. Guided by this task, the government of national defense must rely on the working class, on the unification of all healthy and democratic national forces of Yugoslavia; resolved to improve the material and cultural living conditions of the working people of town and village, it must immediately restore democratic freedoms and brotherly relations among the peoples of Yugoslavia on a basis of national equality; it must comprehensively consolidate friendly relations with the Balkan states and support Yugoslavia's friendly connections with all countries prepared to fight German and Italian Fascism, and above all with the Soviet Union."

Being politically shortsighted, Prince Paul and Stojadinović wanted to exploit the new situation in Central Europe, and determined to hold elections. You should have been in Yugoslavia in those times to see how very little democracy there was. First of all, voting was not secret. Instead of casting his vote and dropping it into the ballot-box at the polling station, each voter had to declare his choice openly. His vote was entered against his name in the electoral register. In many parts of the country civil servants lost their jobs for voting for the opposition. There was also flogging, corruption and bribery. In some parts of Serbia the government candidate offered the peasants a pair of "opankas" (peasant footwear) if they voted for them. To be sure of their vote they would give one of the opankas before the voting and the other only after checking the vote. Nor was this enough: there were forgeries in many regions during the vote counting. Despite all this the regime was defeated at the polls. Stojadinović hesitated several days before announcing the returns. Finally came the statement, a false one, of course, that the government had polled 1,600,000 votes as against the opposition's 1,300,000. According to the electoral system, the party with a relative majority got at once two thirds of the seats in Parliament, and the rest was divided according to the votes cast. And so it happened that the government received three hundred seats, the opposition only seventy. A government candidate in Croatia who got only 95 votes was elected, while his opponent from the opposition who got 28,500 votes was defeated.

But nothing could conceal the regime's defeat. Prince Paul decided to make Stojadinović his scapegoat, replacing him with a new prime minister in the person of Dragiša Cvetković, a colorless person. But the policy remained unchanged.

In order to strengthen his power in the country, Prince Paul made an agreement with Maček, the leader of the Croat Peasant Party, giving some autonomy to the Croat bourgeoisie. But Maček, from his side, worked full speed for a destruction of Yugoslavia, leaning heavily on Berlin and Rome.*

Since it was unmistakably fighting for the defense of Yugoslavia's independence and integrity, for equality among her peoples, for elementary democratic freedoms and for better living conditions for the working class, the Communist Party rapidly gained the attention of the people. As our political influence increased, our underground work grew easier. The fact that the leadership was now at home made it possible to react quickly to the changing course of events. Assistance was given in districts where the Party organizations had been wrecked. Organizations were set up, consultations were held beginning with local groups and concluding in nation-wide consultations and conferences. A conference was held in the summer of 1939 which elected the first Provincial Committee for Bosnia; in Macedonia a provincial leadership was elected. Thus Party organizations were established in all parts of Yugoslavia. The members of the Central Committee lived with the people and con-

---

* According to Mussolini's Foreign Minister, Count Galeazzo Ciano, Maček even asked for financial help from Mussolini. In his diary, American edition, page 84, Count Ciano said under date of May 18, 1939: "Carnelutti, sent by Maček, wants information as to our conversations with and commitments to the Regent Paul. Nothing is changed on our part, since Belgrade has made no formal commitment of adherence to the Axis. Then he informs me: (1) Maček no longer intends to come to any agreement with Belgrade; (2) he will continue his separatist movement; (3) he asks for a loan of 20,000,000 dinars; (4) within six months, at our request, he will be ready to start an uprising. I make an appointment with him following my return from Germany, in order to continue our negotiations."

Count Ciano further states that Mussolini authorized him to give financial help to Maček. According to Count Ciano, the following accord was reached with Maček's representative, Carnelutti, at a meeting on May 26, 1939. In his diary under that date, Count Ciano made the following entry:

"A meeting with Carnelutti, who has just returned from Zagreb; he confirms Maček's full decision to turn down every agreement with Belgrade and to refuse to prepare the rebellion. We agreed and embodied in a memorandum the following points: (1) Italy will finance Maček's Croat revolt with twenty million dinars; (2) he undertakes to prepare the revolution within four to six months; (3) he will quickly call in the Italian troops to insure order and peace; (4) Croatia will proclaim itself an independent state in confederation with Rome. It will have its own government but its ministries for foreign affairs and of national defense will be in common with Italy; (5) Italy will be permitted to keep armed forces in Croatia and will also keep there a lieutenant general as in Albania; (6) after some time we shall decide on possibilities for union under a single head."

stantly went round to the Party organizations. Zagreb was my headquarters, for communication with the whole country was the easiest from that central point.

To avoid discovery by the police, I called myself Ivan Kostanjšek. I got an identity card made out in this name, and professed to be an engineer employed in the Ministry of Forestry and Mining. Later, during 1940, I took the name and title of Slavko Babić, licensed engineer, and had all my documents made out in that name. I rented a small house in Zagreb and all my neighbors believed me to be an engineer.

Many militants joined the Party straight from the factories and workshops. The rapid approach of war increased the cost of living and conditions were becoming harder for the working class; strikes lasting a month or more took place. One of our big successes between 1937 and 1941 was establishing our Party in the rural areas. But for the correctness of our policy and the way we explained it to the peasants during the war in 1941, the Party could never have played the part it did. Much of the credit for this must go to the Party organization in the University of Belgrade. The University had long been known for its freedom of thought, especially between the two wars. To begin with, most of the students were the sons of peasants and workers, usually from Montenegro, Bosnia and parts of Serbia. Most of these students lived at home and came to Belgrade only to sit for their examinations; they were in constant touch with the people. Besides this, the Party organization at the University had come through the general exposure in 1936 unscathed, and its work had gone on.

A special and most important sector of our work was the army. This made Prince Paul's regime extremely touchy, for in the army lay its hope. But from 1937 resentment grew steadily in all ranks, especially among the young officers, over Prince Paul's policy and his reliance on Hitler and Mussolini. I was in charge of a special military commission whose task was to organize Party work in the army.

Our influence in the forces grew rapidly, chiefly in the air force, though contact with the higher-ranking officers developed slowly.

Special attention was paid to the ideological training of Party members. Since 1925 the central Party paper had no longer been printed at home but in Vienna and later in Paris and Brussels, and delivered by messengers or by post. Now, however, we began to print the paper in an underground press in Yugoslavia. A good deal of our literature was published in semilegal editions. In this way we published Lenin's *Imperialism*, Engels' *The Origin of the Family* and a number of similar books. Party courses were also held. Such work made the Party an increasingly serious factor in the country.

We did not found a Popular Front on the French model, because developments in our country followed a different pattern. We proposed to some parties that we should found a Popular Front to fight for national independence, internal democracy and improved living conditions, but some of the bourgeois parties had become too involved with various great powers, and neglected the interests of the homeland. Consequently they rejected all suggestion of co-operation, even a Popular Front, fearing it would be a danger to them. But we launched a campaign among the people for the formation of a Popular Front to defend the country against Fascism and to create better living conditions. The common people rallied around this platform, and the Communist Party became a leading patriotic and revolutionary force in the country.

In the meantime Yugoslavia was threatened by ever-growing danger. In April Mussolini occupied Albania; Prince Paul and Dragiša Cvetković, the new Prime Minister, agreed to this Italian imperialistic move. Returning from Albania, where he had fought against that small country, Count Ciano boasted in the Italian Assembly on April 15, 1939:

"The attitude of Belgrade is particularly important. It is inspired by the friendship pact, and even more by the sympathy and confidence that have existed between the two nations for two years. Belgrade realizes that Italy's presence in Albania in no way means hostility toward Yugoslavia, but is on the contrary a means of strengthening solidarity and successful co-operation."

As the Italian papers reported, this part of Count Ciano's speech was cheered by all the Italian senators. The official text records that the Yugoslav Minister in Rome, Hristić, who was present during Count Ciano's address, rose from his seat at these words and greeted Ciano and the Italian Assembly with the Fascist salute.

That is one example of how the most responsible figures in the

government of that time worked against the most elementary interests of their country. In Yugoslavia the people were indignant over
the Italian attack on Albania. We issued several statements on this
event. Our organization at the University of Belgrade published the
following statement on April 8, 1939:

"The attack of Italian Fascism on little Albania is the natural continuation of the criminal policy of conquest of the aggressive Rome-
Berlin Axis. Only twenty days have passed since the fateful moment
when the brotherly Slav peoples of allied Czechoslovakia fell into
slavery to Teutonic imperialism. Today the tragic fate of the Czech
and Slovak peoples threatens to become evil reality for the peoples of
Yugoslavia.

"More than ever our country is in deadly danger. Along our frontiers, from Mount Triglav to Salonika, from the Drava to the Banat,
from Ulcinj to Djakovica, stand the enemies of our country, the
mortal enemies of the independence of our peoples, preparing to
attack our territory.

"Taught by the experiences of the Czech and Slovak peoples, the
heroic people of Albania, poorly armed, are resisting an incompara-
bly stronger enemy. The struggle of the Albanian people for freedom and independence is at the same time a struggle for the vital
interests of our country. Mussolini is not occupying Albania for the
sake of Albania; he needs to enter Albania to block Yugoslavia on
all sides, so that the imperialists of the Rome-Berlin Axis can more
easily overcome and occupy her. Mussolini will not stop at our frontiers. He has entered Albania today in order to enslave Dalmatia,
Montenegro and Croatia tomorrow."

Then came August, 1939: the Soviet-German pact. We accepted
the pact like disciplined Communists, considering it necessary for the
security of the Soviet Union, at that time the only Socialist state in
the world. We were ignorant at the time of its secret clauses, counte-
nancing Soviet interference in the rights of other nations, especially
small ones.

But the Soviet-German pact did not for a moment weaken our
vigilance in preparing for the defense of the homeland in the event
of attack, nor did it alter our Party line in the general struggle
against German and Italian imperialism. To be sure, we simultaneously opposed the attempts to draw Yugoslavia into the war as a

pawn of Chamberlain and Daladier and supported all the measures necessary for home defense. When partial mobilization was proclaimed in Yugoslavia, we advised its support. At the same time we fought fiercely against fifth-column elements in the army, especially the unpatriotic generals who revealed themselves as saboteurs even over these partial mobilizations. I personally wrote an article in the central Party paper, *Proleter*, criticizing the method of building fortifications along the Italo-German frontier.

Our actions provoked the wrath of Hitler and Mussolini; it is no accident that on June 22, 1941, when Germany declared war on the Soviet Union, Ribbentrop widely quoted the proclamations of the Communist Party of Yugoslavia issued after the conclusion of the Soviet-German pact, as evidence of Soviet hostility toward Germany. Here is one of the places in his speech analyzing the activity of our Party in 1939 and 1940:

"Thus in connection with the anniversary of the German-Russian pact, August 23, 1940, a pamphlet was issued attacking the Yugoslav Government for 'pursuing a policy of rapprochement with Rome and Berlin and for wanting to hitch itself to the imperialist cart of Germany and Italy.' Foreign policy propaganda recommends that Yugoslavia should lean toward Russia. Accordingly, a Communist pamphlet distributed in Zagreb in November attacks Maček for 'wanting to sell the country to the Fascist imperialists in Berlin and Rome.' A pamphlet circulating in Slovenia in connection with the day of the Russian Revolution, November 7, 1940, protests 'against the flirting of Cvetković's regime with the imperialist governments of Berlin and Rome.' "

The regime of Prince Paul mercilessly settled accounts with the mounting movement of the people. In December, 1939, during the demonstrations in Belgrade, the police opened fire on the demonstrators, killing six and wounding more than fifty. Prince Paul ordered the building of concentration camps, in which many of our Party officials caught by the police were interned.

I went to Moscow twice during 1938 and 1939. Remaining there a short time, I had talks with Dimitrov. There still prevailed a feeling of distrust toward the Yugoslav Communists. I remember during lunch in the Lux, I was sitting at a table with Veljko Vlahović, a student from Montenegro who had lost a leg in Spain on the Jarama, and had come to Moscow as our representative in the Comintern. Vlahović had observed: "Do you see how no one wants to sit at our table!?"

"It doesn't matter," I replied. "One day they'll be grabbing chairs from each other to sit with us."

My 1939 trip to Moscow was a brief one and I returned to Yugoslavia in March of that year. I had a forged Swedish passport this time, in the name of John Alexander Karlsson, an engineer born in Stockholm on December 23, 1897. I left Moscow by ship for Le Havre, and thence went by rail through Switzerland to Italy. In Venice I left the train and boarded a boat for the Yugoslav port of Sušak, because control was less rigid there than at the land border.

I visited Moscow for the last time before the war late in 1939. The atmosphere over there as far as Yugoslavia was concerned was rapidly changing. Our Party was going full speed ahead. We were able even to help other Communist parties. For instance, one of the secretaries of the Central Committee of the Czechoslovak Communist Party, Schwerm, was helped by us by forged passports and other facilities to proceed to Moscow. He spent more than two months in our country, living illegally in the quarters of our Party members. He took part in many illegal local and regional Party conferences, and had a firsthand opportunity to witness the growth and the strength of our Party. Arriving in Moscow, Schwerm delivered a full account of the political situation in Yugoslavia and the role played by our Party. He was an objective witness and his statements helped us a lot in the Comintern. At the same time, we were able to help our comrades in Italy and Austria.

I returned from Moscow at the beginning of 1940, after staying there more than four months. The war broke while I was preparing to return. Unable to return by way of Poland, I went to Turkey boarding a ship at Odessa and landing at Istanbul. But the control was extremely rigorous, and although I had a Canadian passport in the name of Spiridon Mekas, I had to stop off for a time at Istanbul because I was unable to obtain the necessary visa for Yugoslavia. Finally, when the Turkish police were already hot on my trail, I took a ticket for the United States on the Italian ship *Conte di Savoia,* then anchored at Naples. This automatically made me eligible for a transit visa through Yugoslavia. Arriving at Zagreb, I left the train. Spiridon Mekas, who had purchased a ticket for the *Conte di Savoia*, never appeared in Naples. The ship left without him. But at Gibraltar, I later learned, the British authorities stopped the vessel, because they thought that Spiridon Mekas must be on board under an assumed name.

New important tasks awaited me in Yugoslavia. It was necessary to prepare for the nation-wide Party conference, which was to discuss the entire situation in Yugoslavia and the adoption of pertinent measures. Working conditions were aggravating because the police had intensified control. Preparations for the conference were made down to ground level: local conferences were held, followed by district and finally by provincial conferences, at which delegates were elected for the national conference, to be held in Zagreb. It was necessary to find space where so many men could meet at once without being noticed. In the city outskirts we rented a one-story house, and began to bring food in for a hundred men, for the conference was to last three days. The delegates were ignorant of the conference site. Each of them was notified of the place by the "grapevine." For instance, comrades from Bosnia came to Slavonski Brod, where they were told to proceed to Zagreb. The delegates came in groups, and finally gathered one evening in October, 1940. There were no difficulties in coming, except that the Montenegrin group had lost its "grapevine" and someone shot at it with a pistol.

We had guards posted on all sides near the house.

The conference lasted three days. No one present was allowed to leave the house. The conference examined our work thoroughly. There were reports on various questions, followed by a lively discussion. Successes in work were noted. The Party membership had grown by over two hundred per cent. The Party now had about twelve thousand members and thirty thousand members of the Communist Youth. Its influence, however, should not be judged by the number of its members. It was a cadre party, composed of hardened fighters who exercised strong influence in the surroundings they worked in. There were cases of strikes in big enterprises with a thousand and more workers being led by cells with only three Party members.

The conference, known as the Fifth National Conference, was of historic significance. It was our last review before the fateful days that came. Four months after the conference, Yugoslavia was attacked by Hitlerite Germany and Fascist Italy. What we had on countless occasions indicated to the people of Yugoslavia from 1937 on had occurred. In the conference resolution this danger had been emphasized several times:

"By transferring the conflagration of war to the Balkan Peninsula, the danger of war directly threatens Yugoslavia. . . . The neighboring totalitarian powers are intensifying pressure upon the small nations of the Balkan Peninsula, especially upon Yugoslavia, requesting complete subjugation to their requirements and aims. In order to increase the economic exploitation of our country, they demand the introduction of the so-called totalitarian system in Yugoslavia, as in Rumania and in other countries. . . ."

The conference also pointed out the traitorous role of the Prince Paul regime, which was preparing to sell the independence of Yugoslavia to the Axis powers.

On the evening of the third day a new Central Committee was elected with thirty-one members and ten candidates, together with a Politburo of seven members. Telegrams of greeting were sent from the conference to Stalin, to Dimitrov and to the victims of the white terror in Yugoslavia. I delivered the closing address, and concluded with the words:

"Comrades, we are faced by fateful days. Forward for the final struggle. We must hold our next conference in a country free from aliens and from capitalists!"

CHAPTER IX

1941:

"Do not lose heart, close your ranks . . ."

YUGOSLAVIA was the twelfth European country to be attacked by Hitler and Mussolini in World War II. They thought, at one time, that they would be able to seize the strategic bridge between Europe and Asia with the aid of the fifth column inside Yugoslavia, as they had been able to do in the case of Hungary, Rumania and Bulgaria. Hitler's and Mussolini's hopes with regard to Yugoslavia rested mainly upon those circles which had gathered around Prince Paul Karageorgevich, the cousin of the late King Alexander, who had been murdered in Marseilles in 1934. (Prince Paul had become regent, because King Alexander's son, Peter, was still under age.) Although he liked to parade as a "British-type democrat," Prince Paul was unpopular in Yugoslavia. In domestic affairs, he pursued a course which did not differ in substance from that followed by his late cousin. Compelled to make certain concessions to the Croatian bourgeoisie led by Dr. Vlatko Maček, he continued to oppress the Macedonians and the Montenegrins. The dictatorial constitution which King Alexander had installed in 1931 and which deprived the people of their elementary democratic rights remained in force. Elections were still conducted by public ballot. In addition, Prince Paul set up concentration camps in Yugoslavia; the beating up of political prisoners continued under his rule.

Although he appeared a cultured, well-read man, he had a characteristic trait which was disliked even in those circles which had supported King Alexander. Prince Paul was a coward. In World War I he had evaded military service. He spent the war years in London, where he traded in paintings. He spoke his mother tongue,

Serbian, with an English accent. The fact that his mother was Princess Demidova of Russia, who had prior to 1917 owned immense estates in the Urals, also had a large part in shaping his character.

Prince Paul's foreign policy was based on a desire to appease the Axis powers. In this he was encouraged by the Cliveden Set, especially while Chamberlain was Britain's Prime Minister. Only when the archives of the various great powers are opened will the portent of Prince Paul's visits to Hitler in the winter of 1939–40 be assessed. It was believed in Yugoslavia at the time that Prince Paul had assumed the role of an intermediary with Hitler for the purpose of seeking a separate peace between Germany and some of her opponents.

Continuing his pro-Axis policy, Prince Paul formally agreed when he visited Hitler on March 1, 1941, that Yugoslavia would accede to the Three-Power Pact, that she would, in other words, follow in the footsteps of Hungary, Rumania and Bulgaria to become an Axis base in the war against the united nations. It would be interesting to find out what it was that influenced Prince Paul to side with the Axis powers. The former Yugoslav Ambassador in Washington, Konstantin Fotich, writes, in his book *The War We Lost*, that Hitler informed Prince Paul in 1941 that the German armed forces would attack the Soviet Union later in the year. Thereupon Prince Paul decided that Yugoslavia should join the Three-Power Pact. According to other sources, Hitler raised before Prince Paul, at their meeting on March 1, 1941, the question of the future ruler of Russia, hinting that it might be a member of the house of Karageorgevich.

Prince Paul considered that Yugoslavia's fate in the World War II had thus been decided. He subordinated the interests of his country and of its independence to his own personal ambitions. In this he was encouraged by the men on whose support he was relying. Their class interests were placed above the interests of the country, above those of the United Nations. On March 25, 1941, Yugoslav Prime Minister Dragiša Cvetković signed, with Ribbentrop and Count Ciano in Vienna, Yugoslavia's adherence to the Three-Power Pact. In Yugoslavia, the people proclaimed that day one of national mourning. The Central Committee of the Communist Party of Yugoslavia issued *on that very day* a proclamation denouncing the betrayal in Vienna, while on the same evening powerful demonstrations broke out in Belgrade, Split, Kragujevac and several other places in the country. The wave of popular indignation swept the country with tremendous vigor.

On March 27, 1941, a group of young air-force officers carried out a *coup d'état*. Prince Paul was arrested and deported, and the Cvetković-Maček government was replaced by a new government under General Dušan Simović. In Belgrade and in a number of other towns demonstrations took place in a manner and on a scale hitherto unwitnessed. The most popular rallying cry was "Better war than the Pact." The windows of the German Tourist Bureau, the Gestapo headquarters for the whole of Yugoslavia, were broken and the swastika flag torn to pieces. Huge meetings in Belgrade were addressed openly by leaders of the Communist Party, who had hitherto led an underground existence. Tito was in Zagreb on March 27, but came to Belgrade the very next day.

When Hitler was told of what had happened in Yugoslavia, he first refused to believe it was true; he thought it a joke. But the telegrams which were coming in from Belgrade soon convinced him of the gravity of the affair. On that very evening, he ordered the High Command of the German ground forces to prepare and carry out military operations against Yugoslavia in order to destroy Yugoslavia "both militarily and as a state." The operations against Yugoslavia were given the code name "Enterprise 25," and the Twelfth German Army under the command of Feldmarschall List was instructed to carry it out. The left wing of this Army was to attack Greece. This Twelfth German Army was concentrated in Bulgaria and was to attack Yugoslavia's flank in order to sever connections between Yugoslavia and Greece. The Second German Army, under Colonel General Von Weichs, was ordered to attack Yugoslavia from the north, from Austria and Hungary.

Hitler immediately informed Mussolini of the decision he had taken. At 2 A.M. the German Ambassador in Rome, Mackensen, called on Mussolini and handed him a personal letter from Hitler. Mussolini accepted all Hitler's proposals. At 4 A.M. Mackensen sent the following reply to Hitler:

"The Duce, who impressed me as being completely rested and serene, seems to welcome, with a view to a later general settlement, the changes which have occurred in Yugoslavia because they afford the opportunity of settling accounts with this artificial creation of Versailles, sponsored by Wilson. This recent instance of Yugoslavia's behavior, which knows of no precedent in history, is an echo of Sarajevo and was caused by the same incorrigible elements."

Hitler thus obtained Italy's help for the attack against Yugoslavia. Similar commitments were obtained from Hungary, Bulgaria and Rumania. The Italian Second Army was to attack Slovenia from the rear. The Hungarian troops were to invade Vojvodina from the north. Rumania's territory was placed at Hitler's disposal as a base for the aggression against Yugoslavia. Bulgaria did the same; Bulgarian troops were, besides, ordered by the German Command to man the frontier against Turkey, in view of the possibility of Turkish intervention.

One question which Hitler discussed in particular with Goering was how to punish Yugoslavia's capital city, Belgrade. It was decided that Belgrade should be attacked by strong formations of the German air force. What made Hitler particularly angry was that the events in Yugoslavia had upset his plans for operations against the USSR. Because of the military action against Yugoslavia, Hitler ordered that the carrying out of the "Operation Barbarossa," the attack on the USSR, be postponed, first for four and then for six weeks. It was this delay that brought the Russian winter into the battle for Moscow.

The Simović government in Belgrade meanwhile was irresolute, primarily because of its own lack of unity. The government consisted, to a considerable degree, of politicians who had basically approved of Prince Paul's policies. Some of them had no idea of what was going on on March 27, and were aghast when officers took them to the General Staff building and informed them they had become cabinet ministers. Nor was the thinking in the General Staff any clearer. It was infested with fifth columnists, who had no faith either in the strength of their country or in the possibility of resisting Hitler.

It was not surprising that the Simović government was unable to steer a firm course either in domestic or in foreign policies. Its first action was to state that it adhered to the pact with Germany and Italy. The Minister of Foreign Affairs of the new government, Dr. Momčilo Ninčić, sent a note to Germany, Italy and other Axis powers in which he formally stated that Yugoslavia recognized all her international commitments, including, of course, Yugoslavia's adhesion to the Axis powers. The government decided also that a delegation headed by Vice-Premier Slobodan Jovanović should immediately be sent to Rome to see Mussolini and confirm once more Yugoslavia's loyalty to the Axis powers. The possibility of dispatching a similar delegation to Berlin was examined. At the same time, a delegation went to Moscow to negotiate a treaty of friendship and mutual assistance with Stalin and Molotov.

Worst of all, the government failed to take measures for the defense of the country. Instead of proclaiming a general mobilization the very first day after March 27, action was delayed until April 7, a day after Hitler's aggression against Yugoslavia. Nor were steps taken to strengthen the unity of the country. In Croatia, forty leading Communists, who had been arrested by Prince Paul for their anti-Axis activities, were left in jail. Vlatko Maček, the leader of the Croatian Peasant Party, and Dr. Ivan Šubašić, the governor of Croatia, stubbornly refused to release them and later handed them over to the Germans and the Ustashi, who shot them. Prime Minister Simović himself and the whole of his government were confident that Hitler would not attack Yugoslavia—so confident, in fact, that the date for the wedding of Simović's daughter was set for the morning of April 6, the very morning when German bombs started pouring on Belgrade. Another example of the erroneous appraisal of the situation by responsible circles was the case of the commanding officer of the Third Army, General Joca Naumović, who called the General Staff at 1 A.M. on April 6, and was told that there was no immediate danger of war, because several Yugoslav cabinet ministers were leaving for Berlin! But Hitler was ready to attack. His troops were already on the move.

April 6 was a bright, sunny Sunday. In Belgrade people usually get up early, even on Sundays, so that all Belgrade markets were crowded. A pact of nonaggression had been signed in the night between April 5 and 6 in Moscow between the USSR and Yugoslavia, and thousands of workers were in the streets, anticipating warm demonstrations of approval in connection with the signing. Shortly before 7 A.M. the roar of the first aircraft was heard, coming in waves from the north, the Rumanian border. Many watched them calmly, believing them to be Yugoslav army aircraft; then the bombs began to drop. What happened after that was hell. Wave after wave of the German air force methodically bombed the whole city. Antiaircraft guns were soon silenced and the few Yugoslav fighter planes were either brought down or destroyed on the ground. Hitler was wreaking a merciless revenge for March 27. The German pilots had been instructed to destroy the city's water system and then to shower incendiary bombs on the houses. The first attack left the whole city in smoke and flames. The Stukas dived practically to the roof level and spared nothing: homes, hospitals, churches, schools and libraries —all were targets.

In the very center of Belgrade, a bomb hit the Church of the Assumption and a shelter in its immediate vicinity, where a wedding party sought refuge, with the bride in white, the groom with rosemary in his buttonhole, the priest in his gold-embroidered robes— two hundred persons in all. The bombs dropped by the Stukas fell in the very center of the shelter, which consisted of a trench protected by about two feet of earth. Nobody emerged alive from the shelter. The first attack lasted for an hour and a half. It left devastation behind it. The people hurriedly left the shelters and rushed toward the suburbs where they hoped to find refuge, jumping over the dead and the wounded. Fire was spreading rapidly. At 11 A.M. came the second attack, more violent than the first. Anarchy in the city was complete. Gypsies from the outskirts penetrated the center of the town and broke into shops, dragging away expensive furs, food, even medical instruments. A bomb hit the zoological gardens, and the wild animals started roaming through the burning city; a polar bear made his way to the Sava River, groaning painfully.

When the attack started, I was in town with Edvard Kardelj. I took him through the burning streets toward the outskirts, to the house of one of our supporters, where I intended to find shelter for him. I passed along Studenica Street, near the building where I had gone to elementary school. It was also in flames. How many times had I, as a child with a school bag on my back, hurried along that street into a one-story house with a stone wall around it, how happily had I run into the street with my little friends, how we had played on that sidewalk, how we had bought grapes from the peasants who were selling them there in the early fall. The same wooden counters where the grapes had been sold were there on the morning of April 6. I saw a peasant in a gray embroidered Shumadian jacket lying dead across the counter amid heads of young lettuce. I was startled by the voice of a fat priest in a black greasy hassock who was dragging two huge suitcases from which hurriedly packed shirts were emerging. He asked me to carry one of the suitcases for him. I waved him away. An elderly woman ran up from somewhere, with her hair all undone and a horror-stricken face. I hardly recognized her. She used to live there, quite near my school. When she came closer, I saw she was carrying something in her arms and smothering it with kisses.

"Oh! Mila, my daughter . . ."

So cried this mother, oblivious to all around her. What she was carrying was the arm of her daughter, who had been torn to pieces by a bomb only a few moments before.

A little farther on there was a wild kind of singing, practically screeching. A young girl with a pimply face and a porter, a powerfully built middle-aged man, were sitting embraced on the doorsill of a half-destroyed tavern. When the first bombing started, they had found refuge in this inn and started to drink until they had become completely drunk. They were now sitting on the doorsill and screeching drunkenly, paying no heed to the sirens which were announcing the third onslaught of Goering's air force. Kardelj and I escaped from the center of the town and reached the suburbs, where we sheltered ourselves in an open trench while the Stukas roared through the air and showered bombs on my native city. Thus, throughout April 6, the attacks of Goering's air force followed one another in close succession.

It was never ascertained how many people were killed that day. A few more than three thousand bodies were buried in the New Cemetery. But how many people were buried under the ruins? How many were buried on the spot, in the streets? As late as three weeks after April 6, living people were brought out from cellars where they had been engulfed in wreckage. One man spent all that time in a cellar subsisting on sauerkraut. The cellar was finally opened up and the unfortunate man brought out into the open air, where he died after a few minutes. And how many houses were there which had been hit and which nobody ever tried to clear up? Thus, the bombing of

Tito

Belgrade took its place in the history of World War II beside Guernica, Coventry, Rotterdam and other martyred cities. Thousands of the inhabitants of Belgrade lost their lives that day, but the Serbs as a nation suffered an even more terrible blow. In Belgrade there was a National Library with a wealth of medieval manuscripts, with the only surviving copies of rare periodicals, without which it is impossible to study the history or culture of my country. The Simović government did nothing to remove these treasures to a safe place, and when Belgrade was bombed a German incendiary bomb hit the roof of the National Library. The precious books thus vanished in the flames. When I returned to Belgrade after the bombing, all that was left were the charred walls, while in the basement one could still see the cinders of the books that had been burnt. A German soldier in a helmet and with a submachine gun slung across his chest passed along the street. Never in my life had I looked with so much hatred at anyone as I looked at this German soldier.

Hitler had achieved his purpose in bombing Belgrade. He had intended to punish the capital city of Yugoslavia for March 27. But beyond the physical destruction he destroyed as well the heart of Yugoslavia's government. No sooner had the first bombs hit Belgrade than certain members of the cabinet climbed into their motorcars and fled headlong from the burning capital. Nowhere did the government pause to review the situation, to take some decision. The High Command was equally paralyzed; there was no longer a center in Yugoslavia from which defense could be co-ordinated.

Where, on that fateful morning of April 6, were Tito, Kardelj, Djilas, Ranković? The majority of the members of the Central Committee were in Belgrade. Djilas was on the streets, awaiting the demonstrations in connection with the signing of the treaty with the Soviet Union. When the bombing began, he took shelter in the gateway of a building, which was a few moments later hit by a five-hundred-pound bomb. He was not injured, but the people who were in the cellar were killed, for the bomb penetrated to the basement before exploding. Djilas withdrew to the outskirts of the city, where he assembled some five hundred Communists and sympathizers whom he ordered to the nearest military headquarters for direction to their respective military units. Kardelj remained in the home of a sympathizer for the first three days of the bombing, hoping to establish contact with the comrades. He then went to Zagreb to see Tito and tell him about the bombing of Belgrade. At that time, a radiogram had been received from Moscow; Dimitrov was inquiring about the bombing of Yugoslavia's capital and whether any of the leading Communists had been killed. A group of young Communists remained in Belgrade throughout that time, to help extinguish the fires. One of their assignments was to put out the fire in the storehouse of the Belgrade police headquarters, which contained, among other things, all the books the political police had banned in recent years. These include *How Steel Was Tempered*, a novel of the civil war in Russia, by the young Soviet writer Ostrovsky. The firefighters made away with all the copies of this prohibited book, and during the war circulated it among Partisan detachments, where the best fighters were given the names of the heroes of Ostrovsky's book.

While Belgrade burned, the Germans were on the march toward the city. The only resistance they met was offered by a group of youths, who ambushed the Germans some ten miles south of Belgrade, in a stone quarry under the mountain of Avala, and attacked the motorized column with rifles and hand grenades. They killed a few Germans, but were soon overcome.

When the war started, on April 6, Tito was in Zagreb, in his apartment, in a small house in the outskirts of the town, which he had rented under the assumed name of Slavko Babić. He heard that the war had started at 11 A.M. from a neighbor who had been listening to the German broadcasts, for the Belgrade station had gone off the air early in the morning. Tito immediately went to town to get in touch with comrades. The confusion was general.

While looking for his friends in the city, Tito passed near the barracks of militia of Maček, leader of the Croat Peasant Party (founded in 1939). Chatting with the militiamen, he soon realized they were looking forward to the coming of the Germans. For this reason, Tito immediately sent a delegation of leading Zagreb workers, among whom were members of the Central Committee of the Communist Party of Yugoslavia, to the Headquarters of the Fourth Army. This delegation requested General Orlović, the Chief of Staff of the Army, to give arms to the workers for them to defend the city against Germans and Ustashi. The General answered that the situation at the front was favorable and that there was no danger from the Ustashi. The workers' delegation insisted on its claims, but General Orlović would not hear of granting them and at the end threatened them with arrest.

Three days later, Zagreb was occupied. The resistance of the Yugoslav army had been short. German tanks very quickly broke down the frontier defense. The army had no unified command. Acts of treason were committed everywhere. Many army commanders were not at their headquarters and there was no efficient liaison with the Supreme Command. It was then that the Italians struck cowardly from behind, but they were halted at the border and managed to resume their advance only after the Germans had broken defense lines from the rear. Yugoslav troops counterattacked in Albania and came to within two miles of Scutari.

On April 10, Hitler's tanks thundered through Zagreb streets on their way south to Bosnia in order to destroy the remnants of the Yugoslav army. On that very day, Tito wrote in the name of the Central Committee of the Communist Party of Yugoslavia a proclamation to the people of Yugoslavia, which contained the following words:

"You who are struggling and dying in this battle for independence, be convinced that it will end in success. . . . Do not lose heart, close your ranks and do not bow your heads under the heavy blows which you are suffering. . . ." A few days later, the Simović government decided to surrender to the enemy. General Kalafatović was instructed to sign an act of unconditional surrender. The King, the government and the High Command drove to the town of Nikšić, where airplanes awaited them, and abandoned their country and their people in their hour of greatest peril. King Peter's actions will never be forgiven; he fled the field of battle. Not even his grandfather, not even his father, had done such a thing. Old King Peter had plodded through the whole of Albania with his army and his people; nobody could deny King Alexander's personal courage.

But the King and the government did not forget to take part of the gold of the National Bank with them, and loaded ten cases into one of the planes. When they were flying over Greece, through a storm, one of the cases fell on the head of one of the ministers and killed him.

Behind them they left a defeated army, an enemy-held country.

The generals and senior officers ordered their men to lay down their arms and give themselves up, but the younger officers refused to comply and some of them led their soldiers into the woods or concealed their weapons in safe places. A number of the older officers chose this same courageous path, but a few days later Hitler declared arrogantly in a speech that he had captured 335,000 Yugoslav soldiers and officers.

Within a period of a few weeks, Hitler fulfilled his threat. Yugoslavia was destroyed not only from a military point of view but also as a state. Italian divisions occupied Montenegro, the greater part of Slovenia, and Dalmatia. The Hungarians seized the fertile Bačka plain in the north, while the Bulgarians took Macedonia and parts of Serbia. Germany occupied the northern part of Slovenia. In Croatia, the Quisling "Independent State of Croatia" was set up under Ante Pavelić, a paid agent of Mussolini. Croatia thus came under Italy's protectorate. An Italian prince was to become King of Croatia. In Serbia, Hitler appointed General Milan Nedić premier of the Serbian Quisling government.

Yugoslavia was thus partitioned. Nor did Hitler stop at that. He goaded the Quisling Pavelić into mass annihilation of the Serbs in Croatia. One of the most ghastly slaughters of World War II thus began. Entire villages were brought collectively before abysses and made to throw themselves into them one after the other, men and women, mothers and children. Elsewhere, people's throats were simply cut with knives. At the same time, Hitler incited the Quisling Nedić to embark upon a massacre of Moslems and Croats. *"Divide et impera,"* watchword of all conquerors, now became a sanguinary reality in Yugoslavia.

The Catholic Archbishop of Croatia, Aloysius Stepinac, openly sided with the Germans and their Quisling in Croatia. On April 12th, 1941, while fighting between the German and the Yugoslav army was still going on in the Bosnian mountains, Archbishop Stepinac openly called on Pavelić's deputy Kvaternik and congratulated him on the formation of the Quisling state of Croatia. At the same time Stepinac sent a pastoral letter to all clergy in Croatia calling them to help the Quisling state of Croatia. At a church conference held later, he as chairman urged a resolution in favor of collaboration. He himself accepted appointment as archvicar of Pavelić's army.

From those parts of Yugoslavia which had come under the direct control of the Third Reich, all Yugoslavs who refused to sign a statement that they were Germans were compelled to leave their homes on twenty-four-hour notice. The only belongings they were allowed to take were those they could carry in their arms. In Belgrade, the capital of Yugoslavia, preparations were under way to make of the city a German fortress. In certain sections of the town the population was already being told to leave, their places to be taken by German families from the Reich. Posters made their appearance on the walls: "For every German who is found killed, one hundred Serbs will be shot."

The roundup of Jews also began. Belgrade, which had always been known for its freedom from any form of anti-Semitism, awoke one morning to find that every Jew was ordered to wear a yellow arm band. Later most of the Jews were mercilessly massacred.

Hours of dire stress began for Yugoslavia. And just then, a communiqué from Moscow spread consternation throughout the country. The Soviet government declared officially that Yugoslavia no longer existed as a state, and that there was therefore no longer need for the Yugoslav Embassy in Moscow. It was difficult to justify such an attitude on the part of Moscow. No explanation that this was being done because of tactical considerations with regard to Hitler sounded convincing to the Yugoslav masses.

Traitors ran riot in Yugoslavia. A civil administration was established throughout Serbia, together with a police force, that Hitler might utilize Serbia as a base in his war against the united nations. Copper and lead mines were again put into operation in Serbia, grains and fats were exported to Germany, workers in Serbia were recruited for the German war industry. Much the same thing was taking place in Croatia. In Slovenia, former Governor Natlačen organized a delegation which went to Rome to swear allegiance to Mussolini. Among the old political parties, all was silenced. Most of the leaders had escaped with the King; those who remained either watched the German actions passively or collaborated in the looting of the country.

Such were the conditions prevailing when Tito convened the Central Committee of the Communist Party of Yugoslavia in Zagreb toward the end of April, 1941. It was extremely difficult to come to this meeting. All Yugoslavia was intersected with new frontiers, and special permits were needed for traveling from one town to another, especially for moving from one zone of occupation to another. In addition, the German command changed the form of the permits every third or fourth day in order to prevent any possibility of their being forged. After careful preparations and after the necessary forged permits had been arranged, the members of the CC of the CPY met for a single day in an apartment in Zagreb. Tito first gave a detailed report on the situation in the country, and then a discussion followed. The question of an uprising against the invaders was raised. It was decided that the uprising should be of the broadest nature and include all those who were prepared to fight the Nazis and Fascists. The foundations of the National Liberation Front were thus finally laid. Edvard Kardelj reported on what had been done in that respect in Slovenia. A meeting had been held there on April 22, between representatives of the Communist Party of Slovenia, of Christian Socialists, of the members of the powerful gymnastic organization Sokol, and of a group of cultural workers, and it was decided to establish a common front in this struggle against the invaders.

The question of the nature of the uprising was discussed extensively at the Zagreb plenary meeting. Tito made a statement on the subject in which he emphasized that the people of Yugoslavia were very bitter against the King and the former government for having betrayed the country, and for having failed to make the necessary preparations for its defense against the invaders. The feeling against those who were collaborating with Hitler and Mussolini was particularly strong. For these reasons, the uprising against the invaders should be linked with the struggle against the fifth column. That meant that the former civil authorities should be destroyed and replaced by a new, people's authority. This portion of Tito's speech reads: "In their struggle against the invaders, the Serbian people will have to wage a no less determined struggle against the traitors to the Serbian people, who have received various functions of government with the aid of the invader and against the will of the people, and are even now preparing to impose upon the people the will of the German conquerors, to persecute the best sons of the Serbian people at the order of the invader and ruthlessly to loot the Serbian people." It was further decided at the meeting to continue intensively the collection of arms throughout the country, to form shock groups under responsible commanders in the towns and in the villages, and to start nursing and first-aid courses.

Such was the attitude of the Central Committee toward the end of April, 1941. The greater part of these decisions were published in a special issue of the *Proleter*, the central organ of the Party, as well as in numerous leaflets. This had tremendous repercussions throughout the country. Until then, all had been silent. Not a voice had been heard in Yugoslavia under Hitler's jackboots. The Communist Party of Yugoslavia was at that time the only party who had called for a struggle against the invaders; the Communist Party of Yugoslavia was at that time the only party which was working in all the provinces of Yugoslavia and which had come out in favor of a united Yugoslavia. This enhanced enormously the prestige of the Communists in Yugoslavia and "Communist" began to connote more and more patriot, fighter for national freedom.

Tito immediately informed Dimitrov in Moscow of these decisions. A radio transmitter had been set up in Zagreb before the war, and Vladimir Velebit,* a Zagreb lawyer, had discovered a villa in which he housed this transmitter and its operator. There was another transmitter in Belgrade for contact with the USSR, concealed in a medical institute; but a German bomb had hit the institute on April 6, destroying the transmitter and killing its operator. The text of Tito's speech was sent to Moscow over the Zagreb transmitter.

It had been decided at the April plenary meeting that the Central Committee should move to Belgrade and form there a center for the struggle against the invaders. It was high time Tito got out of Zagreb, for the Ustashi police were already on his heels—Engineer Babić had begun to appear suspicious to them. They traced Tito through a small Ford he had bought before the war and by means of which he could move easily about the town and its surroundings, since the police never suspected that Communists drove about in motorcars. When the Germans and the Ustashi entered Zagreb, they requisitioned all motor vehicles. Tito was not prepared to give up his car, but instead called a few masons to build up the garage where the motorcar was located. One of the masons informed the police. For-

---

* Vladimir Velebit is now Yugoslav Minister in Rome.

tunately, one of Tito's relatives noticed the police moving around the house and rushed to town, where he found Tito and told him not to return home. The same evening Tito left Zagreb for Belgrade with a forged identity card and with forged permits. He was accompanied by a girl, whose task was to see whether the Germans had established a new kind of permit. They successfully passed through German control posts at two spots, and reached Belgrade in the beginning of May. In Belgrade, Tito lived in the suburb of Dedinje, first in Rumunska Street 16A, and then in Gladstone Street, both located near the home of the German military commander in Belgrade. The second of the two apartments had been carefully designed for emergencies: when the washbasin was removed, an entrance appeared which led into a hiding place concealed under the roof. In this apartment Tito had sixteen hand grenades and two revolvers, with which he intended to defend himself if the Germans found him.

News from all parts of Yugoslavia showed that the preparations for the uprising were progressing satisfactorily. Most of the weapons had been assembled in Montenegro, because it was there that the larger part of the old Yugoslav army had been disarmed. A number of shock groups were already in action. The Central Committee decided to address proclamations to the German, Italian and Bulgarian armed forces and leaflets were printed in the respective languages of these armed forces; they had little effect, except to bring about the arrest of several Communists caught distributing them. All Communists who were known as such went underground.

In the middle of May, German military convoys began moving through Yugoslavia at an accelerated pace, traveling from Greece through Belgrade toward Rumania. A senior German officer told a Russian refugee that Hitler was preparing to attack Russia. This information reached Tito, who sent a radiogram to Dimitrov toward the end of May bringing it to his notice.

Such was the situation in Yugoslavia as June 22 approached. In certain parts of the country, such as Herzegovina, there had already been armed clashes when the Ustashi arrived to massacre the Serbs. The Communists led the uprising and were briefly successful. In the other parts of the country, the people awaited only the signal to begin the struggle against the Germans, the Italians, the Bulgarians and the other invaders. The people were wholeheartedly in favor of a revolt. Within the previous hundred and fifty years, there had been twenty-eight uprisings against occupiers and ten wars of liberation in various parts of Yugoslavia. In the summer of 1941, as Yugoslavia lay prostrate, the people looked for a call which would announce to them the time had come to rise in arms.

CHAPTER X

1941:

"The attack against the USSR only hastened the beginning of our struggle . . ."

THE uprising in Yugoslavia broke out at one of the most critical moments of World War II. Hitler's attack against the USSR had started, and his troops had penetrated deep into Russian territory encircling large units of the Red Army. The rest of Europe was, with the exception of Great Britain, under Hitler's control.

On June 22, 1941, Hitler's orders to the German army to move against the Soviet Union were being read over the loud-speakers in almost all the cities of occupied Europe. That afternoon, the Politburo of the Yugoslav Central Committee met in a house in the outskirts of Belgrade. It was unanimously decided that the time for the uprising had come. While the meeting was still in progress, Tito began to write a proclamation to the peoples of Yugoslavia to rise in revolt against the German, Italian, Hungarian and Bulgarian invaders. That very night, that proclamation was printed in secret presses in Belgrade and carried by courier to all parts of Yugoslavia.

The proclamation began with the words: "The hour has struck to take arms for your freedom against Fascist aggressors. Do your part in the fight for freedom under the leadership of the Communist Party of Yugoslavia. The war of the Soviet Union is your war, because the Soviet Union is fighting against your enemies, under whose yoke your necks are bent." The proclamation appealed to the workers: "Do your proletarian duty unfalteringly and with discipline. Get ready now for the last and decisive battle. Do not let the precious blood of the heroic Soviet people be shed without your participation."

Tito

Communists of Yugoslavia have sometimes been reproached abroad for having led armed revolt only after Germany had attacked the USSR. In a speech delivered in December, 1951, Tito replied to these reproaches: "It is sometimes held that the uprising of the Yugoslav peoples was provoked by Hitler's attack against the USSR. That is not so. The fact is that we wished to assist the Soviet Union with our uprising. The fact is that we availed ourselves of the attack against the USSR in order to mobilize the broadest possible forces at the very outset of the uprising, which had been carefully prepared for several months, and which had in certain places started before the attack against the USSR. It should be understood that the Soviet Union's entry into the war against Hitler, even if involuntary, constituted a very considerable moral support for our peoples, in the same way as the liberation struggle in Yugoslavia was a moral support to the peoples of the Soviet Union. Nor should it be forgotten that we began our uprising in 1941, at a time when the Red Army was retreating on all fronts, when the majority of the people throughout the world were haunted by the somber thought that nothing could resist Hitler and that his war machine was invincible. The attack against the USSR only hastened the beginning of our struggle. Nothing more. To those who ask today why the uprising did not begin before the attack against the USSR, I can reply only that they seem to ignore the fact that so difficult a struggle cannot be prepared in a day, especially when the entire armed force of the country and its weapons had fallen into the hands of the enemy. Rare indeed are the instances in history of a country organizing an armed insurrection of the people so well and so rapidly, after only three months of occupation.

"There are also other unfriendly explanations of our struggle sometimes offered abroad. It has been said that the uprising broke out irrationally or out of despair, or spontaneously. What is implied is that it all happened without any form of organization—that is what Cominform propaganda is at present asserting with unfaltering perseverance—that we could not foresee that the people would listen to us and would enter the struggle, that we could not foresee that we would come out victorious. The height of absurdity is the claim that our peoples entered the struggle only because Stalin had called upon them to do so. Everybody, including Stalin himself, saw later the extent to which our people obeyed Stalin. When Stalin called upon our peoples in 1948 to overthrow the leaders of their country, our people did not respond to his call, and they have not responded through almost three and a half years despite the untiring propaganda efforts of the Soviet leaders and of the Cominform to incite our peoples to revolt."

Only a few days after the proclamation of June 22, 1941, was issued, action against the invaders began. In the night between June 23 and 24, the first act of sabotage was committed on the Belgrade-Zagreb railway line. The Central Committee met again on June 27 in Belgrade. General Headquarters for the armed struggle against the invaders was established under the name of the GHQ of the National Liberation Partisan Detachments. Popularly, the new people's army was known as the Partisans, a name taken from the uprisings of the Spanish people against Napoleon in 1808, and from the Russian revolts against Napoleon in 1812. This GHQ included all the members of the Politburo of the Central Committee, and was subsequently expanded to include certain military leaders. The Military Committee of the Party ceased to function, and its chairman assumed command of the new GHQ. Tito was appointed to this command by unanimous decision of the Politburo. It was also decided that the flag of the National Liberation Movement should be the Yugoslav flag, with a five-pointed star in the middle. Tito had already worked out instructions for the formation of detachments for the scope and nature of their activities, for sabotage, for raids, for the organization of quartermaster and medical services. It was also decided that the GHQ should immediately start issuing an official bulletin.

The atmosphere in Belgrade was particularly bleak in those days. German propaganda provided tremendous publicity for the communiqués in which the High Command registered its advances into Russia. Huge maps showing the break-throughs of German tanks were posted on large boards; the whole city, all the trolley cars, all the walls were covered with German posters. Loud-speakers were installed in the streets blaring communiqués from the eastern front. Quisling newspapers brought out special editions.

To counter this, young Communists of Belgrade decided to burn publicly the Quisling newspapers. Groups of three approached more than a hundred newsstands; one seized the papers, the second poured gasoline over them, the third touched a match to the sodden mess. The effect of this act was tremendous throughout the city, for few well-frequented newsstands had been missed. Of the hundred groups which had taken part in this burning of Fascist papers, only one was caught. All three young men were shot the following morning by the German command.

Two days later, the young Communists decided to repeat the action on a larger scale. The leaders of the organization themselves went to the most crowded spot in town in order to be the first to take part in the action. The Germans did not expect that the first action and their reprisals would be followed by a second wave. This mass burning of Quisling newspapers had a huge political effect on all Belgrade. The common people were proud of this action of the young people of Belgrade, who were prepared to face death in order to accomplish such things. And, suddenly, many of these people started to do similar things, in a spontaneous, unorganized manner. Someone had been brave enough to begin.

The wave of sabotage swept ahead with tremendous vigor. Telephone wires serving the Germans were cut, German soldiers were attacked in dark streets and their weapons wrenched from them, the burning of German military trucks and motorcars began on a mass scale. The most effective weapon was a small incendiary which set gasoline aflame after a brief delay. Young people crept near German trucks, surreptitiously opened the gasoline tank and tossed in an incendiary, then moved away. A few minutes later, while the truck was rumbling through the streets, it would burst into flame.

High explosives, too, were being put to good use. All these weapons were prepared by young people whose previous experience in that field had been very limited. Many died in their primitive laboratories and workshops.

Meanwhile, ruthless persecution of all Communists and other suspicious persons began in Belgrade. The former Yugoslav political police rendered tremendous services to the Gestapo, drawing up lists and carrying out the arrests in association with German officials. The procedure was an extremely summary one. As the majority of Communists had already left their homes, German military cars, manned by soldiers with light machine guns, circled the town. When the Yugoslav agents pointed to a Communist whom they recognized in the streets, the German soldiers would open fire from their light machine guns without warning.

The German command also ordered a curfew. All citizens had to be in their homes before seven o'clock P.M., later changed to six o'clock. Mass searches of sections of the town and of all the houses and apartments were carried out. In reprisal, the Partisans decided that all Yugoslav policemen should be punished by death. They were shot in the street, and a number were killed. One of them was lucky. A student approached him from behind and attempted to fire a bullet into his temple. The revolver missed fire, however, and the student was immediately caught and shot.

The greatest criminal of all, Svetozar Vujković, an old police agent, was shot at while riding a motorcycle. Two bullets hit him but he remained alive. After the war, Vujković was captured alive and brought to trial. His conduct at the trial was extremely cowardly; he said he had been merely an employee, that he had been forced to serve the occupiers, that he had killed no one. This same Vujković had been commander of the concentration camp on Banjica where tens of thousands of people from Serbia, particularly Jews, were murdered. Vujković was sentenced to death and shot.

In this situation, a meeting of the GHQ was convened on July 4, in the home of a friend of the Party in Dedinje, a wealthy residential suburb of Belgrade. In order not to attract the attention of the police, Party members entered the house one by one at fifteen-minute intervals. A detailed plan for the further development of the uprising was worked out at this meeting and Tito explained the main tasks of this phase of the struggle.

With a view to a successful development of the uprising, it was essential, in the first place, to destroy the governmental machinery of the old Yugoslavia, which had completely placed itself in the service of the invaders, and particularly the police, the municipal administrations, and so forth. In this way the occupier's mainstays in the villages and smaller localities, where the power of their army or military police could not as a practical matter reach, would be destroyed. In disarming the police and destroying their headquarters, the Partisans would also obtain the weapons of which they were so badly in need.

In the towns the sabotage, diversionist activities were to be pursued with unabated vigor, and a hell was to be created for the enemy in which he could never feel safe. The Partisan detachments, however, were to be created outside the towns, in the countryside, where detection and arrest were less likely than in the towns. The activities of the detachments outside the towns would have considerable effect in the towns themselves.

At this meeting it was decided where the leaders were to go in order to assume the direction of the uprising in the different parts of the country. Edvard Kardelj was already in Slovenia. Milovan Djilas was designated for Montenegro, Svetozar Vukmanović for Bosnia and Herzegovina, and Tito himself and Aleksandar Ranković-Marko were to take over the leadership of the uprising in Serbia.

Only a few days after this meeting, the first results began to be felt. The wave of sabotage activities in Belgrade increased. A German military garage was blown up, and over a hundred German military motor vehicles were burned. The first six Partisan detachments were founded in Serbia. The manner in which the Partisan detachments obtained their weapons is highly characteristic. Some weapons which had been hidden at the time of the April catastrophe were recovered, but there were not enough to equip a large detachment. The main source of supplies was the enemy. Thus the Kragujevac detachment obtained its first six army rifles by disarming a police post, into which they suddenly broke armed with unloaded sport rifles. The police immediately surrendered, and the Kragujevac Partisan detachment, which later increased to six hundred fighting men, had six army rifles. In the town of Kraljevo, in central Serbia, a young peasant was standing behind a tree, at the side of the road with an ax in his hands. When a German motorcyclist drove past him with a submachine gun flung across his back, the young Serbian peasant struck him on the head with his ax—and the detachment thus got its first submachine gun. The wave of attacks on police stations and municipalities swept over Serbia, and the Partisan detachments were very soon armed.

One summer day a Partisan detachment arrived armed at a people's carnival in the village of Bela Crkva near the town of Valjevo. When the police opened fire, a Belgrade journalist and veteran of the Spanish civil war drew his revolver and killed two policemen, while the rest fled. That was the first open clash between the Partisans and the German flunkies in Serbia. That day, July 7, is now celebrated as Serbia's national holiday.

The uprising developed in other parts of the country. Violently in some places, steadily in others, the whole of Yugoslavia was swept by the wave of resistance to the Germans, the Italians, the Bulgarians and the Hungarians. In Montenegro, where most weapons had been hidden at the time of the short-lived war against the Germans in April of that year, the uprising soon broke out and spread to the whole of this mountainous area. Beginning July 13, 1941, when the Italians were organizing a parliament in the capital city of Montenegro to proclaim Montenegro's unification with Italy, Partisan detachments were flooded by peasants asking for arms to fight against Italians. The peasants said to the Partisans: "Why do you think you are our betters? Why do you not let us fight the invaders?" Within two days and two nights the whole of Montenegro, with the exception of three towns, was liberated from the Italians. Two Italian divisions were disarmed. Huge quantities of weapons fell into the hands of the Partisans. Captured Italian soldiers were very well treated, told about international brotherhood, and released; these same divisions were armed again by the occupation authorities and sent back to fight the Partisans. The rapid growth of the revolt in Montenegro was, to a very large extent, a result of the general conviction prevailing there that the war would soon end by a decisive victory of the Red Army over Hitler's hordes. Woe to those who in Montenegro at that time ventured to prophesy that the war would last as much as another six months.

Uprisings spread rapidly in Bosnia and Herzegovina, as well as in certain parts of Croatia, such as Lika, Kordun, Gorski Kotar, Banija and Slavonija. In many parts of the country, the population rose to fight with hoes and wooden forks, closing in on the police in a wide circle, and attacking them from all sides. The police usually surrendered before the weight of the onslaught. The uprising developed with particular rapidity in the parts of Croatia populated by Serbs, whose complete annihilation Pavelić had vowed. At the same time, the Roman Catholic Church in Croatia with Archbishop Aloysius Stepinac at its head began forcibly converting Orthodox Serbs to the Catholic faith. Those who were not prepared to change their religion were in danger of physical destruction by the Ustashi. In the town of Glina 700 were executed in the church itself. Many Orthodox churches were desecrated, some even being turned into stables. But

Stepinac uttered not a word to stop these conversions and persecutions. On the contrary, he issued political statements in favor of the Pavelić regime and even ordered special masses of thanksgiving that the Ustashi had taken power. Afterward hundreds of priests served with Pavelić's Ustashi troops—some of them even putting on Ustashi uniforms—and joined actively in the attempts to force the conversion of Orthodox Serbs to Catholicism. These activities of the Roman Catholic clergy were particularly intense in Slavonia. A Partisan detachment had just gone into action in that area and was defending the Serbs from the attempt to convert them by force. When the news got around that forcible conversions were to take place in one of the villages, this Partisan detachment, at the time only five men, sent a threatening letter to the local Catholic priest, a very fat man. When the priest read the letter, he was so upset that—the heat aiding—he had a stroke. He was found dead with the Partisan's letter in his hands.

Pavelić persecuted the Croatian workers with equal violence, shooting the most prominent Croatian intellectuals, Prica, Keršovani and Adžija, who had been handed over to him by the old Yugoslavia. The reply was a series of actions in Zagreb. A group of members of the youth movement ambushed an Ustashi military company as it marched along behind a band, and flung hand grenades at it. Shortly afterward, the telephone exchange was blown up.

From Belgrade, Tito continued co-ordinating the uprising throughout the country. He was living in Gladstone Street in Dedinje and did not move much about the town unless it was absolutely necessary, carrying always a revolver and two hand grenades. On August 10 the bulletin of the GHQ appeared bearing the initials "TT" for Tito. In this first issue of the bulletin, Tito's article, "The Task of the National Liberation Partisan Detachments," laid down in detail the lines along which the uprising was to develop.

The article took the form of sixteen brief items. It proclaimed that the main purpose of the Partisan detachments was the liberation of the peoples of Yugoslavia from the occupation forces, and the struggle against those who were assisting them in oppressing and terrorizing our people. Tito stressed that the Partisan detachments were called National Liberation Detachments because they were the fighting formations not of any political party and group—not even the

Communist Party, although the Communists were in the forefront of the struggle—but were the fighting forces of the people of Yugoslavia and should therefore include all patriots, whatever their views, who were capable of waging an armed struggle against the invaders.

Tito proceeded to enumerate the tasks of the detachments: the destruction of railways, bridges, factories, preventing the enemy from collecting grains, cattle, or taxes. The detachments must defend the villages and towns from the enemy with their arms, they must destroy Fascist detachments everywhere, and particularly officers and Gestapo men, Black Shirts, and the Quislings who were the faithful dogs of the foreign invaders. The Partisan detachments must further promote the resistance of the people, and must kindle a general people's uprising, lest they become isolated from the masses. The number of men in the detachments must be increased. There must be iron discipline in the detachments. Any form of looting must be punished with the utmost severity. As the uprising increased in scope, it would be necessary to develop commanding officers capable of leading large units into battle. Finally, where strategic and other conditions were favorable, several Partisan detachments should be merged when necessary into large military units for the purpose of carrying out large-scale operations.

News arriving from all Yugoslavia showed the uprising was growing constantly. The German command resorted to the most ruthless measures in order to quell it. One morning four Partisans were hanged on Belgrade's main square, Terazije. Their bodies swung from the gallows all day, with German soldiers and Serbian Quislings on guard. At the same time, the Belgrade broadcasting station gave the names of the "Communists and Jews" who had been shot. There were mass arrests. One day, toward the end of July, Aleksandar Ranković, member of the Central Committee, was arrested while organizing the dynamiting of the Belgrade broadcasting station. In the course of this sabotage, he had come in contact with a technician at the broadcasting station who denounced him. The Gestapo set up an ambush for Ranković—where he was to meet the radio technician. Four Gestapo men suddenly jumped on Ranković and after a brief struggle knocked him to the ground. They did not know whom they had caught except what the technician had told them: that the unknown man wished to blow up the Belgrade radio station. Ranković was immediately taken to the Gestapo prison, where they began to interrogate him. They found him in possession of an identity card bearing the name of Stanišić. Ranković refused to say who he was. The Gestapo officials were impatient and began to club Ranković on his body and head. One blow hit him on the temple, and he fainted. That evening he was transferred to the hospital for political prisoners, which was guarded by the Gestapo and the old Yugoslav police, in Vidinska Ulica, in the center of the town.

As soon as Tito heard of Ranković's arrest, he immediately ordered the Belgrade Party organization to take all possible steps to free him. The day after Ranković's transfer to the hospital, the Party organization was notified by prisoners in the hospital. A plan for his escape was immediately drawn up. A doctor, who was employed in the hospital, sent a sketch showing the location of the corridors and rooms. Forty Partisans armed with hand grenades and revolvers were designated for this important action.

The hospital in which Ranković was held was located in the very center of the town. On Tuesday, July 29, at 10 A.M. the Partisans, dressed in ordinary civilian clothes, took up their positions in groups of three at all approaches to the hospital, while a party of ten entered the hospital. They had handcuffed one of their group to make it appear that they were detectives escorting a prisoner. Thus they entered the hospital. The policemen at the gate let them through, as did the policemen at the entrance to the hospital, but a policeman in the corridor tried to resist. He was immediately shot down and the Partisans broke into the room where Ranković was located.

This is the story of his escape as he told it to me.

"I did not know that the comrades were coming that day. About ten o'clock I heard the shooting. I immediately understood what was going on. At my side there were four guards and a Serbian male nurse. I got ready. Five members of the shock group appeared at the door holding revolvers. I immediately jumped up. They ordered the guards: 'Hands up!' And to me: 'You are Ranković? Come with us.'

"Two of the group took me by the arms, while two others protected our rear in the corridor. We went out of the building, walking not toward the gate but toward the wall, where I mustered all my strength and leaped over it, or rather, fell into the street. Two Gestapo men were standing there and they opened fire on our group.

They wounded two comrades, one in the arm and the other in the stomach, but our people shot them down. A motorcar should have been waiting for us, but it was nowhere to be seen. The confusion around the hospital was general; our guards, who were posted at the corners, had stopped all traffic and pedestrians. As there was no motorcar, I set out in my hospital clothes, accompanied by the comrades, after removing my bandage. We walked a few hundred steps to a house with two exits and there in the corridor I attempted to put on the clothes which the comrades had brought along. They were too small, except the trousers. We left the house at the other exit. Noises and shooting could be heard from the direction of the hospital. We then went to the house of a sympathizer where I finally found a jacket and a hat. I washed hurriedly and went out in the street, where a horse-drawn cart was waiting for me, into which I climbed with two armed comrades and drove through the streets of Belgrade until we reached one of our illegal apartments on the outskirts of the town."

None of the Partisans who took part in this action was killed. This feat caused tremendous enthusiasm in Belgrade. A few days later in the town of Šabac, in Serbia, a large Partisan detachment attacked the prison and liberated eighty comrades.

Many villages and even a few smaller towns were liberated in Serbia. What was known as the liberated territory, cleared of the invaders, was established. In Slovenia the German authorities themselves put up a signboard a few kilometers before the liberated territory began, with the warning "*Achtung! Banditengebiet*" (Beware! Bandit territory!). The time was approaching when it would become imperative to move the GHQ from Belgrade, where conditions were becoming increasingly difficult, to the liberated territory. Tito left Belgrade in the beginning of September—no easy thing to do. Tito traveled with a forged identity card and in the company of an Orthodox Priest and another man who was carrying the identity card of the German minority in Yugoslavia. The latter was armed, and it would have been difficult to find better camouflage. Tito traveled by train to a small station, situated some hundred miles south of Belgrade, and there hired a horse-drawn carriage to take him to the liberated territory. He drove for a few hours in this peasant carriage, until he reached the first Partisan sentries. The sentries did not know whom they had before them, examined Tito suspiciously, expressed doubts about his identity card and were about to arrest him when Tito demanded that he be taken to the nearest Partisan HQ. There he met a Partisan commander who recognized him. The Partisan sentries began to apologize, but Tito told them they were doing their duty well; had they acted differently he would have called them to task.

Tito entered liberated territory at the beginning of September and did not return to Belgrade until October, 1944, when the capital of Yugoslavia was finally liberated from the Germans. Upon his arrival in liberated territory, a meeting of the members of the GHQ with Partisan commanders from all parts of Yugoslavia was arranged in western Serbia. Beforehand, Tito sought direct contact with the colonel of the former Yugoslav army, Draža Mihailović, who had gone to the woods with a group of his men after the April surrender. His supporters were called Chetniks, "One who is in the company." His units were organized in many parts of Serbia at the same time when the Partisan units were formed. But there was a marked difference between the two military organizations. I remember when I was in the field in Serbia in late summer of 1941, as a political commissar of the Kragujevac detachment, I used to pay visits to the Headquarters of the Chetnik units. There was a strong contrast between these units and Partisan ones. The Chetnik units were usually made up of older men, married men, peasants from rich families. They remained in their villages, they slept at home, and from time to time they were called to the Headquarters where they drilled. I had great difficulty persuading the Chetnik commanders around Kragujevac to take part in the fighting against the Germans. They said they had no orders. On the other hand they criticized our command because we "wasted mercilessly the blood of the Serbian people fighting against the Germans in an uneven struggle." They advised us that we should wait until the Germans were weaker to fight against them. The Partisan units were usually made up of younger people who wanted to fight against Germans. On the other hand, there were some Chetnik units who did fight Germans in some other parts of Serbia, like Vlado Zečević, Colonel Misita and some others. But Colonel Misita was killed fighting Germans and Vlado Zečević joined Partisan units because he did not want to accept orders of Mihailović to stop operations against Germans.

A meeting was arranged, and Tito set out to visit Draža Mihailović, accompanied by a few Partisans. Their first meeting took place in a peasant house in the village of Strugarik, where they plunged directly into the question of action against the invaders. Draža Mihailović's point of view was that the time for the struggle had not yet come, and that it was better to wait for the Germans to be weakened and to save one's forces until that moment arrived and a fatal stroke could be delivered. Actually, Draža Mihailović's purpose was to maintain in Yugoslavia the pattern that had prevailed prior to 1941, and then, after the Germans had been defeated, to hand the country back to King Peter and to the Government in Exile. Tito proposed to Draža Mihailović that they launch joint operations against the occupation forces. But no agreement could be reached.

A few days later, the first meeting of the Partisan commanders took place in the village of Stolica. Commanders from practically all Yugoslavia except Macedonia attended this meeting. Most of them arrived on horseback or by foot through liberated territory; commanders from Slovenia and Croatia came illegally by train. They were all dressed as Partisans, in half-military, half-civilian clothes, furnished with chest straps and belts from which hung submachine guns and revolvers. The majority of them had yielded to a short-lived custom that dictated the wearing of fierce mustaches. The most fierce adorned the commander of a detachment from Serbia, Koča Popović. Tito had no mustaches.

The meeting lasted several days. The political and military situation in every part of Yugoslavia was examined in detail. Several important decisions were taken:

First, it was decided to establish a GHQ in each of the provinces of Yugoslavia, to facilitate the co-ordination of the activities of the numerous detachments, while the existing GHQ was to be transformed into Supreme Headquarters of the National Liberation Partisan Detachments of Yugoslavia.

Second, a detailed plan was worked out for the creation of new liberated territories in Yugoslavia, as had been done in Serbia. A plan was also worked out for extension of the liberated territory in Serbia, and decisions were taken with regard to the points which were to be attacked, the timing of the attacks and the forces which were to be involved.

Third, it was decided that new National Liberation Committees were to be established in the place of the former authorities throughout the liberated territory.

Fourth, it was resolved to form larger Partisan units, in battalion strength, and to avoid frontal clashes with an enemy superior both numerically and in fire-power, but to rely instead on numerous, mobile and closely connected Partisan detachments capable of simultaneous action. Such detachments could, when the need arose, be welded into powerful shock units for the purpose of waging a battle which they had been compelled to accept, or could disperse and strike suddenly at the enemy and at definite objectives, only to disappear again from the area of the attack. The essential point was to keep the man-power as intact as possible, while dealing the greatest possible blows to the enemy. The enemy should be compelled to strike into a vacuum.

The fifth decision of the Stolica meeting was approval of Tito's report on his interview with Draža Mihailović. It was decided to pursue the talks with Draža Mihailović in order further to investigate the possibility of a common struggle against the invaders.

The decisions taken at the meeting in Stolica speedily showed their effect. The twenty-four Partisan detachments in Serbia began to coordinate their activities, and a German garrison was soon captured by the Partisans, who took more than three hundred German soldiers prisoner and appropriated their weapons. Tribute must be paid to the enemy, and it must be recognized that the Germans in Serbia in 1941 fought with extraordinary determination. When they attacked the positions of the Partisans they advanced calmly as if they were on parade ground; when one fell, another soldier immediately took his place and continued to advance with the same calm, deliberate step. In order to avoid the further loss of isolated garrisons, the German command was compelled to evacuate the whole of western Serbia including the principal town, Užice. The Supreme HQ immediately moved to Užice and remained there for almost two months. The town of Užice thus because a kind of symbol of the first liberated territory in Yugoslavia, which the people called the "Užice Republic." While evacuating Užice, the German garrison was compelled to leave behind it an armament factory, whose capacity amounted to four hundred rifles and a large quantity of ammunition daily. The workers of this factory soon reassembled, the machines were transported to an underground shelter near Užice, and the rapid production of rifles bearing a special Partisan sign began. These rifles meant a lot to the Partisan detachments.

The liberated territory in Serbia was linked with the liberated territory in Bosnia and the latter was in its turn connected with the liberated territory in Montenegro. A very considerable part of Yugoslavia was thus liberated; with ordinary care to avoid the larger enemy-held towns, it was now possible to travel from the Adriatic Sea to the outskirts of Belgrade without leaving liberated territory. A Partisan railway ran one hundred miles through this territory, and a mail service was established throughout.

People's committees replaced the local governments which had placed themselves in the service of the invaders. These committees were formed by people who were in favor of the struggle against the occupation forces and against the Quislings. They were elected by the people themselves at meetings. In Serbia, a National Liberation Committee for the whole of Serbia was established, and became the embryo of the future government. Schools were opened in liberated territory. The newspaper *Borba* was published three times a week in Užice. All this was going on right in the midst of Hitler's European fortress, at a time when his triumphs were at their peak, when his forces were on the threshold of Moscow and Leningrad, and had already occupied Kiev.

One day, four men landed from a submarine off the Adriatic coast in Montenegro, which was part of the liberated territory. They were a captain of the British army, two officers of the Royal Yugoslav Army and a noncommissioned officer. With them they brought a radio transmitter and other military equipment. Escorted by Partisans, these unusual guests crossed the whole of the liberated territory, over two hundred miles, without encountering a single Chetnik unit. In Užice, the British captain informed the Supreme HQ that his name was Hudson and that he had been instructed to join Draža Mihailović's HQ. The two officers of the Royal Yugoslav Army left with him. The fourth man, however, refused to go to Draža Mihailović and remained with the Partisans. Captain Hudson was not without acquaintances in Užice, for he had served as an engineer in one of the mines of western Serbia, owned by the British. After the arrival of this mission, relations between Partisans and Chetniks began to deteriorate more and more. Chetnik commanders drifted away from Draža Mihailović as they did not share his unwillingness to come to grips with the Germans, among them the Orthodox priest Vlado Zečević and Lieutenant Ratko Martinović. They placed their detachments under the command of the Supreme HQ.

The situation in Serbia was causing concern to the German command. It had at its disposal in the whole of the territory of Serbia only three divisions of occupation and some police units. It therefore began bringing in reinforcements in the middle of September, in order to wipe out the liberated territory in Serbia. The German command launched its attack from the north, but its front column, which had been provided with tanks, encountered the determined resistance of the Partisan detachments, which put fifteen tanks out of commission with the aid of land mines and hand grenades. The attempts of the German infantry to penetrate into liberated territory also met with failure. Meanwhile, Tito proposed another interview with Draža Mihailović. He suggested that they meet in Užice, but Draža Mihailović refused to come to this Partisan town. Tito then offered to hold the meeting somewhere halfway between Užice and Draža Mihailović's HQ. This proposal was also rejected. Tito then decided to go and see Draža Mihailović personally in the latter's HQ in the village of Brajice on the Ravna Gora mountain, and set out with tall, swarthy Sreten Žujović-Crni,* a member of the Supreme HQ, Mitar Bakić, a Montenegrin Partisan and eight Partisans armed with submachine guns. They traveled in two motorcars. Sreten Žujević-Crni relates this meeting as follows:

"The meeting was held in a large peasant house. There was a big table in the middle on one side of which Tito and the rest of us were seated, while on the other side there was Draža with his men—his political adviser Dragiša Vasić and his second in command Lieutenant-Colonel Pavlović. Our eight bodyguards were standing behind us

---

* Žujević after the war became Minister of Finance of the Yugoslav government. In 1948 he joined Stalin, when the conflict broke out between the Soviet Union and Yugoslavia. Later he recanted.

with their submachine guns, while Draža Mihailović's bodyguards were aligned along the wall behind him. Our boys were young, clean-shaven, with a mustache here and there, while Draža's men all wore long beards.

"At this meeting, we proposed a twelve-point agreement with Draža Mihailović: joint operations against the Germans and the Quislings and the setting up of a joint command; a joint supply system; a joint division of booty in accordance with the slogan 'all for the front, all for the struggle'; a joint local command; a joint commission for the settling of controversial questions; the creation of provisional authorities in the place of the former municipalities which had gone over to the service of the invaders, these authorities to consist of representatives of all political groups which were willing to fight the invaders; voluntary rather than compulsory mobilization; and so forth.

"The negotiations advanced painfully. In the course of the discussion, our bodyguards, who were Partisans and accustomed to political activities in their detachments, began to take part in the discussion, to give their views—in a very quiet voice, it is true, but still loudly enough to make it impossible to ignore. The Chetnik bodyguards noticed this and started to do the same, until Draža Mihailović suddenly took off his glasses, pulled nervously at his beard, and snapped at them:

" 'Shut up, you there. Nobody is asking you anything. . . .'

"This silenced the Chetniks. One could still, however, hear the groaning of a big husky Chetnik whose job it was to carry on his back the huge wooden crate containing Draža Mihailović's treasury. This man had to keep the crate constantly on his back so that he could run away immediately in case of danger or take it to safety from the covetous eyes of others. . . .

"Meanwhile, there was a slight pause in the talks. Draža Mihailović had before him a military map and various colored pencils. He began marking the Chetnik positions on the map for Tito, telling him how many Chetniks there were in the different positions. He thus came to a position somewhere above Valjevo. He asked his second in command Pavlović how many men there were there, but Pavlović could not say. Nobody in the room could offer any information on this matter. Suddenly somebody remembered that a lieutenant who had recently come from that position was in the village at the time. They called for him, and a young man in an officer's uniform entered the room and saluted smartly. Draža Mihailović asked him:

" 'How many men do we have there, Lieutenant?'

" 'Two, sir,' replied the Lieutenant.

"Draža glared at him angrily: 'Don't joke.'

" 'Exactly two, sir.'

" 'Get out at once,' yelled Draža Mihailović.

"After that, Draža Mihailović offered Tito a drink of 'Šumadija tea.' Tito accepted and the 'tea' was brought in. Tito took a long sip from the glass and started coughing violently. It was no ordinary tea, but warm and sweetened plum brandy. Draža Mihailović burst into laughter, while Tito wiped the 'tea' off his uniform.

"During supper, the British Captain Hudson came in. The talks were continued after supper but without substantial results. The following three of Tito's proposals were found especially unacceptable by Draža Mihailović: joint operations against the Germans, the setting up of provisional authorities and the question of mobilization. Draža Mihailović promised to fight the Germans only if he was supplied with weapons from our factory in Užice. Tito promised him five hundred rifles and twenty-five thousand rounds of ammunition.

"The Partisans then spent the night in Draža Mihailović's headquarters.

"Tito spoke very little at this meeting. Draža Mihailović always listened to him very carefully and was surprised that Tito spoke Serbian with an accent found occasionally in Croatia. This led Draža Mihailović to suspect that Tito was a Russian, a conviction he retained for a long time."

By then, the German command had embarked on the second phase against the liberated territory. They had for this purpose brought reinforcements from other areas: the 342nd Division from France, the 125th Regiment from Greece, and the 113th Division from the eastern front, where the offensive against Moscow was in full swing. The liberated territory was thus attacked on a 125-mile front by the complete 342nd and 113th Divisions, considerable elements of the 714th and 717th Divisions, the 268th Artillery Regiment and the 125th Regiment. These forces were strengthened with tank units and more than fifty light bombers. The German forces were joined in the attack by large Quisling formations consisting mainly of Milan Nedić and White Guard units.

This time the Germans changed their tactics. They advanced cautiously along the main lines of approach, clearing the way with artillery and aircraft, while endeavoring to outflank the Partisan positions by means of powerful infantry elements.

Partisan reinforcements were dispatched to the north from Užice. Suddenly on the night of November 1–2, the alarm was sounded in Užice. Enemy units had made their appearance only two and a half miles from the town! They had already been engaged by our forces. Partisans hurried from the town to the scene of the fighting, and workers from the arms factories seized rifles and rushed to the battlefield. Toward dawn, the enemy attacks had been repelled and the Partisans were beginning to encircle the enemy, who was by now in full flight.

They had not been Germans but Draža Mihailović's Chetniks! With the rifles and ammunition we had given them to fight the Germans, they had now struck at the heart of the liberated territory at the very moment when a violent German offensive was threatening us from all sides. After they had been defeated near Užice, the Chetniks began withdrawing rapidly and were soon in desperate flight. They rallied momentarily at the town of Užička Požega but were again defeated. It was there that Sreten Žujević-Crni, a member of the Supreme HQ, was wounded in the stomach by a Chetnik dumdum bullet. The Partisan units pursued the Chetniks, surrounded them on the mountain Ravna Gora, where Draža Mihailović's headquarters were located, and awaited Tito's instructions.

That evening I was with Tito in his Užice headquarters, a large building which had been a bank in prewar days. Tito was in touch by telephone with the commanders of the units which had surrounded Draža Mihailović's HQ. They were awaiting a reply. Tito was walking up and down the large room while I was sitting near a wireless set listening to a Moscow broadcast in Serbian. Suddenly I jumped up and told Tito:

"Listen, Moscow is speaking of the fighting in Serbia against the Germans. Listen, listen! They say Draža is leading all the forces of resistance."

Tito stood still, aghast. I had never seen him so surprised, either before or after that day. He merely said: "But that's impossible."

I repeated what I had heard. Tito was shaking his head, pacing the room, when the telephone rang again. It was commanding officer Jovanović-Bradonja calling. Tito ordered: "Cease further troop movements. Send representatives to Draža and start negotiating." Lola Ribar entered the room at this moment. Tito told him of Radio Moscow's broadcast and then added: "We must not destroy Draža Mihailović, although we have surrounded him. We must be careful not to cause difficulties in the foreign relations of the Soviet Union."

I frowned from my chair near the radio. Negotiations started the next day. I was in one of the commissions, but I had little to say, for I was thinking of my comrades who had been killed by the Chetniks and of the increasingly violent German onslaughts against our liberated territory.

The German offensive developed steadily. First our positions near Valjevo, north of Užice, fell. The German infantry carried out broad enveloping movements against our positions. The German air force was a particularly heavy menace, for there was nothing we could do against it, lacking as we did antiaircraft guns or even effective small arms. The Germans dived to a hundred yards above our positions, and the best we could do to retaliate was to open rifle fire against them.

An ever-growing number of wounded was arriving in Užice. The Germans were advancing methodically, and it was obvious that Užice could not be held. One cloudy day, about 3 P.M., a terrible explosion shook the town. I was in the Supreme HQ, in a large hall divided into a conference room and a ten-bed hospital. I was lying on one of the beds, for I had been wounded by Chetniks only a few weeks previously and found it difficult to move about. Suddenly, as the explosion rent the air, the wall crumbled on me. Everything around me tumbled, and the debris covered me. I wondered about Tito, who had been in the adjoining room.

The armament factory, which was in a tunnel not far from Supreme HQ, had exploded. It was later found out that the enemy, whether Gestapo agents or Chetniks, had placed a bomb in a tunnel where the civilian population sought refuge during air raids. The resulting explosion spread to a gunpowder dump, and the entire factory went up in a tremendous explosion. Two hundred people were killed, including ninety women and children who had taken shelter from an air raid.

The burning gunpowder spread from the factory into the adjoining streets and houses. Many people were burnt alive, and the building in which the Supreme HQ was located was also set ablaze. Tito was injured, but soon managed to get up. I was lying on a bed which had been crushed under the wall which had crumbled on me. It was then that Aleksandar Ranković remembered that I had been in the hospital ward. Two volunteers rushed into the burning building, reached the mass of bricks under which I was lying and began to dig me out. How distant their voices sounded! At long last, I was delivered. I had suffered severe concussions, but I wept for joy that the comrades had not forgotten me.

Four days later, the German tanks were rapidly approaching the town, and evacuation was ordered. I was moved to the Zlatibor mountain, twenty miles from Užice, and joined three hundred other wounded. All day German aircraft bombed Užice and the road leading from Užice to the Zlatibor mountain, while their forces broke through the front immediately defending the city. Members of the Supreme HQ had taken up positions and were endeavoring to stop the Germans by placing land mines on the road, but the tanks were rushing ahead.

Only twenty minutes before the German tanks entered Užice Tito left—one of the last of the fighting men to go. He was at a front-line position overlooking the town when the German tanks broke into Užice. Without pausing, they continued along the road to Zlatibor. The bridges had not been well mined and the tanks soon crossed them, followed by trucks carrying infantry. In a few moments, Tito and a handful of men were cut off by German infantrymen who leaped from the trucks and deployed in battle formation while the tanks continued on their way along the road up the mountain. Tito was only about one hundred and fifty yards from the German infantry and came under their direct fire. He began withdrawing up the mountain with the German infantry in hot pursuit.

Milovan Djilas attempted to mine the road a little higher up, but he was prevented by German aircraft, and immediately after by German tanks.

Tito

It was growing dark. I was sitting alone in the house on the Zlatibor mountain, with a lone candle burning in the big room. The sound of shooting could be heard from Užice, along with the sound of bomb explosions. But no member of the Supreme HQ arrived. Only ever-lengthening streams of wounded were being brought to the mountain.

At that moment Kardelj arrived. He, too, had been attacked by German aircraft on that very road. Several members of his party had been killed. He asked me what had happened to Tito. I just spread my hands. Kardelj went to see how the evacuation of the wounded was progressing, for the German tanks were expected to appear any moment on this plateau. The time was passing. Kardelj returned. Suddenly Djilas appeared. There was no news of Tito. I went out to help with the wounded, and when I came back Djilas and Kardelj jumped up to ask: "What has happened to Tito?"

I again spread my hands. The second candle was burning out. It was almost midnight. Suddenly the door opened. Tito came in. Djilas embraced him. Kardelj could hardly speak from joy. Tito was terribly tired. He laid down his submachine gun and sat down. After the clash with the German infantry on the hill overlooking Užice, Tito had made his way through the mountains for more than twenty miles, all of it on foot and at times under enemy fire. Tito took stock of the situation and said: "All the wounded are to be evacuated as quickly as possible. Take up defense positions. The Germans will attempt to break through here."

He then again leaned back on the chair and asked for water. The minutes were going by more easily now. Aleksandar Ranković entered. One hour later the Supreme HQ moved on from Zlatibor; long columns of wounded had already left. Only the severely wounded were waiting for trucks to transport them. It was already dawn. The engines of the German tanks could be heard. The first German offensive against the heart of the liberated territory in Yugoslavia was thus coming to a close. The Supreme HQ and the decimated units around it were retreating. It was in the last days of November, and already freezing in the mountains. The first snow was about to fall. But the German command had not achieved its purpose. At that very moment, ninety-two Partisan detachments numbering eighty thousand men were fighting in the mountains and in the plains of Yugoslavia.

CHAPTER XI

1942:

"If you cannot help us do not hinder us . . ."

THUS ended the first year of the uprising in Yugoslavia. It had started in one of the most difficult moments in the struggle against the Axis powers, when the prospects of victory over Hitler seemed more remote than ever. It would undoubtedly have been one of the moral contributions to the war effort of all the united nations, had it become generally known in Allied countries to what extent this uprising had developed, what were its successes, how much territory had been liberated and how severe had been the losses of Hitler's troops.

But at that time Yugoslavia, at least as regards the National Liberation Movement and Partisan Tito, had been black-listed by the leading powers of the united nations. Not a single word about it was publicly mentioned in Allied countries, in their press, their broadcasts or their public observances. One had to be in Yugoslavia, fighting the Germans, to understand the painful impression it made upon us. Even silence might have been borne, but instead of silence, attacks were made on Partisans, and the greatest tribute was paid to the very man who had the least merit in the struggle against the Germans in Serbia in 1941: to Draža Mihailović.

The Yugoslav refugee government was in close and constant contact with Draža Mihailović, and it gave wide publicity to his "victories." Thus, for instance, the Official Gazette of the royal government ascribed the entire First Offensive to Draža Mihailović. One can imagine the bitterness we felt in Yugoslavia, among the Partisans, when we heard these foreign broadcasts, when we heard the following official communiqué from London about the battles in Yugoslavia around Užice:

Tito

"Serbian front. Three German and Fascist divisions assisted by tanks and planes have started a general offensive against our positions in the valley of the western Morava. Our troops under the command of General Draža Mihailović are resisting successfully the bitter enemy attacks, although units in the Užice sector have been obliged to retreat before the attack of enemy tanks. . . ."

The Draža Mihailović Chetniks not only failed to offer any resistance to the Germans but suddenly attacked Užice in the course of this very offensive. This was the beginning of one of the greatest frauds of World War II. The communiqué was printed in all the great Allied daily newspapers and a campaign began for the popularization of Draža Mihailović. In Yugoslavia we were informed that several months later *Time* magazine selected Mihailović as the most popular Allied general in 1942, together with MacArthur, Timoshenko and Chiang Kai-shek.

This is how the West reacted. The myth of Mihailović soared to unbelievable proportions. The people in these countries were indoctrinated to such an extent about Mihailović's deeds that later, when the true story came from Yugoslavia, a great majority of them could not believe what they now heard about Mihailović and continued to think him a great hero.

Perhaps one must have been in Yugoslavia in 1941, in the middle of the struggle against the Germans in Yugoslav mountains, as I was, in order to understand fully the role played by Mihailović. I can hardly be expected to forget how he tried to kill me, just because I was a political commissar of a Partisan detachment, which was fighting against the Germans. I was wounded for the first time by a time bomb placed by Chetniks and a comrade of mine was killed. I still have a piece of the time bomb in my knee.

But after the war the truth about Mihailović broke through to the West. If one reads the fifth volume of the memoirs of Winston Churchill, he will find many proofs of the role of Mihailović, and of collaboration of Chetniks with the Germans and Italians. Winston Churchill reveals, for instance, the following facts: "Under this pressure Mihailović drifted gradually into a posture where some of his commanders made accommodations with the German and Italian troops to be left alone in certain mountain areas in return for doing little or nothing against the enemy." If this had been the view of

Winston Churchill in 1941 about Mihailović and his Chetnik commanders, how much blood would have been saved in Yugoslavia.

In the USSR, the situation was no better. They too spoke only of Draža Mihailović. With the exception of a speech by Voroshilov in November, 1941, in which he mentioned the Partisans of Yugoslavia, the whole Yugoslav uprising, our entire efforts were ascribed to Draža Mihailović.

Essentially, a conflict had already arisen between the National Liberation Movement in Yugoslavia and Stalin. The latter was displeased by the fact that we had proceeded to establish new forms of authority against his will. Stalin undoubtedly desired the struggle in Yugoslavia to develop, but only in order to render the operations of the German army more difficult. Stalin never wanted a new progressive movement to be created with roots of its own, which would rely only on its own forces, and would not await liberation from the Red Army. It was for that reason Stalin did not encourage the development of the uprising in Yugoslavia and for that reason the Soviet propaganda never mentioned the Partisans, although Stalin received detailed daily reports on the situation in Yugoslavia, broadcast through the secret transmitter in Zagreb.

These were difficult days for the Partisans in Yugoslavia. They were fighting to the death, they were giving their lives not only for the freedom of their own country but for the general war effort of all the united nations, and all was hidden and distorted. When Moscow was boosting Draža Mihailović, there arose a conflict between the Communist Parties of Yugoslavia and Bulgaria concerning the character of the struggle against the invaders. The Bulgarians ordered the Secretary of the Communist Party of Macedonia, Šarlo, to take no directives from the Yugoslavs regarding the necessity of an armed struggle against the invaders. In a letter written in September, 1941, Tito denounced such an attitude on behalf of the Yugoslav Central Committee, saying: "The Macedonian Central Committee has failed to organize Partisan detachments, it has failed to organize any actions or sabotages, it has failed to act according to the request of the Comintern, but on the contrary, it has deliberately sabotaged these actions and run off to Sofia in order to escape our control. The people are awaiting the arrival of the Red Army, they are watching with equanimity how Soviet soldiers are giving their lives and dreaming of the day when the Red Army will come and put them into power."

The experience gained in the first German offensive, in a frontal struggle with a technically very superior enemy, was extremely valuable to the Partisans. The Supreme HQ and nine Serbian detachments withdrew to the frontier between Serbia and Sandžak and liberated several towns held by the Italians. The detachments, which were somewhat exhausted by considerable losses in their struggles against Germans and by the immense efforts they had made, rested briefly on the mountain Zlatar. Tito visited almost every company of his forces, and talked to the soldiers. In some of these companies, the majority of fighting men were workers from Belgrade or miners from Serbian mines. These inspections led Tito to form proletarian brigades: special Partisan units characterized above all by their firm discipline and by their methods of warfare. These proletarian units differed from the detachments in that they would not be bound to the regions where they had originated, but would fight in all parts of Yugoslavia. In a way, the proletarian units became the symbol of the struggle of all the peoples of Yugoslavia. To distinguish them from other units, the proletarians carried a sickle and hammer over the red star. In the first encounter with the enemy, in a battle against Italians and Chetniks, the First Proletarian Brigade achieved a considerable victory, in which more than 120 Italians and many arms were captured. This encouraged the Partisan units considerably, after their losses in the fights against the Germans.

It was then that Tito almost lost his life in a fight against the Italians. The Supreme HQ were at the foot of Zlatar Mountain, in the village of Drenovo, in a wooden peasant cottage. Tito was sleeping in a large room in this house with other members of the Supreme HQ, the wireless operator and two or three bodyguards. They slept in Partisan fashion: on the bare wooden floor, with their bags for pillows and their coats for cover. Those who had a real blanket were considered well off. We were listening to the radio after a dinner which had consisted of boiled potatoes and rye bread, and had just heard the news of Pearl Harbor and of the entrance of America into the war. We talked of this until midnight. A sentry stood outside. He was relieved every four hours. It was winter. The first snow had already fallen.

In the morning the sentry left, as it was not customary to post sentries in daytime. Tito was one of the first to get up, together with Sreten Žujević. He shaved, as he did this every day even in the Partisan days, whether it was winter or summer, whether we were marching or in camp, whether there was an offensive or a lull. I never saw him unshaved.

At this moment, Žujević looked out of the window and cried: "Look, there are soldiers advancing toward us!"

Tito recognized the Italians deployed in battle array. They were 250 yards from the house. Tito immediately ordered the documents and the transmitter to be removed, as the Italians opened fire against the house in which the Supreme HQ were located. Tito seized his submachine gun and ran out of the house with several comrades, taking positions on a hillock some ten yards farther off, while the comrades with the transmitter and the archives were retreating.

We were no match for the Italians, and soon had to retreat. Luckily, the Italians did not advance immediately, but continued their mortar and machine-gun fire on the house. Everybody dashed from the house, except a woman, the farmer's daughter-in-law, who had been delivered of twins on the night before. She could not leave the house, but a Partisan took the babies along under his greatcoat. When the Italians entered the house they found nothing belonging to the Supreme HQ except Tito's camera, which had been forgotten in the rush. They also found Tito's horse in a stable nearby and took him away. When leaving, the Italians set the house afire, and the unfortunate mother was burnt alive. The babies that had been born on the night of the attack and rescued by the Partisans were later returned to the village, to the family of the mother who had lost her life. The children were baptized Slobodan and Slobodanka (variations of the name of freedom), and today live with their father.

As the First Proletarian Brigade had been formed in the meanwhile, Tito left for Bosnia with this brigade. Their arrival meant a lot for the uprising of this part of the country. Winter had already come. There was deep snow in the mountains and the temperatures sank to 20 degrees below zero.

The German command, however, did not heed these adverse weather conditions, but ordered the launching of a new offensive against those portions of territory where the Supreme HQ and the

First Proletarian Brigade were to be found. This time, the Germans threw ski battalions into the battle. In an unexpected attack on the Romanija Mountain, in snow so deep that even wild beasts could hardly be expected to move through it, a German ski battalion took by surprise a battalion of the First Proletarian Brigade and inflicted heavy losses upon it. The Partisans could not make use of their rifles and machine guns because these weapons had been frozen. But this German offensive failed and the proletarian brigade broke through the German ring. During the retreat to Igman Mountain, 150 of the fighting men were put out of action by the cold. Toes—even the entire feet—had subsequently to be amputated. Most such operations had to be carried out in the absence of any form of anesthetics, because the Partisan medical units lacked both medicaments and surgical instruments. On one occasion, when in a village a Partisan was to have his leg amputated, the doctor for lack of proper instruments borrowed a saw which he boiled and then put to use on his operating table.

No sooner had it emerged from this offensive than the First Proletarian Brigade entered the town of Foča, which had been occupied by Italians and Chetniks and which housed the Supreme HQ for more than three months. This beautiful small eastern Bosnian town on the rapid Drina River, surrounded by mountains, changed hands several times during the first eight months of the war. It was there that I met a man who owned a small store and kept several flags under his counter: a German flag, an Italian flag, an Ustashi flag, and a Yugoslav flag with a star. Whenever he heard fighting going on around the town at night, he would listen intently and then pull out the appropriate flag. Poor man. When the Partisans withdrew, he was shot by the Italians, because they found him in possession of a Partisan flag.

In Foča, the Supreme HQ were accommodated in a hotel. For the first time in two months, we were able to take off our clothes when we went to bed at night. Radio communication with detachments in other parts of the country was maintained uninterruptedly. Messengers also arrived on foot with more detailed reports, as well as copies of newspapers which were being published in various parts of the country. In the town itself, life underwent considerable change. A newspaper began appearing twice a week. The first concert was held in the largest hall in the town. A Partisan mail service began functioning. The stamps were the old Yugoslav stamps which had already been marked with the emblem of Pavelić's "Independent State of Croatia." Now, in addition, the Partisan emblem—a five-point star—was superimposed, making three layers in all. Telephone communications were established throughout the liberated territory.

Just before we entered Foča, direct radio communications were finally established with the Comintern. Up to then, contact had been maintained through Zagreb, but now Supreme Headquarters began sending radiograms directly to Moscow and receiving its replies. The radiograms which were sent from Yugoslavia were sent by Tito under the assumed name of Walter, while those which came from Moscow were signed by Dimitrov, usually under the pseudonym of Deda (Grandpa). As soon as direct contact had been established, Deda requested detailed information concerning our proclamations, our newspapers, our articles. Throughout the night, radio operators used to dispatch lengthy telegrams. In February we received the following radiogram from Moscow: "There is a possibility that we shall be sending people to you in the near future. . . . Let us know exactly where our plane could land. What signals could you arrange so as to make it possible for the plane to land properly and without difficulty? Do you have aircraft gasoline?"

The Partisans would, of course, have been glad to welcome Soviet men on their liberated territory, but what we needed above all were medicaments and ammunition. On February 17, 1942, Tito sent the following radiograms to Moscow:

"February 17, 1942. We urgently require medicaments, particularly antityphus serum. During offensive, 160 serious cases of frostbite.

"Send us ammunition, automatic weapons, boots, and material for uniforms for the men. Send this by air and parachute to us at Žabljak at the foot of Mount Durmitor in Montenegro. Here snow has fallen again and airfields are unfit for use unless aircrafts are fitted with runners.

"The Supreme HQ is in the town of Foča, on liberated Bosnian territory. Anything you can send would be of great moral and material significance."

Later Tito added: "With regard to my telegram concerning directions for parachuting arms and men at Žabljak in Montenegro, wish to add: The site is fully safeguarded, on completely liberated territory. Both men and material can be dropped immediately.

"To enable large aircraft at future date to descend urgently send us fair quantity automatic weapons, machine guns, ammunition, signals material, rockets, light infantry guns and ammunition. Co-ordinates for navigators: 43.8 degrees Lat., 16 degrees and 48' East of Paris.

"To your three red rockets, we shall reply wth three beacons at fifty meters' distance from each other, commencing February 23."

Tito immediately sent Moša Pijade to the Durmitor mountain to arrange all that was required for reception of the Soviet plane. Pijade went through snow six feet deep and prepared the landing ground for the aircraft or for the reception of material, should the planes be unable to land. He waited there for no less than thirty-seven days and thirty-seven nights in expectation of the moment when he would be able to light the fires and receive Soviet aid. This aid, however, was not forthcoming, and Tito constantly warned Pijade to be patient.

". . . I believe you when you speak of your impatience at waiting in vain like this, but you had better resign yourself to much more waiting. Things do not go so simply. Today I sent a telegram to Deda, pressing the urgency of it, and hope soon to have a favorable reply.

". . . Don't get worried by having to wait on."

On March 14, Tito wrote: "You be patient just a little longer, for I still do count on the visit coming off."

Tito again urged that help be sent.

On March 19 he sent the following dispatch to Moscow:

"We are in a critical situation owing to insufficiency of ammunition. Please do all possible to send us ammunition and military material. Tell us if we can expect anything and when."

On March 29 Tito received the following telegram from Moscow:

"All possible efforts are being made to help you in armament. But the technical difficulties are enormous. You should, alas, not count on our mastering them in the near future. Please bear that in mind. Do all you can to try to get arms from the enemy and to make the most economical use of what armament you have."

Tito then wrote to Pijade, still waiting on the Durmitor:

"Today a telegram came from Deda in which he tells me they are doing all they can to aid us with armament but that the difficulties are so tremendous that they will not be able to overcome them for a little time. They request us to bear that in mind and do all we can to acquire ammunition from the enemy and to make economical use of what we have.

"So, as you see, they will gladly help us, as soon as it is feasible. But for the present, for some time, you need do no more night duty, and had better explain to the men as you think best."

Finally, on April 23, Tito asked for the last time what was happening to the aid. He was brief:

"Can we hope for ammunition soon?"

To this he received the following final reply:

"As we informed you earlier, for reasons which you understand, you unfortunately cannot expect to get either ammunition or automatic weapons from here at an early date. The principal reason is the impossibility of getting them to you.

"It is therefore necessary for you to make the best and most economic use possible of all possibilities that do exist, including the slenderest and most difficult possibility of obtaining supplies there on the spot. You will have to carry on like that, regardless of the devilish hard conditions, developing a war of liberation, holding out and beating off the enemy until it becomes possible. It is certainly necessary to unmask the Chetniks to the people, completely, with documentary proof convincingly, but for the present it would be politically opportune for you to do so through a general approach to the Yugoslav government, emphasizing that the Yugoslav patriots who are fighting have a right to expect support for any Serb, Croat, Montenegrin and Slovene fighters who are waging a struggle, either in Yugoslavia or abroad, on the basis of a National Liberation Partisan Army.

"Please consider our advice and communicate your observations, also what concrete steps you may take in that direction."

So the Partisans fought throughout that winter and spring in all parts of Yugoslavia without Soviet help. The proletarian brigades on liberated territory around the town of Foča ran out of ammunition. The enemy jeered, calling us "five-bullet men" because there were five bullets to each soldier. At that very time, Tito was receiving the following suggestion from Moscow:

"It would be desirable for the Supreme HQ of the Partisans to address, on behalf of the Yugoslav people, a brief proclamation to the peoples of the occupied countries, especially of Czechoslovakia and France. In that proclamation, after pointing out that your people are fighting for liberty and independence, the Supreme HQ should call on those people to cease making war materials or supplying the bloodstained Hitler with raw materials or foodstuffs and to do all they can to disrupt his war machine in every way and develop a Partisan movement against the invader, sparing no effort to achieve a total defeat of the deadly enemy of all the peoples of Europe, German-Fascist imperialism. We could give such a proclamation the widest publicity in the press and by radio. Inform us of your opinion. . . ."

Tito immediately replied:

"We have received your telegram of February 13, 1942. We welcome your suggestion about the issuing of a proclamation in the name of the Supreme HQ of the Partisan Army of Yugoslavia. Also give the proclamation by radiogram in the Yugoslav or English language, for publication in our language in the press."

At the same time, we sent all our proclamations and excerpts from articles published in our press to Moscow. We received the following reply:

"Study of all the information you sent gives one the impression that the adherence of Great Britain and the Yugoslav government have some [justification? *] in suspecting the Partisan movement of acquiring a Communist character and aiming at the Sovietization of Yugoslavia. Why, for example, did you need to form a special Proletarian Brigade? Surely at the moment, the basic, immediate task is to unite all anti-Nazi currents, smash the invaders and achieve national liberation.

"How is one to explain the fact that supporters of Great Britain are succeeding in forming armed units against the Partisan detachments? Are there really no other Yugoslav patriots, apart from the Communists and Communist sympathizers, with whom you could join in common struggle against the invaders?

* The word could not be properly deciphered.

"It is difficult to agree that the London and the Yugoslav governments are siding with the invaders. There must be some great misunderstanding here. We honestly request you to give your tactics serious thought, and your actions as well, and make sure that on your side you have really done all you could to achieve a true united national front of all enemies of Hitler and Mussolini in Yugoslavia, in order to attain the common aim—the expulsion of the invaders and would-be conquerors. If anything remains to be done, you should urgently take measures and inform us."

In another telegram from Moscow, we were requested to delete a number of paragraphs from our proclamation, including the following:

"Long live the uprising of all enslaved peoples of Europe against the invader!"

Our proclamation was, of course, never published. The Soviet government was at that time strengthening its relations with the Royal Yugoslav Government and had even agreed that the Royal Yugoslav Legation in Moscow be raised to the rank of an Embassy. Tito was quite openly told in a telegram from Moscow that the publication of the proclamation was postponed until "the relations between the Soviet government and the Yugoslav government in London were clarified." At the same time, the Moscow broadcasting station consistently refused to refer to Draža Mihailović as a man who was fighting on the side of the Axis powers against the people's liberation movement in Yugoslavia. It appears clearly from the archives of the royal government, which were transferred to Belgrade after the war, that the reasons why Moscow was unwilling to send aid to the Partisans in 1942 were of a political and not of a technical nature! Not only in the spring but even in the fall of 1942 Moscow was proposing to the Royal Yugoslav Government a Soviet military mission to Draža Mihailović, the dispatch of matériel to the Chetniks, and even joint broadcasts. This is revealed by a radiogram of the Prime Minister of the Royal Yugoslav Government, Slobodan Jovanović, to Draža Mihailović on November 30, 1942:

"Top Secret No. 40, January 11, 1943.

"Supreme Command: No. 152 of November 30, 1942.

"The Russians have suggested they send high-level officers to your HQ to set up direct contact with you, and form a squadron of yours in Russia to get assistance to you and organize joint broadcasting. Have rejected proposal. We are insisting first on immediate cessation of radio and press campaign against Yugoslav army under your command; second, on the Partisans' being told not to attack our armed forces; third, for Partisans to be placed under your command. Only when this is done can there be talk of further co-operation. We shall inform you of further developments.

"(signed) Jovanović"

The course taken by the negotiations between Stalin and King Peter are confirmed by the following exchange of telegrams between the Foreign Minister of the Royal Government in Exile, Momčilo Ninčić, and the Ambassador to Moscow, Stanoje Simić.

"Cipher telegram:

"London, December 1, 1942; Kuibyshev, December 1, 1942.

"The Prime Minister sends you the following, personally for the Military Attaché.

"There can be no talk of co-operation until the campaign against General Mihailović is called off, since it is now at its height. As a preliminary toward further work, the situation in the field demands that this campaign be called off. All efforts of the Ambassador and Military Attaché are to be directed toward achieving the aim set out in my top secret telegram No. 958.

"Top Secret No. 579.   (Signed) Ninčić"

To this Ambassador Simić replied:

"Cipher telegram:

"The Ministry for Foreign Affairs, London, reference your top secret 579.

"Please keep me informed how campaign against General Mihailović is developing. Here in Russia, impossible to read or hear anything against Mihailović.

"If there is a campaign in the foreign press, it is not reported here. What is more, uninformed persons in the Ministry for Foreign Affairs, here, speak of Mihailović as a national hero. The only thing one does notice is that his name is not mentioned in press and radio.

"Kuibyshev, December 3, 1942. Top Secret, No. 49."

These were the relations between Moscow and Yugoslavia during 1941 and 1942. Stalin thus, in one of the most difficult periods of the

Yugoslav uprising, instead of sending all possible aid to the Partisans made every effort to seize key positions in Draža Mihailović's HQ in order to make use of him in the interest of Soviet foreign policy. The Yugoslav people, the interests of the progressive movement in Yugoslavia, were of secondary importance to him.

CHAPTER XII

1942:

"We have been fighting for twenty months without the least material assistance from any quarter . . ."

BECAUSE of the constant strengthening of Partisan detachments and the growing of liberated territory in the face of repeated offensives, Hitler and Mussolini decided to take even more drastic action. Toward the end of December, 1941, Mussolini wrote to Hitler:

"Balkans. It is necessary to eliminate all the hotbeds of insurrection before spring. They might cause the broadening of the war in the Balkans. We should pacify Bosnia first, then Serbia and Montenegro. It is necessary for our armed forces to collaborate according to a common plan, in order to avoid a loss of energy and to reach the desired results with the least amount of men and material." *

The preparations for the offensive against liberated territory around Foča ended at the end of March, and passed over to the beginning of the so-called Third Offensive. Italian, German, Ustashi and Chetnik forces took part in this offensive. For the first time in the course of this war, the Draža Mihailović Chetniks openly collaborated with Italian troops against Partisans. The offensive developed sluggishly and the Italians advanced slowly. We first had to withdraw from Montenegro and then the enemy encircled us around Foča. The Germans advanced only up to a certain point and then stopped, while the Italians had to withdraw from several spots. But it was clear that we could not maintain Foča. Our tactics consisted

* *Diary*, Cavallero, p. 177.

of attacking the enemy at night, offering the strongest possible resistance, but refusing to accept a frontal battle, and destroying all communications. We finally withdrew from Foča at the beginning of May, 1942. The date for Partisan Olympics had been set for May 1, 1942, in Foča. All the fighting men from the battalions of the First Proletarian Brigade, the Supreme HQ, the other units, the city youth and members of other institutions were to take part in the Olympics. But the enemy offensive occurred in the meantime. The Olympics took place nonetheless, although with a smaller number of participants. They competed in track and field, soccer and volleyball, the final matches being held when Italian units were about seven miles from the town. The Supreme HQ had its own team on which Aleksandar Ranković, Sreten Žujović and Arso Jovanović played, among others. I was the center forward in the final soccer match, and a battalion team was beaten by our Supreme HQ team. Tito watched the last match, but had to leave before the end, as new reports were coming in from the front.

The number of proletarian brigades had increased. Three more brigades had been constituted from detachments from Montenegro and Sandžak, so that the Supreme HQ had direct command over five proletarian brigades. The enemy tried to encircle these units in the high mountains on the border between Bosnia and Montenegro, but failed. It is true that our units suffered immensely from lack of food. Neither bread nor fats could be found in the mountains. The Partisans used to drive herds of sheep before them, and for weeks our only food consisted in lean, boiled mutton. The worst was that there was no salt. We also suffered from scurvy, for there were no fruits or greens in the mountains. We could only eat young beech leaves, or press the juice out of the beech bark and drink it. When we broke through the enemy ring, our brigades found themselves in the valley of the Sutjeska River. This is one of the most beautiful spots in Yugoslavia. This mountain river cuts its way through a canyon over one thousand meters deep and then flows through a fertile plain surrounded by high mountains which are always covered with snow at that time of the year. The Partisans saw there one of the most desolate pictures of war. This region had been formerly peopled with Moslem villages, but in 1941 the Chetniks had massacred everybody and fired the houses. For almost one year no human being had passed there. The ruins of the burnt houses where only chimneys stood were covered with thick grass. There was not a living soul to be seen. Here and there, one could come across a broken barrel, or a cup or saucer. Trees loaded with fruit grew around the dead houses. Thus we passed through one and then another deserted village. This made a terrible impression on the Partisans. Not a living soul, not a single man with whom to talk. At last, we stopped near one of these villages. The quartermasters had found somewhere about one hundred quarts of milk, but Tito ordered everything to be sent to the wounded who were lying in a wood nearby. Tito took us to a mountain and said, "And for us there is a whole mountain of strawberries."

Strawberries alone could not quench our hunger, but this was all the food we had that day. We called a conference and discussed the situation. The problem of hunger was a special item to be discussed. It was decided that nothing should be taken from the villagers under any conditions, and that a drive should be started among Partisans not to talk so much about famine and to concentrate on other matters. This was somewhat the method of fakirs.

When we ended the conference, we heard Tito's voice, coming from the direction of a nearby stream. Some of us went there. Tito showed us a small mill, a building about five feet tall. This was the only house we could see that was not destroyed in a distance of fifty kilometers. Tito entered. The mill was apparently not damaged. Tito felt an old urge—to repair mills. He worked on it for about half an hour, and then the wheel started working. The mill was repaired. In this desert in which we were living, the rattling of the little mill was comforting.

That night the Supreme HQ held a meeting in which it was decided to start a long march to the north, toward the liberated territory of western Bosnia, at a distance of about two hundred miles. It was planned on this occasion to make a powerful attack on an important enemy line of communication, the railroad between the Adriatic Sea and Sarajevo, as well as on a series of enemy garrisons.

Thus began the "long march" of Yugoslav Partisans. The attack on the railroad over a stretch of thirty miles achieved complete surprise. Many trains were captured together with the material they were carrying, a great number of enemy places were destroyed and there was little resistance. At the railroad stations we also got hold of many enemy newspapers with large communiqués of the Italian Second Army, describing the total defeat of the Partisan forces! I looked forward to only one prize for myself from these attacks, a bottle of ink. My fountain pen was almost empty. I thus had to limit the writing of my diary before the attack as much as possible, because of the lack of ink. Imagine my joy when I discovered a bottle of ink on the table of an office in the Bradina railroad station.

A few days later, the Partisan brigades liberated Konjic, an important junction of the Adriatic-Sarajevo railroad. Arms with adequate ammunition were also captured. There two Partisan soldiers of the First Battalion of the First Brigade entered a house and by force took food from a woman. She then came to the battalion HQ to complain. The entire battalion was gathered and the two soldiers admitted what they had done. They were summoned before the battalion and condemned to death. Both requested to be permitted to speak before the entire battalion on the eve of their being shot, and one of them said:

"Comrades, I consider the punishment to be just. I have committed a grave crime. You see, our brigade has gone from one end of Yugoslavia to the other, liberating one city after the other from the invader. It carries freedom, and I have soiled its name, I have soiled this star with the sickle and hammer. . . . Shoot at me without compunction, comrades, do not allow your hand to tremble, because the punishment must be imposed. . . ."

And both stood quietly before the guns. A shot was heard. The soldiers who did the shooting had their eyes full of tears. But there was no other way. The only assistance the Partisan brigades had came from the population. A conflict with the people would mean the end of the brigade, the end of the struggle against the invaders.

The enemy did not expect our offensive. Tito selected his line of advance in a masterly fashion, the demarcation line of the occupation zone of the Italian and German army. While the enemy generals were making up their minds who should attack and where, and who would stop the advance of the brigades, town after town fell, garrisons surrendered and hundreds of new fighting men joined the proletarian brigades. Thus the five brigades of Tito's advanced rapidly to the north, toward western Bosnia, where extensive liberated territory was located. The Partisans freed several large cities there in the spring of 1942. The first Partisan aviation was founded there too. Three light German bombers had been captured on an Ustashi airfield. There were some pilots among the Partisans, and a few days later the Partisan aircraft made their first flights. The enemy did not expect it, and only when they were bombed did they realize these were not their own planes. However, the Partisan aviation could not remain active long, since there was not enough gasoline or bombs. But its moral effect was immense. The population believed that Stalin himself had sent those aircraft to the Partisans.

German fighters soon discovered the Partisan aircraft on the ground and destroyed them. At the same time the enemy began an offensive from all sides against the liberated territory. Partisan units as well as over fifty thousand women, children and old people took refuge on Kozara Mountain, which the enemy promptly encircled in strength. After several weeks of heavy fighting, the Partisans broke through the ring and freed themselves. A considerable part of the population was saved with them, but many women and children fell into enemy hands. Some were immediately shot and the rest taken to concentration camps.

At this moment five proletarian brigades broke through in the south. Thus, the liberated territory was saved and considerably extended, as the proletarian brigades overpowered several strong enemy garrisons. The Supreme HQ was located first in the town of Glamoč, and later in Bosanski Petrovac. A courier connection was resumed with all parts of Yugoslavia. *Borba* was again published as the organ of the Communist Party of Yugoslavia, appearing three times a week. People's committees functioned in all the liberated territory. The first elections for these committees were held in October, 1942, and for the first time women were granted the right to vote. Many women became members of committees, a matter of real consequence in these mountainous regions, where relations toward women were of a conservative kind. But war brought on many changes, including this one. Women worked very efficiently in the committees.

In many parts of western Bosnia, particularly in those inhabited by Serbs, all churches had either been destroyed by the Ustashi or closed since the first days of war. When the Partisan brigades arrived, the army chaplains who accompanied every brigade were kept busy. They first cleaned the churches where the Ustashi had not allowed service, then found the bells and hung them in the belfries. On the following Sunday, the bells rang, and the peasants in their white dresses crowded from everywhere. The chaplains first said mass, and then proceeded to baptize children. The churches had been closed for almost a year, the Ustashis had killed or driven away the priests, and there was no one to baptize the children. Father Vlado Zečević, member of the Supreme HQ, a former commander of Draža Mihailović, baptized more than a hundred children in Glamoč in one single day. The parents wept for joy while Father Zečević effected the ritual, clad in a Partisan uniform with his revolver, over which a vestment was thrown. He wore a Partisan cap with the five-point star and over it a golden cross. The chaplains had no work to do in the proletarian units, since most of the fighting men were atheists. Apart from Orthodox priests there were Moslem imams (priests).

In the fall of that same year, the Supreme HQ decided to form larger units, and corps were organized, composed of several divisions each. This rendered possible more complex military operations, where the co-ordination of larger units was needed. The ancient Bosnian capital, Bihać, was liberated in the autumn of 1942, during some large operations of our divisions. On this occasion more than one thousand enemy soldiers were taken prisoner with a considerable quantity of guns, machine guns and ammunition.

Thus, in the fall, the National Liberation Army increased to over 150,000 fighting men, divided into two corps with nine divisions, 36 brigades, 70 separate battalions in 70 detachments. It was decided at the same time to convene the AVNOJ (Anti-Fascist Council of the National Liberation of Yugoslavia). The most outstanding representatives of the National Liberation Movement from all parts of Yugoslavia attended this assembly in the city of Bihać. It was originally intended for the AVNOJ to elect a provisional government, but Moscow requested that this be done under no conditions. The idea was thus given up, and the council had only the character of a manifestation.

The convention of the AVNOJ had a great effect in all Yugoslavia. The enemy again made preparations for the final liquidation of the Partisan movement. In October, 1942, Hitler invited Lieutenant-General Alexander von Leer to his Supreme HQ on the eastern front at Winitza. Von Leer was then the commander of the German Twelfth Army, and later commander of the entire German southeastern front. His troops were chosen to lead the offensive against the Partisans. Ante Pavelić, the head of Quisling Croatia, attended this meeting, according to the testimony of General von Leer at his trial. A final plan of operations was set up and it was decided to invite the Italians to participate in the operations. On January 5, 1943, a special meeting was held in Rome. General von Leer represented Germany, and Italy was represented by General Hugo Cavellero, and the commander of the Second Army, General Roata. An Ustashi general was also present. General Roata declared that in the winter of 1941–42 when his garrisons had been surrounded he had to be supplied by air. At this consultation, the Italian generals suggested that Chetnik units be used, but General von Leer declared that he was not authorized to do so by his command.

All the preparations were finally made and the offensive started in the second half of January, 1943. The following German divisions advanced from the north: 7 SS Prinz Eugene, the 369 Legionary Teufel Division and the 714 German Division. The 717 German Division attacked from the east. The Italian Fifth Corps was to attack from the west with the divisions Lombardia, Re and Sasari, and Chetniks. The main blow was to fall on the liberated territory in western Bosnia and Lika. This is a mountainous wooded region.

The enemy had powerful aviation at its disposal. The Supreme HQ immediately worked out its operation plans. It was decided to offer the toughest possible resistance to the enemy, but to accept no frontal battles under any conditions. At the same time, the order was given to all units in the other regions of Yugoslavia to start day and night attacks on enemy communications and garrisons. The Supreme HQ also ordered the First Proletarian, the Second Proletarian and the Third Division to assemble in order to break through the enemy ring and to liberate Herzegovina and Montenegro, which were at the time completely occupied by the enemy. This meant changing from an enemy offensive to a Yugoslav offensive.

Several thousand wounded Partisans lying in various hospitals in the liberated territory represented a great difficulty for the maneuvering of Partisan units, since it was impossible to let them fall into enemy hands. The enemy usually killed all our wounded soldiers. All the wounded were divided into separate battalions, those with light wounds who could move without help in one kind of battalion, those more severely wounded but who could ride a horse in so-called cavalry battalions, and those who were very severely wounded in stretcher battalions. All wounded soldiers were armed against enemy attack.

Another very difficult problem was that of the population of the liberated territory. No one wished to remain when the enemy came. Although the mountain paths were covered with snow, one saw grandparents and their grandchildren, driving a cow before them. The cow would be covered with a blanket, the only property they had managed to rescue from the German tanks. The fathers and mothers had joined the Partisans.

The number of refugees increased every day and soon amounted to over a hundred thousand persons. All the ways were blocked, hampering the army and creating a serious food problem. There was also the problem of housing. In former offensives, the enemy had burnt down all the villages in liberated territory. We had tried to reconstruct some of them, but thousands and thousands of families were crowding in. Most of them remained out of doors in the bitter cold. When the refugees assembled again in the morning there would always be a few old people so frozen that they could move no more and had to be left behind. German aircraft represented another danger for the refugees. The long columns were excellent targets both for bombing with light bombs and for machine-gun fire.

I was assigned the task of helping with the evacuation of the wounded, whose number had increased to four thousand. They were scattered over sixty miles of front in a mountainous region. It was necessary to organize a more rapid transportation of those who were in the forefront, for they were slowing our military operations.

The horrors of those days will never leave me. They were so plentiful that they flood my memory. I recall, for example, a young mother with three children who was standing at a turning, under a pine tree. She could go no farther, night had fallen and the mountain was wild and desolate. If she remained there, she would freeze to death with her three children. And she could not go on carrying two children on her back and dragging the third one by the hand. She had made up her mind to abandon one child in order to rescue the two others. She begged some of the other refugees to assist her, but nobody took any notice of her. All were starving and exhausted. Many had become apathetic. Thus the mother begged for help, while taking leave of her youngest son, a black-haired child with big eyes:

"My Peter, your mother has to abandon you."

Two middle-aged peasant refugees came along, quite exhausted. They gave the scene a blank look. I begged them to take one child. They agreed without enthusiasm.

The German offensive developed powerfully. On the other hand, the measures undertaken by the Supreme HQ proved efficient. The proletarian divisions attacked toward the south, liberated the city of Livno, then Imotski, captured a large amount of armament, and then attacked in the Neretva valley, where the units of the Italian Sixth Corps were located in several fortified towns. It became necessary to stop the German advance in the north, and also to break through the Italian ring along the Neretva.

We made a strong attack on the town of Prozor, where a regiment of the Italian Division Murge was located, but the town did not fall on the first night. There was a pause during the day and on the next night we again attacked the Italian pillbox. Victory was achieved at dawn. The Italian regiment surrendered, and our units broke into the valley of the Neretva River, where Italian garrisons fell one after the other. In three days the entire Italian Division Murge was defeated, fifteen tanks were captured, a great many cannons, huge quantities of ammunition, food and medical supplies. Almost two thousand Italian soldiers were taken prisoner in that sector.

Our proletarian divisions could easily ford the Neretva and disappear in Montenegrin mountains. But it was necessary to rescue the wounded, whose number had now increased to forty-five hundred. The evacuation went on slowly. We also had to rescue hundreds of thousands of old peasants and mothers with children who were fleeing before the enemy. This was pitiless war. At some spots, the enemy discovered refugees and massacred them. A Dalmatian unit found a group of about fifty women and children slaughtered in a cave. Only a one-year-old baby crawled among the dead bodies. It had somehow remained alive through the massacre. The Partisans took the child and an army nurse took care of her. The child had no name. The news reached us that day that the Russians had liberated Vjazma from the Germans. Somebody suggested that the child should be named Vjazma. Little Vjazma was sent to an Allied hospital in Italy in 1944, and now is living in a painter's family in Belgrade, ten years old and sickly.

Tito and his staff were at the time housed in a small mill near the Neretva River. One day I found him walking up and down near the stream. When we had greeted each other, he asked me about the wounded. I reported on the situation and told him particularly of the position of the refugees. Tito showed me a telegram which he had sent to Moscow immediately after the beginning of the enemy offensive:

"Am obliged once again to ask you if it is really quite impossible to send us some sort of assistance? Hundreds of thousands of refugees are menaced by death from starvation. Is it really impossible, after twenty months of heroic, almost superhuman fighting, to find some way of helping us? We have been fighting for twenty months, without the least material assistance from any quarter. I do assure you that this wonderful, heroic people, of Bosnia, the Lika, the Kordun and Dalmatia, have to the full merited the maximum of aid. Typhus has now begun to rage here, yet we are without drugs, people are dropping like flies from starvation, yet do not complain. These starving folk give our fighting men their last crusts, and themselves drop like flies, they give their last sock, shirt or boot, and themselves, now in midwinter, go barefoot. Do your utmost to show us assistance."

He then showed me the answer he had received to the above telegram:

"You must not for an instant doubt that, were there the least possibility of granting your wonderful, heroic struggle any material aid, we should long ago have done so.

"The Soviet people, together with its leaders, is in its entirety on your side, full of enthusiasm and profound fraternal sympathy for the National Liberation Army.

"Josif Vissarionovich and myself have [many times?] discussed ways and means of helping you. Unfortunately, hitherto we have not been able to find a satisfactory solution to the problem on account of the insurmountable technical difficulties [for aircraft?] [here some words could not be deciphered] . . . possibility of affording you assistance.

"The moment the conditions exist, we shall do all that is most urgent.

"Is it possible you doubt this?

"Please grasp the present situation correctly and explain it all to your fighting comrades. Do not lose heart, but gather all your forces to bear the present exceptionally hard trials. You are doing a great thing, which our Soviet land and all freedom-loving peoples will never forget.

"With fraternal greetings to yourself and best wishes to all the comrades in their heroic struggle against the accursed enemy."

Tito then took out of his bag a notebook used for writing radiograms and reports, and composed the following telegram for Moscow:

"Can we expect at least some assistance from the Allies? Please answer, as it is not clear how long we can stand a strain like the present. We are suffering huge losses, and our wounded are badly in the way of the fighting."

Tito then told me about the plans of our further operations. We were to await the arrival of all the wounded and destroy all the bridges on the Neretva River, so that the enemy might think that we had given up the idea of a crossing. We should then send our basic forces to the north to push back the Germans as far as possible, and then unexpectedly break through the Neretva River.

Tito's order was quickly carried out. The German divisions in the north were amazed by our counterattack. In this battle we used the fifteen Italian tanks we had captured, as well as the entire artillery that had been captured in the Neretva battle. The Germans had to retreat ten miles and we took many prisoners, a lieutenant colonel among others. I watched this Prussian standing calmly before us. He asked us:

"Where did you get such a huge artillery?"

"We captured it from your allies, the Italians."

He waved his hand. "*Oh, liebe Italiener!*" (Oh, the sweet Italians!)

When the Germans had been pushed away, the Second Dalmatian Brigade received the order to break through the Neretva River first, and to establish a bridgehead. There were fifteen thousand Chetniks of Draža Mihailović on the other side of the river and on the neighboring hills. They had been sent here by the Italians to close the front after the defeat of the Division Murge. The Chetniks had not expected our attack, believing that we were forcing our way to the north. A group of Dalmatian Partisans carrying unfused bombs in their teeth crept over a destroyed railroad bridge which was standing practically erect. When they reached the other end of the bridge, where a Chetnik pillbox was located, they threw two bombs into it and then jumped in. Thus a bridgehead was established after a struggle which had lasted only three minutes. Our engineers immediately erected a wooden bridge over the ruins of the old iron one, and then unit after unit crossed the river at the run and landed on the other bank, broadening the bridgehead. At dawn our first units had already reached the mountain summits on the other side, pursuing the defeated Chetniks.

Columns of wounded followed. The crossing of the river lasted for seven days. German and Italian aircraft bombed the bridge violently but the crossing went on. And thus our last wounded soldier and our last unit reached the other side of the river. The morale of Partisan units was very high. I remember talking to a courier, a shepherd boy from Sandžak. He was very gay because we succeeded in breaking through the enemy circle. He spoke about the end of the war and the fighting in Russia. "It is true they are bombing us mercilessly here," he said. "Here are six German planes dropping bombs. It means six bombers less on the eastern front. And the victory will be achieved sooner."

The German commander of the southeast, Alexander von Leer, described the issue of this operation in the following manner:

"The Partisans managed to cross the River Neretva and to retreat with all their men in the northern part of Montenegro. They broke through a section of the front which was held by Italians and Chetniks. There were neither prisoners nor booty. No wounded Partisans could be found, not even dead ones, although they must have had severe losses, if we are to judge from those we suffered ourselves."

After the break across the Neretva, the Partisan divisions advanced rapidly through Herzegovina and Montenegro, liberating town after town. The problem of the wounded Partisans was a very difficult one. There was a severe epidemic of typhus. We all lived in villages in which the majority of the houses had been burnt down. There were no medicaments whatsoever. The food was insufficient. Those who recovered from typhus were suffering especially from hunger. I remember many scenes from these days: a peasant plowing a field and sowing oats, and as soon as he went away, a wounded Partisan throwing himself on the furrow and digging out the oats with fingers. We had more victims from typhus in March and April, 1943, than we had from encounters with the enemy.

In other parts of Yugoslavia which had not been included in the offensive, Partisan units made violent attacks against the enemy, especially in Slavonia, where the main Balkan east-west railroad line runs.

The fighting was extremely severe in western Bosnia, where German divisions succeeded in surrounding two Partisan brigades in the mountain of Grmeč. This happened in the middle of the winter and the whole mountain was covered with six feet of snow. Partisan brigades and German columns lost their way in the snow-bound mountain. The Fifth Partisan Brigade marched once for more than seventy-two hours without food or rest. From exhaustion, hunger and sleeplessness, mass hallucinations developed. Suddenly a Partisan would shout, pointing to a tree in the distance: "Here is a chimney, let's go and rest in a warm house," and the whole column would start to run toward the trees. Or another Partisan would stop in front of a bush covered with snow and say: "Here is a field kitchen, let's take some hot food." He would take out his spoon, waiting for his turn. German units which took part in pursuit were also struck by mass hallucination. At last the Partisan units and the enemy found their way out of the mountain to the valley, where the units rested and got some hot food.

The victory achieved in this offensive, as well as the size of the Partisan movement in other regions, forced Hitler to start immediately a new offensive against the Partisans. On the other hand, it became clear in Allied circles that the Partisans were the most powerful force in Yugoslavia, that Draža Mihailović was not as strong as it had been believed, especially after the defeat in the Neretva valley. The British government therefore decided to send an observer to the liberated territory. And so, one night, as a "Liberator" was flying over the liberated territory in Lika, an officer in a British uniform parachuted from the aircraft, accompanied by three noncommissioned officers. He landed in a forest in the dark and at dawn reached the fringe of a village where he found a sentinel who directed him to the Supreme Partisan HQ for Croatia. The officer in the British uniform sat in a motorcar and drove some forty miles over liberated territory before he reached the HQ. He introduced himself there. He said his name was William Jones, that he was a Canadian, a volunteer in this war, since he had remained an invalid after the First World War, where he lost an eye, and that he had been sent here as an observer. Major Jones made an excellent impression from the very beginning, because of his sincerity and his courage. The Partisans liked him because he was very brave, and never wanted to bend down or to take cover in a battle. He always stood erect, wearing his beret defiantly. Major Jones was remembered among the Partisans to the end of the war as the most popular Allied officer in Yugoslavia.

Supreme HQ were informed through Major Jones that a special British military mission would be sent them. Meanwhile, in mid-May, the Germans started a new great offensive against three proletarian divisions and several other units which were located with the Supreme HQ on the border between Montenegro and Bosnia. The enemy effected a very deep pincer movement. Twelve German and Italian divisions and one Bulgarian regiment took part in this offensive, which was marked by the bloodiest of battles. The Germans no longer limited themselves to lines of communication, but entering the territory itself climbed upon mountain summits, the way we did. They sent supplies to their units by plane. They fortified themselves powerfully in some sections.

When the offensive began, we had to delay our break-through, because we were expecting the arrival of the British military mission. When it parachuted at last, the Supreme HQ was located on Durmitor Mountain. William Dicken, a don at Oxford, who was then a captain of the British army, was the head of this mission. He gave the impression of being a quiet and courageous man. Dicken arrived with his mission in the middle of one of the most terrible battles fought by the Partisans in World War II.

This offensive was a short one, but it was more violent than any previous campaign. The basic Partisan forces broke through after a bitter struggle, and suffered tremendous losses. Tito himself was wounded in the arm, a member of the British mission, Captain William Stuart, was killed and the head of the Dicken mission was also wounded. The Germans also suffered heavy losses. This is what General von Leer wrote about the result of the battle:

"The fights were extraordinarily heavy. All the commanders agreed that their troops were going through the most bitter struggle of the war. A ferocious Partisan attack which struck the Second Battalion of the 369th Division in particular effected a break-through on this front near Jelašca and Miljevina. All the enemy forces managed to retreat through this front and to disappear in the mountains toward the north. The German troops were too tired and exhausted to be able to do anything about it, and there were no reserves."

Thus the First and Second Divisions with the Supreme HQ and some other smaller units broke through the ring, but the main enemy blow fell on the Third Division, which was protecting the wounded and acting as the rear guard. Milovan Djilas was at the head of these columns. When the tired fighting men of this division crossed the River Sutjeska, everything seemed to be quiet and the enemy had apparently retreated. When the Partisans found themselves in the valley on the other side of the Sutjeska River and were approaching the first hills, Germans behind hidden pillboxes opened fire with all their weapons. To return would have meant sure death. Therefore Milovan Djilas and Sava Kovačević, the commander of the division, ordered an assault. They were both the first to advance toward enemy pillboxes. More than half the Partisans fell before reaching the pillbox and throwing bombs into it. It was necessary then to capture an entire system of pillboxes in order to widen the break-through. The Partisans destroyed more than thirty pillboxes, but when they reached the very summit, Sava Kovačević, a huge, stout man, fell mortally wounded by a bullet in the forehead. His nephew Dragan, a fourteen-year-old Partisan courier, fell at the same time. Confusion overtook the division. Down in the valley, the Partisan wounded had already crossed the river, hoping that a break-through had been effected. Milovan Djilas remained behind with a group of thirty Partisans. The Germans descended into the valley and began killing the wounded. Beside the river lay a wounded Montenegrin

Partisan girl, with a broken thigh. At her side was her husband, a Partisan of the Fifth Montenegrin Brigade. He refused to leave his wounded wife, and the Germans were approaching. When the Germans came within a distance of twenty feet, this Partisan shot a bullet into his wife's temple and then turned his gun upon himself.

Milovan Djilas attempted to break through with the thirty men who had remained at his side, but all passes had been occupied. The whole group hid in a small woods and then, when darkness came, began to advance. They encountered several German ambushes, there were severe clashes and at dawn Djilas again found himself looking up at German pillboxes on a rock. He was advancing at the head of the column when suddenly, at a turning, he confronted two German soldiers, literally face to face. There was no time to get hold of one's rifle. The German drew his knife. Djilas did the same, and he was quicker on the draw. The other German was killed with a rifle blow on the head by a Partisan. All this was happening only fifty yards under a German pillbox, where a German soldier could be seen on guard. It was not until the following night that Djilas finally managed to break through, and a week later he reached the Supreme HQ.

Thus ended the Fifth Offensive. The crack units had been decimated. Tremendous losses had been suffered. But moral victory was achieved. New fighters soon flowed into the ranks of the units.

Tito ordered attacks to be carried out on the garrisons in central Bosnia, new weapons were captured and the song of the proletarian brigades echoed again. In the course of the Fifth Offensive came the news of the disbanding of the Comintern. Tito received the following radiogram from Moscow:

"On the second of May a proposal was sent to the sections for the disbanding of the Comintern as the leading center of the International Workers' Movement. The proposal is explained by the fact that this centralized form of international organization no longer corresponds to the needs of the further development of the Communist Parties of the different countries or of the national workers' parties, and has even become an obstacle to this development. Please examine this proposal in detail in your Central Committee and inform us of your decision."

At the same time, Stalin's statement was received in which he gave his reasons for the disbanding of the Comintern to world public opinion:

"a) It puts an end to the lie that 'Moscow' intends to interfere in the life of other countries and to 'Bolshevize' them. This lie has been done away with.

"b) It puts an end to the slanders of the enemies of Communism and of the workers' movement who allege that the Communist Parties of the different countries were acting not the interest of their own people but on instructions from abroad. This slander too has now been done away with.

"c) It will make it easier for the patriots in the freedom-loving countries to unite all the progressive forces in their country, respective of the latter's party allegiance or religious convictions, in a common national liberation front for the purpose of developing the struggle against Fascism.

"d) It will make it easier for the patriots of all countries to unite all the freedom-loving peoples in an international front in the struggle against the threat of Hitlerized world domination, thus paving the way for future friendship and co-operation among nations on a basis of equality."

The Central Committee of the Communist Party of Yugoslavia considered this Moscow dispatch and sent the following reply:

"After having considered the proposal of the Executive Committee of the Communist International concerning the disbanding of the Comintern, the Central Committee of the Communist Party of Yugoslavia finds itself in full agreement with this proposal as well as with the reasons given. The Central Committee of the Communist Party of Yugoslavia is profoundly convinced that this historical decision will not fail to yield tremendous results in the very near future in the struggle for victory over the enemies of mankind, the Fascist invaders.

"Thanks to the assistance of the Comintern, the Communist Party of Yugoslavia has grown into a powerful mass party which in these fateful days is conducting the struggle for national liberation and has won the good will of the people, of the majority of the masses of the Yugoslav people.

"Under the banner of Marx, Engels, Lenin, Stalin, our Party will continue to do its duty to its people, regardless of sacrifices, in the struggle against Fascism and for the liberation of the oppressed people of Yugoslavia.

"The Communist Party of Yugoslavia will remain faithful to the principles of the International.

"On behalf of the Central Committee of the Communist Party of Yugoslavia:

> "Secretary General: Tito
> Members of the Politburo:
> Aleksandar Ranković
> Milovan Djilas
> Edvard Kardelj
> Ivan Milutinović
> Franc Leskovšek."

During the Fifth Offensive, the operations in other parts of the country were developing successfully, because the enemy had concentrated all his forces against the bulk of the Partisan units. The liberated territory continued to increase. The British government then decided to supplement its mission to the Supreme HQ. Brigadier Fitzroy MacLean, a tall Scotsman, then became head of the mission. The Partisans had the opportunity to judge him on the very first day. A German plane came along. The Scotsman looked at it calmly. This meant that this British brigadier general was not lacking in courage. When it came, however, to the question of Allied supplies, there were misunderstandings. We did not receive the help we had requested, or when something was sent to us it was only in small quantities.*

Then came the surrender of Italy. Although our Supreme HQ had not been informed in advance of this event, eleven Italian divisions were disarmed, which was of tremendous significance for the arming

---

* Arms supplies from the Western Allies began arriving in larger quantities only in the second half of 1944. Brigadier Fitzroy MacLean has stated that 100,000 rifles were sent to the Partisans in 1944. In order to get the facts corrected, one should, however, bear the following in mind: In the beginning of 1944, the Partisan base in Bari was instructed to take over 40,000 Italian rifles from a depot in Sicily. These rifles were transported in cases on small Yugoslav ships through German-controlled waters to the Dalmatian islands which were held by the Partisans. When these cases were finally opened, they were found to contain old models of Ethiopian rifles, captured by Mussolini in 1936, as well as a certain number of breechless Italian rifles. The whole quantity of 40,000 rifles was unserviceable.

of Partisan units. One day, a rather strange man appeared on Partisan territory. He was an officer of the United States Army, a major, who said that his name was Huot. He asked to see Tito, but inquired all the time whether there were any British officers in the vicinity. At that very moment a British officer came along. The American immediately asked the town major to hide him in another room so that the Englishman should not see him. The town major did as he was asked, but was at a complete loss to understand what the American officer was after.

The facts were simple, however. Major Louis Huot had not obtained permission from the Allied Command to come to Yugoslavia. He had come on his own initiative to assist the Partisans, whose representatives he had met in Bari. Huot was received by Tito and had a long talk with him, after which he returned to Italy. He kept his word. He sent us over four hundred tons of uniforms, medical supplies, ammunition and other items, which could not be found in Yugoslavia, from certain U.S. quartermaster stores and by means of the small Yugoslav boats. This assistance amounted to more than the total aid we had hitherto received from the Allies. We were planning on further quantities of supplies when one day this energetic American disappeared from Bari. He had been posted elsewhere.

CHAPTER XIII

1943:

"Recognition by the Soviet people and their army of our struggle—that was our dearest recognition . . ."

THE crucial year of the war was 1943. Hitler's fate was sealed. In the east the Red Army had advanced from Stalingrad for a year, in pursuit of the Nazi divisions. The Allies had driven Rommel from Africa, and Italy had been put out of action. It was a matter of time before Hitler would capitulate.

In Yugoslavia the people were yearning for an end to their sufferings, the burning of villages, the bombing, and the blood. The great Allied victories held out hope that the end of the war was near. How they were celebrated, how the news of Mussolini's fall was received, what rejoicing there was over the liberation of Kiev on November 6, 1943. Supreme Headquarters was then at Jajce, an old town in Bosnia. Milovan Djilas had heard the voice of the announcer Levitan that evening over the Moscow radio reading Stalin's order in connection with the liberation of the Ukrainian capital. He ran out to the top of the tower of the old town and fired three pistol shots into the air, a traditional Montenegrin manner of announcing good news.

The fighters in the town had also heard of the liberation of Kiev, and when Djilas fired from the fortress, they began to fire first their pistols, then rifles and machine guns until the whole town resounded with shooting. The people came out into the streets and began to dance, and the firing went on steadily. Not knowing what was happening, Tito came out of his room, and then the shooting grew even wilder. The news spread from the town to the surrounding positions, where even the Partisans in the mountains began to let loose their artillery. It was an hour before the din died down. Telephone orders flew over the wires, explanations were given. That evening the quantity of ammunition wasted would have been sufficient for a battle, and every bullet was precious—everything had to be captured from the enemy.

Such was the mood in the army and among the people in the autumn of 1943, when the National Liberation Army numbered three hundred thousand fighters after successfully overcoming two heavy German offensives. The liberated territory was half the size of Yugoslavia.

Partisans were already discussing means of preserving the achievements of the struggle. After Italy's surrender the Central Committee decided to reconvene the AVNOJ, the national parliament made up of the most prominent members of the National Liberation Movement, to adopt suitable decisions for founding a temporary government of new Yugoslavia.

In October, 1943, hearing that a meeting was to take place in Moscow between the British Foreign Secretary, Anthony Eden, the American Secretary of State, Cordell Hull, and the Commissar of Foreign Affairs, Molotov, Tito sent the following telegram to Moscow:

"In connection with the preparations for a conference between the representatives of the USSR, Britain, America, it is probable that the question of Yugoslavia will be raised.

"In this connection I beg you to inform the Soviet government of the following:

"The Anti-Fascist Council of Yugoslavia, and Supreme Headquarters of the National Liberation Army and Partisan detachments of Yugoslavia have empowered me to declare:

"First, we acknowledge neither the Yugoslav government nor the King abroad, because for two and a half years they have supported the enemy collaborationist, the traitor Draža Mihailović, and thus bear complete responsibility for this treason to the peoples of Yugoslavia.

"Second, we shall not allow them to return to Yugoslavia, because that would mean civil war.

"Third, we speak in the name of the overwhelming majority of the people, who want a democratic republic based on National Liberation Committees.

"Fourth, the only legal government of the people at the present time are the National Liberation Committees headed by the Anti-Fascist Councils.

"We shall give a statement to this effect to the British mission attached to our Headquarters.

"The British general has already informed us that the British government will not insist on supporting the King and the Yugoslav Government in Exile."

The results of the conference in Moscow were awaited impatiently at Jajce, the one-time capital of the Bosnian kings, in the valley of the Vrbas River, where Supreme Headquarters was situated in October, 1943. The conference lasted from October 13 to October 30, but the Soviet government did not place Tito's statement on the agenda.

Nevertheless, it was decided in Yugoslavia to convene the AVNOJ in Jajce. During the war this town had changed hands several times. The Partisans freed it in 1942, the Germans took it again toward the end of the same year, and the Partisans recaptured it in the autumn of 1943. Tito and his staff took up their quarters in this town, on a plateau beneath the fortress where there stood two barracks with offices. Tito lived in a small room in one of the barracks, not far from a tunnel that served as an air-raid shelter.

On the eve of the AVNOJ meeting German bombers raided the town. Tito, together with some civilians of the town, took refuge in the air-raid shelter. Some of them were killed and one was badly wounded. His stomach was torn away. In the air-raid shelter there was stationed a first-aid ambulance, with a Partisan surgeon, Dr. Papo. He undertook the operation immediately. Tito was holding the head of the wounded Partisan, while the doctor operated on him. The case was hopeless. Tito remembers this day. "I was holding the head of the boy. He was sweating. The operation was done without anesthetics. The wounded Partisan did not want to show how much he suffered. I told him: 'Never mind, you'll get through all right.' A few seconds later his head dropped and so he died in my hands."

The delegates to the meeting of the AVNOJ came from the remotest parts of Yugoslavia, traveling under arms, for the routes passed from the liberated territory through districts in German hands and some had to fight their way through. The Montenegrins had made the longest trek, traversing two hundred miles of mountains and canyons, all on foot, carrying arms.

The AVNOJ met in the hall of the former gymnastics society "Sokol." During their first attack on Jajce the Partisans had set fire to the building, but three weeks after they freed the town they had restored it and converted it into a cultural center. It was there that the Partisan theater performed Gogol's *Government Inspector* and various short plays on Partisan life. The hall was now adapted for the session of the AVNOJ. The platform was decorated with flags: Yugoslav with the red star in the center, Soviet, American and British. The session was held at night because of the danger from air raids.

It was on the eve of opening the second session of the AVNOJ that Ivo-Lola Ribar, a member of Supreme Headquarters, was killed by a German bomb. He had been nominated, with Vladimir Velebit and Miloje Milojević, for the first Partisan military mission sent to Allied Headquarters for the Near East. They were to have gone to Italy by air, but British planes were unable to land. A few days previously a home guard officer had fled Zagreb on a German light bomber Dornier 17. It was then decided that the Yugoslav delegation, as well as two British officers, were to be taken to Italy by this plane. It was already preparing to take off from a Partisan airfield near Jajce when a German reconnaissance plane appeared from over a mountain. It dived at the group of men who were boarding the plane, dropping two bombs from an altitude of about a hundred yards. Ivo-Lola Ribar, the British officers Captain Donald Knight and Major Robin Weatherley, and a Partisan were killed. Lola Ribar's younger brother, Jurica, a painter, had fallen a month earlier fighting the Chetniks in Montenegro.

Lola Ribar's father, Dr. Ivan Ribar, had just arrived from Slovenia for the AVNOJ session. He was ignorant of the death of his two sons. When he called on Tito to exchange greetings, Tito told him of Lola's death. Old Ribar did not shed a single tear. He only said, "Is Jurica far away, and has he been told of Lola's death? It will be a heavy blow for him. . . ."

Only then did Tito realize that the old man knew nothing of the death of his younger son. He was silent a few moments, wondering what to do. Then he approached Ribar, took him by the arm and in a soft voice said:

"Jurica was killed too, fighting the Chetniks in Montenegro, a month ago. . . ."

Old Ribar was silent. He embraced Tito. "This fight of ours is hard. . . ."

Lola Ribar was buried that same evening. A battalion of the First Proletarian Brigade was lined up on the square at Jajce. The last to take leave of Lola was old Ribar. With a strong voice that trembled only occasionally, he spoke to the fighters of the First Proletarian Brigade: "No force will be able to stop the people of this country in their struggle for liberation. . . ."

Later the coffin with Lola Ribar's body was taken to a sheltered spot where it was buried temporarily, because there was danger that the Germans and Chetniks would discover the grave and destroy the body.*

For Yugoslavia, the second session of the AVNOJ was the most important event in the war, for it was there that the foundations of the new state were laid. The day of the session, November 29, had been adopted as the national holiday of new Yugoslavia. It was at this session that the National Committee was founded as the executive organ of the AVNOJ, with the functions of a temporary cabinet. The AVNOJ adopted a decision depriving the exiled government in London of the powers of government in Yugoslavia. It was also decided that King Peter and other members of the Karageorgevich dynasty should be prohibited from returning to Yugoslavia, and that the question of the form of the state, whether a republic or monarchy, would be set aside for decision after the war. The principle was proclaimed that Yugoslavia was to be a federated state.

It was decided to send an appeal to the American government to freeze Yugoslavia's gold reserves, which had been removed to Wash-

---

* Lola's and Jurica's mother learned of the death of her two sons in a village in Srem, where she had taken refuge from the Gestapo. During the summer of 1944 she was discovered in the village, taken to the square near the church, where she was asked to betray the men who had helped her to flee from Belgrade. She vigorously refused. A German soldier who was attached to her as escort became impatient and shot the old woman on the spot.

ington out of Hitler's reach, and were now being selfishly squandered by the Royal Government in Exile. On the proposal of the Slovene delegation the title of Marshal of Yugoslavia was conferred upon Tito.

The most distinguished representatives of the National Liberation Movement were elected to the Presidium of the AVNOJ and to the National Committee. A member of the National Liberation Army from the first day of the uprising, Dr. Ivan Ribar, was elected President of the AVNOJ. A member of the Democratic Party, he had been Speaker of the Constituent Assembly of old Yugoslavia in 1921. Tito was elected President of the National Committee and Commissioner of National Defense. Dušan Sernec, one of the leaders of the Catholic Clerical Party in Slovenia, was elected Commissioner for Finances. He had been Governor of Slovenia in 1932, but from the outbreak of the resistance served in the National Liberation Movement. Father Vlado Zečević, a former commander in Draža Mihailović's detachments, who in 1941 had refused to fight against the Partisans, was elected Commissioner for Internal Affairs in the National Committee. Edvard Kardelj was elected Vice-President of the National Committee. Anton Augustinčić, a well-known sculptor, was elected also a Vice-President.

The session of the AVNOJ was held at the same time as the conference between Roosevelt, Stalin and Churchill at Teheran, where in addition to questions of the second front and general Allied strategy against Hitler, there was some discussion of Yugoslavia's contribution in the war against the Axis powers. Roosevelt, Stalin and Churchill agreed at Teheran that the basic force fighting the Germans in Yugoslavia was the National Liberation Army under Tito's command.

Finally, after two and a half years of steadfast struggle and efforts, after the plot of almost the whole world to conceal the truth about Yugoslavia, this injustice was now remedied. By the formal decision of the three leaders of the anti-Hitlerite coalition at Teheran the Partisans of Yugoslavia were factually recognized as an Allied army. In the announcement of the Teheran decisions, first place was given to the recognition of the Yugoslav Partisans. The second point dealt with the prospects of Turkey's entering the war, the third with Bulgaria, the fourth with the second front, "Operation Overlord," to begin in May, 1944, the fifth with continued consultation among the military staffs of the Allied powers regarding imminent operations of the Allied armies.

Tito did not notify the representatives of any of the big powers in advance of the concrete decisions at Jajce, although he had given the outline to General Fitzroy MacLean, the chief of the Allied Military Mission with Supreme Headquarters, and to the Soviet government in the telegram previously mentioned. It was a Yugoslav affair, exclusively the right of the Yugoslav peoples, and based on the principles for which the United Nations were fighting. The resolution of the AVNOJ says word for word:

"The peoples of Yugoslavia joyfully accept and greet the decisions of the Moscow conference of the representatives of the governments of the Soviet Union, Great Britain, and the United States, which assure all peoples the right to solve the question of their internal order according to their freely expressed will. These decisions are of the utmost importance for the peoples of Yugoslavia, who have by their steadfast struggle demonstrated their will and readiness to build up their common homeland on new foundations of genuine democracy and equality of nations."

Thus, it was only after their adoption that Moscow learned of the decisions of the AVNOJ, and particularly that the Royal Government in Exile had been deprived of powers, and King Peter forbidden to return to Yugoslavia. Moscow's first reaction was furious. The "Free Yugoslavia" radio station had orders not to broadcast the resolution prohibiting the King's return; Yugoslavia's representative in Moscow, Veljko Vlahović, was reprimanded and his broadcasts for "Free Yugoslavia" and the Moscow radio were censored. Manuilski delivered Stalin's message:

"The Hazyahyin* is extremely angry. He says this is a stab in the back of the Soviet Union and the Teheran decisions."

Stalin's reaction took the Yugoslavs by surprise. It was not clear to them at the time. They recalled Stalin's opposition to the formation of the National Committee at the first session of the AVNOJ a year before. Not to create the National Committee, not to give the people in Yugoslavia a clear indication that they were fighting for a

* In familiar circles in Moscow Stalin is called "Hazyahyin," which means "the host."

new Yugoslavia different in every way from the old Yugoslavia under the Karageorgevich dynasty, would have meant to renounce everything that had been achieved in two and a half years. It would have meant the end of the Yugoslav revolution. It was only later that Stalin's opposition became clear: he opposed the principle of Yugoslavia for the Yugoslavs; he wished the country to be a "sphere of influence" for one big power or another.

In the West the foundation of the National Committee was also received with surprise, but in that part of the world they had to reconcile themselves to a *fait accompli*. The relation of forces in Yugoslavia was such that it was clear to every realistic politician what sort of Yugoslavia would emerge from the war. Moreover, everyone in London and Washington was firmly convinced that Tito had the approval of Stalin before the decisions of Jajce were announced. Since commentaries in the Western press were not so sharp but on the whole even favorable to Yugoslavia, the decision was altered in Moscow, and on December 14, two weeks after being notified of the decisions of the AVNOJ, the People's Commissariat of Foreign Affairs released the following announcement:

"The events in Yugoslavia which have already met with understanding in Britain and the United States are considered by the Government of the Soviet Union to be positive facts that will contribute to the further successful struggle of the peoples of Yugoslavia against Hitlerite Germany. These events also bear witness to the remarkable success of the new leaders of Yugoslavia in the cause of uniting all the people's forces of Yugoslavia."

It was simultaneously announced that the Soviet government would send one of its military missions to Yugoslavia.

Meanwhile, a military mission of Supreme Headquarters had arrived in Cairo, where it made a number of contacts with leading figures in Allied Headquarters. The talks were chiefly concerned with the question of supplying the National Liberation Army with arms and ammunition. The main decision taken was to help to evacuate the Partisan wounded to Allied hospitals in Italy.

The military mission was besieged by correspondents of the big newspapers and agencies in America and Great Britain. Almost nothing had been known in those countries about the struggle of the Partisans: all credit for the resistance against the Germans in Yugoslavia had been given to Draža Mihailović. There were wildly impossible versions of the person of Tito. Some Catholic papers wrote that the name TITO was an abbreviation meaning "Third International Terrorist Organization." Even serious papers such as the New York *Times* were involved in such conjectures. After the Teheran conference, at which President Roosevelt had personally presented to Stalin the report of Major Ferrish, a liaison officer attached to Supreme Headquarters, on the fighting in Yugoslavia and on Tito, Cyril Sulzberger, in the New York *Times Magazine*, wrote on December 5, 1944, that there were rumors that Tito was a woman!

Shortly afterward Sulzberger corrected his wild guesses in a long article in the New York *Times* which had a great effect in the United States and helped to inform American public opinion on the development of events in Yugoslavia.

For the German command, the National Liberation Army of Yugoslavia constituted a growing danger. With a shortened front, lines of communication through the Balkans became of vital importance to Hitler. Consequently, toward the end of 1943 he assigned twenty-two German divisions, nine Bulgarian and twenty native satellite divisions, totaling about six hundred thousand men, to the struggle against the National Liberation Army. He simultaneously planned an offensive against those parts of the National Liberation Army that threatened the most important lines of communication. Thus began what is called the Seventh Offensive. It was prosecuted on a fairly broad sector, the main blow being leveled against the Third Corps of the Partisan forces in eastern Bosnia. In their documents the Germans called this offensive "Operation Kugelblitz" ("thunderbolt"). Parts of the Second German Armored Army Corps, the Fifth and Fifteenth Corps, carried out this attack in cold weather. The fighting was fierce; the Partisans lost Tuzla, the chief town in this area, but they saved their striking force and went over to the offensive again. Tito ordered attacks in all parts of Yugoslavia.

At the same time Tito decided to find a safer place on liberated territory for the National Committee and for Supreme Headquarters, in order to facilitate the discharge of ever-growing state business. Jajce was abandoned and headquarters were set up in the town of Drvar, 125 miles or so to the west, in a protected valley.

During the evacuation of Supreme Headquarters toward the end of December, 1943, an incident occurred that might have ended tragically. In deep snow the column of Supreme Headquarters was moving along a trail above Jajce. The horses were loaded with records and radio sets; the members of the Supreme Staff were riding. The head of the Engineering Department, Colonel Vladimir Smirnov, a Russian engineer who had come to Yugoslavia as a young man in 1919 and joined the Partisans in 1941, wanted to dismount. His tommy-gun was slung across his back. As he was getting off his horse, the bridle rein looped round the trigger and sprayed an endless volley on all sides. The bullets whistled past Tito's ears. The unlucky Smirnov was unable to stop the volley, for his horse took fright and began to toss his head, and the firing continued until the magazine was emptied. Fortunately, no one was hurt. When it was certain that everybody was alive, it even seemed funny, and Smirnov's attack became one of the stories of the war.

The winter fighting in 1943 and 1944 meant complete failure for Hitler in Yugoslavia.

The National Liberation Army of Yugoslavia inflicted blow upon blow on the enemy, each heavier than the last. This was reported by the officers of the Allied military missions who were attached to all the corps of the National Liberation Army.

The reputation of the National Liberation Movement steadily grew in the world. The communiqués of Supreme Headquarters were now published by all the big newspapers in the West. The Soviet press also began to write more about the fighting in Yugoslavia. In February, 1944, in connection with the anniversary of the Red Army, the Central Committee of the Soviet Party said:

"Stalwart patriots of Yugoslavia: Your struggle for the freedom and independence of your country is an exhilarating example to all the enslaved peoples of Europe. Long live the heroic people of Yugoslavia with their gallant National Liberation Army which is fighting with such selflessness against the Fascist invaders!"

Simultaneously, for the first time during the war, Stalin personally answered Tito's greeting for the anniversary. In his telegram Tito had said:

"Our fighters, fighters for the freedom and brotherhood of the Yugoslav peoples, have always been conscious that the Fatherland War of the Soviet Union is at the same time a struggle for the liberation of all enslaved countries. They have been conscious that their sacred duty to their homeland enjoins them to fight shoulder to shoulder with the Red Army. They have felt all the great honor and responsibility of fighting together with the army led by the great Stalin. They most gladly grappled with the German bandits as they set out for the eastern front or returned from it. Recognition by the Soviet people and their army of our struggle against the German Fascists—that was our dearest recognition."

Stalin's reply ran:

"The heroic struggle of the brotherly Yugoslav peoples and their glorious National Liberation Army against the German invaders rouses the deep admiration of the people of the Soviet Union and is an example inspiring all the enslaved nations of Europe. I wish further success to the Yugoslav patriots who under your leadership are fighting gloriously for the liberation of their country."

The official Soviet military mission arrived at last in Yugoslavia a day later. How it had been awaited, what joy it gave the Yugoslavs to see the representatives of the Red Army! Headed by Generals Kornieyev and Gorskov, the mission came by plane through Persia, Egypt and Italy. The journey was very slow, especially the last stage, because the winter in Yugoslavia had been severe; deep snow had fallen, and the planes were unable to land at the mountain airfield near Petrovac, not far from Drvar, and the Soviet military mission transferred to gliders which were cut free over Petrovac, where they slowly landed on the thick blanket of snow. That same night there was a formal public gathering in observance of the anniversary of the Red Army. The Soviet generals were the guests of Petrovac. The people carried them shoulder-high, and afterward danced the Kozara kolo.

On February 24, in honor of the arrival of the Soviet military mission, Tito gave the first gala reception for the representatives of a foreign state in his new capacity of President of the National Committee and Marshal of Yugoslavia. He appeared for the first time in his Marshal's uniform with a gold-embroidered wreath on the shoulders and round the collar. General MacLean, as head of the Anglo-American mission, was an honored guest.

This was the first official contact between the representatives of the three leading powers in the anti-Hitler coalition and the representatives of Yugoslavia on liberated territory in Hitler's so-called "Europafestung."

The National Committee was now confronted by a difficult task, which called not only for courage but for tremendous statesmanship. That was to get recognition of the status of legal government of Yugoslavia. It was an extremely complex problem, for the big powers continued to recognize the Royal Government in Exile as the only legal government, although in the Teheran decision they had recognized the National Liberation Army as an Allied army.

As President, Tito applied himself together with Edvard Kardelj that winter to one of the most difficult tasks in his life, that of winning recognition for the National Committee as the *de jure* government of Yugoslavia. Tito was thus starting a new page in his activities: as head of a new government, he opened negotiations with the heads of other countries with the aim of gaining recognition of the legality of the government he headed.

He had contact with the Soviet leaders only through the telegrams he exchanged with Moscow, although a representative of the General Staff of the Red Army was present in his Headquarters. During that same winter Tito entered into correspondence with Winston Churchill. In connection with the Prime Minister's illness after the Teheran meeting, Tito sent him wishes for a speedy recovery through General MacLean. Churchill responded with a personal letter and his photograph, which Tito answered immediately. In these letters Churchill acknowledged the merits of the National Liberation Army in the struggle against the Germans, but insisted that the National Committee could not be recognized as the legal government of Yugoslavia.

Tito decided to send out two military missions, one to London and Washington, and the other to Moscow. The first, headed by Vladimir Velebit, left for London, where it was received as a mission with an exclusively military character. It did not go on to Washington because the official attitude of the United States in the spring of 1944 had strangely begun to alter on Yugoslav matters. Until then American policy toward events in Yugoslavia had not differed from the British, which had the initiative. But when, toward the end of 1943, Churchill realized that the Partisans were the basic force in Yugoslavia, that nothing could be expected of Draža Mihailović, that obviously a new Yugoslavia would emerge from the war, he changed his tactics and began to establish contact with Partisan Supreme Headquarters. Moreover, Churchill decided early in 1944 to extend no further military assistance to Draža Mihailović. However, at that moment there began an independent policy of the United States toward events in Yugoslavia. Far from stopping further assistance to Draža Mihailović, they sent him a military mission headed by a colonel. Later events proved Washington's political shortsightedness.

Supreme Headquarters also sent a mission to the Soviet Union, headed by Milovan Djilas. He stayed there during most of April and May, 1944, and brought back positive impressions. To be sure, Stalin gave him no promise of recognition for the National Committee as the legal government of Yugoslavia. Djilas recounted the details of his visit to the Soviet Union: "One of the things that had to be settled in Moscow was the organization of supplies from the Soviet Union. Stalin personally ordered that an air route for Yugoslavia should be set up directly from the Ukraine. When the first crew was called to undertake this dangerous route over the Carpathians, German-occupied Rumania and Hungary, more than a hundred fliers volunteered. Some of them told our mission: 'We shall not fly by night, but in broad daylight!'

"Shortly afterward, toward the end of April, several Soviet planes arrived in Yugoslavia, dropped material and returned to their airfields in the Ukraine. The Soviet government had further decided on our suggestion to send ten Soviet transport planes to Bari so as to fly assistance to Yugoslavia.

"Stalin took an interest in the development of our struggle. To my question as to whether our line was correct, Stalin replied: 'You yourself know best, and you yourself should judge.' Then he spoke of the enormous significance of our struggle, emphasizing that 'The eyes of the whole world are turned to you!' He had only one criticism to make: 'What do you need the red stars for? You are frightening the British. The form isn't important.'

" 'But our fighters would not fight without them. They are a symbol of the anti-Fascist struggle!' I replied.

"Stalin showed special concern for the safety of Tito and the other members of the Central Committee. He warned me that we should be on our guard against assassinations and similar provocations organized abroad!

"The Presidium of the Supreme Soviet gave me a gold sword as its gift to Tito.

"Our mission toured the Ukrainian front. It was cordially received by everyone, from general to private. I had an interesting meeting with the Bishop of Uman, who said to me, 'You must realize that Stalin is the unifier of all the Russian lands.'

"Marshal Koniev gave me his own binoculars for Tito, which he had carried since the first day of the war, and a pistol to each of the members of the mission.

"A brigade was formed of Yugoslav citizens resident in the Soviet Union and of prisoners of war and refugees. There was some trouble in connection with the brigade's insignia. The Soviet authorities had decided the brigade should wear the royal emblem on their cape. Our comrades pointed out what a political error this would be, saying that our people would rebel if the brigade appeared on our territory with the royal emblem, which was worn by Draža Mihailović's Chetniks. Only after persistent representations by Veljko Vlahović, our representative in Moscow, were the royal emblems replaced with the five-pointed star. All this had occurred before our mission arrived.

"In Moscow I had a disagreement in connection with an article about Tito. The editors of the review *War and the Working Class* had asked me to write an article about Tito for them. When I handed in the manuscript, they made many observations on the text, and changed the style of my every sentence. I refused to sign such an article and only after an hour and a half's discussion did I consent, when the editor openly told me that such an article about Tito in the Soviet press would be disagreeable to Stalin. I later published the original text of this article in the Yugoslav papers."

CHAPTER XIV

1944:

"It was then for the first time in my life that I met Stalin . . ."

THE summer of 1944 was approaching. The opening of the second front was in the air. In the east, Hitler's divisions were rapidly retreating. In Italy, Allied troops had at last captured Cassino and stood before Rome. In Yugoslavia the National Liberation Army had grown to ten corps and a large number of detachments. The German High Command then decided once again to attempt to paralyze the development of the struggle in Yugoslavia. Preparations were made for an attack on Supreme Headquarters in the town of Drvar, in western Bosnia.

The German command called this operation "Rösselsprung" (the Knight's move in chess). The objective of the operation as given in the order was: "The command of the Fifteenth Mountain Army Corps with strong motorized units, with parts of the Seventh SS Mountain Division and SS Airborne Jaeger Battalion, will advance with a number of task forces concentrically in the region of Petrovac-Drvar, will overcome the resistance of the Red forces and occupy the center of the Red command. In this operation the airborne Jaeger Battalion will parachute at dawn and overcome the resistance of the enemy command, putting them out of action for a long time."

The Germans fixed May 25, Tito's birthday, as the date of the attack. Several days earlier German reconnaissance planes had flown over Drvar taking photographs.

Tito was living in a clapboard house at the mouth of a cave, above Drvar. Through the cave ran a brook, which was dry at this time of the year. On the morning of May 25, just at dawn, the Germans launched a heavy air raid over the whole town and its surroundings.

When the bombers flew off, big Junkers transports arrived and airborne troops began to drop. Then came other planes drawing gliders with additional troops, ammunition, machine guns and mortars.

There were no Partisan units in the town at that time. The Soviet and British missions were in the villages near Drvar, and no direct danger threatened them. The Germans soon broke the resistance in the town. The District Committee of the Communist Youth League of Yugoslavia (SKOJ), consisting of six men, was surrounded in a building in the center of the town. They refused the German appeals to surrender and fought to the last round, returning German hand grenades through the window. They fought until the last man fell.

A German squad advanced toward the mouth of the cave where Tito and Kardelj had taken shelter when the bombing began. The Germans opened fire at the mouth of the cave, and effectively sealed it off. A courier of Supreme Headquarters went forward to survey the terrain and discover the whereabouts of the Germans, but was wounded in the head and fell at Tito's side. The Germans slowly approached the cave.

Late in the morning, Tito and Kardelj managed to make their escape. Deep in the cave they discovered that water had worn an opening through the roof. With the aid of a rope they made their painful way up the narrow channel and emerged on the plateau over the cave, where they found Aleksandar Ranković and a group of Partisans holding off the Germans. Meanwhile a Partisan brigade had arrived outside the town and began to tighten the ring around the paratroopers. In the town the Germans had shot everyone they caught, women and children included.

The attack had been badly planned. Had airborne troops been dropped on the plateau above the cave, Tito might well have been captured. But in the end, the attack failed. Supreme Headquarters saved its records and radio station. The Germans captured only a new uniform of Tito's (which was at a tailor's in town) and a pair of top-boots, which they took at once to Vienna where they displayed them as trophies at an exhibition. The German airborne battalion suffered heavy losses, and was driven into the cemetery near Drvar, but at dawn strong German tank forces arrived and rescued these survivors.

During the attack on Drvar, the heaviest losses were suffered by

the civilian population. Two Allied correspondents, Stojan Pribičević of the American press and Talbot of the British press, were captured. Later Pribičević was freed by Partisan units, but Talbot remained in captivity. Randolph Churchill, the son of the British Prime
Minister, who had parachuted to the liberated territory as a British
liaison officer, was not in direct danger, for he had retreated with
one of our units.

The German High Command was silent about the results of the
Drvar attack until the opening of the second front. Then on June 6
it released with great pomp an announcement of the attack on Supreme Headquarters immediately after the report about the opening
of the second front. It said:

"In Croatia units of the armed forces and SS units under the command of Colonel General Rendulic, supported by strong fighter and
bomber units, attacked and destroyed the Headquarters of the Tito
bandit groupings after several days' hard fighting. The enemy lost, as
far as can be ascertained, 6,240 men. Besides this, many different
weapons were seized, in addition to stores."

What the inner circle around Hitler thought of Tito and fighting
in Yugoslavia is best shown by a statement made by Himmler to the
Commanders of Wehrkreise and Chief Training Officers on the 21st
of September, 1944, at Jägerhöhe. The extracts of this speech were
captured in Germany and handed over to the Yugoslav government
by the British Ambassador in 1945 after the end of the war. This is
Himmler's opinion of Tito as expressed in that speech:

"I would like to give another example of steadfastness, that of
Marshal Tito. I must really say that he is an old Communist, this
Herr Josip Broz, a consistent man. Unfortunately he is our opponent.
He really has properly earned his title of Marshal. When we catch
him we shall do him in at once. You can be sure of that. He is our
enemy, but I wish we had a dozen Titos in Germany, men who were
leaders and had such great resolution and good nerves that though
they were forever encircled they would never give in. The man had
nothing, nothing at all. He was between the Russians, the British and
the Americans, and had the nerve actually to fool and humiliate the
British and Americans in the most comical way. He is a Moscow
man. He had arms delivered from there. He was always encircled,
and the man found a way out every time. He has never capitulated.

We know better than anyone how he gets under our skin in the Serb-Croat district, and that is only because he fights consistently. He has the cheek to call a battalion a brigade, and we fall for it straight away. A brigade? In Heaven's name. The military mind at once imagines a group of 6–8,000 men. A thousand vagabonds who have been herded together suddenly become a brigade. Divisions and corps are knocked to pieces by us, and the man forms them up again every time. Be sure he only succeeded in doing that because he is an uncompromising and steadfast soldier, a steadfast commander."

The attack on Partisans' Supreme Headquarters in 1944 provoked great attention. Goebbels' propaganda spread its interpretation of this attack. The most amusing account was published by Franco's paper, *Madrid*, on June 13, under the headline, "Tito Surrounded by German Troops Loses Morale." Franco's paper first said that Tito "escaped on a horse he had stolen that morning from a farm near the town," and then continued:

"Passing through villages and settlements, Tito is committing every possible crime. A captive gave an account of the incredible crimes committed by Tito, who kills for the sake of killing. For this reason Tito is greatly feared in Partisan ranks. Nor do the Partisans, following Tito's example, shrink from murder, robbery and other inhuman deeds. Tito wears a long, utterly unkempt beard, his features are hard. He wears trousers of cloth, boots and a jacket of leather, and on his head a winter cap with a big five-pointed star in the middle. On his breast he wears a badge with the hammer and sickle."

The Allied press, for its part, published extensive and in the main objective accounts. *Pravda* also wrote of the attack on Drvar. It published a report by Tass from Cairo headlined "Unsuccessful Hitlerite Attempt to Capture Marshal Tito's Headquarters."

The attack on Drvar marked the opening of the Seventh Offensive, which developed exclusively in the area of western Bosnia. Units of the First, Fifth and Eighth Corps were engaged on our side in this offensive. The fighting lasted some ten days; the Germans charged stubbornly and there were fierce encounters. In this offensive we had for the first time the help of Allied planes, which appeared in large numbers and hampered the operations of the German air force. Supreme Headquarters, headed by Tito, and the Allied military missions, were with our units during this offensive. Then Tito decided to find a more secure place for the National Committee and Supreme

Headquarters, where it would be easier for them to work. Early in June the National Committee and a part of Supreme Headquarters with Tito took off for Bari from an airfield in the Bosnian mountains near the town of Kupres in a Dakota flown by the Soviet pilot Shornikov; Tito was transferred several days later by a British destroyer to the Yugoslav island of Vis, which the Partisans had freed in September, 1943. The National Committee and Supreme Headquarters came to the island later. From here connections were much easier, both with the outside world and the interior of the country.

Supreme Headquarters took up a position on a hill in the middle of the island. There were several caves in the rock which became the offices, and sleeping quarters were set up in tents in front of them.

Vis became a veritable beehive. Partisan commanders arrived every day from the remotest parts of Yugoslavia: from Macedonia, Vojvodina, Slovenia. Anglo-American and Soviet transports landed on improvised airfields in the mountains and plains of Vojvodina on liberated territory, and from there took Partisan commanders or political workers to Bari, where they went on by sea or air to Supreme Headquarters on the island of Vis. In addition to this, there was daily radio connection with all the corps.

There was always the chance that the Germans would attempt a landing on the island, so it was fortified.* A group of British Commandos was also stationed at Vis, chiefly to man the antiaircraft artillery.

Basic political activity was continued about the question of the recognition of the National Committee as the legal Yugoslav government. The Royal Yugoslav Government, headed by Božidar Purić, with Draža Mihailović as Minister of War, was in Cairo. It no longer enjoyed a reputation abroad. General Dušan Simović, who had been head of the government on March 27, 1941, when Yugoslavia entered the war, made a statement over the London radio in which he said:

"Not to recognize the National Liberation Army and the National Liberation Movement means to work against the Allies for the enemy. The National Liberation Movement enjoys the support of

---

* According to reports captured in the German archives the German High Command had prepared a new attack on Supreme Headquarters on the island of Vis, but this action was upset by the attempt on Hitler's life on June 20, 1944, and was postponed.

Russia, Great Britain, America. This movement must co-ordinate the activity of all patriots both at home and abroad with one chief purpose—to defeat the enemy."

In Moscow the Ambassador of the royal government in the Soviet Union, Stanoje Simić, had tendered his resignation, and had written a letter which *Pravda* published, sharply attacking the royal government. Our people in the Soviet Union pursued action for recognition of the National Committee. Yugoslavia's representative in the Soviet Union, Veljko Vlahović, wrote an article for the Soviet magazine *War and the Working Class,* asking for recognition for the National Committee as the legal government of Yugoslavia. The editors of this semiofficial organ of the Soviet Ministry of Foreign Affairs accepted the article but said it would be inconvenient if Veljko Vlahović, a Yugoslav, signed it and asked the Soviet historian and academician Derzhavin to sign it. But when the article was published, a subsequent number carried a criticism of it, and *War and the Working Class* withdrew its request for the recognition of the National Committee. The unfortunate Professor Derzhavin was astonished and called on Veljko Vlahović, to complain about the mess he had got him into, because to be publicly refuted by a review or paper in the Soviet Union is the first step toward liquidation. Vlahović explained that no responsibility attached to the old professor, that the editors of *War and the Working Class* had suggested him and that Vlahović as a Yugoslav regretted the whole affair, especially since the Soviet Union had so drastically withdrawn her support of the National Committee at such an important time in Yugoslavia's struggle.

Events developed rapidly. King Peter and his Prime Minister Božidar Purić were summoned to London. Consultations were held in connection with the reconstruction of the royal government. The choice of a new Prime Minister fell on Dr. Ivan Šubašić, a Croatian politician, who had been Governor of Croatia till 1941. The first particulars of this were announced by Churchill in the House of Commons on May 24. He also declared that Draža Mihailović would not be Minister of War in the new cabinet, and that supplies to the Chetniks had been stopped by the British.

In the meantime the attack on Drvar had taken place, and as soon as the National Committee and Supreme Headquarters had moved to

Vis, steps were taken for the creation of a joint government of the National Committee and the Yugoslav Royal Government. Tito had received a telegram from Churchill saying that King Peter's representative, Dr. Ivan Šubašić, would come to Vis. It is characteristic that the Soviet government had given its consent about this project, through their military mission in Yugoslavia. At that time something had already been heard in Yugoslavia about an agreement between the Soviet Union and Great Britain to divide Yugoslavia into spheres of influence.*

Dr. Ivan Šubašić arrived in Vis in June, 1944, where he was re-

---

* In my *Partisan Diary*, published in three volumes after the war in Yugoslavia, I speak about this matter on page 165 (third volume of *Diary*):

"An American journalist well versed in the political situation explained to me the line of American policy. He told me that an agreement had been reached between the Soviet Union and Great Britain dividing Yugoslavia into spheres of influence, and that the negotiations between Šubašić and Tito were the outcome of this agreement. That an agreement had been arrived at between the Russians and English for work in the Balkans is borne out by the fact that the British propaganda organization for the Balkans has already adjusted its work in the spirit of this agreement. It has discontinued all propaganda work in Rumania, and intensified it in Yugoslavia, where it will work fifty-fifty with the Russians. Similarly the Russians will stop all propaganda work in Greece.

"I answered this American that I did not believe in such arrangements. The Russians would never make arrangements behind the back of other nations."

Below this text in the same edition of my *Diary* a footnote was added, written after the war:

"However, an agreement between the Soviet Union and Great Britain on a division of spheres of influence in the Balkans against the interest and without the knowledge of the Balkan nations had really been reached. During the war we met many indications that there was such an agreement, but in our boundless faith in the Soviet Union we considered such arrangements impossible. Besides the instance of the talk with the American journalist in Bari, I know that during the summer of 1944 Randolph Churchill boasted on the liberated territory in Croatia that his father had written him a letter informing him of the division of Yugoslavia between the Soviet Union and Great Britain on a fifty-fifty basis.

"One of the telling consequences of this arrangement is the Tito-Šubašić cabinet, whose formation was officially confirmed at the Yalta Conference, and even extended to compelling us to admit into the AVNOJ a number of members from Stojadinović's Assembly of 1938, elected under the 1931 constitution of Petar Živković.

"After the war several documents were published that corroborate the agreement between the Soviet Union and Great Britain. These facts were revealed by Cordell Hull in his memoirs, as well as by Edward Stettinius in his book *Roosevelt and the Russians*."

Moscow never denied this deal with Winston Churchill.

ceived with all honors. He was accompanied by the British Ambassador to the Yugoslav Royal Government, Ralph Stevenson.

Šubašić arrived with a proposal that the Partisan National Committee should be abolished, that is to say, that it should be incorporated with the Royal Yugoslav Government. The first plenary meeting took place in Tito's cave, where the whole National Committee had assembled. As far as the mouth of the cave Šubašić was accompanied by the British Ambassador, Stevenson, who then withdrew to the house of the chief of the British Military Mission, Brigadier Fitzroy MacLean. The meeting opened with a report by Šubašić, who began by saying that King Peter was the actual commander of all the armed forces in Yugoslavia, invoking the Constitution of 1931.

From the Partisan side, Edvard Kardelj took the floor first and then Tito, Bakarić and others. They rejected the proposals of Šubašić. At the end the old Dalmatian, Josip Smodlaka, the Commissioner of Foreign Affairs of the National Committee, added a dose of his irony to his statement.

In well-chosen words Smodlaka drew Šubašić's attention to the fact that he had passed in silence over the National Committee, that it was impossible to make an arrangement between two governments in one nation, that there could be no talk of a joint command, "because you have no army," that the agreement was a sacrifice for the Partisans, "because you would not hear a single voice for it among the people."

Smodlaka concluded with the following words:

"You have neither people, nor an army, nor territory."

Then the meeting was adjourned. Šubašić and Kardelj withdrew and had a private meeting in order to try to find a joint solution. After long and laborious work, they succeeded at last. Almost all the proposals of Šubašić were rejected. All the proposals of the National Committee were agreed upon, except a few technicalities.

In the plenary meeting Šubašić accepted at last all our proposals. Over the question of the monarchy there were the greatest difficulties. Šubašić accepted the wording that the question of monarchy would be solved after the war by the free will of the Yugoslav people. This formulation did not appeal to the British Ambassador and he later made an official visit, asking that this wording be changed. But the National Committee rejected this demand.

Finally an agreement was signed by which Šubašić, on his part, in the name of the royal government recognized the National Committee as the sole authority in the country, and the National Liberation Army under Tito's command as the sole army, condemning all those who publicly or covertly collaborated with the Germans, and agreeing to form a new cabinet in London and to broaden it with democratic elements. On its part the National Committee undertook not to raise the question of monarchy during the war, since both parties had decided to leave this question for the final decision of the people after the liberation.

The new cabinet formed in London did not include Draža Mihailović. Two adherents of the National Liberation Movement, Vukosavljević and Marušić, were taken into it, not as representatives of the National Committee but in their own names, so that no coalition government was formed.

After these important decisions, life on the island of Vis became more animated. Visitors from abroad were ever more frequent. One day a vessel arrived with Greek sailors who kissed the "free Balkan soil" on landing. Shortly afterward the EAM (the National Liberation Movement of Greece) sent its representative, A. Dzimas, as delegate to the National Committee in Yugoslavia. Talks for the exchange of military missions began with the French National Committee and the Czechoslovak government.

The small airfield on the island was soon expanded and became an auxiliary airfield for bombers of the Fifth American Air Force during its attacks on military and industrial centers in Central Europe and the Balkans. Bombers returning from these tasks damaged or short of fuel would land at Vis. One day in August nine Liberators made forced landings on the Vis airfield.

About that time the Allied Air Force carried out one of its largest rescues of Partisan casualties. On Mount Durmitor a number of our units, with about nine hundred wounded, were surrounded by the Germans. Tito personally asked the Allied command to save these wounded because of the danger that Germans would kill them all, and to restore the mobility of our units. Tito's request was granted and about noon one day in August, twenty-five Dakotas escorted by fighters landed on Mount Durmitor, on an improvised airfield. All nine hundred wounded were rescued. The German positions were a few miles away, but the whole operation was accomplished without incident.

The formation of a joint government remained one of the basic questions with which the National Committee had to contend. Pressure came from several quarters. One day General Wilson, the Allied Commander of the Mediterranean, invited Tito to visit him at Caserta, in Italy. It was also learned that King Peter was in Italy and there was a possibility of Tito's being faced with a *fait accompli;* that is, of being obliged by the circumstances of his visit to General Wilson to meet the King. Other reasons too dictated that Tito should not accept the invitation.

Consequently the Central Committee, at Tito's suggestion, decided that Tito should not visit General Wilson on this occasion. This was received with indignation in General Wilson's Headquarters, for they had been convinced Tito would come.

The visit was postponed for a time and finally took place on August 10. The meeting with General Wilson was extremely formal. General Wilson's manners left an impression quite different from that of other Allied commanders in Italy, such as General Alexander or the American General Eaker. In General Wilson's behavior the Yugoslavs felt something offending. The only cheerful moment of the meeting occurred during the luncheon General Wilson gave in Tito's honor. Italian waiters were serving and two of Tito's bodyguards, armed with tommy-guns, watched them suspiciously, because they had heard one of them speaking Serbian. They feared he might be a Fascist who had been in Yugoslavia with the occupation troops, and fearing for Tito's life they stood near him with their tommy-guns during the luncheon. The situation was extremely trying. First, the host began to laugh softly, followed by Tito, and then by the whole assembly. Tito then signaled his escorts to withdraw.

That same evening General Ira C. Eaker, commander of the Fifteenth American Air Force, gave a reception in his Headquarters in Tito's honor. Eaker gave Tito the impression of being a frank man, a soldier who said clearly what he thought.

Tito received also an invitation from General Alexander, the Commander of the Eighth Army, to visit him at the front, in his Headquarters near Lake Bolsena, north of Rome. Tito left on this journey by plane, together with General MacLean and with his escort.

"Tiger" went, too. On the way the plane circled various battlefields in Italy, staying longest over Cassino.

Tito was sitting forward next to the pilot, who asked him if he would care to take the controls. He showed Tito the rudimentary moves, and put the control lever into his hand just as the plane was making a wide circle over Cassino.

At that moment the pilot smiled at Tito and said:

"Excuse me, I must go back for some cigarettes. Will you please right the plane."

"I wasn't a bit pleased," Tito said later. "It was easy while the plane was keeping a straight course, but now it had banked, and I had only had two minutes' 'flying time.' "

The pilot returned after a few moments. Tito laughed happily and the plane flew on toward Rome. There it ran into a storm; the clouds were pitch black, lightning streaked around the plane. Tito suggested to MacLean: "Let's head for the sea; if we fall it will be softer!"

The wind grew stronger. Tito was given a parachute. He was airsick too, and when they landed near Lake Bolsena he was not feeling his best. But General Alexander was an excellent host in every way.

After a stay at the front, Tito returned to Rome. He had never been to the Italian capital before, and set out to see St. Peter's, the Colosseum, accompanied by two Partisans with their tommy-guns across their breasts.

Emerging from the Colosseum, he was recognized by some Italians, who began to wave and shout: "Tito, Tito."

From Rome Tito returned to Naples, where on August 12 he met Winston Churchill. The meeting took place in what was once Queen Victoria's villa. Tito had several talks with Churchill, first attended only by Tito, Churchill and an interpreter, and later attended on the Yugoslav side by Žujović, Vladimir Velebit, Šubašić, Sava Kosanović and others. The talks covered a wide range of questions. Tito was impressed by Churchill's strength and lucidity. The British Prime Minister began by praising our army; then they passed on to the operations in Yugoslavia. Churchill said he was sorry he was so advanced in age and could not land by parachute, otherwise he would be in Yugoslavia fighting.

"But you have sent your son!" said Tito.

At that moment tears glistened in Churchill's eyes.

Tito

The fundamental matter upon which the talks centered was King Peter. Churchill asked Tito whether he would meet the King. Tito invoked the decision of the AVNOJ prohibiting King Peter's return, stressing that he was unpopular because of his wartime record, and that we should do nothing to weaken the struggle against the enemy.

Churchill asked again if Tito would meet King Peter on a warship, if nowhere else. Tito replied that he had no objection to visiting Churchill on a warship, and if King Peter was present he would of course meet him, too.

Churchill saw that nothing could be done and waved his hand. During further talks Churchill asked Tito what he thought about receiving King Peter in Yugoslavia as a flier.

Tito said: "Let him come, and fight as we are fighting!"

The talk went on to relations between Yugoslavia and Bulgaria. Churchill asked: "What are your relations with Bulgaria?"

Tito replied that the relations would develop in the direction of brotherhood in spite of the present situation.

Churchill suddenly asked in the course of the conversation whether it was our intention to establish socialism in Yugoslavia on the Soviet model.

Tito's reply was that Soviet experience would be useful, but that we should take our own conditions into consideration. Churchill went on to say that the situation in Serbia was different, that the peasants there wanted not the Partisans but Draža Mihailović, that the Serbian people should be given the opportunity of expressing their free will, that Stalin had had the greatest difficulties with the peasants, etc.

There was also discussion about Istria and Trieste. Churchill was noncommittal. He said Trieste would be important for Allied operations against Austria.

Churchill then took Tito to his study and showed him a chart of the operations on the Allied fronts. That very day had been fixed for the invasion of southern France by Allied troops.

The British Prime Minister asked Tito whether he would like to take a picture with him and the Prime Minister of the Royal Government Šubašić. Tito gladly accepted this offer. Churchill placed Tito at the right of him and Prime Minister Šubašić to the left of him. But Tito remarked at once to Churchill:

"Prime Minister, aren't you making a mistake? Your Tory Party will be very angry if they see this picture. You have placed a Prime Minister of a King to the left of you."

Churchill laughed heartily and placed Šubašić to the right and Tito to the left. The same day the British Prime Minister gave a gala banquet in Tito's honor.

During the second meeting with Churchill, Tito received a report from Supreme Headquarters that the Second, Fifth and Seventeenth Yugoslav Divisions had penetrated into Serbia, routed the Germans, Bulgarians and Chetniks on Mount Kopaonik, and joined up with the Serbian divisions at Toplica. Further operations had developed favorably. The Partisan units were driving steadily toward the Sava and the Danube. Tito immediately ordered other units of the Fifth and Sixth Proletarian Divisions to enter Serbia, as well as the Twelfth Corps.

He then returned to Vis. The big Soviet offensive in Rumania had begun. Units of the Red Army soon routed the Germans and Rumanians and descended toward the Danube. The day was approaching when they would unite with the units of the National Liberation Army of Yugoslavia. That junction took place on September 6. To mark it Tito issued an Order of the Day.

In connection with the meeting of the Red Army and units of the National Liberation Army, Ilya Ehrenburg wrote an article entitled "Together" which was published in the Soviet press and read over the Moscow radio. The article was read in all the units of the National Liberation Army, in the whole of Yugoslavia, until the men knew it by heart. In this article Ilya Ehrenburg said among other things:

"A friend is not tested at the feasting table but in adversity. Nations are not tested at conferences but on the field of battle, in terrible war, in days of tribulation. In those days the strong have proved weak, and some of the weak strong. . . .

"Let the diplomats at the peace conference revise the map. In 1941 Yugoslavia was marked as a small country. On the scales on which the diplomats attempted to find the famous balance of power, Yugoslavia was a small weight, like Rumania. Two years have elapsed and we now see a miracle. Yugoslavia has penetrated to the front ranks. The whole world is talking about the Yugoslav National Liberation

Tito

Army. The name of Marshal Tito has reached the five continents of the world. When the war ends, Yugoslavia will go to the peace conference not with the supply train but with the vanguard. She has not only freed a whole series of districts of her territory but has won a new honorable place in postwar Europe.

"On this glorious eve, our Soviet people and our army think with elation of the epic of new Yugoslavia. We were together in adversity —we shall be together at the celebration!"

The end of September was approaching, and Tito decided to leave for the Soviet Union in order to confer with the Soviet representatives on the co-ordination of operations between the Red Army and the National Liberation Army. He left for this journey on his own initiative but with the obvious approval of Moscow, for when he informed the chief of the Soviet Military Mission, General Kornieyev, of his intention, the Russian said with satisfaction: "Very pleasant news. Only keep the time of your departure strictly secret."

Tito boarded a Dakota on September 21, at eleven o'clock at night. The plane was flown by Soviet pilots. The night was dark, the take-off from the small airfield at Vis rather difficult. Tito had first to fly across Yugoslavia to Krajova, Marshal Tolbukhin's Headquarters, and then on to Moscow. He was accompanied by General Kornieyev, Ivan Milutinović of Supreme Headquarters and his secretary Mitar Bakić. As he was leaving, his dog "Tiger" refused to keep still. He was constantly by his master, and Tito had to take him on the plane. In case the dog barked when they were boarding, a sack was pulled over his head.

The flight to Rumania was without incident, although they passed over several towns still in German hands. At Krajova Tito received a delegation from Bulgaria headed by Dobri Terpeshev. This delegation asked the National Committee to sign an armistice in order to help Bulgaria clear her honor. It further requested that the Bulgarians should be permitted to send their army to fight with ours in the final operations against Hitlerite Germany. Finally an agreement in this spirit was made and signed at Krajova. After that Tito left with General Kornieyev for Moscow. They flew by day escorted by fighters, for the front was still close and there was danger of aircraft attack. Thus after five years Tito was in Moscow again, not as an underground worker this time, a man who had to hide from the police, not with a forged passport, but under his full name, as Marshal of Yugoslavia and as the President of the National Committee. Behind him were five years of hard struggle and efforts, and sustaining him was the support of the overwhelming majority of the Yugoslav peoples, united in the National Liberation Movement.

This is how Tito describes that journey to Moscow in 1944:

"It was then for the first time in my life that I met Stalin and talked to him. Until then I had only seen him from a distance, as during the Seventh Congress of the Comintern. It seemed to me that he looked much shorter than he appeared on the photographs. On the other hand, he gave me the impression of a man full of energy, although a little bit tired. During my stay, I lived in a villa in which Winston Churchill stayed during his visit to Moscow.

"This time I had several meetings with Stalin, two or three in his study in the Kremlin, and twice at his private house, where I had supper with him.

"One of the first things we discussed was the question of joint operation between our two armies. It was in his study in the Kremlin. I asked for a tank division to help our units during the liberation of Belgrade. In the eastern parts of Yugoslavia we had no tanks or heavy artillery while the Germans were armed to the teeth with the most modern weapons. Stalin agreed to my request, and said:

" 'Walter (as they called me in Moscow), I shall give you not one division, but a whole tank corps!'

"We also reached an understanding as to how much of Yugoslavia to free with our joint forces, what point their troops and ours were to go to, and, finally, how long their troops were to remain in our country. We agreed that they were to give us a tank corps to liberate Belgrade with, and then their forces were to withdraw from Yugoslavia after Belgrade was freed, their left flank being thus strengthened for the attack on Budapest.

"After these talks we wrote a joint communiqué in which this understanding was defined. The communiqué was published by Tass on September 28, 1944. It read:

" 'Several days ago the Soviet command—bearing in mind the interests of the development of operations against the Germans and Hungarian troops in Hungary—asked the National Committee of Liberation of Yugoslavia and the Supreme Headquarters of the Na-

tional Liberation Army and Partisan Detachments of Yugoslavia to
consent to the temporary entry of Soviet troops into Yugoslav territory, which borders on Hungary. The Soviet command on this occasion declared that Soviet troops, having completed their operative
task, would be withdrawn from Yugoslavia.

" 'The National Committee and Supreme Headquarters of Yugoslavia agreed to meet the request of the Soviet command. The Soviet
command accepted the condition advanced by the Yugoslav side that
the civil administration of the National Committee of Liberation of
Yugoslavia should be operative on the territory of Yugoslavia in the
areas where the units of the Red Army are located.'

"Otherwise, the first meeting was very cool. The basic cause, I
think, were the telegrams I had sent during the war, especially that
one I began with the words, 'If you cannot send us assistance, then
at least do not hamper us.' This was confirmed to me by Dimitrov
when I visited him immediately after my first meeting with Stalin.
He told me:

" 'Walter, Walter, the Hazyahzin was terribly angry with you
because of that telegram. . . . He stamped with rage.'

"Dimitrov wanted to let me know by this that he had actually
defended me before Stalin.*

"As I have said, tension arose at this first meeting with Stalin. We
were more or less at cross purposes on all the matters we discussed. I
noticed then that Stalin could not bear being contradicted. In conversation with the men around him he is coarse and touchy. Of all
the members of the Politburo of the Soviet Central Committee it is
only Molotov to whom he turns occasionally to ask an opinion, but

---

* Dimitrov in general was favorable to Yugoslavs. It is true that in 1938 he fell
for the intrigues of some Bulgars in Moscow against Tito, but later he changed
his mind. For a very long time Dimitrov was married to a Yugoslav worker by
the name of Ljuba Jovošević. They didn't have children. In 1933 when Dimitrov
was arrested in Germany by the Gestapo, and when the news of his arrest
arrived in Moscow, his wife thought that he would never return from Hitler's
prison, and in despair she committed suicide. She jumped through the window
from the third floor of the Hotel Lux, in which lived all the officials of the
Comintern. Later Dimitrov married for the second time. His wife was of German origin. They had a child, a son, of whom Dimitrov was very fond. According to Ivan Karaivanov, Dimitrov's friend and co-worker in the Comintern,
when the boy was born, Dimitrov announced proudly to his friend: "Listen, I
got a son." During the war, in 1943, the boy died. That was a very hard blow
for Dimitrov. After that he changed a lot.

he never listens to him to the end, but goes on with his own idea.

"I was not used to such conversation, which led to simply uncomfortable scenes. For instance Stalin said to me:

" 'Walter, be careful, the bourgeoisie in Serbia is very strong!'

"I answered calmly:

" 'Comrade Stalin, I do not agree with your view. The bourgeoisie in Serbia is very weak.'

"He was silent and frowned and the others at the table, Molotov, Zhdanov, Malyenkov, Beria, gaped.

"Stalin then began to inquire after different bourgeois politicians in Yugoslavia, where they were, what they were doing, and I replied, 'He is a scoundrel, a traitor, he worked with the Germans.'

"Stalin asked about another one. I gave the same answer. Stalin flared up:

" 'Walter,' he said, 'to you they are all scoundrels!'

"I replied, 'Exactly, Comrade Stalin: anyone who betrays his country is a scoundrel.'

"Stalin frowned again, while Malyenkov, Zhdanov and the others looked at me askance.

"The talk proceeded in a very painful atmosphere. Stalin began to assure me of the need to reinstate King Peter. The blood rushed to my head that he could advise us to do such a thing. I composed myself and told him it was impossible, people would rebel, that in Yugoslavia the king personifies treason, that he had fled and left his people in the midst of their struggle, that the Karageorgevich dynasty was hated among the people for corruption and terror.

"Stalin was silent, and then said briefly:

" 'You need not restore him forever. Take him back temporarily, and then you can slip a knife into his back at a suitable moment.'

"At this moment Molotov returned to the room, which he had left a moment back. He carried a telegram from a Western news agency reporting that the British had landed in Yugoslavia.

"I leaped to my feet: 'That's impossible!'

"Stalin, angrily: 'Why impossible! It is a fact!'

"I repeated that it was impossible and probably the agency was mistaken; that we had asked General Alexander to send us three batteries of heavy artillery to help our Fourth Army in its operations toward Mostar and Sarajevo, and the arrival of this artillery had probably been mistaken for an invasion of Yugoslavia by the British.

"Stalin was silent, and then he asked the direct question: 'Tell me, Walter, what would you do if the British really forced a landing in Yugoslavia?'

" 'We should offer determined resistance.'

"Stalin was silent. Obviously this answer was not to his liking. Was he at that moment pondering over the arrangements he had made for a division of spheres of influence in Yugoslavia?

"That evening Stalin was permanently angry. He phoned Marshal Malinovsky in my presence. Malinovsky had been halted by the Germans at that time.

" 'You're asleep there, asleep!' said Stalin over the wires.

"Malinovsky must have said something to the effect that he had insufficient tank divisions, for Stalin retorted, 'You say you haven't tank divisions. My grandma would know how to fight with tanks. It's time you moved. Do you understand me?'

"Stalin put down the receiver, and invited me to his villa for supper. The servants in white aprons brought in covered dishes of food, and we all helped ourselves. There we drank toasts deep into the night. I had not been used to drinking, and I felt sick. At one point I went outside because I felt so bad. I cursed myself out loud for having drunk so much, and I heard Beria's voice behind me: 'That's nothing, these things will happen. . . .' "

Tito returned to Yugoslavia across Rumania several days later. The fighting for Belgrade had begun. The Germans resisted fiercely. Our First, Fifth, Sixth, Eleventh, Sixteenth, Seventeenth, Twenty-first, Twenty-eighth and Thirty-sixth Divisions, composing the First Army Group, and the Soviet Fourth Moto-mechanized Corps under General Zhdanov supporting our divisions with its tanks, were engaged in this operation. The battle lasted six days and ended with the final liberation of Belgrade. Both we and the Russians had suffered considerable losses. In connection with the liberation of Belgrade Stalin issued an Order of the Day, and *Pravda* carried it with a banner headline across the whole of the front page:

"Troops of the Third Ukrainian Front, together with Troops of National Liberation Army of Yugoslavia Liberated Belgrade, Capital of Our Allied Yugoslavia, from German Invaders."

Tito also issued a similar Order of the Day. Directly afterward the

Soviet Central Committee issued its rallying cries in connection with the anniversary of the October Revolution. One was dedicated to Yugoslavia: "Greetings to the Yugoslav people! Long live the heroic National Liberation Army of Yugoslavia, which is liberating its homeland from the German conquerors shoulder to shoulder with the Red Army."

In one of Belgrade's suburbs, not far from the German concentration camp at Banjica, where the Germans had put more than thirty thousand people to death, Tito reviewed the units that had taken part in the liberation of Belgrade. The First Proletarian Brigade, founded in 1941, marched past and then the Belgrade Battalion which, three and a half years earlier, had started out from Serbia, fought over almost the whole of Yugoslavia, and now returned to its native city. Of those who had set out with it in 1941 only two were left. Some had been promoted to the command of other units, but most had been killed. Tito ended his review of the troops with the words:

"In the most difficult hours of the war, in the most terrible offensives, I always thought to myself, 'In Belgrade we began the uprising; in Belgrade we shall end it in victory!' That great day has now come. Among us there are very few of those who set out in 1941. They built their lives into the foundations of this country that it might be free and what the people wish it to be. Their example was followed by thousands of others. Every fallen rifle was seized by ten other hands. Glory to the fighters who fell for the liberation of Yugoslavia, for the liberation of her capital Belgrade!"

The liberation of Belgrade thwarted the German High Command's plan to establish the southern flank of the German eastern front on Yugoslavia's eastern frontiers by uniting the groups "F" and "E" which had been south of Belgrade, mostly in Greece, with the group "Serbian."

While the Belgrade operation was being prepared, units of the National Liberation Army in Macedonia, with the co-operation of units of the First and Fourth Bulgarian Armies, began the battle to liberate Macedonia from the German group "E" (the 11th, 22nd, 41st, 104th and Skenderbeg divisions and the 40th Independent Battalion), which was withdrawing from Greece along the Vardar valley. By November the whole of Macedonia had been freed. The German group "E" was unable to retreat along the Vardar and

Morava valleys and had to turn toward Kosovo to pass through Bosnia. Shortly afterward Montenegro was also free. The front stood about one hundred kilometers west of Belgrade in Srem, and extended southward to Sarajevo and westward to the Adriatic Sea. There were no longer any Soviet units in Yugoslavia; only in the north, on the River Drava, were there the Bulgarian units.

Then came the meeting between Roosevelt, Stalin and Churchill at Yalta, in the Soviet Union. The National Committee had not been informed of this meeting. On February 12, 1945, the British and the Soviet Military Missions in Belgrade informed the National Committee that the heads of the three governments had discussed the Yugoslav question at the plenary meeting of the Yalta Conference on February 10, and had agreed to make the following recommendations to Marshal Tito:

"a) That the Tito-Šubašić agreement should be enforced immediately, and that a new government should be formed on the basis of this agreement;

"b) That upon formation the new government should declare:

1. That the AVNOJ should incorporate members of the last Yugoslav National Assembly who had not compromised themselves by collaboration with the enemy, thus creating a body to be known as the Provisional Assembly, and

2. That the AVNOJ's legislative acts should be subject to subsequent ratification by the Constitutional Assembly."

This decision provoked the deepest indignation among the supporters of the National Liberation Movement in Yugoslavia; people were particularly indignant that the AVNOJ had to incorporate members of the 1938 Assembly, which had been elected during the regime of Milan Stojadinović, an Axis man.

Nevertheless, after much persuasion this decision was accepted and the joint government was formed after long negotiations. But the National Committee made the reservation that the new government should not be responsible to the King, but to a regency; and that the regency should not be appointed without the approval of the National Committee. These reservations were accepted by the King. The regency was made up of men well known for their liberalism. The National Committee was impelled to accept this decision because the country was faced with serious difficulties; hard fighting with the Germans still lay ahead.

At that time, the armed intervention of British troops in the Greek internal affairs produced quite a commotion in Belgrade. Public opinion was very much disturbed. This move of Winston Churchill was regarded as an act of sheer intervention. In Belgrade, it was stated that his action was equally aimed against the People's Liberation Movement in Yugoslavia.

The German command endeavored to stabilize the front in Yugoslavia by linking it with the fronts in Hungary and Italy. In January, February and March the Germans launched a number of offensive operations on this front remarkable for the scope and number of the troops engaged.

Toward the end of February, 1945, Field Marshal Alexander, the Commander of the Mediterranean, arrived in Belgrade on an official visit. He had a number of meetings with Tito, at which a plan of coordinating operations between the Yugoslav army and the Allied armies was established. An agreement was reached that the Allied forces in Italy should supply the Yugoslav Fourth Army, operating in western parts of the country. Tito gave a reception in the Officers' Club in Belgrade in his honor which was attended by the Soviet General Kisselyev, the American General Lemnitzer, and by the British General MacLean, who was leaving his mission after two years' work. The Yugoslavs remember MacLean as a courageous officer.

The day of the final downfall of Hitler's Germany was approaching. The Allied armies had already crossed the Rhine and penetrated deep into the heart of Germany. The Red Army was fighting at the approaches to Berlin.

Just before the beginning of the general offensive of the Yugoslav army for the final liberation of the country, there were seven German army corps in Yugoslavia (the 15th Mountain, the 15th Cossack, the 21st, 34th, 69th, 91st and 97th) with seventeen divisions (the 1st and 2nd Cossack, the 11th, 41st, 104th, 22nd, 181st, 7th SS, 369th, 373rd, 392nd, 237th, 188th, 438th, 138th, 14th SS Ruthenian and the Division Stefan). In addition to these forces the Germans in Yugoslavia had naval forces to defend the coast and strong police forces to secure the rear. Under their command stood armed Quisling formations of about twenty divisions.

At that time the Yugoslav army was about eight hundred thousand strong, organized into the First, Second, Third and Fourth Armies, and the 2nd, 3rd, 4th, 5th, 6th, 7th, 9th and 10th Corps outside army composition.

The general offensive of the Yugoslav army for the definitive liberation of the country began on March 20, 1945, and developed mainly on the following lines:

The Fourth Army, under the command of Petar Drapšin, broke through the enemy front in Lika from March 20 to April 16, liberated Lika and the Croatian littoral, including the islands, and reached the old Yugoslav-Italian border.

Fighting for Rijeka took place from April 16 to May 7. The enemy front was pierced in the northern direction April 27, and Trieste was liberated (May 1), the 97th German Army Corps was surrounded and forced to surrender (May 7) and a motorized detachment of the Fourth Army penetrated into Carinthia and the Celovec sector and, linking up with the units of the Third Army, closed the ring around the enemy forces in Yugoslavia.

The Third Army, under the command of Kosta Nadj, forced the Drava on April 12, fanned out through the Podravina, reached a point north of Zagreb, crossed the Austro-Yugoslav border in the sector of Dravograd, and closed the ring around the enemy forces in Yugoslavia with the motorized detachment of the Fourth Army in Carinthia.

The First Army, under the command of Peko Dapčević, penetrated the enemy fortified front in Srem on April 12, and on April 22 smashed the enemy defenses and continued its advance toward Zagreb.

The Second Army, under the command of Koča Popović, went to the offensive on April 5, forced the Bosna River (April 16–17), liberated Doboj and reached the Una River. Continuing its operations for the liberation of Zagreb in co-operation with units of the First Army, it freed Zagreb on May 8. From May 10 to 15, together with the First Army, it took part in capturing and destroying the surrounded enemy forces in Slovenia. It is characteristic that the Germans resisted in Yugoslavia even after the surrender of May 9.

They fought till they were destroyed or captured up to May 15, the date upon which Victory Day is now celebrated in Yugoslavia.

The liberation of the whole territory of Yugoslavia was completed during the period from March 20 to May 15, when the Yugoslav army inflicted losses of 99,907 dead and 209,639 captured, including many commanders led by the commander of the German front for the southeast, Colonel-General Leer. It seized 183,622 rifles, 24,454 automatic weapons, 1,520 guns, 3,651 trucks, 40 planes and much other war material.

Thus ended the war in Yugoslavia. During the final battles alone about 30,000 Yugoslavs were killed and 70,000 wounded. During the whole of the war, Yugoslavia had about 1,700,000 dead, who lost their lives on the battlefield, in concentration camps or in German captivity. Every ninth Yugoslav gave his life in the past war. Material losses were indescribable. More than 820,000 houses were destroyed or burned. Twenty per cent of the railways were made useless. Two-thirds of the livestock was plundered. Almost all the big industrial units were damaged.

I met Tito for the first time after the war when I returned from San Francisco in September, 1945, where the United Nations session had taken place. We spoke about our losses in the war, about the prospects of rehabilitating the country, about the possibilities of further assistance from abroad. Tito suddenly interrupted me:

"The houses will be rebuilt, the railways restored, but we can't give back a million and seven hundred thousand human lives. Each of those men had his personal life, his hopes, his hardships, his joys. That is the tremendous price we had to pay for our freedom."

I was holding a letter which Ivo-Lola Ribar, a member of Supreme Headquarters and Secretary of the Youth of Yugoslavia, had written before going to the war to his fiancée, Sloboda Trajković, a student of Belgrade University. He did not want to send the letter to Sloboda immediately, but left it in trust with a friend, asking him to send it to her only if he was killed.

The letter reads:

"My dearest and only one: Writing this letter I confidently hope —I am an optimist as always!—that it will never reach you, but that the two of us will meet again and remain always together. That is why I am writing this letter.

Tito

"At this moment, when we are going to the final, decisive stage of the battle upon which our personal future and happiness, in addition to everything else, depends, I want to say a few simple and ordinary things to you.

"In my life there are only two things: my service to our sacred purpose and my love for you, my dearest. Our happiness and the life we wanted we were unable to realize in isolation, like so many millions of others, but only through our struggle and our victory. That is why these two things are in essence one and the same within me.

"Know, my heart, that you are the only one I love or have ever loved. I have dreamed and still dream about our happiness together—the happiness which we wanted, a happiness worthy of free men. That is the only real happiness, the only happiness worth wishing for.

"If you receive this letter—if, therefore, I do not see that great hour, do not mourn, my dearest! In the world you will be living in then, you shall always find living the best part of me and all my love for you.

"I am sure that your way will be straight and what it must be. In that, in your way of life, you will find both vengeance and happiness.

"I love you very, very much, my only own! And I hope you will never receive this letter, but that we shall welcome the hour of victory together. I wish to make you as happy with my love as you deserve."

Ivo-Lola Ribar did not live to see the end of the war. He was killed by a German bomb on November 28, 1943. But his letter was never delivered. Sloboda Trajković, together with her father Svetislav, well-to-do pharmacist in Belgrade, her mother Milena, her sister Vera and brother Miroslav, was arrested by the Gestapo, driven into the terrible gas-chamber truck, and suffocated with poison gas, with all her family.

The letter could not be delivered. A mutual friend of Lola Ribar and myself brought it to me after I returned home at the end of the war. That autumn day in 1945 I had wanted to show the letter to Tito, but after his words about the one million seven hundred thousand human lives, I refrained. Tito had dearly loved Lola Ribar ever since the first day they had met in the autumn of 1937.

CHAPTER XV

1945:

"The most dangerous thing for us now is to stop midway . . ."

I HAD not seen Tito from April to August, 1945, because I was abroad. He didn't change much, with the exception that he was a little heavier than during the war. He had too many meetings to attend, too much desk work, so he didn't have a chance to move around as he did during the war. His aunt Ana had just arrived from Kumrovec to see her nephew Tito. He showed her around the stables of the Guards. She was greatly impressed by the beautiful horses.

When Aunt Ana left Tito's study I asked him, in the course of our conversation, what was the first thought to cross his mind as the war was ended in May. He told me the following:

"I recalled an event occurring sometime just before the war, when I had returned from living in the underground abroad longing for my birthplace, my cousins and friends. I arrived at Kumrovec secretly one evening just at sunset. I stole into an orchard near my old home and from there watched the Kumrovčani ending their day's toil. The village looked as if I had never left it in my early childhood. There lay my Kumrovec with its muddy streets, its pretty houses; there meandered the Sutla through the meadows, where once I had tended the cattle and horses; there before my eyes passed my peasants in their heavy boots, tattered clothes, their backs bent by strenuous life. Nor had the life of my ancestors from generation to generation been any different in this mud and misery. My contemporaries with whom I had grown up were no longer at Kumrovec, for there had been nothing to keep them there, and there was not enough bread to feed them. As I stood gazing at my village in the setting sun, I knew there were still hungry children in those small, shingle-roofed houses, as my brothers and sisters had been, and that these children would perhaps also have to leave their village one day in quest of a better life.

"I remained in that orchard till darkness had descended upon the surroundings. The dogs were barking ceaselessly from one end of the village to the other as I pondered the wilderness and backwardness that had been weighing upon us for centuries, and thought of the day when Kumrovec and thousands of similar villages and towns in Yugoslavia would at length wrench themselves from their squalor, when their young men would finally have an equal chance in life, when they would be able to live happily and in peace raising their families. At that time—it was in 1934—I had no idea when opportunity would offer itself; but I was firmly convinced that the realization of that goal called for the exertion of every ounce of strength and for supreme sacrifices.

"I recalled this visit to Kumrovec when for the first time after the war I met Miroslav Krleža, the writer from Zagreb, to whom I had recounted my visit and my meditations sometime in 1937.

"And indeed, we all of us together had invested the utmost efforts in this war. The war is over, and now the opportunity is at hand not only to restore what has been destroyed, but also to create something new.

"The most dangerous thing for us now is to stop midway. What we achieved in the war is only the beginning. Now we are confronted with tasks almost unimaginable, with overwhelming hardships, and you yourself can see what means we have to combat them with: We have nothing save our strong will, high morale and our sinews. I have been touring the country during these past several months. In the Lika everything has been razed to the ground: there are villages that have been burned a dozen times over during the war. You can cover a hundred kilometers without seeing a single house standing. But on the other hand, what enormous strength emanates from the people! On all sides the people ask for nails, for lumber: they are patching houses and schools the best they can. I went over the Belgrade-Zagreb railway, which the Germans plowed up almost over the whole of its four hundred and fifty kilometers. They broke its every single tie like match-sticks with that plow of theirs. Nothing but devastation lay along the whole route: on all sides the twisted rails, broken ties, gutted stations. In no more than two months the whole line was fit for traffic: hundreds of thousands of people worked on it voluntarily day and night until the first train was able to run between the two chief towns of our country. These are the qualities in our people that will help us to overcome even greater hardships and to build a firm foundation for the future progress of this country."

Such were Tito's words in 1945. Those were indeed difficult times. A cake of soap, an ordinary needle, a spool of thread were the dream of every housewife. There is no doubt that the aid UNRRA extended Yugoslavia during those days played an enormous role in alleviating neediness. It was sent urgently, when it was most required. True enough, when negotiations began with UNRRA in 1944, there were some difficulties owing to the request that UNRRA should distribute aid to Yugoslavia through its own organs. The National Committee was unable to agree to this proposal, and it was even held that under such conditions it would be better to turn UNRRA's aid down. Later Yugoslavia's requests were accepted: UNRRA's aid was distributed through the people's committees to all those persons requiring it, no matter what their political convictions. In Yugoslavia this aid was received not only as a humanitarian gesture but also as tribute paid to the heroism and sufferings of Yugoslavia by all the countries which had fought against Nazism. UNRRA's aid totaled more than $400,000,000, mostly in food. Director General Fiorello La Guardia visited Yugoslavia and together with Tito toured the Lika and other regions ravaged during the war. Tito cherishes his memories of La Guardia.

"La Guardia was not only a humanitarian but a genuine democrat. He was always open-minded. There was nothing haughty about him. What especially attracted me was his sense of humor. While we were at a meeting at Korenica in the Lika, a young peasant galloped after our car with his horse. The automobile steadily gained in speed, the young peasant spurred his horse onwards, as he shouted his catchwords at us. La Guardia said, 'It is easy to be a Tito in a country with men like these.' La Guardia saw a large part of Yugoslavia and gained an even more vivid impression of the sacrifices these people had made during the war. La Guardia and I separated with feelings of profoundest friendship. Before he left we played a game of chess, which he lost."

The problem of rehabilitation was not the only problem confronting Yugoslavia with the termination of the war. It was necessary to bring to a successful conclusion those goals for which the people had fought. It was necessary to realize equality among all the peoples of Yugoslavia, to consolidate brotherhood and unity. It was necessary to punish those most responsible for the fratricidal struggle, for having provoked conflict among the several nations or religions, so as to free ourselves in the future of similar dangers to the existence of the nation, to the preservation of Yugoslavia as a whole; and on the other hand, to pardon those who had been blind tools in the hands of their masters.

But all those who were guilty had to be punished, in particular one of the most guilty among all Quislings, Draža Mihailović. The task was to capture Draža Mihailović alive and to bring him before the trial.

When the units of the National Liberation Army liberated Serbia in 1944, Draža Mihailović, together with the Germans, withdrew from these parts of Yugoslavia and settled with a few thousand of his men, mostly officers, noncommissioned officers, and police, in Central Bosnia. His left flank was protected by the Germans, whose most extended units were located thirty miles to the east. His southern flank was protected by the Germans and Ustashis.

During the winter of 1944–45, there were in Draža Mihailović's staff great confusion and inner frictions caused by his political defeats. On his staff were some who realized the treachery he was involved in, and these people acted against his interests. They had as their task not to allow Draža Mihailović to escape abroad. The first success was achieved when Draža Mihailović came to believe that all Serbia was for him and that the people were anxiously awaiting him. All this was calculated in order that Draža Mihailović in his planning should choose not to abandon Yugoslavia but to return to Serbia; in this way time would be gained for the realization of the plan of his arrest.

In April, 1945, when the Yugoslav army commenced its final offensive against the Germans and when they were pushed back in

Srem, the left flank of Draža Mihailović's forces became exposed. Then he decided to escape with a few thousand of his men into Serbia.

He set out from northern Bosnia to the south in order to by-pass the River Bosna and then to turn eastward in the direction of Serbia. This maneuver of his was possible because almost all our forces were engaged in the final battles with the Germans. Against Draža Mihailović fought only individual units of the Corps of the National Defense and local militia.

Thus Mihailović forced his way down the River Bosna but he suffered great losses. The morale of his troops was weak. Food vanished. Moreover, he led his units badly. On the day of May 12th Draža Mihailović with his halved troops came to the approaches of the River Sutjeska, the famous scene of the battles against Germans and Italians of the Fifth Offensive in 1943. The final battle began; Chetnik columns were cut through. During the morning of May 13th, Draža Mihailović's command was attacked. Here he lost all of his radio stations, personal luggage, rucksack, and even his binoculars.

After the battle Mihailović was left with only a group of a hundred men with whom he attempted to escape to the north. During the night of May 19–20, 1945, he ran into a Partisan ambush, not far from the scene of the main battle, and lost forty of his men. At the next ambush he again suffered heavy losses, and finally he remained with only seventeen men.

Among the things he preserved to the end were English gold pounds. Out of the battle at Sutjeska he saved 250 of them. He was compelled to divide that money among those seventeen men of his. Then started a wandering from village to village and hiding from the pursuers. One after the other of his escort started to run away from him together with money. They surrendered or were caught, giving valuable information about Mihailović's movements. Here is the story told by one of his escorts, a former sergeant who surrendered to the Yugoslav authorities:

"We were continuously moving. We had great difficulties finding food. For instance in the village Bejić we stopped for half an hour and got a little milk, but we were soon discovered by the local militia and were fired on by a few rifles. The same night we moved farther and tried to take food in the village Radjević, but were noticed again and we escaped to Mount Devetak, where we waited the morning. Three out of our group separated from us that night and departed on their own.

"We spent the day on Devetak and in the evening we came downhill into the village Džimrije and purchased flour and milk. We cooked our meal and when we divided it among us, rifles could be heard above the village, and we withdrew uphill. We remained in the mountain two days and two nights for Mihailović had become ill. The soldiers protested because they were hungry.

"The second or third night we arrived in village Plana around ten o'clock. Here we slaughtered a cow, which belonged to a woman. She protested and did not want to sell the cow. Before dawn, after having eaten, we went on to the Mount Žepa. From here we continued over Mount Javor and moved a couple of days and nights meeting no one, until we arrived in the village Gunjaci where we purchased corn and flour from cottagers. But soon after we arrived pursuers fired on us and we returned once more to Mount Javor. At this point our guide fled, taking along one of our soldiers. We moved farther toward the village Džile where we ran into an ambush. This life was too hard for me, and I decided to surrender."

Draža Mihailović with a few of his men went to a remote district on the border of Serbia and Bosnia, in a village around Višegrad, where he decided to hide himself for a time.

In his escort remained only four men. They dug a bunker for him in a small forest above the village. It was a simple foxhole, half open, with a little straw on the bottom, roofless so that it rained into the hole. During the day, Mihailović lay in this hole freezing, for he could not make fire, and when the night came he went to a house in the village. When the pursuit neared, Mihailović remained in his hole at night, too.

Thus Mihailović hid in this hole. The main question for him was how to feed himself and how to save his life. And, while the foreign press wrote about Draža as leading sixty thousand men, communicating with countries abroad, even having gone to a meeting with King Peter, he was freezing in this foxhole.

Several times, from May, 1945, till March, 1946, the pursuit groups could have killed Draža Mihailović, but they had strict orders to capture him alive.

The ring got closer around Mihailović. Unable to sustain himself, he finally was captured one evening when he emerged from his foxhole. He entered the peasant house and soon after it was all over. He did not resist, because the capture was too sudden. He realized the situation only when manacles were on his hands. Mihailović was terribly filthy, and pretty much starved.

After some days, on March 13, 1946, during a discussion in the Parliament, Aleksandar Ranković, the Minister of Interior, disclosed for the first time the news that Draža Mihailović had been caught.

From the village Mihailović was brought by car to Belgrade. Among the first to come to his cell to see him was Aleksandar Ranković. Mihailović stared for a moment and said:

"I know you from somewhere!"

"Quite possible," answered Aleksandar Ranković. "I came once to your headquarters on Ravna Gora, when Comrade Tito sent me in the autumn of 1941, to try once more to speak with you and to invite you to fight against the occupier. You became the worst traitor to your fatherland in its most dreadful days."

Draža Mihailović remained silent. He asked for better food, for permission to take a bath and for clean underwear. All these requests were granted.

On the day Mihailović was seized, Aleksandar Ranković cabled to Tito, who was on his way to Poland: "The plan is fulfilled."

When Tito arrived in Warsaw, he spoke by phone with Stalin on some political questions, and he told him that Mihailović had been caught. Stalin expressed his satisfaction because of this news, but on the other hand immediately called to account the representatives of N.K.V.D. in Yugoslavia. They had learned of Mihailović's capture from the Yugoslav papers, for they knew nothing about preparations for his capture.

The chief representative of N.K.V.D. in Yugoslavia, Timofejev, came to Aleksandar Ranković completely depressed and began to complain that Stalin strongly rubbed their noses and that they ought to have been informed about the plans to seize Draža Mihailović. Aleksandar Ranković responded, "The main thing is that Draža has been caught."

The trial against Mihailović began in July, 1946, in the Guard Hall in Topčider. He did not confess all the things he was accused of by the public prosecutor. He defended himself very unskillfully.

His entire archives were discovered and brought to the court. Here were his war dispatches, written by his own hand, showing how he collaborated with the occupier and how his units, first together with the Italians and later with the Germans, participated in the fight against the Partisans. This he could not deny. He was betrayed by his own handwriting in which he wrote the orders to his units to tie themselves with the occupier's forces.

The trial was held in public, and a great number of foreign and domestic journalists attended. The entire procedure was transmitted by the radio stations. Witnesses came in the hundreds, mothers of slain peasants, orphans of massacred victims.

For his crimes Draža Mihailović was condemned to death. When he heard the sentence he wrote an appeal for pardon. It could not be granted to him. He caused Yugoslavia tremendous damage and was directly guilty for the death of ten thousands of people. His appeal was rejected. Until the last minute, even when he went to his execution—entirely upset and almost out of his mind—he had hoped to be pardoned. But the life of a man who caused his homeland such great trouble, as Benedict Arnold did to America, could not be spared.* Draža Mihailović was a man of limited intelligence and was not very courageous.

It was necessary after the war to undertake a number of measures requested by the people during the war and constituting the fundamental basis of our struggle. It was necessary to raise the country out of its semicolonial position, to develop its huge natural resources. There is no country in Europe of Yugoslavia's size with Yugoslavia's natural wealth. It contains all the strategic raw materials, although it has not yet been thoroughly prospected. It has immeasurable water-power. With its deposits of nonferrous metals it ranks among the world's top producers, being first in the production of bauxite in Europe, and second in the world; first in Europe in the production of lead, fifth in the world; in chromium first in Europe, sixth in the world; in antimony first in Europe, fourth in the world; in mercury second in Europe, second in the world; in copper second in Europe,

---

* In Great Britain, for instance, after the Second World War, people were condemned to death for lesser crimes. Lord Haw-Haw was executed simply because he talked over the German radio during the war. A similar fate befell the young Amery.

eighth in the world; in zinc second in Europe, eighth in the world. One of the most valuable metals, molybdenum, used in the steel plating of warships and tanks, is found in Europe only in Yugoslavia and Norway, and elsewhere only in the United States and Canada.

Plans were consequently made for the industrialization of the country, that it might no longer be a country of muddy roads and general backwardness.

Foreign capital in Yugoslavia held the key positions. For instance, in mining 77.9 per cent of the capital was foreign, in the metallurgical industry 90.9 per cent, in the metal-processing industry 55.8 per cent, in the ceramics and glass industry 28.3 per cent, in the timber industry 51.4 per cent, in the paper and printing industry 15.1 per cent, in the chemical industry 73.6 per cent, in the food and agricultural industry 27.1 per cent, in the textile industry 61.4 per cent, in the leather and fur industry 40.9 per cent, in the power-generating industry 43.5 per cent, in other industrial branches 32.3 per cent.

Thanks to its domination in the essential branches of industry and in banking, foreign capital was in the position to pursue its own economic policy. This policy led to favoring particular economic branches at the expense of others, and intensifying the inequality of development in our economy.

For instance, although the country is extremely rich in bauxite ore, aluminum was virtually not produced. The cause was the economic policy of the aluminum cartel, which controlled 99.7 per cent of our bauxite mining. Lest the production of aluminum should develop independently of the wishes of this monopoly group, foreign monopoly capital bought up bauxite concessions and refrained from exploiting them. There were thirty-five such grants on the territory of the mining inspectorate of Split alone which had been bought up but never exploited.

It was necessary to erase those huge inconsistencies existing in the country between different sections of the population: abundance on one side, and wretchedness on the other.

The land was redistributed. The large estates were divided among the peasants. No one in Yugoslavia could have more than sixty acres of land after redistribution. This hit the interests of the large landowners, especially of the Catholic and the Orthodox Churches, which possessed vast areas of land. In Croatia and in Slovenia alone the Catholic Church had to cede over a hundred and sixty thousand acres of land to the peasants. Churches and monasteries of historic value were allowed to retain up to sixty acres of land in order to preserve these monuments.

The realization of these tasks progressed with relative ease, because the majority of the people had declared themselves for their enactment during the war. That is why our People's Front easily accepted nationalization after the war: had the Communists been alone in seeking to carry out this task, they would have been in the minority, and civil war would have been inevitable.

In the autumn of 1945 elections were held for the Constituent Assembly, and the overwhelming majority of the population voted for federation, for the republic against the monarchy, for the legalization of all those proposals which were advanced and realized during the war.

In order to carry out these tasks, it was necessary to make the country secure from outside. But the moment the war ended there were difficulties, in more than one quarter. In some Western countries certain influential quarters considered they could arrest Yugoslavia's free and unhampered development. They believed that as a country which had suffered such losses Yugoslavia was extremely needy and therefore weak. Pressure was brought to bear on the country in various ways. For instance, the justified requests of the Yugoslavs to unite the whole of their national territory met not only with no aid but on the contrary with vigorous opposition, as in the case of our requests for Trieste.

War criminals were helped to pass through the Western countries unmolested, to avoid their due, such as the Quisling leader of Croatia. Support was extended to former King Peter, although it was clear to every objective observer that the overwhelming majority of the people no longer wanted him as ruler of Yugoslavia.

The gold of the Yugoslav National Bank, which had been removed to the United States during the war lest it fall into Nazi hands, was frozen.

For these reasons Yugoslavia's early postwar attitude toward events in Greece was dictated by the danger which threatened its independence and free development from that quarter.

One part of the Western press wrote the worst possible fabrications about Yugoslavia; it was said to be the most obstinate of the Soviet satellites, and Tito himself to be not a Yugoslav but a Soviet general. This was happening at a time when Yugoslavia was already deeply involved in a struggle against the Soviet government's attempts to subjugate it.

Relationships with the Soviet Union had begun to aggravate with the very first day of the war. Moscow refused to tolerate any movement independent of it, any movement that primarily had the interest of its country or of its people in view; it wanted such a movement as would be blindly obedient to and in fact a weapon of Russian foreign policy, an unjust foreign policy which had no regard for the interests of small countries, being only concerned for big power expansionist interest. That is what Yugoslavia did not want. That is why there was conflict between the Yugoslav leadership and the highest Soviet leaders, headed by Stalin, not only after the termination of the war but even during it.

Yet, during the first postwar months we thought it necessary to push these disputes and disagreements with the Soviet Union into the background because during the early postwar years Western pressure against us was heavier and the greater danger threatened us from that quarter. Let us take the incident with the American planes in 1946. The situation in connection with Trieste was extremely tense. Very little understanding had been shown at the Paris Peace Conference for the efforts Yugoslavia had exerted during World War II to unite all the Yugoslav lands once and for all. Moreover, those efforts were belittled. The people in Yugoslavia were agitated. On the other hand, American planes by the squadron continued to fly over Yugoslav territory. This was a serious violation of our sovereignty, and on several occasions Tito had personally spoken in the National Assembly advising the cessation of this practice.

The Department of the Ministry of National Defense for Liaison with Foreign Missions had on several occasions vainly drawn the attention of the military and air force attachés of the United States to these cases.

Owing to the systematic character which these flights had assumed, violating the sovereignty of Yugoslavia's territory, the Chief of the General Staff of the Yugoslav Army personally sent a letter to the United States Military Attaché on July 10, warning him of the seriousness of these cases.

The American military and air force attachés in their answers to these intercessions sent letters on July 16 and August 7 limiting themselves to the statement that they had received no replies from the competent American military authorities in Italy and in Austria on this matter. In his letter of August 7 the Military Attaché even stated that the American government had recently issued a circular prohibiting American fliers from flying over the territory of friendly countries without permission. The unauthorized flights, however, continued. Between July 16 and August 8, 172 planes, among them 87 bombers, 40 fighters and 45 transports, flew over Yugoslav territory without authorization. On July 22 alone Yugoslavia's territory was violated by 18 planes, of which 11 were bombers; on July 23, 12 planes flew over Yugoslav territory, of which 11 were bombers; on July 29, 18 planes, of which 11 were bombers and 1 fighter; on July 30, 29 planes, of which 22 were bombers; on August 7, 11 planes, of which 3 were bombers and 7 fighters; and on August 8, 8 planes, of which 3 were bombers and 3 fighters.

The Yugoslav Foreign Ministry had presented a dozen or so notes protesting against these flagrant violations of Yugoslavia's sovereignty. Tito himself spoke in Parliament, asking that this violation of the Yugoslav territorial sovereignty stop. It was useless: the planes continued to fly over Yugoslav territory. Then one plane was compelled to land, and, regretfully, another one was shot down, the result being the death of its crew. Even after this incident, which occurred on August 9, Anglo-American planes continued to fly over Yugoslav territory. Thus during the period from August 10 to August 20, a total of 110 Anglo-American planes flew over Yugoslav territory, of which 34 were fighters, 57 bombers, 19 transports and unidentified types. On August 13 alone a total of 33 planes flew over Yugoslav territory, of which 9 were fighters, 22 bombers, and 2 transports. During August 16, there was a total of 17 planes that violated Yugoslavia's territory, of which 2 were fighters, 11 bombers, and 4 transports and unidentified types. On an average, 10 military planes violated Yugoslav territory during these eleven days, combat planes among them averaging 8.3.

All manner of pressure intensified. The bulk of Yugoslavia's river shipping, which the Hitlerites had removed to Germany, was deliberately held back although these vessels were indispensable to Yugoslavia.

Such were Yugoslavia's relations with the Western countries up to 1948.

CHAPTER XVI

1946:

"The cause of the conflict . . . is the aggressive tendencies of the Soviet Union toward Yugoslavia . . ."

WE HAVE seen that during the early postwar years Yugoslavia had difficulties in her relations with some of the big Western countries, reflected in attempts to restore King Peter and to reinstate the old regime, in the nonrecognition of Yugoslavia's justified national demands, in various discriminatory measures against Yugoslavia, in freezing Yugoslavia's gold, in holding up Yugoslav shipping on the Danube and so forth.

At that time there were deep differences between Yugoslavia and the Soviet Union. To be sure, it was rather difficult to perceive them not only for observers outside Yugoslavia but also for many people in this country. Taught as they had been for so many years to regard the Soviet Union as a socialist country, the Yugoslav Communists were at first unable to comprehend the unjustified and hegemonic Soviet acts, which clearly showed that the Soviet Union was taking measures toward Yugoslavia incompatible with a socialist country.

However, the open conflict that broke out only in 1948 had begun to develop far earlier. What were its causes? What was it that led to such a fierce clash between the two countries that had considered themselves socialist? What was hidden behind these hegemonic Soviet moves? Was it only a passing conflict?

Such are the questions many people ask themselves in the world today. Here is what Tito has to say about it.

"The cause of the conflict is simple. It is the aggressive tendencies

254

of the Soviet Union toward Yugoslavia. The first state of the workers and peasants, which had roused such enthusiasm among the working masses of the whole world and had achieved such material success, had reached a stagnation point in its development. The domination of tendencies toward state capitalism was disenfranchising the workers and causing the loss of much that had been gained in the October Revolution, as well as oppressing the non-Russian nations in the Soviet Union; and abroad it was giving rise to expansion, to a policy of spheres of influence. All this is the consequence of a line introduced by Stalin, especially from the thirties, when instead of expanding the rights of the working class he relied on a state machinery which had become not the servant of the community but its master.

"During the past fifteen years an important role has been acquired by the intelligence service—the N.K.V.D. Instead of a weapon to fight counterrevolution, it has grown into a force in itself; instead of being an instrument of the revolution, it has become a power above Soviet society. The entire activity of the country, the Party, the whole foreign policy—all this rests upon the intelligence service; its reports are given priority, it really rules the country.

"Stalin himself has become a slave of the intelligence service he created and developed—its willing slave. Consequently, in the Soviet Union today no one trusts anyone else, everything is a source of suspicion. Whoever in the least earns the displeasure of the N.K.V.D. is erased from the social community. Hundreds of thousands of people have thus been unjustly liquidated. Progress toward socialism has been arrested, and the Soviet Union has become an enormous terror state.

"The fundamental question on which Stalin failed is the problem of the freedom of the individual in socialism, for there can be no socialism without the freedom of the individual. These two concepts are identical. And we see that developments in the Soviet Union during the past ten years and more have followed the dangerous course of suppressing individual freedom. Never in history has the individual been so subjugated to the state machinery as he is in the Soviet Union today. Nowhere are men so inhumanly treated as they are in the Soviet Union after thirty-four years of Soviet rule, when the whole world expected the Soviet Union to become a model country for all, not only materially but also as the embodiment of free socialist men. Instead she has betrayed socialism.

"The Soviet Union has betrayed the hopes put in her. It was difficult to appreciate these changes in the Soviet Union, because long years of teaching and training about the Soviet Union had prevented us from perceiving the negative traits in the life of that country. We constantly endeavored to justify them by citing Russia's backwardness, the enormous difficulties with which she had had to contend, surrounded as she was by enemies. But it was practice, life itself, the arrival on the stage of history of other countries where the workers had come to power, that finally revealed the sad course upon which Stalin had set the development of social relationships in the Soviet Union.

"When did the conflict between us and the Soviet leaders really begin?

"When we review the history of that conflict today, we can rightly say that there were elements of disagreements between us back in 1941, from the first day of our revolution. As early as that the Soviet leaders revealed a tendency to steer our whole uprising neither in the interest of the Yugoslav peoples nor of the struggle against Hitlerism in general, but chiefly in a way that best suited the interests of the Soviet Union as a state and her Greater-Russian policy.

"In 1941 there were already elements of conflict between ourselves and Moscow as to the character of our revolution. Several weeks after the German occupation of Yugoslavia, when preparations were being made to launch the uprising against the enemy, I said in an address to the plenary meeting of the Central Committee in Zagreb that from the first day of the struggle against the occupying forces we had to begin creating a new, people's government instead of the old government that had brought the country to ruin in 1941, and with the occupation had for the most part placed itself at the service of the Germans and Italians.

"What did this mean? It meant that we wanted not only to drive the Germans and Italians out of our country, but also to create a Yugoslavia that would no longer be the satellite of some big country or other, a Yugoslavia that would develop its immeasurable natural resources, a Yugoslavia in which there would no longer be exploitation of man by man.

"My address and all the decisions of the plenary meeting were forwarded to Moscow, whose reaction was quick in coming. The Comintern warned us not to forget that an anti-Fascist war was being prosecuted and that it was a mistake to found new organs of government.

"What did this mean? What would have happened had we accepted these instructions? It would virtually have meant suicide. We should have been unable even to launch the uprising, we should have been unable to mobilize the majority of the people unless we offered them a clear prospect of a new, happier, and more equitable Yugoslavia rising out of that terrible war. In fact the Comintern, at the Kremlin's orders, wanted a resistance movement in Yugoslavia that would serve the interests, not of the people of Yugoslavia, but of Russian great-power policy and its bargaining position with the other great powers.

"It was this, the first disagreement as to the character of our revolution, that sowed the seed of conflict between Yugoslavia and the Soviet Union. And the more the revolution grew in Yugoslavia, the more these disagreements necessarily increased, and finally when Yugoslavia emerged from the war as a new, independent state, they led to open conflict. Only, I repeat, this was not a simple process; at the beginning things were not as clear as they are today, but the thread of the conflict can be followed from day to day during the war, at each of its most important turning points. Bearing this in mind, it is obvious why the Comintern actually concealed the scope of our struggle from the Soviet public during the first year of our revolution, although it was notified daily of the events in Yugoslavia. Until December, 1941, Draža Mihailović was always mentioned as the leader of the resistance movement in Yugoslavia, the first attack on him only being permitted from the Free Yugoslavia radio station in the summer of 1942, after we had proved our strength by successfully emerging from three enemy offensives. Moreover, the Soviet government had refused to give us any military assistance at all, even a symbolical one. On the contrary, during this period it was negotiating with the Royal Yugoslav Government in Exile.

Tito

"Today it is logical and obvious to us why the reaction was so fierce in Moscow, late in 1943, when we finally laid the foundations of the new Yugoslavia of today at the second session of AVNOJ at Jajce, when we ceased to acknowledge the Yugoslav Government in exile, prohibited the return of King Peter and proclaimed the principle of 'Yugoslavia for the Yugoslavs.' We took counsel with none of the great powers regarding this step, because it was the Yugoslav people's affair, because with it we had taken our fate into our own hands and simultaneously demonstrated that new Yugoslavia was unwilling to be small change among the great powers. Moscow's reaction to our step was savage. They called the decisions of the second session of AVNOJ a stab in the back of the Soviet Union.

"And when new Yugoslavia emerged from the war as she had been conceived at the historical meeting at Jajce, it was obvious that she would clash not only with some of the Western powers which had been endeavoring to hamper our free development, but that her very existence as an independent and socialist country would be at cross purposes with the hegemonic policy of the Soviet Union. Yugoslavia's position among the countries of Central Europe and the Balkan Peninsula also greatly contributed to this, for she has a unique strategical position and after 1945 she gained a unique political influence owing to the struggle of her people during the war.

"This in essence is a conflict between two conceptions of the relations between states; it is a conflict between Soviet bureaucracy and the Yugoslav common people. For full thirty years people in our country had looked upon the Soviet Union as a socialist country, as the ideal for which they had been flogged in prisons, languished in confinement, perished in the war. By their behavior toward new Yugoslavia, a socialist country, the Soviet leaders showed tremendous inconsistency between their words and deeds.

"It is evident Stalin had been preparing to settle accounts with new Yugoslavia from the first days of her inception. When we look now at all the actions of the Soviet Union toward Yugoslavia from 1944 on, although they seemed accidental to many Yugoslavs who had illusions about the Soviet Union, we can clearly see their logical connection.

"Stalin coolly and systematically prepared to subjugate Yugoslavia as the central point in Southeastern Europe. Not satisfied with having annexed six European states with over eighty million inhabitants to the Soviet Union after the war, he reached out for Yugoslavia.

"The actions of the Soviet Union toward Yugoslavia from 1944 onwards show that Stalin wanted first of all to seize the key position in our country, to capture Yugoslavia's economy in order to seize the whole state leadership, to destroy all those moral-political values the people had gained during the war, to wreck Yugoslavia's unity, to plunge us into fratricidal war for his benefit, and then to get the shattered country completely in his own hands.

"He made abundant use of the fact that during the early postwar years Yugoslavia was threatened by other great powers; he himself endeavored to complicate these relations so as to make us easier prey. And indeed, we were compelled to be silent for a long time because a greater danger at one time threatened us from the West. Finally, considering that the conditions were ripe, Stalin resolved upon an open blow.

"It is clear today that Stalin prepared these steps with considerable cunning. First, he endeavored to attract all responsible officials in the economy, in his Party machine, in the army, in the UDB * to his service, and this accomplished, to deliver the final blow and turn Yugoslavia into a Rumania, Bulgaria or some other East European country which had met a fate like that prepared for Yugoslavia. Those were the direct intentions of Stalin and the other leaders of the Soviet Union, those are the causes of the conflict between the Soviet Union and Yugoslavia."

As Tito says, there was a whole series of actions from Soviet quarters insulting Yugoslavia as a country, her participation in the war, and the sacrifices her army had made.

In November, 1944, while the war was still being fought, Edvard Kardelj, the Vice-President of the National Committee of Liberation of Yugoslavia, and Ivan Šubašić, the Prime Minister of the Yugoslav Government and Foreign Minister, went to Moscow where they were received by Stalin. During a conversation Stalin, suddenly, for no apparent reason, began to speak about our army, about our contribution in the war. He spoke disparagingly about the Partisans, their fighting spirit, even their numerical strength.

---

* UDB—Uprava državne bezbednosti (Bureau of State Security), police for the defense of the security of the country.

"I know those Partisan figures. They are always exaggerated."

On the other hand, he praised the Bulgarian army. Kardelj reminded him that it was a Fascist army fighting against the united nations, that almost all its old commanding staff remained, that it could not change overnight. Stalin answered that it was a regular army, a good army, with officers' cadres.

Naturally, Stalin's opinion of our army was not received with approval by our National Committee, nor were we willing to convey it to the people because we were still involved in a hard fight and it would have demoralized the men.

But there were other Soviet actions that could not be concealed, which struck the people unfavorably when they heard about them. With the arrival of the first Soviet missions, some of the officers began to engage Yugoslav citizens for work in the Soviet intelligence service. The Soviet missions could have obtained all the information of interest to them from our National Committee. But they were not satisfied; they wanted to set up their own men in our Party and state machine to be at their service when a convenient moment arrived. They engaged Yugoslav citizens behind the back of the Yugoslav authorities, advising every agent to keep quiet about this work. There were a considerable number of such inveiglements during the war and immediately after it. The Soviet officers had recourse to various means. They enticed some people with their faith in the Soviet Union, some they attracted with money and promises of better posts, still others they blackmailed into working for them. They would usually discover something regrettable in a man's life, or something he concealed from his neighbors, and then threaten him with exposure unless he worked for their intelligence service.

This activity was pursued in all directions, starting with members of the Central Committee and ending with coding officials in the Party and state machine. Andrija Hebrang, member of the Politburo and Secretary of the Central Committee of Croatia, very quickly fell into their trap. Hebrang was arrested in Zagreb in 1942 by the Ustashi police. He gave way under torture and to save his life consented to work for the Ustashi intelligence service and the Gestapo. His dossier was sent to Gestapo headquarters in Berlin. On the orders of the men he had signed an obligation to work for, he joined the Partisans in the autumn of 1942 ostensibly as an exchanged prisoner.

Nothing was then known about what he had done in prison; he was imagined to have behaved well, so he became Secretary of the Central Committee of the Communist Party of Croatia. When war ended, Hebrang's dossier was found in Berlin by the Russians. We in Yugoslavia learned in 1945 that something was wrong with Hebrang, but the Russians gave us no information about him, although they possessed evidence of his treachery. Even when Kardelj and Djilas met Molotov in 1946 and told him that Hebrang was under Party investigation about his behavior in prison, Molotov said nothing. Hebrang was tightly in N.K.V.D. hands, and did what they ordered him.

Stalin's intention was to cover all the key positions in Yugoslavia with his intelligence network, especially the army, the economic apparatus, the Party machine, Transport and Home Office. Various means were employed to this end. For instance, Dušanka Perović, a Partisan girl of twenty who was employed in the coding department of the Home Office, was approached in the autumn of 1945 by Colonel Ivan Stepanov, a member of the Soviet military mission, and asked to work for the Soviet intelligence service. She told him she would first have to ask for the Party's permission. Colonel Stepanov, however, insisted that she should say nothing about it. "Colonel Stepanov," says Dušanka Perović of this incident, "tried to flatter me into accepting by saying I was a good Communist and was right as far as that went; but in this case I should take a broader view of the matter, because a higher aim and a great duty I was to perform for the common struggle were involved. He mentioned a number of well-known instances of treason in the Bolshevik Party. He implied that the enemy might be hidden in the highest leadership, that a man should never be too sure and so should choose the bigger and better tried organization: service for the Soviet Union. If I consented, my decision would be greeted by the highest Party leaders, like Dimitrov. I told him I did not think our responsible comrades would refuse aid to the Soviet Union and considered it best to ask them for advice on this question. During the whole conversation Colonel Stepanov had spoken about the leaders of the Communist Party of Yugoslavia in disparaging terms. He said there was at present nothing to suspect Comrade Tito of, that he was working as he should for the time being, but that this was not the case with others."

Tito

General Soldatov, the Soviet military instructor attached to Headquarters of the Fourth Yugoslav Army, exclaimed in the summer of 1947 to persons whom he had engaged for the Soviet intelligence service:

"Yugoslavia is a small country which can exist only with the Soviet Union. We Russians and no one else liberated Yugoslavia, and we are entitled to request you to do what we require and what we tell you to."

This is only one example of the means the Soviet intelligence service used to penetrate our Party and organization. In a brigade formed in the Soviet Union of Yugoslav nationals who while fighting in the German army were taken prisoner by the Russians, almost every one of them had to sign an undertaking to work for the N.K.V.D. on joining the brigade and before its departure for Yugoslavia. This was also the case with the White Guards in Yugoslavia who had fled from Russia after the October Revolution and settled in Yugoslavia. These men had a poor record; they had been in the service of King Alexander and during the war most of them worked for the Gestapo. They had even formed a special military detachment that fought against the Partisans. After the liberation of Yugoslavia in 1945, the Soviet representatives asked to interrogate all these men. Naturally, during the inquiry they were all compelled to sign an undertaking to work for the Soviet intelligence service.

The N.K.V.D. stopped at nothing to achieve its ends. It cajoled the young Communists in Yugoslavia into working for it with slogans about loyalty to the Soviet Union, the country of revolution, and cajoled the White Guards who had fled from the revolution with blackmail and appeals to serve "eternal Mother Russia."

All these things could not be concealed. There were many who refused to work for the N.K.V.D. and spoke to others about it. People asked with astonishment what this could mean. Why did the Soviet Union countenance the use of such methods? Were those the methods the Soviet Union used in Yugoslavia, an allied and friendly country that had made such sacrifices in the war?

There were conflicts on other matters, too. Some units of the Red Army had been taking part in operations against the Germans in the north of Yugoslavia at the close of the war. It must be said that they fought bravely and suffered heavy losses. On the other hand, the behavior of many officers and men from these units while passing through Yugoslavia was not such as our people imagined worthy of fighters of the Red Army. Wherever the units of the Red Army passed, the people complained about their behavior. Many women were assaulted, many were raped, there were cases of murder and robbery. At first we tried to explain these things to the people as isolated instances, but the number of crimes steadily grew. This did enormous harm to the prestige of the Red Army and Soviet Union, and hampered us in our political work, because not only during the war but even before it broke out we had been telling our people quite different things about the Red Army. The misbehavior had assumed such proportions that it was becoming a grave political problem. Reports were received by our authorities that Red Army officers and men had committed 1,219 violations on Yugoslav territory, 329 attempted violations, 111 violations with murder, 248 violations and attempts at murder and 1,204 robberies with violence. The Secretary of the County Youth Committee of Vojvodina was among the violated girls. Even the wife of a member of the National Committee had been assaulted. In Belgrade itself there were several cases of rape which provoked indignation in our army and among the civilian population. During the battle for the liberation of Belgrade in October, 1944, while a girl courier of the Sixth Lika Division was carrying orders to the front line, a Russian captain stopped her and attempted to rape her. As she resisted, he wounded her with a knife and then raped her while she was unconscious. Two cases at Čukarica, the workers' suburb of Belgrade, profoundly agitated the population of our capital. Several Russian soldiers one after the other had their will with the daughter of a woman worker in the sugar factory, who had been a member of the Communist Party of Yugoslavia since 1939. The girl was so deeply demoralized and depressed by this brutality that she abandoned all political work. A citizen from Čukarica had invited a group of soldiers, N.C.O.'s and officers of the Red Army to be his guests. After supper, a drunken major assaulted the man's wife before his very eyes. Rising in the defense of her honor, the Russians threw him out of the house, and while he was rushing about the suburb seeking help, his wife was raped by seven Russians. This event provoked indescribable horror in Belgrade.

Tito

After an extremely shocking incident the Politburo invited the chief of the Soviet Military Mission, General Kornieyev, to a meeting in order to draw his attention to these unworthy acts which were damaging the prestige of the Red Army. The meeting was attended by our Generals Peko Dapčević and Koča Popović. We made our observations in a friendly and comradely way, and Milovan Djilas said the acts were all the more unfortunate as the bourgeoisie in Belgrade was using them against the Red Army, saying that the British officers (attached to our Supreme Headquarters at that time) were more civil than the Soviet.

But Kornieyev refused to listen to our remarks. He promptly began to protest: "In the name of the Red Army Command I protest against these things because they are untrue!"

Kornieyev forthwith presented this matter to Moscow in another light; we got a telegram saying that Djilas had declared that Soviet officers had lower morals than the British.

We thought the whole affair had finally been settled in April, 1945, when Tito went to Moscow to sign a treaty of friendship and mutual assistance with the Soviet Union. Tito was accompanied by Milovan Djilas, who told Stalin in detail how this incident had occurred and what different Red Army officers and men had done in Yugoslavia. Surprised by this account, Stalin said to Djilas, "Why did you not write to me about all this? I did not know it. I consider the dispute now settled."

When Tito was in Moscow again in 1946, Stalin asked why Djilas was not in the delegation. He told him that he was ill, that he was suffering from permanent headaches. Stalin said:

"Give my regards to Djilas and tell him I will cure him. Ask him if he would care to spend his summer holiday at Socha on the Black Sea; he will soon be cured there."

We imagined that the dispute was settled in this way. But in 1948, when the conflict began openly, one of the first things with which Stalin charged us was ingratitude toward the Red Army and with having insulted the memory of fallen Red Army fighters, accusing them of things they never did. But the best witnesses, who were right in this case, were the people in those parts of our country the Red Army had passed through in 1944 and 1945.

This was one kind of disagreement and conflict with the Russians.

There were others, however, in different forms and on various matters. The Soviet leaders considered it their right to withhold information on foreign-policy questions directly concerning us, on
questions of vital interest to Yugoslavia. Thus, during the work of
the Council of Ministers in Paris in the spring of 1946 when the
Trieste issue was being discussed, Molotov talked the whole night
through about the frontier with our representative Edvard Kardelj
on the eve of the decisive session, never by a single word conveying
his intentions. And the next day Molotov gave his consent to the
French proposal of frontier, so unjust to Yugoslavia.

All these things increased the tension in our relations with the
Soviet Union, while Russian pressure steadily mounted. What can
be said about the behavior of Soviet military and civil experts in our
country? Their duty was to help us with their experience; their approach was quite different. First of all, their chief object was to make
a thorough study of our conditions purely for intelligence reasons.
They attempted to corrupt our men. For instance, during the construction of the bridge across the Danube near Belgrade, destroyed
during the war, which we had begun to rebuild together with Soviet
experts, they inveigled Yugoslav engineers and men into working for
the Soviet intelligence service. Working on this bridge, Soviet agents
built up a whole espionage network in our railway service and when
in 1948 the clash came this group of agents caused heavy damage to
our railway transport.

As to advice, the Soviet experts were extremely rigid, and deliberately so. They wanted to transplant everything as it was in the
Soviet Union, making no allowance for conditions in our country.
They worked deliberately to cause us more hardships. But our
people would not have it. They were prepared to accept useful advice but they were unwilling to tolerate the blind transfer of experience from Russian conditions to ours. The absurdities this led
to is best seen from the following example. A Russian legal expert
suggested to our public prosecutor that secret courts-martial should
be instituted to try members of the Communist Party. Our public
prosecutor argued that it was impossible to set up such courts in
Yugoslavia, that our people would receive such a practice with indignation, and the Communist Party members with protests; that revolts had broken out in Serbia sixty years ago because the King had

wanted to institute secret courts. The Soviet expert insisted, even invoking Stalin, but our public prosecutor refused to yield.

Then there were many problems with the Soviet experts in the army. First of all, they had engaged our officers in their service in great numbers and then there were always clashes of opinion over the development of the Yugoslav army. The Soviet experts considered that we had to transplant all the experiences of the Red Army to our own. Our people said it was true the Red Army had a wealth of experience but it was wrong to belittle the experiences we had gained in the Second World War, that to abandon our experiences and to imitate the Red Army blindly would harm the development of our army. Then the Russian officers wanted to have orderlies. But in the Yugoslav army orderlies do not exist and our soldiers were unwilling to clean the boots for the Russians or to go to market with the basket in hand accompanying wives of Russian officers.

How little the views of us Yugoslavs were respected can be seen from an incident with Tito while he was in Moscow. He says:

"The representatives of the Soviet press asked me to write an article for their papers. I did so, and when I got the text, I noticed that eight tenths of my views had been completely altered according to the wishes of the editors. I was already familiar with such methods in the Soviet Union but I never imagined that Soviet journalists could alter to their own formula the text of an article written by the Prime Minister of a friendly and allied country. The same thing happened to Djilas, Moša Pijade and Rato Dugonjić, the Secretary of the People's Youth of Yugoslavia. The latter had written an article about the Brčko-Banovići railway which the youth of Yugoslavia had built by voluntary work. The editor of the *Komsomolskaya Pravda* had changed the article considerably, even shortening the railway from fifty miles to thirty-seven. Strange logic!"

In contact with the most responsible Soviet representatives a tone of disparagement toward the Yugoslavs as a people was noticeable, disparagement of our culture, complete ignorance of our history and our reality. For instance, Zhdanov once asked Djilas whether opera existed in Yugoslavia. There were twelve opera houses in Yugoslavia, and Yugoslav composers, Lisinski for instance, had been writing operas more than a century ago. It was not merely a matter of belittling our culture, our language, our press in words, but in deeds.

1946

The Soviet representatives in Yugoslavia proposed including as many Russian songs in our radio programs as possible. Had we accepted their suggestion there would have been two or three times as many Russian songs as Yugoslav. They also requested of us to increase the number of Russian plays in our theaters. We have always esteemed Gogol, Ostrovsky, Gorki, but we refused to flood our theaters with third-class modern Soviet plays. As for films, in 1946 they imposed a block booking contract, so that we had no choice of the films they sent; and we had to pay the rental in dollars, at three, four or five times the prices we paid for films from the West. Thus we got Laurence Olivier's *Hamlet* for about two thousand dollars, but for *Exploits of a Soviet Intelligence Agent* we had to pay some twenty thousand dollars.

Different Soviet representatives especially pounced on our press as one of the most powerful instruments of propaganda. Almost every week a representative of the Soviet Information Bureau would come around with several hundred articles written in Moscow on various topics, mostly about life in the Soviet Union, birthdays of Russian writers, composers, scientists, life in the collectives; there were also many articles about other countries, and he obstinately asked for all this material to be published in our dailies and weeklies. Had we printed them all, we should almost have had no space left for our own journalists, who would soon have been out of work, leaving the people to be informed of world events only through the eyes of writers in Moscow.

On the other hand, we asked the Soviet government to publish at least something about Yugoslavia in the Soviet press on a reciprocal basis. This was always avoided. Some articles waited a year for publication, then were returned without having seen daylight. The same thing happened with books. We published 1,850 Soviet books; they published two of ours.

In daily contact with representatives of the Soviet Union after the war, not only our leaders but all our people who met them were convinced at every step of the great difference between the words and deeds of the Soviet government. The fundamental matter on which the conflict began was the attempt of the Soviet government to exploit our country economically. We could not allow it because we should have earned the hatred of all our people. What sense would there have been in our revolution, why should we have made so many sacrifices in the war against the Germans, Italians, Hungarians, Bulgarians, if our exploiter, one great power, was to take the place of another? No, this we could not possibly allow.

Economic enslavement was only a part of the general Soviet plan of East European integration. Immediately after the war the Soviet government endeavored to set up a sealed-off economic area in the East European countries. The plan was to turn the Soviet Union into a vast market, absorbing the entire production of Eastern Europe. With such a market the Soviet Union would have absolute mastery over economic life and development in these countries.

Intensive trade had been developing between Yugoslavia and the Soviet Union from 1945 on—based on a series of trade agreements. These agreements were similar to those in Western Europe. The Russians insisted on doing trade on the basis of world-market prices. There were people in our country who considered it incorrect for trade between socialist countries to be based on world prices, because the underdeveloped country (in this case Yugoslavia) would be an unequal partner; its lower productivity of labor would compel it to give extra profit to the more developed country (in this case the Soviet Union). But none of us objected seriously to trade being carried on with the Soviet Union at world prices, although we knew that the Soviet government required the world-price clause to be inserted in all the trade agreements with us, although this is not customary in trade agreements between states.

But another thing was rather damaging to us in these trade agreements with the Soviet Union: this was the question of the goods to be exchanged. The Soviet government firmly insisted on our giving it essential items which our country could have sold without any difficulty on foreign markets, such as nonferrous metals, ores, hemp, hops. In 1948, for instance, our exports to the Soviet Union consisted of from 40 to 50 per cent ores and metals, although they constituted only 25 per cent of our over-all exports.

There was no particular trouble on this point, but we perceived the real Soviet intentions when talks began in connection with the foundation of Soviet-Yugoslav joint-stock companies in our country. We were not opposed in principle to the foundation of these companies because we were under the illusion that the Russians would help us to develop our industry through them, to begin the systematic exploitation of the vast natural resources of Yugoslavia. Consequently, we accepted the principle of joint-stock companies at first, although in fact it meant that profit would be flowing from Yugoslavia into the Soviet Union.

CHAPTER XVII

1946:

"They sought to exploit us economically . . ."

DURING the spring of 1946, on the occasion of Tito's visit to Moscow, a detailed discussion took place with Stalin and Molotov on economic affairs, including the establishment of Soviet-Yugoslav joint-stock companies. The Yugoslavs consented in principle to the creation of joint-stock companies, since, despite the fact that a part of the surplus labor-value of the Yugoslav working class would be turned over to the Soviet Union, the companies would contribute to the industrialization of Yugoslavia.

On this journey to Moscow Tito was accompanied by Aleksandar Ranković, Boris Kidrič, Koča Popović and others. They were met at the Moscow railway station by Molotov. Of all Tito's meetings, this one appeared to be the most cordial, if there can be any talk of cordiality on Stalin's part. When one regards that meeting in 1946 through the prism of the present it will be seen that on this occasion Stalin behaved diplomatically, slyly, and in great measure demagogically.

Koča Popović, who was also in Moscow on this occasion as one of Tito's escort, gave an account of these meetings and talks. He gave his description from notes he had made at the time:

"When one is to be received by Stalin, notification of such a reception is made almost on the eve of it. Once we were even called to leave the Bolshoi Theater, where we were attending an opera, and half an hour later we were with Stalin. The same custom was followed on the occasion of our present visit. On the evening of May 27 Tito set out for the Kremlin. He was accompanied by Ranković, Kidrič, Vladimir Popović, Nešković and myself. Entering the Kremlin, we passed through a whole maze of corridors and antechambers. The first impression of the Kremlin is that everything is polished, rather simple, all the corridors and rooms covered with carpets, footsteps being inaudible; as if one were in a sanatorium.

"Finally, we were led into a room with a long conference table and some ten chairs. There stood Stalin, at his right Molotov, at his left Lavrentyev, Soviet Ambassador in Belgrade.

"I looked at Stalin. He is a man of middle height, far smaller than he appears in photographs and portraits. He has unusually narrow sloping shoulders, almost a physical deformity, and he holds his arms a little away from his body. As we entered, he smiled at us with yellow and jagged teeth. It struck me that his hair is rather sparse, the strands being thin. He moved toward Tito, quite easily—jauntily almost. Having shaken hands with him, Tito presented the Yugoslavs. Stalin shook hands with all of us, making simultaneous appraisal of the stature of each, especially of Vladimir Popović and Ranković. Stalin turned to Molotov and said, 'Vyacheslav Mikhailovich, see what handsome men, strong men, a strong people!'

"Molotov nodded.

"Stalin then sat at the head of the table, the rest of us following. He grabbed his notebook and began to doodle. He asked Tito about the journey, then went on to the question of Šubašić and Grol, inquiring what they were now doing since they had left the government, made a joke or two about them, calling them 'comrades.' As he did so he steadily doodled, crossing out and beginning over again. He asked after Kardelj's and Djilas's health.

" 'They are well,' Tito replied. 'We could not bring them along, but half of the government is here.'

"Then came a question about Trieste.

" 'The English and the Americans don't want to give you Trieste?' asked Stalin, smiling.

"Again he switched suddenly over to another topic. He inquired about the harvest in Yugoslavia and whether we had succeeded in sowing all the land. Finally began a serious political talk. Tito described Yugoslavia's prospects of economic development while Stalin nodded and interjected, 'We'll help.'

"The discussion marched along to the problem of joint-stock companies in Yugoslavia.

" 'Our people have informed us,' said Stalin, 'that your comrades engaged in economic matters do not agree with plans for the organization of joint-stock companies?' He was silent a moment, as if awaiting Tito's reply, and then continued, 'We have nothing against your not wanting to. Nor were the Poles, for instance, willing to found such companies, lest the Americans on their part raise the question also of founding some.'

"Tito: No, that is neither my own nor the opinion of the other Yugoslav leaders. We consider that such companies may be formed, naturally such companies as will help the industrialization of our country.

"Stalin: Yes, yes. I agree that the kind of companies you want should be founded. Is that right, Vyacheslav Mikhailovich?

"Molotov: Quite, quite, such joint-stock companies should be founded in those branches that will be the most useful both to you and to us.

"After this Stalin asked where we had deposits of oil, bauxite, copper, lead. 'You have good bauxite,' he said, ceaselessly doodling in his notebook.

"Tito explained where lay the various deposits of nonferrous metals in Yugoslavia, and then spoke in detail about several mines.

"The conversation continued on military problems, and then veered to foreign-policy questions. Stalin was especially curious about Albania, and asked details about relationships in the Central Committee of the Albanian Party, about different factions, going into the minutest trifles.

" 'Do you know Enver Hoxha?' he asked. 'What kind of a man is he? Is he a Communist? Have they any internal problems? What is your information?'

"Tito: I have never seen Enver Hoxha. He is a young man, but during the war he won popularity. On the whole, the leadership of the Albanian Party is made up of young men. As far as we know, there are no special problems among them.

"Stalin: They asked to come here, but they do not want to let Enver come alone; they want to send Kochi Dzodze with him, as a sort of control.

"Stalin was silent for a moment, and then: 'What do you know about this?' he asked.

"Tito: We are not informed of any deeper disagreements.

"Stalin: We are constantly putting off their coming. What do you think: should we receive them here in Moscow? It seems to us there is no need to do so. It would now be unpleasant for them to come, both for themselves and for us. Better if we helped them through you. But, nevertheless, things aren't in order in the Albanian Politburo.

"Ranković: There are no matters of import, except that the comrades in the Albanian Politburo do not consider Enver Hoxha a sufficiently firm Party man and always endeavor to have Kochi Dzodze going about with him as the eldest member of the Party in the Politburo. During the April plenum they discussed the Party line, especially in relation to Yugoslavia and the Soviet Union, and exposed some errors, and, holding Seyfoul Maleshov responsible, evicted him from the Politburo. The leadership has been more compact since.

"Tito: We can settle those questions with them.

"Stalin: Good.

"And so the talk continued on foreign-policy matters, on Bulgaria, Hungary.

"Midnight was long past. Stalin turned to Tito:

" 'What are your plans for tonight?'

"Tito: We have none.

"Stalin (laughing): Ha, a government without a state plan.

"Vladimir Popović: We have adapted our plans to the meeting with you.

"Stalin: 'Then a morsel should be eaten,' he said, inviting the whole assemblage.

"All consented, and Molotov added, 'If that is an invitation, with the greatest satisfaction.'

"Stalin summoned a secretary of his in the uniform of a colonel, a small, fat man, completely bald, a typical Russian, and ordered him to have automobiles ready. Then he turned to his guests and continued to jest. He was extremely courteous, witty. Not two minutes passed and he summoned the colonel again. He asked whether the automobiles were ready. The colonel became fidgety. Stalin suddenly changed. That pleasant, witty host had turned into another man. He trembled with rage, he shouted, his features distorted, he sharply motioned with his hand and poured invective into the face of his secretary who was trembling and paling as if struck by heart failure.

"So we set off for Stalin's supper. It was dark, the guests entered the automobiles, drove somewhere about Moscow, and emerged upon the so-called 'Pravitelstvyushchi Chaussée,' or 'The Government Road,' which no other automobiles except the automobiles of the highest Soviet leaders may use. There was a barrier across the road at one point, where the automobiles had to halt for a moment, and then they resumed their way.

"Supper began in the dining room. A long table had been already laid out. Stalin sat in the middle. To his right sat Tito, opposite Stalin sat Molotov, and then the rest of us where we chose. Zhdanov, a man with a red puffy face, with rather lively movements, was also there. Traces of illness were visible on him. He was suffering of angina pectoris. Beria was there also with his scrutinizing gaze, and so was Bulganin, a quiet, rather deaf man.

"The dining room was clean, not richly furnished, the impression always being that one was in a hospital, dead quiet, apart from the outer world. A buxom woman, middle-aged, with a white apron, brought in silver lid-covered vessels with the food and placed them on the table. Each removed the lids and helped himself. The food was mostly Georgian. After an hour the woman with the white apron came in again with clean tableware, gathered up the soiled dishes and left without uttering a word.

"The supper began with toasts. The first was proposed by Stalin. It was a glass of pertsovka, fiery vodka with a red-hot pepper at the bottom of the glass.

"And so hour after hour passed in eating and drinking toasts. It attracted my attention, the attention of a foreigner, that Stalin spoke Russian with a Georgian pronunciation. His pronunciation of the letter 'r' was not soft as the Russians pronounce it, but exceedingly hard. The conversation unwound about different leaders of the Communist Parties: about Thorez, Duclos, Pieck, La Passionaria and others. Stalin gave his opinion of all of them. He appraised Togliatti as a theorist, a professor who can write a good article but does not know how to rally the people and lead them to a goal.

"He said Thorez and Duclos were good comrades, but that Thorez had one big shortcoming: 'Even a dog,' said Stalin, 'which does not bite, bares its teeth when it wants to frighten someone. Thorez can't do even that much.'

"He said that Pieck had grown so old he had become a 'Grandpa' who was capable of slapping people on the back, but was ignorant of how to lead them to a definite goal.

"He praised José Diaz, who had died in the Soviet Union as Secretary of the Spanish Party. He said he had been a good and wise comrade.

" 'That is what La Passionaria lacks,' he added. 'She is unable to pull herself together and is incapable of leading the Party in this difficult situation.'

"Much later in the night Stalin rose from his chair, went to a corner where a gramophone stood and began to play record after record. He selected the records himself, mostly Russian folk music.

"Singing softly, he began to dance to the gramophone music. Molotov and the others shouted out to him, 'Tovarish Josif Vissarionovich, how strong you are.'

"But Stalin's mood suddenly changed. 'Oh, no, no, I won't live long,' he said. 'The physiological laws are having their way.'

"Molotov and the others got to their feet: '*Nyet, nyet*, Tovarish Josif Vissarionovich, we need you, you still have a long life ahead of you.'

"Stalin shook his head in denial. 'No, no, the physiological laws are having their way,' he repeated. Then he looked at Tito, and continued. 'Tito should take care of himself lest anything happen to him. Because I won't live long, and he will remain for Europe. Churchill told me about Tito, that Tito is a good man. He repeated this three times and at last I answered him, "I don't know, but if you say so, he must be good. I shall do my best to get to know Tito, too." ' He turned toward Molotov. 'Vyacheslav Mikhailovich will remain here.'

"Stalin then raised his small glass of pertsovka and invited Tito to drink *Brüderschaft* with him. They clinked glasses and embraced. Then Stalin straightened up and said, 'There is still strength in me!' and slipping both hands under Tito's arms, lifted him off the floor three times to the Russian folk melody coming from the gramophone.

"Stalin then invited the other Yugoslavs to drink *Brüderschaft* with him. He invited me also: 'Serb, *preedyi soudah*' (Serb, come here).

"I approached with my glass in my left hand, but he struck me gently on that hand, and told me, '*Brüderschaft* is drunk with the right hand.'

"And so we exchanged *Brüderschafts*. Stalin had a word or two to say to each of us. He spoke with Kidrič about the Slovene intellectuals, making puns on the words '*podlaya intelligentsia*' * and '*podlinaya intelligentsia*.' †

"He turned suddenly to Ranković, advising him to be careful of Beria, and then to Beria, asking him:

" 'And you two? Which of you will trap the other?'

"Then toasts again. Stalin afterward recommended that we Yugoslavs plant the eucalyptus tree, that he would send us seedlings, because the eucalyptus tree was the best timber for shipbuilding. Many years ago he had read a book saying the tree grew in South America. He had acquired seed from there and had it sown in the Crimea, where the tree took excellent root and grew rapidly.

"The conversation then passed on to history. Stalin spoke in detail about the Chechens, about the great migrations in the fourth and fifth centuries, about the Avars, about the arrival of the Slavs in Europe, about the Langobardi.

"Supper was over at five the next morning."

Stalin gave this supper the day Tito arrived in the Soviet Union, on May 27. During his stay in Moscow, Tito met Stalin several times, once during an official lunch given by Stalin in the Kremlin, and again at a supper in Stalin's villa. Aleksandar Ranković recounts this second supper and the talks that took place:

"This time the Bulgarians Dimitrov, Kolarov and Traicho Kostov were invited to the supper in addition to the Yugoslavs. They had come to Moscow to attend the burial of Kalinin, who had died early in June that year.

"The main topic during the supper was the foundation of the Cominform. What struck me was the sharpness, almost the malice, with which Stalin spoke about the work of the Third International, shooting his darts at Dimitrov. As he did so old Dimitrov grew so

---

* *Podlaya*—base.

† *Podlinaya*—genuine.

red and was obviously so uncomfortable that the rest of us squirmed.

"This supper ended like the first. We stayed until five in the morning with the customary toasts and pertsovkas. It was obvious, at least to me, that Stalin was attempting to cause a rift between the Yugoslavs and Bulgarians. That evening Stalin had some bottles of Yugoslav and of Bulgarian wine among the heap of bottles of wine, whisky, cognac, liqueurs. From time to time he would leave his chair, go to the table where the drink stood, and selecting a bottle from the heap ask, 'Is this Bulgarian wine?'

"When one of the Bulgarians said it was, he exclaimed, 'It is not, it is the Yugoslav wine the Bulgarians stole from Yugoslavia during the war.'

"All the Bulgarians were moody in consequence. The other Russians took up Stalin's cue. For instance, old Kolarov left his chair to pace the dining room a bit, and stopped before a cupboard on which stood some kind of a bust. Unable to see it well, he raised his glasses from his eyes, when Beria shouted at the top of his voice, 'Look at him, he lost all his senses forty years ago.'

"That is how we spent the night in Stalin's villa.

"During the Yugoslav delegation's stay in Moscow Stalin was untiring in trying to demonstrate that he held Tito in higher esteem than he did Dimitrov, in order to provoke distrust and conflict between them. President of the Presidium Kalinin had just died in Moscow. The Yugoslav delegation was called on to be guard of honor at the catafalque. On the day of the interment, Tito and the other Yugoslavs as well as all the guests from abroad were standing to the left of the main stand, which was occupied by Stalin and the members of the Politburo. Suddenly, just as the ceremony had begun, Stalin invited Tito to come up and stand with the Politburo. This honor was conferred only on Tito. All the other foreign guests remained on the stand at the left."

After Tito's return from Moscow, negotiations were opened in August of that year for the foundation of joint-stock companies. From the outset, it was clear what the Soviet Union wanted from us. The Russian representative Yatrov made it clearly understood that he had orders from his government to found such Soviet-Yugoslav joint-stock companies in Yugoslavia as would on the one hand give the Soviet Union a monopoly in whole branches of our industry, and even in our economy in general, and on the other as would exploit Yugoslavia's natural resources and in particular her raw materials, which meant that we should have remained a source of raw materials for developed countries, with no opportunity to develop our own industry. And without the development of industry in our country, there would be no foundation for the building of socialism in Yugoslavia.

During negotiations Yatrov openly said, "What do you need heavy industry for? In the Urals we have everything you need."

However, we stood firmly by the view that Yugoslavia's natural resources had to be exploited, that it was economically possible to do so, but that we were not striving for autarchy, because autarchy is impossible and very dangerous in a world where the economies of all countries constitute a whole. We favored the closest economic co-operation with the Soviet Union and with the other East European countries, provided our resources were developed, because such development was economically feasible and necessary in the interests of the people of Yugoslavia.

A particularly long and trying discussion developed over the joint-stock companies. Oil was first to be considered but the Soviet representative stated that such a company was unnecessary; in his opinion the production of oil could not be raised to 450,000 tons annually during a period of five years on the basis of the established reserves. Consequently he proposed a lesser number of drilling sets. But our representatives insisted, advancing proof that there was sufficient oil in Yugoslavia for exploitation on a large scale. Moreover, Boris Kidrič, our Minister of Industry, had already told Parliament of the favorable prospects revealed in a study of potential Yugoslav oilfields. The Soviet representative then consented to discuss the founding of such a company, but during the discussion advanced impossible conditions.

According to Soviet plans, the value of the oilfields in Yugoslavia was not to be recognized as Yugoslavia's share in the undertaking; he invoked Marx, saying they were natural wealth with no direct social value. Our negotiators produced copies of agreements between the Soviet Union on one side, and Hungary and Persia respectively on the other. According to these agreements the Soviet Union had recognized the value of oilfields as representing 50 per cent of Persia's nominal share capital in the joint-stock company, and in the case of Hungary as representing 15 per cent.

Moreover, the Soviets demanded that any oil products exported by Yugoslavia should go to the Soviet Union in accordance with Soviet requirements, free of all fiscal burdens and export duties during the first five years. The five-year period expiring, the Yugoslav government was entitled only to income tax and to no other fiscal dues or to customs. Yugoslavia could use the remainder of production for herself. As oil production in Yugoslavia was in its infancy this would have meant the establishment of a Russian monopoly in production.

On top of all this, the Soviet plan required that all oil distribution in Yugoslavia, that is, the whole retail network for gasoline and other oil derivatives, would be in the hands of this company. In point of fact, this Soviet proposal to a socialist country contained conditions much more difficult than the Soviet Union had proposed to a semifeudal country, such as Persia.

The Soviet proposal for the founding of the joint-stock oil company contained principles characteristic of all the other companies the Soviet Union wanted to found in Yugoslavia. In addition to the given characteristics, the Soviet proposal clearly stipulated two additional principles typical only of relationships among capitalist countries and colonies at the beginnings of the export of capital. They were, first, the Soviet request for a monopoly in Yugoslavia; and, second, the right to "capitulations," or to a treaty under which these companies would be exempt from local jurisdiction.

In the draft agreement on the founding of a joint-stock oil company the monopoly position was evident in article 8, proposing provisions that "the Government of the Federal People's Republic of Yugoslavia shall grant the company the right of prospecting and exploiting oilfields on the whole territory of Yugoslavia."

Another instance was evident in article 10: the company was to have been guaranteed the special right of availing itself of all rights granted to enterprises with exclusively Yugoslav capital. Simultaneously, no obligations were stipulated for the company to bring its work into conformity with Yugoslav legislation like the other Yugoslav enterprises. Retaining all the rights of Yugoslav enterprises, the company was exempt from the application of existing Yugoslav laws, which in fact constituted a violation of Yugoslavia's sovereignty.

Endeavoring to release the company from the laws and measures of the Yugoslav government, the Soviet representatives sought in the discussion to avoid provision of any obligations which would have meant the application to the company of the Yugoslav economic plans. This would have meant that the Yugoslav government would not be able to lay down its annual plans without the approval of the Soviet representatives in the joint-stock companies, and in the final analysis would not be able to plan its economic development independently.

The Soviet delegates on the one hand requested that land rent should not be calculated in determining the Yugoslav share in the oilfields or mines, and that the mining deposits and oil-bearing fields should be treated as ordinary land, which meant no payment would have been made for the exploitation of Yugoslav national wealth. On the other hand they required in the case of the oil company among others that regardless of outside market conditions, the company work on a paying basis; namely, internal prices would have to meet all production costs, plus the profit; and then the Soviets categorically requested throughout the discussions that in exporting the company's products, Soviet requirements be covered under the most favorable conditions. This meant that when it was a matter of satisfying Yugoslav requirements, the prices had to cover production costs and the profit, but when it was a matter of selling these same products to the Soviet Union, the products would be shipped to the Soviet Union under the most favorable conditions regardless of costs and profits; Yugoslavia would have had to cover losses rising out of such business.

The Russians also advanced the condition that the company should not pay social insurance of the workers according to Yugoslav legislation, but only "insofar as the company was able to do so," which would in all probability be less than prescribed by Yugoslav legislation. They also wanted to treat security payments on the basis of a "world average" and not according to our socialist laws, which grant full social and health insurance to the workers. Obviously in this case we should have had to make good the difference.

This same Soviet tendency was evident during the negotiations for the foundation of joint-stock companies for steel, iron and nonferrous metals. The same line was pursued everywhere: the purpose was to prevent the industrialization of Yugoslavia, to found only such companies as would turn Yugoslavia into a raw-material base of the Soviet Union, to take over the existing going enterprises in Yugoslavia which required very little additional capital and were already profit-yielding, such as the biggest copper mine in Europe, Bor, the big lead mine Trepča, and the iron works of Zenica.

But the Russians reached the climax with their proposal to found a Soviet-Yugoslav bank. This bank, which would actually not have been a joint-stock bank but a pure Soviet agency, was to penetrate to the heart of Yugoslavia's economy; Soviet organs were to take the Yugoslav central financing and credit body into their own hands. Through this bank they would control Yugoslavia's economy from one central point, subjugate it to their requirements as they thought fit.

According to the Soviet proposals, the Yugoslav-Soviet bank was to transact the following business:

1. Credit, clearing, and cash business for all Yugoslav-Soviet joint-stock companies;

2. All clearing transactions in trade between the Soviet Union and Yugoslavia;

3. Other business carried on by local banks.

It is immediately clear what the consequences of such an agreement would be. The joint-stock companies would embrace the most important economic branches, which means almost the whole economy, so that through credit and financing the Soviet-Yugoslav bank would have complete control over our economy. Furthermore, Yugoslavia's financial and foreign-exchange autonomy would be violated, because international clearing transactions by a specially privileged mixed company, in which the Russians would have the main say, are considered the prerogative of a sovereign government.

Yugoslavia's economy would gradually become dependent on this bank, in which the Russians would soon achieve complete domination, for Yugoslavia's trade balance with the Soviet Union would for a time be adverse and of very high volume and the bank would come into possession of substantial clearing funds, increasing its working capital and strengthening the Russian position. Besides, this would strengthen its credit business for the whole amount of Yugoslavia's debit balance, and with its transactions, as a second automatic source of credit in Yugoslavia, it could paralyze the independent credit policy of the Yugoslav bank of issue.

Given the third authorization, the bank would be permitted to transact any banking business with any client, since the proposed agreement provided for no restrictions in this respect. Thus it would amass further substantial funds, enabling it to interfere in any transaction in Yugoslav economy. It would have the same rights as the Yugoslav bank and, in view of its special financial power, could become the strongest competitor in the country in every form of banking business. All this would be brought about without hindrance through its organizational structure, and through the privileged position of the director general, who was to be a Soviet citizen.

Naturally, we immediately rejected this proposal. In Moscow this was taken as a hostile act. Some of their representatives in contact with ours began to talk about megalomaniac Yugoslav plans, about utopian industrialization in our country. Those were the first signs of the gathering storm.

The negotiations dragged on until the beginning of 1947. We still had illusions about the Soviet Union. Finally, early in February, 1947, we signed an agreement founding two Soviet-Yugoslav companies: the "Justa" Air Transport Company, and the "Juspad" River Shipping Company. We did so in the hope that agreements on other Soviet-Yugoslav companies would be signed as we had proposed, and that they would help the industrialization of our country. Above all we had hopes of receiving oil, aluminum and steel installations.

In order to give the reader a clear picture of the conditions imposed upon us by the Soviet representatives with the foundation of the two companies, I shall here explain the matter in detail.

First of all, the "Justa" Air Transport Company appropriated the most profitable lines in Yugoslavia. It assumed the monopoly of all lines between Yugoslavia and other countries, so that our own company, the Jugoslavenski Aerotransport, did not run a single line outside our country. Moreover, "Justa" appropriated the most profitable lines inside the country, leaving our own company in an entirely subordinate position, to vegetate on the trifling traffic conceded to it by "Justa." Thus the Soviet-Yugoslav company established a complete monopoly for its own benefit.

However, matters did not stop there. The Director General of "Justa," a Soviet citizen, began to interpret the agreement arbitrarily, assuming functions which were in the direct jurisdiction of the Yugoslav authorities. He appropriated almost all installations at the airports and all means of communication and navigation for "Justa," thus taking over the control of Yugoslavia's entire air traffic, although according to the agreement "Justa" was entitled only to commercial exploitation of the airfields. It even ceased to inform the local authorities of the arrival of foreign aircraft, so that the Director General of "Justa" became a sovereign in his own domain.

"Justa's" share capital amounted to one hundred million dinars ($2,000,000) on each side. Yugoslavia invested the airports, the means of communication and five million dinars ($100,000) in cash. The Soviet Union invested the aircraft and technical installations, and five million dinars in cash.

All profits were to have been divided according to the capital invested and were exempt from rates and taxes.

The method of estimating the assets other than cash was one that yielded the Russians high extra profits. They valued their own assets high and the Yugoslav assets low. Our assets were estimated at 1938 prices, when the dinar stood considerably higher and was more stable, and theirs at prices prevailing in 1946 and 1947, when prices were very high. Here the Soviet Union really did Yugoslavia heavy damage and prevented her from taking her share of the profit according to her share capital. With far less capital, unjustly inflated, the Russians were able to collect greater profits than their Yugoslav partner, and more than the real value of their share capital warranted. For instance, Yugoslavia built an airport for "Justa" near Belgrade estimated at only seventy-one and a half million dinars ($1,430,000), although its real value was something like twenty times as much. Again, during the valuation of the airports, the Russians acknowledged only the value of ordinary land, and not of landing strips; that is, they did not acknowledge the labor invested in that land. Further, by wrongly interpreting the agreement they appropriated all the installations, buildings and other fixtures at the airports. Consequently, all this together with the airports went at the price of ordinary land. Naturally, the Yugoslav share in this way dropped enormously and an equal division of the profit was only an illusion.

A similar tendency to monopoly, and to the prevention of the development of Yugoslav companies in different economic branches, was seen also in the case of the "Juspad" River Shipping Company.

As is well known, Yugoslavia is one of the chief Danubian countries. This great European artery flows for a considerable length of its course through Yugoslavia, and our country has always had well-developed river shipping. Of all the countries through which the Danube flows, Yugoslavia had the largest tonnage. By founding "Juspad" the Soviet Union in fact deprived Yugoslav shipping of the place and importance it had held on the Danube until then.

Under the agreement founding "Juspad" each side was to contribute the shipping and shipyards, the Soviet the shipyard equipment. Thus "Juspad" appropriated the best Yugoslav vessels on the Danube, the Soviet Union giving not a single ship. In business, as it turned out, the Russians did not even keep to the obligations they had accepted under an extremely favorable agreement for them. For instance, up to the end of 1948 Yugoslavia had invested 76.20 per cent of its contemplated capital in craft, installations and funds, or 305 shares (craft, shipyards and funds). During the same period the Soviet Union had invested 9.83 per cent of its capital in kind and money, or 39 shares. Under the agreement the Soviet Union was to have invested 67.5 million dinars' ($1,350,000) worth of equipment and material for the construction and repair of craft through a period of five years, but during the two years of the company's existence she invested only 3.4 million dinars ($68,000). Because of this, the company had to utilize additional Yugoslav funds amounting to 15 million dinars ($300,000) in foreign currency, which was a heavy burden and loss for Yugoslavia considering the trouble she had in obtaining foreign currency. The agreement provided that the Soviet Union should also invest machinery and installations for the construction of a shipyard with the purpose of developing the Yugoslav shipbuilding industry. Instead of meeting this provision, the Russians sent trucks, linen, glass and similar items to Yugoslavia. This caused double damage, for unnecessary material was imported, the construction of this important branch of industry came to a standstill, and the Yugoslav economy is still suffering considerable difficulties. The company also began to carry on motor transport instead of confining itself to river shipping, which was completely contrary to the agreement. It is quite clear that this was an act of sabotage, revealing the real features of Soviet intentions.

Let me give an example. In determining the goods transport tariffs for different countries the Director of "Juspad" discriminated against Yugoslavia. He fixed the tariffs of one ton-kilometer for Soviet goods at 0.19 dinars (38¢), for the goods of all the other Danubian countries at 0.28 dinars (56¢), and for Yugoslav goods at 0.40 dinars (80¢), so that Yugoslavia had to pay 52 per cent extra to carry her own goods on her own vessels invested in "Juspad." This alone cost Yugoslavia 38 million dinars ($760,000) in 1948, although the craft in the possession of the company were solely Yugoslav property and intended for Yugoslav requirements.

Hence, instead of assisting the economic development in Yugoslavia, the existence of "Justa" and "Juspad" proved to be a pure loss. The Soviet Union in this manner sought to establish a monopoly in Yugoslavia and deprive us of economic independence and sovereignty.

This deeply embittered our people. These agreements on the joint-stock companies, more than anything up to then in our experiences with the Soviet Union, opened the eyes of our people to Russia's real intentions toward Yugoslavia, her unwillingness to see Yugoslavia develop its economic potential freely, and her endeavors to enslave us economically.

The stalwart attitude of our negotiators also opened the eyes of the Soviet leaders. They saw that Yugoslavia was resolved to follow her own course in the development of her independence, that we regarded socialism as something serious, that we were tough and persistent.

Consequently the Soviet leaders began to change their tactics in negotiations on the joint-stock companies. On the one hand, they were partly satisfied because they had achieved quite a lot with the foundation of "Justa" and "Juspad"; they had gained a monopoly in air and river transport. On the other hand, they realized they had shown their hand too soon, that their negotiator Yatrov had been premature.

Tito

This was most evident during Edvard Kardelj's visit to Stalin in March, 1947, when the Yugoslav delegation was in Moscow in connection with the four-power talks on the Austrian peace treaty. Kardelj was prepared, in the name of the Yugoslav government, to point out to Stalin that the joint-stock companies, as far as they were proposed by the Soviet economic experts, were unacceptable to the Yugoslavs. However, before Kardelj started to express the views of the Yugoslav government, Stalin suddenly declared that joint-stock companies were unsuitable for Yugoslavia and should be established only in former enemy countries. The talk took place in Stalin's office in the Kremlin. It was attended by Stalin and Molotov for the Soviet, and by Edvard Kardelj, Vice-President of the Yugoslav Government, Stanoje Simić, the Foreign Minister, and Vladimir Popović, the Yugoslav Ambassador in Moscow.

This is an excerpt from their conversation as shown in notes made by the Yugoslav group. Kardelj delivered greetings in the name of Tito, who had just undergone an operation, at the hands of a Soviet surgeon that Stalin had sent to Yugoslavia, and said:

"First of all, I wish to express Marshal Tito's cordial greetings.

"Stalin: How is Comrade Tito?

"Molotov: Is he well after the operation?

"Kardelj: He is feeling very well, and the operation was a complete success. Only we are deeply sorry that Dr. Smotrov has died.

"Stalin: What did he die of?

"Kardelj: A heart attack.

"Stalin: Did he drink too much, perhaps? Surgeons like to drink, you know.

"Kardelj: No, he did not drink, as far as we know.

"Stalin (laughing and addressing Molotov): Did you send Tito a note about it?

"Molotov (also laughing): You know, it didn't come to that because there was no time, as Tito told us about it first. So we consider the matter closed."

After these and similar exchanges, the conversation turned to the real business, the problem of Yugoslavia's industrialization, and of the joint-stock companies. Stalin was the first to broach this question:

"How do matters stand with industry in your country? What about the production of pig iron, steel? Are you producing oil?

286

What is the capacity of your factories? Have you any oil refineries? How do you stand in electric power stations?"

Kardelj gave him information on our productive capacity both then and as envisaged under the Five-Year Plan. In connection with oil he said, "We are producing oil, to be sure, in small quantities, and we have an old type of refinery at Rijeka."

At these words Stalin and Molotov looked at each other, and Stalin said he was pleasantly surprised to hear that oil was being exploited in Yugoslavia even in a small way. Then he asked, "Do your oilfields lie near Hungary?"

Kardelj: "The oil belt extends from Rumania through Hungary and Yugoslavia and runs down to Albania. According to studies which were made earlier, as well as those made by Germans during the war, there is a great deal of oil in our country. As for the steel industry, it is small and out of date."

Having given the information Stalin asked for, Kardelj went on: "I wanted to speak to you about the joint-stock companies, and some misunderstandings that have arisen during negotiations. We were unable to accept the proposals of your delegation for both political and economic reasons. For example, we asked you to build an aluminum plant at Mostar, but your delegation did not consent."

Stalin: "When was our delegation there, and who headed it?"

Kardelj was unable to recall the name of the head of the delegation immediately, and continued, "We are interested in founding a joint oil extraction refining company."

Stalin raised his hand and asked Kardelj, "Is it not your opinion that joint-stock companies should not be set up because judging by everything they are not useful to you?" Without waiting for an answer, he added, "How would it be if we did not set up joint-stock companies, but helped you; how about our giving you an aluminum factory and a steel plant, and helping you extract and refine oil? Of course it is not a good form of co-operation to found joint-stock companies in an allied and friendly country like Yugoslavia. There would always be misunderstandings and differences; in a way the very independence of the country would suffer and friendly relations would be spoiled. Such companies are suitable for satellite countries."

The Yugoslav Ambassador in Moscow, Vladimir Popović, broke

in at this point, "Joint-stock civilian air transport and river shipping companies have already been formed."

Stalin: "Yes, but that is another thing. They are not productive companies, and they may continue with their work. We shall help you in this other way."

Molotov: "Yes, that is better and simpler."

Stalin: "Have you any plan? What capacity of aluminum and steel do you require?"

Kardelj: "I could not tell you at the moment, but in a few days we shall present you with our proposal in writing, and our delegation will come to complete this work. We agree fully to your proposal; I was just about to mention it, as the official view of the Yugoslav government, but you were first. We also believe such a solution is better and more suitable for us, and we thank you very much."

Stalin: "We shall let you have this on credit; we shall also help you with men, with specialists, and you shall pay something in money, or however you can." Stalin laughed as he concluded this part of the talks with the words, "However, we should get something from you."

In point of fact, Stalin had acted the demagogue at this meeting. He was satisfied that he had two joint-stock companies set up in Yugoslavia, giving him a monopoly in civilian air transport and in river shipping. He waived the other companies because he realized that we would not consent to companies such as the Soviet representatives planned. Seeing that we were adamant and unyielding in our resolve to follow a course of our own, he changed his tactics. That is why he magnanimously offered Yugoslavia capital goods credits, wanting to throw us off our guard so as to make the final reckoning more easily.

This visit was followed by negotiations which ended in the summer of 1947, when the Soviet Union agreed to grant Yugoslavia capital goods credit of 135 million dollars. Out of this credit the Soviet Union was to supply Yugoslavia with heavy industry installations, steel plants complete with a coking plant, installations for extracting and refining oil, a zinc electrolysis plant, a sulphuric acid factory, copper and aluminum rolling mills, molybdenum installations.

The agreement was a mere ruse, for the Soviet Union had no intention of honoring it. The terms for the manufacture of the installations under the agreement covered a long period, and did not meet capital expenditures even for the First Five-Year Plan. Of the 135 million dollars promised, the Soviet Union sent us installations valued at only $800,000. Then this agreement was renounced by the Soviet Union in 1949, causing heavy damage to Yugoslavia's economy, for we were dependent on the Soviet Union for all these enterprises.

There was exploitation also in the field of technical assistance. We paid our scholarship recipients, cadets and experts on study in the Soviet Union in roubles calculated at the official rate of 5.30 roubles for a dollar, although the real purchasing power of the rouble had been far less. We had to create the funds with exports, consisting on the whole of essential goods sold at Soviet prices, so that the Soviet Union for its services received our most valuable products in payment.

We wanted to regulate the question of technical assistance under an agreement between the Soviet and the Yugoslav governments. But the draft agreement which was submitted by the Soviet government toward the end of February, 1947, contained the three following principles: first, everything must be paid for; second, payments shall be made in a way and to an amount determined by Soviet organizations; third, calculations should be in dollars through the clearing account at the rate and conditions stated.

Yugoslavia was unable to accept such conditions.

But in the matter of technical "assistance," the difficult conditions of payment were not so important; what was important was the circumstance that the Soviet Union made use of it in order to develop its intelligence and similar activities, as has already been described.

Such was the character of the economic relations between the Soviet Union and Yugoslavia. They clearly indicate that the Soviet Union intended to subjugate Yugoslavia economically, to turn it into a raw-material appendage of Soviet economy, to prevent Yugoslavia's industrialization and to delay the further socialist development of our country. The Yugoslav government headed by Tito was firmly resolved not to permit such a turn of events.

CHAPTER XVIII

1947:

"We extended the hand of friendship . . ."

BEFORE resolving upon the final conquest of the countries he considered his sphere of influence in Eastern and Central Europe and the Balkan Peninsula, Stalin considered the possibility of bringing this area closer to the domination of the Soviet Union. But to do so it was not enough to bring to bear the pressure of the armed forces of the Soviet Union. He employed the tried and tested method so familiar to great powers involved in this part of the world: he incited one country against another by inflaming ancient differences. Finally, he counted on the fanaticism of many Communists, on their faith in the Soviet Union, on their faith in him personally. Among them he included the Communists of Yugoslavia, whom, as Tito says, he often called "chasni duraki," or "honest fools."

But first Stalin had to settle accounts with some of the Communist Parties in those countries where they were in power. His intention was to increase his grip on them with the help of his men. In Hungary, Rumania and Poland this was not difficult, for there had been no Communist Parties worth mentioning in those countries during the war. They appeared only with the bayonets of the Red Army when the Germans were driven out in 1944. The great majority of the leaders of those Parties had passed the war years in Moscow under the watchful eye of the N.K.V.D., and after 1944 they were simply moved to the capitals of their countries. But this was not the case with the Communist Party of Yugoslavia, whose leadership had steeled itself at home in the course of the struggle and had remained with the people, sharing good and evil with them. Stalin now had to penetrate this leadership and, failing that, it had to be isolated from other Balkan Communist Parties and forced into a new international workers' organization which would again be under Moscow's direction.

It is true that after the war there was no powerful instrument to control the other Parties and dictate their political line that the Comintern had been. Stalin himself had dissolved it in 1943 under pressure of the other great powers. Now, in his view, it was necessary to create something like the Comintern, different in form in view of the altered conditions, but essentially a more undemocratic, more obedient tool in Moscow's hands. The new body could also be usefully employed in the international workers' movement, as a powerful moral-political weapon for pressure on all the more developed and self-reliant Parties, especially the Communist Party of Yugoslavia, should they resist the demands of the Soviet Union.

In Yugoslavia there was for entirely different reasons a disposition to see such an international organization re-established. Such a consultative body could be of major service in the exchange of views, and in the exchange of the wealth of experience brought by the development during the past years.

Tito himself, in 1945, had submitted this idea to Stalin, who had welcomed it with open arms, although he failed to note that his own conception of a new International in the workers' movement was quite different from Tito's.

The matter was also discussed in June, 1946, when a Yugoslav delegation headed by Tito, Ranković, and Kidrič visited the Soviet Union. At that time a Bulgarian delegation including Dimitrov, Kolarov and Kostov had also arrived in Moscow for the funeral of the President of the Supreme Soviet, Kalinin.

During this visit Tito had several talks with Stalin, who on one occasion asked Tito whether he still thought that a new International, but informative in character, should be founded. Tito agreed, and then Stalin suggested, "It would be best if you Yugoslavs took the initiative."

That same evening Stalin invited the Yugoslavs and Bulgarians to his villa to dinner. One of the first topics that Stalin broached was the work of the Third International. On his left sat Dimitrov, the former Secretary General of the Comintern, on his right Tito, whose memories of the Comintern's work were not of the pleasantest. Stalin did not mince matters. He spoke about the Third International in sharp terms, and he rebuked Dimitrov to such an extent that the old man turned first pale and then red, to the acute embarrassment of the other guests. Dimitrov dared not justify himself, and Stalin continued his maneuvering, designed to win over the Yugoslavs. He developed the idea that the revival of the Third International in any form was altogether out of the question. But something else had to be created, he said. It was necessary to organize an informative body, that would meet from time to time, exchange general experiences, and make various decisions. Naturally, said Stalin, the decisions of this body would not be binding for any Party that did not agree to them.

Stalin continued his game. He wanted to deepen the gulf between Dimitrov and Tito even more by setting up a contest for the honor of initiating the new body. He hoped that the Bulgarians and Yugoslavs would quibble over the matter, and although before this meeting he had suggested to Tito that he should be the initiator, he now asked Dimitrov in Tito's presence, "What do you think? Who should be the initiator: you, Walter, or the French?"

Stalin used the name "Walter" by which Tito had been known in Moscow during Comintern days.

Dimitrov replied, "Walter could."

Tito, however, did not agree. "Let it be the French," he said.

And so the talk ended.

In the end, the Information Bureau of the Communist Parties was actually founded a year later, in the autumn of 1947. It is characteristic that Stalin's decision was carried out just when the Soviet Union had finally decided to take under her direct control a number of East European countries—Yugoslavia, Czechoslovakia, Poland, Bulgaria and Rumania—which until then had enjoyed to a greater or lesser extent far more freedom than do those which remain today Soviet satellites. Stalin considered the international situation ripe. The whole world had disarmed after the war except the Soviet Union; she had the obvious advantage.

Nor should it be forgotten that Stalin showed his hand exactly toward those countries which had been acknowledged during the war to be his sphere of interest. Invitations to the inaugural meeting of the Cominform were sent to the representatives of the Communist Parties in the countries that lay in the sphere of interest of the

Soviet Union: Yugoslavia, Bulgaria, Rumania, Hungary, Czechoslovakia and Poland. In addition, the consultation was attended by the representatives of the Parties of France and Italy, two of the strongest in Europe, which showed certain tendencies to follow an independent road to socialism that could have been exceedingly dangerous for Moscow, particularly in the case of France, a country so rich in revolutionary traditions.

No other Communist Party was invited to the founding of the new organization. Many Communists wondered that no representative of the Greek Party was present although it was carrying on an armed struggle in its country at the time and was attracting the attention of the whole of international public opinion. Bearing in mind the agreement on spheres of interest that the Soviet Union had concluded during the war with the other great powers, when it was decided that Greece should not fall within the Russian sphere, it is easy to understand why Stalin did not invite the Greeks.

A number of other Parties had not been invited, such as the Chinese, which was involved in a hard struggle with Chiang Kai-shek, the Communist Party of Great Britain and so on.

The Cominform meeting began in western Poland toward the end of September, 1947, in a small spa called Sklyarska Poremba, or Schreiberschau in German. The meeting was attended by Zhdanov and Malyenkov for the Soviet Communist Party, by Kardelj and Djilas of the Yugoslav Central Committee, Chervenkov and Poptomov for the Central Committee of the Bulgarian Workers' Party, Gheorgiu Dezh and Anna Pauker for the Communist Party of Rumania, Jacques Duclos and Etienne Fageon for the French Central Committee, Gomulka and Minc in the name of the Central Committee of the Polish Workers' Party, Luigi Longo and E. Reale for the Italian Communist Party, and Rudolf Slansky and S. Bashtovanski on behalf of the Czech Central Committee.

The meeting lasted seven days, and all the participants and their staffs stayed in a convalescent home of the Ministry of State Security of Poland in the middle of a park measuring five or six hundred yards across. The conference hall and dining rooms were in the same building. The building and the park were strongly guarded.

A report on the international situation was read by Zhdanov. His chief topic was the existence of two camps in the world: the imperialists headed by the United States, who were making large-scale preparations for war against the anti-imperialist bloc, and the anti-imperialists led by the Soviet Union.

He was followed by a representative of each country, who reported on the activity of his Party. Two resolutions were adopted toward the close of this meeting to found the Information Bureau of Communist Parties, as the new organization was to be known officially. The first declaration contained the political line, the second established the organizational principles. The second resolution read:

"It is confirmed that the absence of connections among the Communist Parties taking part in this consultation is a serious drawback in the present situation. Experience has shown that the absence of such connections among Communist Parties is incorrect and harmful. The need for the exchange of experiences and for voluntary co-ordination of action among the Parties has grown particularly pressing today by reason of the complex postwar international situation, in which the lack of connections among the Communist Parties can do harm to the working class.

"Guided by this, the participants in the consultation have agreed on the following:

"First, to found an Information Bureau of the representatives of the Communist Party of Yugoslavia, the Bulgarian Workers' Party (Communists), the Communist Party of Rumania, the Hungarian Communist Party, the Polish Workers' Party, the All-Union Communist Party (Bolsheviks), the Communist Party of France, the Communist Party of Czechoslovakia, and the Communist Party of Italy.

"Second, the Information Bureau shall be charged with the task of organizing the exchange of experiences and, if necessary, with the co-ordination of the activity of the Communist Parties *on the basis of mutual agreement.*

"Third, the Information Bureau shall be composed of representatives of the Central Committees, to the number of two members from each Central Committee, the delegations of the Central Committees being determined and replaced by the Central Committees.

"Fourth, the Information Bureau shall found a fortnightly and later a weekly organ, to be published in French and Russian, and if possible in other languages.

"Fifth, the headquarters of the Information Bureau shall be in Belgrade."

The full text of the announcement is given because it indicates that this was to have been only a consultative body, and that coordination between the Communist Parties was to have been promoted only on a basis of mutual agreement. The Cominform was to have been something altogether different from the old Comintern, which had been in essence an instrument in Stalin's hands. But it was evident from the first day of the Cominform's existence that Stalin intended to create under this cloak something worse than the Comintern had been.

It is typical that the Communist Party of Yugoslavia was named first in all the communiqués. When the seat of the new organization was discussed, there were proposals that it should be in Prague. However, Zhdanov telephoned Stalin, who replied himself to establish it in Belgrade.

It was no accident that Yugoslavia was given top place at the first meeting. The intention was to bind her as tightly as possible to this organization in order to facilitate the blow that was to follow. Not only this: the first Cominform consultation is typical in that its aim was to create a gulf between the Yugoslav Party and those of France and Italy, the most independent Communist Parties in Europe at the time. Zhdanov cleverly instructed our representatives Kardelj and Djilas to speak first in the discussion after the reports delivered by Duclos and Luigi Longo, the French and Italian representatives, and to criticize the policy of their two Parties. Kardelj and Djilas needed no persuading, because the Yugoslav Party had deeply critical observations to make on the work of these two Parties during the war and immediately after.

In his report Duclos defended the policy of being in the government, opposing strikes and demonstrations, and supporting the government's economic measures. Even as he spoke, Zhdanov flung at him, "While you are fighting to stay in the government, they throw you out."

Zhdanov also had remarks to make during Longo's report. During the discussion the Italian Party's policy was criticized by Edvard Kardelj and the French Party's by Milovan Djilas. Duclos and Longo reacted differently to the attitude of the Yugoslav delegation: Duclos was angry, and huffily refused to speak to anyone. After the meeting he withdrew into the park and sat on a bench alone, restlessly swinging his short legs, which could not reach the ground. Longo, on the contrary, asked for a meeting with the Yugoslav delegation to hear their criticism in more detail. As to their wartime policy, he said, they had acted on Moscow's instructions.

Work was resumed. After Zhdanov's observations, during which he upheld Yugoslav criticism, Duclos admitted that the line of the French Party had been opportunist. Longo did the same. Zhdanov remarked again, "You Italian comrades are bigger parliamentarians than de Gasperi himself. You are the biggest political party, and yet they throw you out of the government."

It is typical that Malyenkov spoke a great deal at this meeting about preparations for the congress of the Soviet Communist Party, which had not been convened since 1938. This congress was to adopt a fifteen-year plan of transition from socialism to communism. After he had completed his report Malyenkov observed that the Soviet Union was drawing in detail upon the utopian socialists. However, the congress has never been held, and it is now more than fourteen years since the congress has met. This undoubtedly indicates the ideological confusion that exists in the Soviet Union. There are many questions that cannot be answered. They speak about the transition to Communism when they are faced by a maze of unsolved questions. The peasant problem, for example, remains a bad headache, as does the question of nationalities.

During the meeting there was also some discussion with Gomulka, who several times came into direct conflict with Zhdanov as to the path Poland should follow. He said above all that collectivization in Poland should be pursued cautiously, that the peasants were resisting strongly. Gomulka also spoke with the Yugoslav delegates about the difficulty of a Partisan uprising during the war in Poland. He spoke of the German terror, the execution in Poland of three million Jews alone, the shooting of hundreds of thousands of Poles. Gomulka was supported by the Czechoslovak delegate. The Yugoslav delegates put forward their view, explaining the Yugoslav experience: that German and Italian terror had reigned in Yugoslavia no less, and that the uprising had developed for that very reason. When the people had taken up arms, more lives were spared destruction by the Germans.

Gomulka had his own opinion on several other questions. He was, indeed, against organizing the Cominform. Later he yielded but requested that no announcement be made of the meeting or the organization of the new body, but that it should remain secret. Everybody opposed his proposal, and finally all the resolutions and decisions were signed unanimously.

Zhdanov and Malyenkov had achieved their object. The Cominform had been founded. Duclos and Longo left Poland offended with Yugoslavia. The seed of discord had been sown among the largest Communist Parties in Europe. That the Cominform was founded by the Russians chiefly as an instrument for their particular policy, primarily against Yugoslavia, is borne out by the fact that after this first meeting the Cominform met only twice during the first two years of its work, and on both occasions decisions were taken against Yugoslavia. Apart from this, a meeting was held in Yugoslavia on December 15, 1947, merely to discuss the purely technical questions of editing the Cominform paper *For a Lasting Peace for the People's Democracy*.

According to this paper's statute, there should have been a representative of each Party in the Cominform on the editorial board. The whole thing, however, was in the hands of Pavel Yudin, the representative of the Soviet Party, a philosopher by profession, who on several occasions had been compelled to admit publicly the fallacy of his philosophical views. In the Soviet Union there was a joke about Yudin, that he is "the best philosopher among the N.K.V.D.-men and the best N.K.V.D.-man among the philosophers." How servile was Yudin toward the members of the Soviet Politburo is best shown by this eyewitness account of Vladimir Popović, then the Yugoslav Ambassador in Moscow:

"At the end of 1947 I paid a visit to Zhdanov in connection with some problems of Albania. While we were discussing the matter, the telephone rang and Zhdanov told me that Yudin would arrive with an issue of the Cominform journal, published in Belgrade. A few minutes later the door opened and Yudin came in, bowing toward Zhdanov while he was approaching him. He left the newspaper on the table and retreated, bowing all the time. He covered that way more than six or seven yards, because the room was rather large, and in going backward toward the door he was still bowing, hitting the door with his back, nervously trying to find with his hand the door-knob to make an exit."

Yudin moved to Belgrade in October, 1947, and asked for one of the largest buildings in the center of the city for the Cominform headquarters. He immediately set up a radio-telephone with Moscow, and a telegraph-radio station. The paper was printed at "Borba," the biggest printing press in Yugoslavia, in Russian, French, English and Serbo-Croat. Lacking faith in the Yugoslav typesetters, Yudin brought his own from Moscow. All the work was done in the strictest secrecy; "Borba" had to allot special rooms for setting and make-up. Yudin employed a Yugoslav worker for make-up, who was carefully watched by Yudin's assistant Olyenin in case he took any of the proofs. After work or during lunchtime he would lock the rooms and even seal the doors, lest anyone should chance to enter.

Yudin had brought several Soviet journalists, or people who called themselves journalists, from the Soviet Union, and arbitrarily brought them to the meetings of the editorial board, although the statute did not entitle him to do so.

The board meetings were devoted to discussing what was to be written in each number; but later the articles were on countless occasions greatly altered from the original text, without the knowledge or permission of the writer and the board. The Polish representative Finkelstein especially protested against the arbitrary alterations in an article by a Polish statesman.

How much equality there was on the editorial board is best illustrated by the fact that the paper had to be censored in Moscow. When the first hundred copies were printed, work was interrupted, the plates removed from the cylinders, the paper assembled and printing postponed for several days. A number of copies, known as "signal impressions," were sent to Moscow by the special plane always at Yudin's disposal. The "signal impressions" were seen personally by Stalin and Molotov. When they had approved, orders arrived over the special radio-telephone that publication should go on.

This happened for every number. At times Yudin himself would go to Moscow with the "signal impressions" and corrections were dictated from there. Occasionally there were so many changes that some of the articles had to be reset, the whole paper made up again, printed, sent to Moscow and returned with new corrections.

On one occasion the paper had passed through all the stages of censorship and orders were given to go ahead. The French, English, and Russian editions had already been printed when orders arrived to withdraw the paper. Yudin ordered the copies to be transferred from "Borba" to the Cominform building. During a whole day and night these copies were carefully burned in the furnace in the presence of Yudin's assistant. He saw to it that nobody took a copy. The reason for this destruction was an article of the General Secretary of the Greek Communist Party, Zachariades, that was not to Stalin's liking.

This is only one instance of inequality on the editorial board, of the esteem in which were held the views of such distinguished and veteran leaders in the workers' movement as Dimitrov, and of how thoroughly the Cominform was really an instrument of Soviet foreign policy.

Yudin's work in Belgrade was not restricted to the paper. He, as well as the Soviet Ambassador Lavrentyev, took an active part in preparing the final settlement with Yugoslavia. He tried hard to poison relations between Yugoslavia and her neighbors, especially Bulgaria and Albania.

In fact, Stalin and the Soviet leaders, in their plans to isolate Yugoslavia, resorted to the old method, used so many times in history: to provoke conflict between the small Balkan states. If we survey the nineteenth and twentieth centuries, we shall see how some of the economically backward Balkan states have always served first one of the great powers and then another, thanks to their internal weakness and their regimes. The Balkan Peninsula earned the name of "Powder Keg" through no fault of its people. Living in a strategic area of tremendous importance, the Balkan nations were the prey of the great powers whose interests clashed here.

New Yugoslavia considered it was high time to put an end to this situation and to develop the idea of brotherhood among the Balkan nations, who should take their fate into their own hands. Such ideas, however, did not suit Stalin's plans. Tito says in this connection: "One thing especially was a thorn in the flesh of the Soviet leaders, and that was our attempts to establish good-neighbor relations with the surrounding peoples in the Balkans, the Bulgarians, Albanians, Hungarians, Rumanians. We had made efforts in this direction before, during and after the war in which those countries joined in the attack on Yugoslavia, or were used by the Germans and Italians as a springboard in their attacks against us. We let bygones be bygones and extended the hand of friendship, because we knew that not the people of those countries but their semifeudal regimes and monarchies were to blame. We demonstrated our desire for sincere relations with a number of concrete facts."

During the early postwar years Yugoslavia concluded a number of treaties of friendship and mutual assistance with her neighbors and other countries in Eastern Europe. The treaty with Poland was signed in Warsaw on March 18, 1946, with Czechoslovakia in Belgrade on May 9, 1946, with Albania in Belgrade on July 9, 1946, with Bulgaria at Evsinograd on November 27, 1947, and with Rumania at Bucharest on December 19, 1947. All these treaties were concluded with a view to consolidating "friendship and close co-operation between the peoples of both countries and of all the United Nations" and "to contribute to the postwar organization of peace and security." The parties to the treaty bound themselves to extend military and other assistance to each other with all the means at their disposal if either of them was involved in military action. Furthermore, each side was under the obligation not to enter into any alliance, or to take part in any action, aimed at the other party.

Such were the treaties. How were they enforced? Let us take the attitude of Yugoslavia, the largest Balkan country, toward Albania, the smallest. Since economic relations are a measure of the intentions of one country toward another, a brief survey of economic relations between Yugoslavia and Albania will be the best comparison with those between the Soviet Union and the East European countries.

It came as a surprise to many Communists in Yugoslavia and in other East European countries when after the war they saw that the economic relations between their countries and the Soviet Union were based on purely capitalist principles: that is to say, trade was regulated according to world prices. This means that the countries with weaker means of production are exploited by the advanced countries trading with them. Mikoyan, a member of the Soviet Politburo, once said openly to a Yugoslav representative: "Trade is trade; I am not engaged in making presents but in carrying on trade."

Let us consider on the other hand the principles on which Albano-Yugoslav economic relations rested. Though she herself is economically underdeveloped, Yugoslavia's economy is far in advance of Albania's, and Yugoslavia could easily have exploited Albania had world prices been the basis of trade as they are in Soviet Union trade with the East European countries. Instead of this, the two countries agreed that Albania should sell her goods at prices prevailing on the Albanian market, and Yugoslavia at prices prevailing on the Yugoslav market. The difference in prices was covered by Yugoslavia out of the price-equalization fund opened for this purpose with special Yugoslav credit.

This prevented Yugoslavia from drawing extra profit deriving from the difference in the economic development of the two countries. Having neither trade relations nor organizations, the Albanians asked Yugoslavia to sell their copper on the world market. At that time the world price of copper was four times less than the price of copper in Albania, because of the primitive methods of mining and of the poor quality of the ore in that country. The difference between the two prices was paid to Albania out of special credits granted it by Yugoslavia in 1947 and again in 1948.

The joint-stock companies were also typical of relations between the Soviet Union and other East European countries. We have seen that the representatives of the Soviet Union refused to found joint-stock companies that would promote Yugoslavia's productive forces, but wanted only companies that would make profits, with no regard for the development of Yugoslavia's industry. We have seen, too, that the Soviet Union was reluctant to invest capital goods in these companies in Yugoslavia. This reluctance was even more marked in Rumania, where the Soviet Union invested former German and Italian assets as its share capital.

But when Yugoslavia founded joint-stock companies in Albania at that country's request, she sought primarily the development of Albania's productive forces. A railway-construction company was founded, because until then Albania had not a single railway line. Certain factories were transferred bodily from Yugoslavia to Albania.

With the help of these joint-stock companies a railway line thirty miles long was built from Durazzo to Petzinj, and preparations were made to construct a line from Durazzo to Tirana. Installations were sent from Yugoslavia for a sugar factory at Korcha, a fruit- and vegetable-processing factory at Elbasan, a hemp and flax factory at Rogozina, a fish cannery at Valona, a modern printing press in Tirana, an automatic telephone exchange in Tirana, as well as machinery for a textile factory.

That is what Yugoslavia did for Albania in two years when she was herself faced with great economic difficulties. During that period the Soviet Union did not send a single factory to Yugoslavia.

Second, Yugoslavia paid Albania ground rent, whereas the Soviet Union refused to pay ground rent to Yugoslavia. Third, during the three-year existence of the joint Albano-Yugoslav companies, Yugoslavia never drew her share of the profit, but reinvested it in the company. Fourth, Yugoslavia went even further and, although in the throes of difficulties, granted Albania a credit of two billion leks (about forty million dollars) in 1947, and three billion leks in 1948.

Yugoslavia also extended Albania technical assistance in the form of 597 experts, including forty-three engineers. The Albanians also asked for the assistance of military experts.

The Albanian Assistant Minister of Finance, Andul Kelezi, declared in the Albanian Parliament on July 17, 1947, "The present valuable aid from the people of Yugoslavia of two billion leks constitutes 56.73 per cent of the revenue of our national budget. The brotherly peoples of Yugoslavia are helping us today with no ulterior motives, with the sole aim of raising our economy, to assure our people a better life, because the road of our peoples is the glorious road to socialism."

In addition to this, Yugoslavia made direct gifts to Albania. In 1946 she sent her 20,000 tons of corn and wheat to relieve the famine. When in October, 1946, there were terrible floods in Albania, 57 million dinars was collected in Yugoslavia and sent as first aid to the victims. She also granted a second credit in equipment and food for the Albanian army amounting to 700 million leks.

When the assistance Yugoslavia gave Albania during three postwar years is added up it comes to far more than Yugoslavia granted her own economically backward republics, Macedonia and Montenegro, out of her central budget.

The development of Albano-Yugoslav relations was followed with close attention in Moscow. There was not a single meeting between Stalin and the Yugoslav representatives at which Albania was not discussed. For instance, when Kardelj met Stalin in 1947, Stalin suddenly asked: "How are things with the Albanians? Enver Hoxha has complained about your political advisers in their army, he says they are weakening discipline, or something of the sort."

Kardelj: "That is news to us. They said nothing to us about it."

Stalin: "What is the origin of the Albanians?"

Kardelj: "They are descendants of the Illyrians."

Stalin: "I remember Tito told me they were related to the Basques."

Kardelj: "Yes, that's right."

Stalin: "They seem to be rather backward and primitive people."

Ambassador Vladimir Popović: "But they are very brave and faithful."

Stalin: "Yes, they can be as faithful as a dog; that is one of the traits of the primitive. Our Chuvashi were the same. The Russian tsars always took them for their bodyguard."

After a few more questions Stalin asked about the religion of the Albanians, and the conversation turned to other topics, to the Yugoslav bourgeoisie, and then Stalin reverted to Albania.

He asked Kardelj: "Do you know Enver well? What is your opinion of him? Is he a consistent man? Will he remain with us to the end?"

Kardelj: "Our opinion is that he is good and honest on the whole, although he has certain characteristics of a petty bourgeoisie intellectual. He has a good war record and the people love him. But he lacks Marxist-Leninist training. Still, we think that he will hold on. But we consider that the best and most consistent man over there is Kochi Dzodze, a worker, although he also lacks training."

Stalin: "They had some disagreement?"

Kardelj: "That's all settled now."

Stalin to Molotov: "What do you think?"

Molotov: "I think that the opinion of the Yugoslavs is right. I saw Hoxha in Paris. He is very handsome and leaves a good impression. He is quite cultured, but you feel Western influence in his upbringing."

The conversation ended there.

At the same time Soviet agents in Albania were actively engaged in provoking a conflict between Enver Hoxha and Kochi Dzodze, and constantly intriguing against Yugoslavia.

Something similar was being done in Bulgaria, Yugoslavia's neighbor. For hundreds of years there had been an effort among the people of Bulgaria and Yugoslavia to unite into one state, for they are related in language and customs.

After the war new Yugoslavia undertook a whole series of steps to normalize her relations with Bulgaria, which had taken part in the attack on our country. For example, not only did we waive reparations claims to the value of 25 million dollars for damage done by the Bulgarian army on Yugoslav territory, but even restitution of a part of the goods Bulgarian troops had taken to their country during the war.

Talks had commenced immediately after the war for the creation of a federation between Yugoslavia and Bulgaria. The initiative, in November, 1944, came from Yugoslavia, which made a draft of the federation, and Kardelj went to Sofia to talk over these matters in detail with the Bulgarian statesmen. The Bulgarian view was not identical with ours; they insisted that Bulgaria should join the federation as one member, Yugoslavia being the other. We pointed out that Yugoslavia consists of six separate republics, which are equal members of the Yugoslav federation; that some of these republics, like Serbia and Montenegro, for example, had been independent states long before Bulgaria, and that a federation could be created only if Bulgaria became one of the seven South Slav states in the new federation.

The Soviet representatives drove the wedge deeper into these opposed views. The Bulgarians proved susceptible to Russian designs. One of their representatives openly said to us: "The federation will be a fine thing: we Bulgarians are clever, you Yugoslavs rich!"

Finally the matter was discussed in Moscow. Stalin said the Yugoslavs were right, agreeing with our views only verbally, for the Russian representatives immediately declared that there were new difficulties and the whole matter was postponed. At the Bled meeting, in 1947, the question of federation was again raised with Dimitrov, and it was decided it should be accomplished gradually.

Yugoslavia consolidated relations with the other East European countries as well, especially Czechoslovakia and Poland. The Polish government had on several occasions urged through its Ambassador in Belgrade that Tito should go to Poland on an official visit, explaining that "political conditions are difficult in Poland and that Marshal Tito has the moral right to speak to the people, because Yugoslavia enjoys great fellow-feeling in Poland." That was in 1946. Tito visited Poland and then Czechoslovakia. In Poland he met Gomulka and Bierut. Gomulka made a favorable impression on him. He was a worker, rather modest and reticent; Bierut was more like an ordinary civil servant ready to carry out every order of his superiors.

Both in Poland and in Czechoslovakia Tito was welcomed by huge crowds, which was immediately noticed by the Soviet leaders. The welcome in Czechoslovakia was especially remarkable. In Prague he had a long talk with Beneš, whose health was already breaking down. Beneš was very slow in answering questions, and frequently skipped from one topic to another. On this occasion a treaty of friendship and mutual assistance was to have been signed between Czechoslovakia and Yugoslavia. But Beneš made reservations about the inclusion of a mutual assistance clause, and the agreement was not signed until later, in Belgrade. Gottwald told Tito about Beneš's misgivings. "When I mentioned the agreement to Beneš," Gottwald said, "he warned me saying: 'I don't know whether we should insert the mutual assistance clause. I am afraid those Yugoslavs might go to war with the Western powers over Trieste and involve us. You don't know the Yugoslavs. They are a strange people. You never know what they are going to do. Somehow they always stick to a course of their own. I know them well from the First World War.' "

Nevertheless, the agreement was signed. After visiting Czechoslovakia and Poland, Tito accepted the invitations of other East European countries. He visited Bulgaria; Rakosi in Hungary insisted that Tito must also come to his country. Again hundreds of thousands of people came out into the streets, this time in the Hungarian capital. The Soviet press hardly recorded this event, although Tito had consulted Moscow about each visit.

Then came an invitation from Rumania. Tito had not the time to inform the Russians. The welcome in Rumania exceeded all expectations. More than half a million people gathered in a driving snowstorm on the main square of Bucharest to hear Tito's speech. In those days Anna Pauker was boss in Rumania. Having been released from a Rumanian jail before the war, she emigrated to the Soviet Union, where she became an obedient servant of the N.K.V.D. Her husband was arrested and sentenced to imprisonment in Siberia. The relations between Anna Pauker and the Soviet organs in Rumania is best illustrated by the following example. Several Yugoslavs had gone to Rumania to discuss particulars in connection with Tito's visit. One of them was talking to Anna Pauker and with members of the Rumanian Politburo late into the night. It was perhaps two o'clock in the morning when the telephone rang. It was the Soviet Ambassador. Anna Pauker excused herself, saying she had to leave to call on the Soviet Ambassador with the other members of the Politburo. The Rumanian Politburo had to report to the Soviet Ambassador, and this on a telephone summons at two o'clock in the morning.

Tito's visits, and the warm welcome accorded him everywhere, provoked irritation in Moscow. In addition to this a treaty of friendship and mutual assistance had been signed in Bulgaria. Yugoslavia's prestige had grown enormously. On all these journeys responsible people praised Yugoslav experience, saying it was closer to them than Soviet experience was because Yugoslavia was a country that had just emerged from a revolution. These conversations were heard by various N.K.V.D. agents in the leadership of the different Parties, such as Bodnarosh in Rumania. This man was an officer in the old Royal Rumanian Army. Then he became a Communist and emigrated to the Soviet Union. He came to Rumania in 1944 as a Soviet officer, and then the N.K.V.D. appointed him to one of the most responsible offices in the Rumanian government. He was its Secretary General.

In Bulgaria Dimitrov was especially enthusiastic over the development of relations between Yugoslavia and Bulgaria, although he was surrounded by men who were in Russian service. He had already given to a narrow circle his view on the need to create a federation or a custom union among the Balkan and Danubian countries. He was preparing to speak openly about it.

However, the Kremlin had already decided to begin liquidating the whole process of *rapprochement* among the nations of Central Europe and the Balkans. It was necessary to strike at the nerve center, at Yugoslavia. Stalin perfected preparations for the final blow. He considered that international conditions were ripe. All the Eastern European countries, especially Yugoslavia, had strained relations with the Western powers. At that time only the Soviet Union, of all the big states, had a huge well-equipped army.

CHAPTER XIX

1948:

"But now . . . the Russians are hindering us . . ."

EARLY in January, 1948, there was apparent calm in Yugoslavia. The winter had been unusually mild, and there were many beautiful sunny days. People were talking about the beginning of production in the machine-tool factory at Železnik near Belgrade, the first big enterprise built in eastern Yugoslavia under the Five-Year Plan, or about the dispute with the United States government over the gold which had been removed from the strong-rooms of the Yugoslav National Bank and shipped to the United States in 1940 to be safe from Hitler. It was a great deal—almost fifty million dollars' worth. The American government was unwilling to return this gold to Yugoslavia after the war, claiming forty-two million dollars, which it later reduced to twenty millions, as compensation for nationalized American assets in Yugoslavia. The two governments exchanged a number of notes; the Yugoslav Ambassador in Washington, Sava Kosanović, said at a press conference, "We entrusted this gold to the United States to keep it from falling into Hitler's hands and being used by the enemy against the Allies. I regret to be compelled to say this: Had we allowed Hitler to plunder this gold, we should not need today to prove our right to it as we must now, having entrusted it to an allied friendly state. The two largest industrial plants built in Yugoslavia with American capital, the Socony Vacuum plant at Slavonski Brod, and the electric power plant at Novi Sad, were destroyed by the Anglo-American air force during the war. Now Yugoslavia is required to pay in gold one hundred per cent of their value."

1948

In Yugoslavia the people were agitated. *Borba* wrote angrily:

"Our public opinion interprets this attitude of the American government as a direct attempt to hamper the construction of New Yugoslavia, whose efforts are a significant contribution to the rehabilitation of all Europe. Our public opinion condemns this latest injustice which is being done us by Wall Street diplomacy, and vigorously demands the return of property belonging to the peoples of Yugoslavia, with which no one has the right to speculate for inadmissible extortionate purposes."

The Yugoslav government made known her intention to lay the issue before the Economic-Social Council of the United Nations.

In the midst of the excitement over this issue, a telegram arrived in Belgrade from Moscow signed by Stalin personally. The Soviet Ambassador in Belgrade, Lavrentyev, a husky man with a diplomatically expressionless face, delivered the telegram personally to Tito. Stalin required that someone from the Yugoslav Politburo, if possible Djilas, leave immediately for Moscow to discuss various current issues, especially in connection with Albania.

No one in Belgrade was surprised by the telegram. There were many questions to be settled: the problem of defending southern Albania; the purchase of war material from the Soviet Union for the Yugoslav army; the question of machinery for the war industry and for the navy, and others. But it was rather unusual that Stalin should ask just Djilas to go to Moscow. Later it was easy to guess why. During both Djilas's visits to Moscow, in 1944 and 1945, Stalin had become convinced that Djilas was a very frank man, who said what he thought. Was it Stalin's intention with this invitation to cause a rift in the Politburo by winning Djilas to his side? Back in 1946 he had invited him to spend his holiday on the Black Sea coast, but Djilas had not gone, thinking it a courtesy invitation. Or perhaps Stalin wanted to extract some statements from Djilas on open questions, and then by distorting them to use them as an argument in the struggle he was preparing with Yugoslavia.

Djilas left Belgrade by train for Moscow through Rumania. He was accompanied by a Yugoslav military delegation, Koča Popović, Chief of Staff, Svetozar Vukmanović, Chief of the Political Department of the General Staff, and several other military figures.

In Bucharest the Yugoslav delegation was welcomed at the station

309

Tito

by Gheorghiu Dezh, Anna Pauker and Bodnarosh. The Yugoslav
Ambassador, Radonja Golubović,* entertained the delegation at
supper, during which a discussion took place between Vukmanović
and Bodnarosh about the development of the army in Yugoslavia
and Rumania. Bodnarosh took the view that the bourgeoisie held its
army together only with the help of the noncommissioned officers,
and that it was now necessary to abolish the N.C.O.'s in Rumania.
Vukmanović, on the other hand, maintained that the noncommissioned officers should not be abolished, but retained and re-educated.
Anna Pauker broke in, saying to Bodnarosh:

"Don't you see that the Yugoslav comrade is right? That's how it
should be done."

The discussion then turned on the value to Rumania and Yugoslavia of the experiences of the Red Army. Bodnarosh stated that
Rumania should make use of Soviet experience. The other Rumanians present at the supper demurred, saying that Yugoslav experiences were more useful to Rumania, because like Yugoslavia, Rumania was only just creating something new, and that the two countries had the same problems. Bodnarosh shook his head.

The Yugoslav delegation made its farewell and left Bucharest
about midnight, proceeding for Moscow by train. At Jassy they
transferred to a parlor car provided by the Soviet government. The
wide Russian tracks ran from there. The train went slowly, never
more than thirty miles an hour, through districts devastated during
the war. The whole journey from Belgrade to Moscow lasted almost five days and nights.

In Moscow the delegation was accommodated in the well-ap-
pointed Moscow Hotel in the heart of the city. Shown to his room,
Djilas said he would rather not be alone but preferred to share a
room with Koča Popović. This made the management uneasy, for
it placed Djilas in a room on the fourth floor, and not the one reserved for him. The management begged him to move into a big
bedroom with a sitting room on the second floor, which he did.
Shortly afterward some electricians arrived to "repair" the suite.

Hardly had the Yugoslavs made themselves comfortable, two or

---

* Radonja Golubović had already been engaged by the N.K.V.D. After June,
1948, he declared himself for the Cominform resolution, and against Yugoslavia.

three hours after their arrival, when Djilas received an invitation from Stalin to call on him at the Kremlin unless he was unduly tired after the journey. Djilas went immediately and was welcomed by Stalin and Molotov. Without many preliminaries Stalin began to speak about the Albanian problem. "The government of the USSR has no pretensions whatsoever concerning Albania. Yugoslavia is free to swallow Albania any time it wishes to do so." At the word "swallow" Stalin gestured: he licked the fingers of his right hand.

Djilas was astonished by this remark, and retorted, "But, Comrade Stalin, there is no question of swallowing Albania, but of friendly and allied relations between two countries."

"Well, that's one and the same thing," Molotov remarked.

Stalin spoke again, saying he considered relations between Yugoslavia and Albania correct, and that a telegram should be sent to Tito to that effect. He suggested that Djilas should write the telegram and have it sent to Belgrade in Stalin's name.

Probably Stalin thought he would thus induce Djilas to write a telegram expressing what he, Stalin, had said about Albania, so as to have an argument about Yugoslavia's alleged imperialist aspirations toward Albania. Djilas sent the text of the telegram to Stalin the next day, but it was never sent to Belgrade, for its contents were not what Stalin had suggested.

At this meeting, Djilas informed Stalin of the arrival of our military delegation and of its requirements. Stalin professed generosity and promised everything the Yugoslavs asked for. He simply waved his hand and said: "*Chepoukha!* [A trifle.] We'll give you everything."

Djilas told him that Yugoslavia asked for no secret weapons from the Soviet Union.

"There are no secrets from a friendly and allied army like the Yugoslav," Stalin replied.

In Djilas' presence Stalin telephoned to Marshal Bulganin, the Minister of National Defense, asking him to receive the Yugoslav military delegation without delay, and to comply with all its requests.

These talks completed, Stalin invited Djilas to supper at his villa. Besides Stalin and Molotov, there were Zhdanov, Voznesenski and

Beria. Voznesenski was silent the whole evening, but Beria was talkative. He is a rather stout man, with a fleshy face and blue ice-cold staring eyes which are always on the alert.

At about five o'clock the next afternoon, Djilas was received with the delegation by Marshal Bulganin. In his room were also present from the Russian side: Marshal Vassilievski, Antonov and other leaders of the Soviet army. Djilas put forward the Yugoslav requests. Bulganin was no less generous than Stalin: *"Chepoukha!* You will have everything!"*

Bulganin immediately told Marshal Vassilievski to form a joint commission of specialists to work throughout Sunday, and to have results by Monday.

A cheerful mood prevailed in the Yugoslav delegation, who thought the whole job would be completed in three or four days. Monday came, then Tuesday, Wednesday, Thursday, Friday, Saturday, and still no results. The Yugoslavs seemed to have been forgotten. Vukmanović interceded with Bulganin, who answered briefly, "Complications have arisen."

The wait continued. Our delegation went to the Bolshoi Theater almost every night, visited museums, saw the city. Svetozar Vukmanović went to see the Red Army Museum, where the N.K.V.D. officer escorting him asked him to write down his impressions. Vukmanović wrote that he was not pleased with the museum, for there was very little material in it from the revolution and civil war. The N.K.V.D. officer agreed with this and himself drew Vukmanović's attention by saying, "Look, there are some more shortcomings. For example, there isn't enough about Lenin's role in 1918."

On their return to the hotel, the Yugoslavs talked to each other about their other impressions of Moscow, not concealing their observations on many things.

Since no reply arrived from the Kremlin, Djilas, Koča Popović and Vukmanović expressed the desire to visit Leningrad. They were warmly welcomed there, given a villa, and received by Popov, the Secretary of the Regional Committee.

"Somehow, in Leningrad one feels different than in Moscow. It is the atmosphere of the city where the October Revolution started, it is the atmosphere of the city which fought bravely in the last war," the Yugoslavs said to their escort Lisyakov, who was employed in the Agitprop of the Central Committee and attached to Djilas.

The military delegation was constantly escorted by an N.K.V.D. major. When General Vukmanović called on the Commissar of the Leningrad Front, a colonel general, the N.K.V.D. major was present. It was a rule in the Soviet Union that even a Front Commissar must not speak to foreigners unless someone from the N.K.V.D. was present.

The Yugoslavs stayed in Leningrad several days, visiting the city's landmarks of the October Revolution, and important spots in the city's heroic defense in the war, and then returned to Moscow. There was still no answer from the Kremlin. Djilas was received by Mikoyan and had a talk about the contract for the sale of Soviet films to Yugoslavia. Djilas emphasized that the contract was very difficult for us, but Mikoyan firmly refused to revise it, saying he did not wish to make any precedent which other East European countries might invoke.

The Yugoslav delegation had been in Moscow nearly one month, and still there were no results. The reasons began to crystallize. The National Assembly in Belgrade had meanwhile ratified the treaties of friendship, co-operation and mutual assistance between Yugoslavia on one side and Bulgaria, Hungary and Rumania respectively on the other. During this session Edvard Kardelj had delivered a long address in which he had summed up the results of Marshal Tito's visits to the neighboring countries. This was new fuel for Stalin's fire. At about that time Dimitrov set out on an official visit to Rumania. In an interview, on this occasion, he made a statement on the Balkan federation. The question read:

"It is rumored that a federation of Balkan nations and a federation of the areas of Eastern and Southeastern Europe to include Hungary, Czechoslovakia and Poland is imminent. In the event of such federation being created, will other countries from these regions also be able to join it?"

Dimitrov replied, "The question of a federation or confederation is premature for us. It is not on the agenda at present, and therefore this question was not a subject of the discussion at our conferences. When the question matures, and it must inevitably mature, then our peoples, the nations of people's democracy, Rumania, Bulgaria, Yu-

goslavia, Albania, Czechoslovakia, Poland, Hungary and Greece—
mind you, and Greece!—will settle it. It is they who will decide
what it will be—a federation or confederation, and when and how
it will be formed. I can say that what our peoples are already doing
greatly facilitates the solution of this question in the future. I can
also emphasize that when it comes to creating such a federation or
confederation, our peoples will not ask the imperialists, and will not
heed their opposition, but will solve the question themselves, guided
by their own interests bound up with the interests and international
co-operation necessary to them and to other nations."

The Kremlin reacted furiously to Dimitrov's statement, although
Pravda published it. Imagine a Balkan federation without the Soviet
Union! Stalin now resolved to attack Dimitrov openly in *Pravda*. On
January 29, 1948, *Pravda* published the following:

"Many readers in the Soviet Union have turned to the editors of
Pravda with questions that boil down to this: Can it be inferred that
Pravda, by publishing Dimitrov's statement, agrees with his view on
the expediency of organizing a federation of Balkan and Danubian
states, including Poland, Czechoslovakia and Greece, and on the
indispensability of setting up a customs union between them?

"In this connection the editors of *Pravda* consider it necessary to
give the following explanation:

"First, *Pravda* could not but have published the statement of Comrade Dimitrov, which had been published in the press of other countries, where, of course, *Pravda* could make no alterations.

"Second, this, however, does not mean that the editors of *Pravda*
agree with Comrade Dimitrov on the question of federation and customs union among the countries mentioned. On the contrary, the
editors of *Pravda* consider that these countries require no question-
able and fabricated federation or confederation, or a customs union;
what they require is the consolidation and defense of their independence and sovereignty by mobilizing and organizing internally their
people's democratic forces, as was correctly stated in the well-
known declaration of the nine Communist Parties."

After Dimitrov's statement and the *démarche* in *Pravda*, telegrams
were immediately sent to Sofia and Belgrade from Moscow sum-
moning new delegations to a consultation. Djilas had known nothing
about this telegram from Moscow, but Tito informed him from

Belgrade that Kardelj and Vladimir Bakarić were on their way. A delegation of the strongest composition, headed by Dimitrov, left Bulgaria. He was accompanied by Vassil Kolarov and Traicho Kostov.

The invitation extended to Tito to send a new delegation to Moscow did not mention who was invited, but the Russians expected that Tito himself would come. This was evidently their wish, for when Lavrentyev again called, he informed Tito that Dimitrov would be a member of the Bulgarian delegation. He thus wanted to intimate that Tito was expected to go. The Central Committee of the Communist Party of Yugoslavia, however, considered it sufficient that Kardelj, Bakarić and Djilas were in Moscow.

While Kardelj and Bakarić were preparing for the trip to Moscow, the Albanian government asked the Yugoslav government to send two Yugoslav divisions to southern Albania, because Enver Hoxha was afraid that the Greeks might occupy some parts of the Albanian territory, which they claimed were inhabited by the Greeks. The Yugoslav government deliberated over this request of the Albanians. In principle, they were in favor of the move, but the date of departure of the divisions had not been fixed. Sometime before, the Albanian government had requested that Yugoslavia send an air force regiment. This Albanian wish was granted and that Yugoslav regiment was already in Albania.

Moscow did not like these moves of the Albanian and Yugoslav governments. Molotov sent a sharp cable to Belgrade, saying that the Soviet government did not agree with the arrangements made between the two governments. The Soviet Foreign Minister even threatened that the Soviet warning would be announced publicly, if the Albanian and Yugoslav governments did not cancel their agreement.

Kardelj and Bakarić arrived in Moscow on Sunday, February 8, and up to Tuesday, February 10, not a single bit of information did they receive from anyone, except a statement that the "top Bulgarians" had arrived, which was obviously an allusion to Tito's absence.

On Tuesday the Yugoslavs were notified to be in Stalin's office in the Kremlin at nine o'clock that evening. Kardelj, Djilas and Bakarić arrived precisely at nine, and were held ten or fifteen minutes in the waiting room of Stalin's office for the arrival of the Bulgarians.

The meeting began at about nine-fifteen. Stalin sat at the head of the table; on his right hand sat Molotov, Malyenkov, Zhdanov, Souslov, and Zorin. On his left hand sat Dimitrov, Kolarov, Kostov, Kardelj, Djilas and Bakarić.

The meeting was opened by Molotov, who stated in his introduction that there were serious differences between the Soviet Union on one side and Yugoslavia and Bulgaria on the other, and that they were "inadmissible either from the Party or from the state point of view."

After Molotov's words there could be no doubt as to the issue. Stalin was glowering and ceaselessly doodling in his notebook. Molotov proceeded to enumerate the causes of the misunderstanding. First, he mentioned the conclusion of the Yugoslav-Bulgarian treaty of alliance; then Dimitrov's statement on the federation of East European countries and Balkan countries including Greece; and finally the interchange of messages between Yugoslavia and Albania.

He stated the Soviet government had advised the Yugoslav and Bulgarian governments "not to conclude the agreement before the peace treaty limitations expired." However, he said, the two governments concluded the alliance, and the Soviet government "learned about it from the newspapers."

Speaking of the second cause of misunderstanding, Molotov gave a detailed account of Dimitrov's statement regarding a federation and customs union, dealing especially with that part of his statement on a customs union between Bulgaria and Rumania.

Stalin broke in at this point, saying, "We see Comrade Dimitrov abandons himself fervently at press conferences; he does not mind his tongue. Whatever he says, whatever Tito says, is thought abroad to have been said with our knowledge. For instance, the Poles were here. I asked them what they thought about Dimitrov's statement. They said, 'A wise thing,' and I told them it was not a wise thing. Then they countered that they also thought it was not a wise thing, since that was the Soviet government's view. They thought Dimitrov had made his statement with the knowledge and at the instructions of the Soviet government, and had approved it in consequence. Comrade Dimitrov tried to correct his statement subsequently with some kind of communiqué released by the Bulgarian news agency. Nothing was corrected with his correction. He alleges even that Austria-Hungary upset a customs union between Bulgaria and Serbia, the inference being: 'The Germans once hindered it, it is the Russians who are doing so now.' "

Stalin added some more comments in the same general sense, and Molotov went on to finish his statement. The next speaker was Dimitrov. His words were constantly interrupted by outbursts from Stalin. Dimitrov began by saying that Yugoslavia and Bulgaria did not release the text of the agreement at Bled, but only an announcement that an understanding had been reached between the two countries to the effect that such an agreement would be concluded. Dimitrov furthermore stated Bulgaria was combating great difficulties and that it could not hope to develop without co-operating with other countries. But he accepted Stalin's criticism regarding his statement, and said, "It is true I was carried away at the press conference."

"You wanted to shine with new words," Stalin interrupted. "That's all wrong, because such a federation is an impossibility."

"There is no essential difference between the foreign policy of Bulgaria and that of the Soviet Union," said Dimitrov.

"There are huge differences," Stalin replied angrily. "The fact should not be concealed. Leninist practice has always demonstrated that it is necessary to realize an error and to mend it as quickly as possible."

Dimitrov: "It's true, we did commit a mistake. But we are also learning on those foreign-policy mistakes."

Stalin: "You are an old political worker, and you have been engaged in politics more than forty years, and now you want to rectify mistakes. Mistakes are not the issue: the issue are conceptions different from our own."

Stalin repeated this observation a number of times, only in sharper terms, and finally said he had nothing against a federation between Yugoslavia and Bulgaria, but there must be no federation and customs union between Rumania and Bulgaria. Evidently he thought he had a large number of his men in the Bulgarian government who had spent ten to fifteen years in the Soviet Union, and imagined that with a federation between Yugoslavia and Bulgaria it would be easier to subjugate Yugoslavia as the strongest factor in this part of Europe. Georgy Dimitrov was already ailing, exhausted, no longer the stalwart fighter he had once been. Now Stalin endeavored to shake his reputation both publicly through *Pravda* and at this meeting. As for the customs union and federation between Bulgaria and Rumania, Stalin was opposed to it because he had special plans for Rumania.

The next speaker was the Bulgarian, Kolarov. He explained that the Rumanians also favored a customs union with the Bulgarians.

"I do not see where Comrade Dimitrov's fault lies, because we had sent the draft agreement to the Soviet government, and it made no observation on the formulation regarding the customs union, but only regarding the definition of an aggressor."

At Kolarov's words Stalin turned to Molotov: "Is it true they sent us the draft agreement?"

Molotov: "Well, yes."

Stalin (angrily): "There, we are also making fools of ourselves."

Dimitrov availed himself of the opportunity, and said, "That is the reason I made my statement, because the draft had been sent to Moscow."

Stalin pounced upon Dimitrov again.

"You've plunged like a Comsomol * Youth," he said. "Whatever you do, you bandy words about like women in the streets. You wanted to astonish the world, as if you are still the Secretary of the Comintern. Bulgaria and Yugoslavia report nothing about what they are doing, and we must learn about it in the streets, and find ourselves confronted with an accomplished fact."

Kostov's turn came to speak. He began with an explanation of Bulgaria's economic situation. He had hardly uttered the words, "It is hard to be a small underdeveloped country. I should like to raise some economic questions," when Stalin interrupted.

"You have definite ministries for that matter," he said. "We called this meeting in order to discuss the differences in the foreign policy between the Soviet Union on one side, and Bulgaria and Yugoslavia on the other."

---

* Used in this sense, "Comsomol" or "Comsomolist" means "childish."

Kostov fell silent. The speaker now was Kardelj. He began to explain how the draft of the Yugoslav-Bulgarian treaty had been sent in advance to the Soviet government. This had been done even before the treaty was signed. After this, from the Soviet government came only one remark—that the time limit of the treaty should be twenty years, not "forever" as it was envisaged in the first project.

Stalin looked angrily at Molotov, who kept nodding his head in approval of Kardelj's statement.

Kardelj continued, saying that he could see no differences in the foreign policy of the USSR and Yugoslavia except the remark made by the Soviet government about the duration of the treaty between Yugoslavia and Bulgaria.

Stalin interrupted Kardelj.

"There exist differences and deep ones. What would you say about Albania?"

Kardelj then gave a review of the Yugoslav-Albanian relations. At that moment the Yugoslavs were not aware of the fact that Stalin purposely was using the Yugoslav-Albanian relations as a pretext and excuse for the pressure against Yugoslavia. Later it became clear that Stalin purposely used Enver Hoxha, his main stooge in the Albanian government, to plant through him the request for sending Yugoslav troops to Albania. Stalin again interrupted Kardelj.

"There remained the fact that you didn't consult us about sending two divisions to Albania."

Kardelj answered that it is true that no consultations between Yugoslavia and the Soviet governments took place about sending two divisions to Albania. He added that the definite agreement on this matter hadn't been concluded, that the Yugoslav government had not even definitely decided whether to send the troops to help the Albanians, although in principle the Yugoslav government was willing to accept the Albanian request. This step on the part of the Yugoslav Government in no way constitutes a threat to the peace, because its sole purpose was to defend Albania's independence from dangers from abroad; the Albanian Government had on a previous occasion requested that a Yugoslav Air Force regiment be sent to Albania and this was done without leading to any kind of international difficulty. Then Kardelj stressed once more that he didn't see one single case of any importance in the Yugoslav foreign policy in which the Yugoslav government did not consult with the Soviet government.

Stalin angrily interjected, "It isn't true. You do not consult with us at all on any question."

After this it was obvious that Kardelj was unable to speak because of the constant interruptions of Stalin. This was no longer a discussion, but an occasion for the transmission of Stalin's orders. Kardelj broke off, and Molotov took the floor. He read the passage from the Yugoslav-Bulgarian agreement that "Yugoslavia and Bulgaria shall work in the spirit of the United Nations and support every initiative directed toward maintaining peace and against all hotbeds of aggression."

Dimitrov answered that the wording of the agreement meant that the struggle against hotbeds of aggression was linked to the United Nations action, whereupon Stalin broke in again: "That is preventive war, an ordinary Comsomolist performance. That is an ordinary clamorous phrase which only brings grist to the enemy mill."

Molotov then dealt with the Bulgaro-Rumanian announcement harmonizing economic plans and said it amounted to the unification of Bulgaria and Rumania.

Stalin interrupted Molotov and said that the customs unions in general are not realistic. Here once more Kardelj tried to speak, explaining that the custom unions sometimes in practice do not give bad results.

Stalin asked Kardelj to give an example and Kardelj mentioned Benelux.

Stalin retorted sarcastically, "Benelux, that's nothing."

"There is Belgium, there is Luxembourg," Kardelj continued.

Stalin: "And nobody else."

Kardelj: "There is Netherlands."

Stalin: "No."

Kardelj: "Yes, Netherlands are in. Look at the name of Benelux. It means, Belgium, Netherlands and Luxembourg."

Stalin, very angry: "When I say 'no' it means NO."

Again Kardelj stopped short, confronted with a man who refused even to recognize the existence of Benelux.

Stalin went on to explain Molotov's previous views, saying that the harmonizing of the economic plans between Bulgaria and Rumania was nonsense and that Dimitrov would see how foolish such an act was because instead of co-operation there would be discord between Bulgaria and Rumania.

At this juncture, Stalin for the first time openly advanced his plan for federations among the East European countries. He said three federations should be created: between Poland and Czechoslovakia, Rumania and Hungary, Bulgaria and Yugoslavia. Turning to Dimitrov, Stalin said, "Bulgaria and Yugoslavia should create their federation tomorrow because Bulgaria is a sovereign state now."

Kardelj replied that the Yugoslavs also favored a federation with Bulgaria; that they had wanted to create it in 1944 before either Yugoslavia and Bulgaria had built their appropriate new state forms, and federation might have eased the road ahead. But in 1944 this wish of the Yugoslavs had not been realized, because of pressure from abroad. In the meantime in both countries new states had been formed, but now the federation should not be hurried in view of international and internal factors. The matter had been discussed between Tito and Dimitrov at Bled in 1947 and it had been decided that federation between Yugoslavia and Bulgaria should come about gradually.

But Stalin was not of this opinion. He insisted once more: "No, the federation should be proclaimed immediately, the sooner the better. The matter is ripe. First, Bulgaria and Yugoslavia should unite and then they should annex Albania." Stalin even went on to suggest a name by which the new state should be known.

Kardelj then tried again to speak. He gave once more the Yugoslav view and then spoke about relationships with Albania, stressing once more that fundamentally there was no difference between Yugoslav and Soviet views on foreign policy.

Stalin again repeated what he had already said to Kardelj and Dimitrov.

"It is not true. There are differences between us. Even we, Lenin's disciples, differed many a time with Lenin himself. Moreover we quarreled on some matters, but later we gave them a good airing, reached a unanimous view and proceeded further. For instance, we do not agree with Yugoslav comrades that they should help further the Greek Partisans. In this matter, we think that we are right and not the Yugoslavs. It is true, we have also made mistakes. For instance, after the war we invited the Chinese comrades to come to Moscow and we discussed the situation in China. We told them bluntly that we considered the development of the uprising in China had no prospect, and that the Chinese comrades should seek a *modus vivendi* with Chiang Kai-shek, that they should join the Chiang Kai-shek government and dissolve their army. The Chinese comrades agreed here with the views of the Soviet comrades, but went back to China and acted quite otherwise. They mustered their forces, organized their armies and now, as we see, they are beating the Chiang Kai-shek army. Now, in the case of China, we admit we were wrong. It proved that the Chinese comrades and not the Soviet comrades were right. But that is not the case with you in the Balkans. It is not the case with the Greek Partisans, and Yugoslav comrades should stop helping them. That struggle has no prospect whatsoever."

Then Stalin put a blunt question to Kardelj. "Are you sure that the Greek Partisans could triumph?"

"Certainly," said Kardelj, "but only if foreign intervention does not increase in Greece and if the Greek Partisans do not make serious political and strategic mistakes."

This topic exhausted, Dimitrov again moved some economic questions between the Soviet Union and Bulgaria. Stalin said curtly, "We shall talk about that with the joint Yugoslav-Bulgarian government."

However, Traicho Kostov reopened the discussion on economic questions. He stated the Soviet government had concluded a technical assistance agreement with Bulgaria unfavorable to his country.

Stalin told Kostov to make a note of it and Molotov would see what it was about.

The discussion then treated relationships between the Balkan countries and Italy. The issue was what kind of answer to give the Italian government in connection with its request to the Soviet Union and Yugoslavia to support its claim to administration of its former colonies in Africa. Stalin said Italy's request should be supported, and even asked Molotov whether a reply had already been sent to the effect. Stalin then explained why this was necessary: "Emperors, when unable to agree on the division of their game, once gave the disputed territory to the weakest feudalist, in order to grab it from him the easier at a suitable moment. The feudalist was usually a foreigner, and the emperors overthrew him with greater ease when he became a nuisance."

Stalin laughed for the first time that evening as he uttered these words.

The talk ended about midnight. Its basic characteristic was Stalin's unusually sharp tone. The rebukes, on the whole, were directed against Bulgarians, although Stalin openly aimed at the Yugoslavs.

Unlike earlier meetings, Stalin invited neither the Bulgarians nor the Yugoslavs to supper at his villa.

When the Yugoslav delegates dispersed after this meeting to their Embassy, their unanimous opinion was that Stalin asked for an immediate federation between Bulgaria and Yugoslavia in order to break the unity of Yugoslavia. Therefore the Yugoslav delegates came to the common conclusion that they should not hurry the federation with Bulgaria.

The next day Dimitrov met Kardelj and Djilas. Dimitrov seemed to have fathomed Stalin's intentions, and at one point said, "It's not a matter of criticizing my statements, but of something else!"

Probably Dimitrov wanted to intimate to the Yugoslavs that Stalin was preparing much more serious steps, perhaps the incorporation of Bulgaria and Yugoslavia into the Soviet Union.

"It will be far easier for you and ourselves to progress because we are starting from a far higher level of productive forces, from a higher cultural level of the population than was the case in the Soviet Union," he continued.

At the meeting of February 10, Stalin stressed several times that Yugoslavs did not make a habit of consulting with the Soviet government about their foreign policy. During that meeting Stalin stated categorically that this should not happen again and suddenly informed the Yugoslav delegates that they should, in the name of their government, sign an agreement about mutual consultation with the Soviet government over the questions of foreign policy.

At midnight, February 11, Kardelj was urgently summoned to see Molotov at his office. When Kardelj entered the room of the Soviet Foreign Minister, everything was ready for the signing of the agreement. Molotov handed Kardelj two sheets of paper. The text of mutual consultation on the foreign-policy questions between the Soviet and Yugoslav governments was already written down. Kardelj remembers that scene very vividly:

"I was looking at two sheets of paper inserted in a blue folder, I was listening to the harsh voice of Molotov ordering 'sign this,' and I was boiling with rage. Why should this whole thing be done in this manner, although the Yugoslav government was not against the mutual consultation on the question of foreign policy? Why should we sign such an agreement when up to that time we had been acting exactly as the agreement provided? The humiliation disgusted and perplexed me—it reminded me only of the dictates of big powers to small and weak ones. I was thinking what to do, whether to sign or not. At last I decided to affix my signature. I did this so that I would not complicate the situation, which was already very tense. Being perplexed, I put my signature where Molotov should have signed, and the whole procedure of signing was postponed for another night because a new text had to be written. The following night I signed this agreement and left Moscow immediately with my comrades."

CHAPTER XX

1948:

"I felt as if a thunderbolt had struck me . . ."

THE meeting at the Kremlin on February 10th marked the beginning of Stalin's open pressure on Yugoslavia. In every country he put his machinery into operation to crush any potential Yugoslav resistance. The first action took place in Rumania, where orders were suddenly given for the removal of Tito's portraits. Soviet propaganda saw to it that the world press took notice of this. For instance, the Paris *Figaro* on February 12, 1948, wrote:

"According to reports arriving from Bucharest, the Communist Party of Rumania has ordered the removal of Marshal Tito's portraits from all windows in which the head of the Yugoslav government appeared in company with Marshal Stalin, Dimitrov and Groza. Various rumors are circulating in Bucharest about Marshal Tito, whose position seems not to be as firm as is generally believed. He appears to have lost Moscow's confidence. These rumors cannot be verified for the time being, but are worth recording."

At a reception in Tirana, in honor of the anniversary of the Red Army, Gagarinov, the Soviet Chargé d'Affaires, replied when the Yugoslav Envoy Josip Djerdja proposed a toast to Stalin and Tito: "I drink to Tito, provided Tito is for unity in the democratic bloc." Josip Djerdja replied vigorously and immediately informed his government of this aspersion.

Not content with the removal of Tito's portraits and the toast in Tirana, Stalin gave the Yugoslavs to understand that he would take more serious steps to make them obey. In those days Yugoslavia's foreign trade depended for the bulk of its volume on the countries of Eastern Europe, and primarily on the Soviet Union.

Over 50 per cent of her exports went to these countries. She especially depended on the Soviet Union for certain essential raw materials, such as oil and cotton.

The time had arrived to renew the trade agreement between Yugoslavia and the Soviet Union for 1948, since the exchanges had been determined only up to April of that year. A Yugoslav trade delegation had been in Moscow for two whole months. Stalin now tightened that screw.

Krutikov, the Assistant Soviet Minister of Foreign Trade, informed his opposite number Bogdan Crnobrnja toward the end of February that Yugoslavia need not send another trade delegation to Moscow. This virtually meant the discontinuation of trade relations between the two countries, and it meant that Yugoslavia would have no more oil or cotton.

Tito called a meeting of the Yugoslav Central Committee for March 1. It began in the morning in Tito's home at 15 Rumunska Street. Among those present was Sreten Žujović, Minister of Finance, whose behavior of late had been very strange. He had withdrawn from the other members of the Central Committee. He maintained only official contact with them at cabinet and Assembly meetings. He never went hunting with them or went to see Tito in the evening for a game of billiards. The agenda of this Central Committee meeting contained four items: first, a report by Kardelj, Djilas, and Bakarić on the results of their talks in the Soviet Union; second, the Five-Year Plan; third, the problems of the army and the war industry; fourth, the federation with Bulgaria.

The first speaker at this meeting was Tito. He gave a brief review of the relations between Yugoslavia and the Soviet Union, and said that lately they had been in a blind alley. He reviewed our economic relations with the Russians, speaking particularly about the joint-stock companies for Danube shipping and air transport. "These agreements put us on an unequal footing," he said.

Then he went on to speak about the Albanian problem and our relations with the Soviet Union, and about the results of the armaments talks. "They didn't want to help us in this matter either. They always asked: 'What do you want a strong army for? We are here.'"

Tito concluded saying that by putting off signing the trade agreement the Russians were now exercising economic pressure upon us, and that we had to endure it.

Tito was followed by Kardelj, who described the course of the talks with Stalin in the Kremlin. Speaking of the tone Stalin had used, Kardelj said, "He spoke as if we were the Comsomol."

Djilas spoke next, followed by Svetozar Vukmanović-Tempo, who had also been in Moscow. He said: "In the Soviet Union they are absolutely uninformed about the Yugoslav army. I went to study Party work in the army there, but they failed to answer many of my questions. I noticed differences of opinion there on questions of building up armies in people's democracies. They clearly intend to make us dependent on them. We differ from them as to whether there should be Party organizations in the army. They are against it, we are for it."

Kidrić then spoke about our economic relations with the Soviet Union:

"The coolness in our relations with the Soviet Union began over the question of the joint-stock companies. The Soviet government has now refused to conclude a trade agreement for 1948. It has informed us that the agreement will not be considered until December, 1948."

The meeting developed more and more in this direction: it was an analysis of the differences between Yugoslavia and the Soviet Union. Kardelj developed the view that there were differences between ourselves and the Russians on the questions of socialist development, namely, whether socialism should develop by the equal co-operation of nations proceeding toward socialism or by further enlargement of the Soviet Union, as the Russians seemed to think, and added:

"Our policy toward the Soviet Union continues unchanged; but we are under an obligation to watch closely over the interests of our country. We consider it improper that some of our people have been engaged for the Soviet intelligence service."

When the second point of the agenda, the Five-Year Plan, was dealt with, Kidrič itemized the immense damage the Soviet Union was causing us by refusing to conclude the trade agreement for 1948. The value of the agreement was to have been two billion dinars ($40,000,000). To overcome these difficulties, he proposed the strictest economy in all fields, including gasoline consumption.

Tito spoke again and declared that the Soviet government had denounced the agreement in order to bring economic pressure to bear on Yugoslavia. But the country's independence was more important.

Then the discussion went on to the federation with Bulgaria. Tito spoke first. He said:

"We fought during the war for the idea of federation with Bulgaria. We must continue working for it. But is this a suitable time to raise the question of federation? Are the conditions ripe for it? There are still many things to be overcome. We should also create one Party with the Bulgarians. Our strength lies in the unity of will and action. We would be burdened. They differ from us ideologically. It would be a Trojan horse in our Party. Yugoslavia is clearly on the road to socialism. The Russians are fostering ideas, and they regard the national question in a different light. We are not a pawn on a chess-board. A federation is not feasible until we see how the whole situation crystallizes. Moreover, the matter is not ripe economically. Our Five-Year Plan is in full swing; Bulgaria would now be a burden. She is a poor country, and besides that she has to pay forty-five million dollars reparations to Greece."

Djilas agreed with Tito. He said that the Bulgarian Party was disunited, but that co-operation along socialist lines should be continued. Then Djilas gave his own appraisal of the further development of relations with the Soviet Union:

"I do not believe the Russians will stop at economic pressure on our country. In my opinion the fundamental question is whether socialism is to develop freely or by the expansion of the Soviet Union."

The next speaker was Aleksandar Ranković-Marko. He also maintained that federation with the Bulgarians should not be formed immediately:

"The Bulgarian Central Committee is split by factions. In the first are Traicho Kostov and Yugov, in the second Chervenkov and Tsankov, in the third Dimitrov alone, swimming between these two. The latest reorganization of the Bulgarian Central Committee indicates that men who were trained in Bulgaria are going under. In Bulgaria the Russians have a finger in everything. The Ministry of the Interior is completely in their hands."

Then followed a discussion on military matters, and the session was adjourned.

The only man who had not said a single word was Sreten Žujović-Crni. He had only made careful notes.

But the Central Committee, except for Žujović, who was silent, unanimously took a firm stand toward the Soviet demands. Moreover, at this meeting Tito emphasized that the issue was the independence of Yugoslavia.

It was decided that not a word was to be said to anyone of the matters discussed at the meeting and that all the issues were to be kept in strictest secrecy, for the consequences would be serious if the matter were made public, especially regarding Soviet economic pressure. There were few people in Yugoslavia at that time who really knew what tremendous events were looming ahead. The papers had been reporting the preparations for the celebration of International Women's Day, the news of sowing preparations, the victory of the Yugoslav runner Stefanović at the cross-country race organized by *L'Humanité* in Paris. *Borba* on March 2 published the speech made by Marcel Cachin, the veteran member of the Central Committee of the Communist Party of France, who had said: "I am not at all surprised that the race was won by a Yugoslav, because I have been to Yugoslavia and have seen with what love and will the Yugoslavs are working and fighting for a better life under the leadership of their beloved Marshal Tito."

At its meeting of March 1, the Yugoslav Central Committee had decided upon complete opposition to the Soviet demands. New measures soon followed from Stalin's side. On March 18, General Barskov, the chief of the Soviet Military Mission in Yugoslavia, informed Koča Popović that by decision of the Soviet government, Marshal Bulganin, the Minister of National Defense of the Soviet Union, had ordered that all military advisers and instructors should be withdrawn from Yugoslavia, for they were "surrounded by unfriendliness, and treated with hostility in Yugoslavia."

A day later Armyaninov, the Chargé d'Affaires of the Soviet Embassy, asked to be received by Tito, to whom he read a telegram from the Soviet Union ordering all civilian specialists to leave Yugoslavia.

These decisions were enforced without delay. The Soviet specialists gave notice that they were ordered to leave. People in the army and in civilian quarters asked what it all meant. Tito was preparing a reply to the Soviet Union when Yudin, the representative of the Russian Communist Party in the Cominform, asked for an interview. Tito received him immediately. Never mentioning the letters or the conflict with the Soviet Union, Yudin only asked Marshal Tito to write an article for the Cominform paper. Had Yudin come to Tito on his own, had he already been informed of the conflict? Obviously, Yudin had deliberately come to put further pressure on him by asking for an article. Tito answered that he would write the article if time permitted.

That same day Tito wrote to Molotov about the withdrawal of the Soviet officers and specialists. In connection with the allegation that the military instructors were being withdrawn because they had been treated with hostility in Yugoslavia, Tito openly told Molotov in his letter that he considered this was not the real reason for their withdrawal. About the civilian specialists Tito wrote:

"Second, on March 19, 1948, I received the Chargé d'Affaires Armyaninov, who informed me of the contents of a telegram in which the government of the Soviet Union orders the withdrawal of all its civilian specialists from Yugoslavia. The explanation of this decision is no less incomprehensible and astonishing to us. It is true that Minister Kidrič's assistant, Srzentić,* told your trade representative Lebedev that according to the Yugoslav government's decision no one was entitled to give important economic information to anyone, and that Soviet citizens should seek such information at a higher level, that is to say, from the Central Committee of the Communist Party or from the government. Srzentić also told Lebedev to ask Minister Kidrič for the information he required. Your people were told long ago that the official representatives of the Soviet government may receive all the important information they require direct from the leadership of our country.

"We took this decision because every official in our ministries had been in the habit of giving necessary and unnecessary information to anybody who asked for it. It follows that various people revealed

---

* Vojo Srzentić had already been engaged by the N.K.V.D.; he was found to be a Soviet intelligence agent only in 1951.

state economic secrets which might, and sometimes did, fall into the
hands of our common enemies.

"We have no special arrangement, such as your telegram mentions,
regarding the right of our people to give information of an economic
nature to Soviet economic workers without the permission of our
government or Central Committee, except, of course, such information as they require in the execution of their duties.

"Whenever the Soviet Ambassador Comrade Lavrentyev asked me
personally for any information, I always gave it without reserve, as
did our other responsible leaders. It would deeply surprise us if the
Soviet government was not in agreement with our attitude from the
viewpoint of political necessity. . . .

"It follows from all this that the foregoing reasons are not the
cause of the steps taken by the Soviet government, and we should
appreciate it if the Soviet government would openly inform us what
the trouble is, and point out what it thinks is not in keeping with
the good relations between our two countries. We consider that such
a state of affairs is harmful to both countries and that sooner or later
everything that hampers friendly relations between them will have
to be removed.

"If the Soviet government obtains its information from other
people, we think such information should be received with caution,
because it is not always unbiased, precise or well-intentioned."

Tito's letter was sent to Moscow without delay. What would
Stalin's answer be?

Day after day passed. World opinion had no inkling of what was
happening. At that very time most of the Western papers were en-
couraging a new wave of propaganda against Yugoslavia, especially
in connection with the elections in Italy. Reports were published that
Yugoslavia had warlike intentions toward Italy, that there were V-1
and V-2 rocket-launching platforms in Yugoslav towns near the
Yugoslav-Italian border adapted to a range of from three hundred
to nine hundred miles, and that Italian towns would be bombed at
any moment. Italian papers also wrote that Yugoslavia was preparing
to attack Trieste and Italy, and that twenty-eight infantry brigades
and nine artillery divisions were prepared for the campaign. Hundreds of thousands of pamphlets were printed and distributed in

Rome to the effect that the Yugoslav army was mobilized and concentrated along the border of the Free Territory of Trieste.

At this moment the governments of the United States, Great Britain and France decided to amend certain provisions in the peace treaty with Italy, and to cede Trieste to her. Stalin made the best of this Western pressure on Yugoslavia, for he considered it would facilitate his work.

Meanwhile Tito awaited Stalin's answer. He had not long to wait. He was staying in his villa at Tuškanac, a wooded suburb of Zagreb, when he was asked to receive the Soviet Ambassador Lavrentyev and Armyaninov.

They entered Tito's study, where he was sitting at his writing desk. Lavrentyev already had Stalin's reply in his hands. Having shaken hands, he presented the letter. Tito and the Soviet representatives remained standing because Tito had not asked them to be seated.

Tito stood behind his writing desk with one hand resting on it, as he turned the pages of the letter with the other, reading it rapidly.

How did Tito feel then, what thoughts ran through his mind? This is what he has to say: "Scanning the opening lines, I felt as if a thunderbolt had struck me. Lavrentyev and Armyaninov, on the other hand, peered at me coolly to see what my reaction would be. I never winced, I contained myself as much as I possibly could.

"Lavrentyev approached half a step in my direction, his gaze steadily fixed on me. He could no longer endure it, and before I had scanned the whole letter with its eight pages, he asked: 'When shall we have an answer?'

"I replied tersely, 'We shall consider the letter.'

"The meeting was at an end. It had lasted no more than three or four minutes."

Then Tito reread the whole letter. It consisted of eight pages typewritten in Russian. At the top in purple ink was "Confidential."

Its tone was extraordinarily crude and commanding, and the contents matched the tone. The letter began with the words, "We consider your answer untruthful, and therefore wholly unsatisfactory." In the first part Stalin and Molotov enumerated the reasons for recalling the Soviet specialists. They recalled the statement made by Djilas at the meeting of the Yugoslav Central Committee in the autumn of 1944 in connection with the cases of rape by officers and men of the Red Army, although Stalin himself had said the case was closed. Moreover, Stalin and Molotov fiercely attacked the Yugoslav government for preventing the Soviet civilian specialists from getting economic information from quarters other than the Yugoslav government. Molotov and Stalin wanted for their specialists the right to go to any Yugoslav ministry and ask for any information they liked from any official. Molotov and Stalin further alleged that Soviet representatives in Yugoslavia were under the surveillance of organs of Yugoslav State Security, as was Yudin, the representative of the Soviet Communist Party on the Cominform paper. Molotov and Stalin concluded: "It will not be superficial to observe that Soviet representatives are under similar surveillance only in bourgeois countries, and not even in all of them."

In the second part of their letter Molotov and Stalin attempted to disguise the whole conflict in the relations between the Soviet Union and Yugoslavia as an ideological discussion. They expressed their anxiety over the position of the Communist Party of Yugoslavia, anxiety that its status was still semilegal, that the spirit of class-struggle policy did not pervade it, that capitalist elements, unopposed by the Party leadership, were growing in town and village; that the Party had been lost in the People's Front; that there was no feeling of inner-party democracy; that the Central Committee was not elected but appointed; that there was no criticism or self-criticism in the Party, that the Minister of State Security was Party Secretary for cadres and that the Party cadres were thus under surveillance of the Minister of State Security.

Furthermore, Molotov and Stalin accused the leaders in Yugoslavia of slandering the Soviet Union behind her back, and added it is "absurd to listen to stories about the Soviet Communist Party, from dubious Marxists of the type of Djilas, Vukmanović, Kidrič, Ranković and others." As a threat they recalled the case of Trotsky.

"We think Trotsky's political career is sufficiently instructive." So the letter read. It was signed: V. M. Molotov—J. V. Stalin.

When later the Soviet government published these letters and the Cominform resolution, for distribution through underground channels in Yugoslavia, they bore the stamp of the Central Committee of the Soviet Communist Party instead of the signatures of Molotov and

Stalin. The Soviet leaders no doubt replaced Stalin's name rather than have the world realize that the Yugoslavs had dared to resist Stalin himself.

Tito immediately phoned and asked Kardelj, Djilas, Ranković and Kidrič to come at once. Having read the letter again, Tito got up and paced his study, pondering its contents. Then he sat at his desk and in his own hand began to outline a reply. It was finished in two hours. On heavy paper, headed "President of the Ministerial Council, Minister of National Defense, Marshal of Yugoslavia Josip Broz Tito," on thirty-three long sheets, in unusually large handwriting Tito had drafted his reply.

Kardelj, Djilas, Ranković and Kidrič had arrived in the meantime. They also read the letter from Stalin and Molotov. They stood unanimously behind Tito. All of them said at once that all the Soviet accusations should be denied, because they were false.

Tito was moved very much. At one moment he said that he was willing to retire, if he were an obstacle to good relations between Yugoslavia and the Soviet Union. Kardelj, Djilas, Ranković and Kidrič unanimously rejected the suggestion.

In history this meeting will go down as a decisive one, as far as the Yugoslav resistance toward Stalin's aims was concerned. At this meeting, the secretariat of the Central Committee of Yugoslavia decided in full conformity that all Soviet demands should be rejected.

It is clear what Stalin and Molotov intended in attacking four men by name in their letter. To begin with, they wanted to split the Yugoslav Central Committee, overpowering first one group, and then the whole Committee. It was not by chance that they began with these four men. They administered just those sectors into which the N.K.V.D. was attempting to penetrate: economy (Kidrič), the army (Vukmanović), the Ministry of the Interior (Ranković), propaganda and the press (Djilas).

Djilas realized Stalin's and Molotov's purpose but thought it necessary to say to Tito, "Stari,* if you think that the four of us who are accused here by name should resign, I am ready to do so at once."

Tito leapt to his feet. "Oh, no!" he cried. "They want to wreck our Central Committee! What the devil should I do if you went?"

---

* "Stari" in Serbo-Croat means "old." "Stari" is a term of endearment meaning "old man."

All five seated themselves and took counsel. They resolved unanimously to place the whole matter before the Plenum of the Central Committee, which they summoned for April 12 in Belgrade. It was decided to discuss the whole situation at the Plenum and to send a reply to the Russians. It was also decided that the Party members should be acquainted with the contents of the letter from the Soviet Party.

As it happened, the third anniversary of the signing of the treaty of friendship and mutual assistance between the Soviet Union and Yugoslavia fell just at this time. It was customary for Stalin and Tito to exchange greetings telegrams on each such anniversary. Nor was this custom ignored in 1948, although the styles were rather cold. (It was, incidentally, the last exchange of telegrams between the two heads of governments.) Tito sent the following telegram to Stalin on April 11:

"On behalf of the people and Government of the Federative People's Republics of Yugoslavia and in my own name, I congratulate you and the Government of the Soviet Union on the third anniversary of the signing of the Treaty of Friendship, Mutual Assistance and Postwar Co-operation between the Union of Soviet Socialist Republics and the Federative People's Republic of Yugoslavia.

"Desiring that this historic act may serve our peoples as an indissoluble link and strong guarantee of peaceful development toward a happy future, I avail myself of this occasion to wish the brotherly peoples of the Soviet Union on behalf of the peoples of Yugoslavia the greatest successes in creating prosperity and further progress in your great socialist country."

Stalin answered Tito on the same day with an even shorter and more reserved telegram:

"I cordially thank you for your congratulations in connection with the third anniversary of the signing of the Treaty of Friendship, Mutual Assistance and Postwar Co-operation between the Soviet Union and the Federative People's Republic of Yugoslavia. I wish success and prosperity to the brotherly peoples of Yugoslavia." *

---

* This exchange of telegrams between Stalin and Tito was printed in the Yugoslav press on the front page. But the Russians were not satisfied with it. General Gunurov, one of the leading officials of the All-Slav Congress, reproached the Yugoslav Ambassador in Moscow, Vladimir Popović, that Stalin's

Tito

On the morning of Monday, April 12, the members of the Yugoslav Central Committee began to arrive for the plenary meeting at Dedinje, a suburb of Belgrade, in the library of King Alexander's palace. This building, erected during the thirties of this century in alleged Serbian style, is squat and tasteless. It is used only for gala purposes, or big state receptions. It was Dimitrov's residence during the visit of the Bulgarian government delegation in 1947.

What decision would the Yugoslav Central Committee take? Would the majority agree with the view held by Tito, Kardelj, Djilas, Ranković, that they would not yield to the authority of the Soviet Union, or to Stalin, when their Party had taught them for so many years that he was the leader of the international proletariat? How did these men feel at that moment? They were faced by a historic responsibility. Upon their decision depended the fate of their country, perhaps the future of the cause of socialism. Moreover, Yugoslavia had never found herself in a harder position: in the East this terribly heavy pressure from Stalin; in the West relations that had perhaps never been worse. The Yugoslav government had only a few days earlier instructed its Ambassador in Washington to protest officially against the statement made by the Chairman of the Senate Appropriations Committee, Senator Bridges, who had called on the United States government to interfere at all costs in the internal affairs of the countries behind the Iron Curtain, including Yugoslavia.

Besides this, there had been incidents on Yugoslavia's western frontiers. During the first three months of 1948, American planes had flown over Yugoslavia twenty-one times. The Yugoslav government had decided to inform Trygve Lie, the Secretary General of the United Nations, of all these violations.

It was in such an atmosphere that the historic session of the Central Committee began on April 12, 1948. It was exactly ten o'clock when Tito entered the library and sat down. The doors were closed. Tito proposed four items for the agenda: the Letter of the Central Committee of the Soviet Communist Party, the Economic Situation, the Fifth Congress, and Miscellaneous. The session was attended only by

---

answer in the Yugoslav press was printed much lighter than the text of Tito's, although both texts were printed with the same type. No one in Yugoslavia had noticed this but the Russians.

members of the Central Committee. There was no stenographer: the minutes were taken in longhand by Krsto Popivoda, a candidate for membership of the Central Committee. Djilas also made notes of some of the speeches.

What did Tito feel when he opened the session? He says:

"I was conscious of its fateful importance. Life had taught me that the most dangerous thing at such critical moments is not to take a stand, to hesitate. In such situations reactions must always be bold and determined."

Tito first gave a brief introduction, explaining the history of the conflict; then he read first the text of the Soviet letter, then the draft of his answer. The last paragraphs of his draft read:

"What exactly is the issue, then? It appears to us that we differ as to how relations should stand between our two countries. There is no doubt we share the view that they should be the best and friendliest; but how to clear them up—there lies the difference of opinion.

"What are the elements we consider indispensable to the firmness of our relations and to indestructible friendship? First, absolute respect for the principle of national and state independence, as explained by Lenin and Stalin in their works; second, absolute mutual trust, without which relations cannot be lasting and firm. The Soviet people and above all their leaders must believe that new Yugoslavia under her present leadership is moving irresistibly to socialism.

"Third, it must be conceded that the Soviet Union has the most faithful ally in present-day Yugoslavia which, under the present leadership, is ready to share every good and every evil with the peoples of the Soviet Union.

"Fourth, although we know that the Soviet Union has enormous difficulties in rehabilitating her devastated land, we rightfully expect assistance from her in the construction of our country and in accomplishing our Five-Year Plan, because we consider it is in the interest of the Soviet Union for new Yugoslavia to be stronger, since she is face to face with the capitalist world, which threatens her peaceful development.

"Fifth, the Soviet people who are in Yugoslavia either as official representatives or in any other capacity should remember that they are in a brotherly independent country and that they should not interfere in that country's internal life.

Tito

"Can the present relations be improved? They can and must, because there is no other way out. Any other outcome would do tremendous damage to both countries. . . .

"How do we regard the possibility of further revolutionary development in the world in the present international conditions, and how can socialism blaze a trail for itself? We consider that small people's democracies like Yugoslavia and others, which are treading new paths to socialism, must in every case, both for internal and external reasons, remain completely independent and sovereign, at the present stage, but firmly bound to each other and all to the Soviet Union, by various treaties. Every hasty unification or federation, before the necessary conditions—economic, cultural, political and so on—are ripe, would be harmful and followed by unpredictable consequences.

"The experiences of successful revolutionary development in every people's democracy should be considered a continuation and addition to the experiences of the great October Revolution, as something new in revolutionary practice, and wholly in the spirit of the science of Marxism and Leninism.

"The role of the Soviet Union should consist in extending full, comprehensive support with her authority to the new democracies, making special use in propaganda of the successes achieved in these new democracies in the realization of socialism.

"The most important thing of all is that full confidence, mutual understanding and comprehensive co-operation should exist between the countries of new democracy (where the Communists are in power) and the Soviet Union."

Tito concluded his address with these words:

"Comrades, remember that it is not a matter here of any theoretical discussions, it is not a question of errors committed by the Communist Party of Yugoslavia, of our ideological digression. We must not allow ourselves to be forced into a discussion of such things. Comrades, the point here, first and foremost, is the relations between one state and another. It seems to me that they are using ideological questions in order to justify their pressure on us, on our state. That, comrades, is the issue."

His last words were:

"This letter is the result of dreadful slanders, misinformation. I beg that the discussion should be conducted dispassionately. Each member of the Central Committee should declare himself here. If the comrades from the Soviet Central Committee ask for the minutes of this session, we shall send them."

When Tito had finished his speech, all the members of the Central Committee declared themselves in the order they sat at the conference table. The first to speak was Edvard Kardelj, who declared his agreement with the answer proposed by Tito. He then analyzed the creation of new Yugoslavia and the role of her Communist Party during the past war, her part in developing the profound faith of the Yugoslav people in the Soviet Union.

"It is with its own hands that our Party has done what it has," he said. "No one denies it did so with the assistance of the Soviet Union. But Yugoslavia was the country that freed almost the whole of her territory during the war with her own forces. Czechoslovakia, Rumania, Bulgaria, Poland, Hungary were freed by the Red Army. We are entitled to ask the Soviet government to have confidence in the Party that has achieved such results. Let us cast a glance at the things we have accomplished during the three years since the war. Land reform, nationalization, the Five-Year Plan. We have proved that our Party is capable of directing the construction of socialism. We shall be loyal not to the letter but to the spirit of Marxism-Leninism. It is simply ridiculous to speak of Trotskyism in Yugoslavia, or of the revival of capitalism. We are moving toward socialism more quickly than any country in Eastern Europe. I consider that the answer drafted by Comrade Tito is appropriate. We should not be sincere men but snakes in the grass if we were to admit that which is not true."

Kardelj was followed by Djuro Pucar, Blažo Jovanović, Boris Kidrič, Milovan Djilas, Svetozar Vukmanović, Stevo Krajačić. They all approved the answer of our Central Committee. Then came Luka Leskovšek, and after him Spasenija-Cana Babović, a woman worker from Serbia.

Next came Lazo Koliševski, Vida Tomšić, and then Miha Marinko, who said:

"The Russian letter leaves a painful impression. I feel like a man

who has been hit on the head by a sledgehammer. In spite of everything, this struggle must be kept up, and I am sure we shall be equal
to it."

Then Vicko Krstulović, a worker from Split, rose:

"I have never experienced harder moments than a few days back
in the Central Commitee while I read this letter. I am no high-level
theorist; I speak with the instinct of a proletarian worker. I see no
comradely warmth in their letter. It is a letter that points out no
shortcomings, but hits us over the head. I thoroughly agree with the
answer read by Comrade Tito."

Krstulović was followed by Ivan Gošnjak, a worker from Sisak,
now a general in the Yugoslav army. He also accepted Tito's answer.
Sreten Žujović's turn came. Before him seventeen members of the
Central Committee had already declared themselves against the letter
of the Soviet Party and in favor of our answer and proposing minor
amendments, such as inviting a delegation of the Soviet Party to
Yugoslavia to convince itself on the spot of the untruthfulness of the
charges in the letter. All seventeen members preceding Žujović had
spoken seated. Žujović, however, rose to his feet, pushed back his
chair and began in a raised voice:

"Comrades, I appeal to your revolutionary conscience. I am
against such a letter being sent to the Soviet Party. Do not forget
that tremendous matters are involved. I am against such an attitude
toward the Soviet Union and the Soviet Party."

Dead silence prevailed in the library of the Old Palace. Only Tito
rose to his feet while Žujović spoke and began to pace up and down
the library, whispering to himself, "This is treason to the people, the
state and the Party."

Tito repeated these words several times: Žujović did not hear him,
but went on with his speech.

"The question is: What next and where from here? Where will
Yugoslavia's place be in the struggle against imperialism? I have
thought deeply about it all. A fateful mistake should not be committed. We did our duty during the war. The present-day situation
has brought us to leadership of the state, and thus into contact with
the Soviet Union. Every word and observation, even the slightest,
from the Soviet Party, should be a warning to us to re-examine
everything before deciding on further action. We must seek the full

sense of Stalin's every word. How can we convince ourselves and
the people that we are on the right path, if the Soviet Party and
Stalin do not approve? I believe it is we and not they who are wrong
in this matter."

Žujović then began to speak about ideological digressions among
us. Djilas jumped up with tears of rage in his eyes:

"Tell me, Crni," he said, "do you think I am a Trotskyist?"

Žujović, hedging, replied, "No, but, you know . . ."

Almost all the members of the Central Committee leapt to their
feet, pointing to Žujović and crying, "Out with it, openly, no beating about the bush."

Tito's voice was also heard:

"Tell us, Crni, are we heading for capitalism, has our Party dissolved in the People's Front, does our government keep spies? In the
teachings of Marx, Engels, Lenin and Stalin we are the Russians'
equals."

Žujović hesitated. Kardelj and Vladimir Popović asked him further
questions. He spoke for another ten minutes and then sat down.

He was followed by Vladimir Popović, Yugoslavia's Ambassador
to Moscow. "What Žujović has said here before us is dishonest and
un-Communist," he began. "We have pursued a correct policy toward the Soviet Union. The system of joint-stock companies is no
good. Stalin himself has admitted it."

All the members of the Central Committee had declared themselves when, by the end of the session, Moša Pijade began, "Comrades, what surprised me most of all was the low level of Stalin's
letter."

His words provoked the only laughter during the whole fateful
meeting. The session adjourned at about two o'clock, and was resumed immediately after lunch. A lively discussion developed. Tito
spoke again.

"It hurts to see and hear Žujović speak as he does, as if to say,
'How dare we pygmies oppose the Soviet Party?' We also made
sacrifices for this country. It surprises me that Žujović can say such
a thing when he sees this youth of ours building railways, building
a future, raising itself from this backwardness. I am sure that none
of those who gave their lives ever thought their country would become nameless after the war.

Tito

"Everything we achieved in this war constitutes a contribution to socialism in the world: both our national equality, and the first real freedom for our people. What would the Italian people, the French or any other people say if we were to renounce all this, if we were to renounce our right to achieve socialism along the path we have chosen? How would that affect them? The road and incentive to socialism are not incorporation into the Soviet Union, but the development of each country separately. That is where we differ from the Soviet Party. And, suddenly, we hear Crni stand up and say: 'You are not right to defend yourselves.' To accept the letter of the Soviet Party is a blunder. They must also realize their letter is a blunder. To accept the letter is to be contemptible—to admit what is untrue. We are entitled to speak on an equal footing with the Soviet Union. There is deep ignorance among them about the things that have happened in our country. You, Crni, have assumed the right to love the Soviet Union more than your country. Our Party is as honest as the day. You, Crni, want to wreck its unity, you want to wreck the leadership that has been working like one man these eleven years, a leadership that is bound by blood to the people. We called upon those people to make the supreme sacrifice. They would refuse to stand by us for a single day if we proved unworthy of their sacrifices." Here Tito hesitated, rose from his chair and said: "Comrades, our revolution does not devour its children. The children of this revolution are honest."

As Tito uttered these words, the eyes of many of the members of the Central Committee filled with tears. Moša Pijade again rose.

"Crni should answer the questions Tito asked," he said.

Žujović was silent. Aleksandar Ranković asked to be allowed to speak. "Here before this Plenum I ask Žujović to answer the following questions: Does he consider our Party is not a Marxist-Leninist Party? Is the Communist Party of Yugoslavia illegal, and has it dissolved in the People's Front, thus losing its leading role?" Ranković asked question after question, and then continued, "What he has said demonstrates profound distrust in the forces of our country and in our people, and especially distrust in the Party. They say that in our country the state security controls the Party. The opposite is the truth. They say that the Soviet military and civilian advisers were surrounded by unfriendliness. The truth is that no one in Yugoslavia watched the Russians. Their organization sought support in our country among the White Guards who had fled from the October Revolution, among the reactionaries and former politicians, among the Party elements."

Addressing Žujović, Ranković reminded him of the time back in 1937 when he had been expelled from the Central Committee as Gorkić's man, and that it had been Tito who afterwards gave him the opportunity to correct his mistake.

"Remember, Crni, if there was anyone who tried to help you and save you for the Party, it was Comrade Tito, who proposed you for election to the Central Committee at the Fifth National Conference in 1940, in spite of what you had done abroad, in spite of your connections with Gorkić."

During the further course of discussion the question was raised whether Žujović had reported anything of the discussion in the Central Committee to Lavrentyev, the Soviet Ambassador in Belgrade, and whether he had submitted a report to him on the Central Committee session of March 1, when Kardelj, Djilas and Bakarić returned from the meeting with Stalin in Moscow.

Several days after the March 1 session of the Central Committee, Djilas was passing the Soviet Embassy in his car about noon when he noticed Žujović's car standing in front of the Embassy. Djilas had told Tito what he had seen, and Tito now asked, "What were you doing at Lavrentyev's?"

Žujović said he had to talk to him about getting a car for him.

Djilas: "A sorry sight for one of our federal ministers to be crawling to the Soviet Ambassador to get a car for him."

Žujović was confused. He attempted to reply to this and the previous questions.

"I didn't tell Lavrentyev a word about the meeting of the Central Committee. But, comrades, I ask you, can Yugoslavia defend herself?"

Kardelj spoke and answered Žujović's doubts. Then Žujović said: "Comrade Stari, may I go to the Financial Committee meeting at the National Assembly? I have to speak there."

Upon that Tito moved that the session be adjourned and resumed the next morning. He further proposed that a fair copy be made of the letter he had drafted and finally said, "Our Plenum must take a stand on the case of Žujović. Further co-operation with him is impossible. Personally, I am not sure he did not report to Lavrentyev. That is treason. No one has the right to love his country less than the Soviet Union."

The session was resumed the next day. It was first decided to found a commission composed of three members, to examine the case of Sreten Žujović and Andrija Hebrang. The letter to be sent to the Soviet Party was finally approved. On this occasion some of the formulations were modified, and a whole paragraph at the close, regarding relations between the Soviet Union and Yugoslavia, was deleted. Instead, an invitation to the Soviet Party was inserted asking them to send a delegation to Yugoslavia to verify the untruthfulness of the charges against the Yugoslav Party. In this way Tito and other Yugoslav leaders tried to stop the conflict, endeavored to find all means for an honest reconciliation with Stalin.

The Yugoslav answer first stated that we were astonished by the tone and contents of the letter, that the Soviet government had received inaccurate and tendentious information from its representatives in Yugoslavia, and also from Sreten Žujović. The letter continued:

"However much any of us loves the country of socialism, the Soviet Union, he should in no case love less his own country, which is also building socialism; to be precise, the Federal People's Republic of Yugoslavia, for which hundreds of thousands of her most progressive citizens have fallen. We know very well that this is also realized in the Soviet Union."

Further, the letter speaks of the Soviet military and civilian experts. It states that the Soviet government had been informed in 1946 that it was difficult for Yugoslavia to pay such high salaries to the Soviet military experts, and asked the Soviet government to revise the conditions. However, the Soviet government replied through Ambassador Lavrentyev that the salaries could not be reduced and that the Yugoslavs should act as they thought fit.

The letter says:

"The salaries of the Soviet experts were four times the salaries of our army commanders and three times the salaries of members of the Yugoslav Federal Government. The commander of an army corps, with the rank of lieutenant-general or colonel-general, had from nine to eleven thousand dinars a month [$180–$220], whereas a Soviet military expert, with the rank of lieutenant-colonel, colonel and general, had from thirty to forty thousand [$600–$800]. At the same time our Federal Minister had twelve thousand dinars monthly [$240]. Of course, we felt this not only as a financial burden but a political mistake, because it was incomprehensible to our people."

Further on, the letter dealt with Stalin's and Molotov's charges in connection with the work of the Communist Party of Yugoslavia. Here are several interesting extracts:

"Many Soviet people labor under the delusion that admiration of people in Yugoslavia for the Soviet Union came of itself, founded on a tradition whose trail goes back to Tsarist times. That is not so. Love of the Soviet Union has not come of itself; it was persistently spread in our Party and among our people by the present leaders of new Yugoslavia, including above all those who were so seriously accused in the letter. The present leaders of Yugoslavia are those who long before the war, sparing neither pains nor sacrifices, persistently revealed to us the truth about the Soviet Union, and implanted love for the country of socialism among the masses of Yugoslavia."

The answer also deals with Molotov's allegation that Djilas had given instructions that the history of the Bolshevik Party should not be studied in the Party schools and courses in Yugoslavia. After stressing the falsity of this allegation, the letter gives statistical data showing that the *History of the Bolshevik Party* had been published four times in Yugoslavia by underground methods before the war and during the war, and that several editions, totaling over 250,000 copies, had since been published in Yugoslavia.

Then the letter said toward the close:

"If you were to ask us whether there is anything we are dissatisfied with on your part, we should openly say that there are a number of reasons for which we are dissatisfied. What are those reasons? It is impossible to enumerate all of them in this letter, but we shall mention several. First, we consider it an impropriety on the part of organs of the Soviet intelligence service to engage our citizens for its intelligence service in our country, in a country on the road to socialism. This we cannot but understand as an action against the interests of our country. This is being done in spite of the fact that our leaders and state security organs have protested against such actions and made it clear that we could not permit it. Our officers are cajoled, so are various leaders and those who are hostile to new Yugoslavia.

"We have evidence that some organs of the Soviet intelligence service, when engaging members of our Party, cast suspicion on our leaders, destroy their good names and represent them as incompetent and suspect. For instance, while dealing with a good comrade of ours in 1945, engaged in the central coding department in our state security apparatus, Colonel Stepanov did not hesitate to sully and question all our leaders, conceding that 'for the time being Marshal Tito is working as he should.' Such instances continue to the present day. This is not a case of pursuing the struggle against some capitalistic country or other, and we must inevitably conclude that it wrecks our internal unity, destroys confidence in our leadership, demoralizes our people, compromises our leaders, and is a source of the daily collection of false information. Such work of the organs of the Soviet intelligence service cannot be termed loyal and friendly toward our country, which is on its way to socialism and the most loyal ally of the Soviet Union.

"It is impossible for us to agree that the Soviet intelligence service should create its network in Yugoslavia. We have our own state security and intelligence service for the struggle against various foreign capitalist elements and the class enemy inside the country, and if the Soviet intelligence organs require any information or assistance in this direction, they can get it whenever they require it, as has always been the case as far as we were concerned."

Signed on behalf of the Central Committee of the Communist Party of Yugoslavia by Tito and Kardelj, the letter was sent to Moscow by the Yugoslav Ambassador, Vladimir Popović. He returned to Moscow immediately and delivered it to Molotov. He was received in Molotov's office in the Soviet Ministry of Foreign Affairs, with a Soviet secretary present at that meeting and taking shorthand notes of what was being said. According to Vladimir Popović, Molotov was very nervous. After handing over the letter, Popović, according to the instructions he received from the Central Committee of the Yugoslav Communist Party, explained to Molotov the reasons for the Yugoslavs' attitude. Popović spoke for about forty-five minutes but Molotov hardly listened to him. He was looking all the time through the window, biting his lips. When Popović ended, Molotov asked, "Is that all?"

"Yes, do you have any questions?" answered Popović.

"I have no questions whatsoever," retorted Molotov.

"I am surprised that you have no questions," said Popović.

After some hesitation, Molotov answered, "I can say only that I thought you, personally, would not share the opinion of the others in Belgrade."

So the meeting ended. Molotov and Popović did not shake hands on departure.

CHAPTER XXI

1948:

"If only we do not lose our nerve, our victory will be certain . . ."

AFTER the answer of the Central Committee of the Yugoslav Party to his ultimatum of March 27th, Stalin realized that he had lost the first round. The Yugoslav Central Committee had proved its unity. The Central Committee of the Communist Parties of all six Yugoslav republics also approved unanimously the stand taken by Tito and his comrades. The only leading Yugoslav Communist who declared himself for Stalin's line was Sreten Žujović, but he was alone.

But Stalin had other pressure he could bring to bear. He had set the Cominform machinery in motion. The letter of Stalin of March 27th was sent not only to the Yugoslav Central Committee but also to the members of the Cominform, together with a request that they declare themselves on the question of the conflict between Yugoslavia and the Soviet Union, and do so simply on the basis of the Soviet material: that is, the first letter sent by Stalin and Molotov to the Yugoslavs on March 27, without the Yugoslav reply. That is how Stalin understood democracy in the Cominform. He did not stop there: he also demanded that the replies of all the Parties be sent to him, and not directly to the Yugoslav Central Committee.

On April 16 Tito received Yudin, who delivered a letter from the Central Committee of the Soviet Party with Zhdanov's signature, to which were attached comments on the Yugoslav case by Matyas Rakosi, Secretary of the Hungarian Central Committee. He had, at Stalin's request, sent it to the Soviet Central Committee. Naturally, Rakosi, who had arrived in Hungary under the protection of the Red

Army in 1944, attacked the Yugoslav Central Committee with all the fury of which was capable, siding with Stalin on every point.

As soon as the letter was received, the Politburo of the Yugoslav Central Committee met, and Tito proposed that replies should be sent to Rakosi and the Soviet Central Committee, or rather to Zhdanov, who had sent Rakosi's letter to the Yugoslavs.

The Yugoslav reply to the Hungarians was furious. The reason was very obvious. Rakosi himself had complained many times to the leading Yugoslav Communists that the Russians were plundering Hungary, and that they had anti-Semitic tendencies. He had asked many times Yugoslav help in clarifying the political situation in Hungary created by various unjust Russian acts, and now Rakosi was the first to throw mud in the faces of the Yugoslav Communists in order to please Stalin.

The following reply was sent to the Soviet Central Committee: "On April 16 Comrade Yudin delivered Comrade Zhdanov's letter with the resolution of the Central Committee of the Communist Party of Hungary, of April 8 of this year, to the Secretary General of the Central Committee of the Communist Party of Yugoslavia Comrade Tito. It follows from these documents that the Central Committee of the Soviet Communist Party sent a copy of its letter of March 27 to the leaders of the other Parties.

"We are astonished at such an act of the Soviet Party for the following reasons:

"First, the Central Committee of the Soviet Communist Party did this without the approval of the Central Committee of the Communist Party of Yugoslavia, without awaiting the reply of the Central Committee of the Communist Party of Yugoslavia, and without verifying the allegations it makes in its letter of March 27 with the Central Committee of the Communist Party of Yugoslavia.

"Second, the brotherly Communist Parties were thus informed of one side of the case, not knowing the opinion of the Central Committee of the Communist Party of Yugoslavia, which has therefore been subjected to general criticism in such a way that it cannot defend itself from the unjust allegations of that criticism.

"For these reasons the Politburo of the Central Committee of the Communist Party of Yugoslavia cannot agree to such an act of the Central Committee of the Soviet Communist Party and considers that such an act cannot contribute to clearing up and explaining the causes which have led to differences between the Central Committee of the Soviet Communist Party and the Central Committee of the Communist Party of Yugoslavia."

Since the Russians had clearly demonstrated that they considered the Cominform to be their personal weapon rather than a consultative body in whose work the nine member Communist Parties were to have participated on an equal footing and of their own free will, the Yugoslav Central Committee decided to send its answer to the first Russian letter to all members of the Cominform, to inform them of the whole course of the dispute so that they could hear both parties before passing their judgment.

But the Soviet representatives in Belgrade had already begun to deliver the replies of other members of the Cominform, which differed neither in substance nor in tone from the letter sent by Matyas Rakosi. Among others, a letter arrived from Rudolf Slansky on behalf of the Central Committee of the Czechoslovak Party, as well as one from the Central Committee of the Rumanian Party. Replies had not yet arrived from Gomulka on behalf of the Polish Party, or from Dimitrov on behalf of the Bulgarian Party. The French and the Italians also remained silent.

The Yugoslavs had not received a reply from the Bulgarians up to April 19. On that day a delegation of the Bulgarian government passed through Belgrade on its way to Prague to sign a treaty of friendship and mutual co-operation between Bulgaria and Czechoslovakia. Dimitrov was one of the members of the delegation. The Yugoslav Central Committee decided that Milovan Djilas should go to greet Dimitrov.

Djilas says of that meeting: "I found Dimitrov in a parlor car at the railway station in Topčider Park near Belgrade. We exchanged greetings. At that moment only he, I and another Bulgarian, whose name for obvious reasons I cannot divulge, were in the carriage. Dimitrov told me he had heard about the letter of the Central Committee of the Soviet Party, that some things in it were correct. Then he gripped me by the hand and said: 'Be firm!'

"I told him we Yugoslavs had plenty of firmness, and asked him what they would do. He said the main thing was to be firm, that everything else would come of itself.

"This talk with Dimitrov lasted only a few minutes. He was extremely cordial, but his tone altered visibly as Chervenkov and some others entered the coach."

It was agreed that Dimitrov should meet some of the members of our Politburo upon his return from Prague and stay in Belgrade two or three days. However, the meeting did not take place. Meanwhile, the letter arrived from the Bulgarian Central Committee, in which the Bulgarians agreed fully with the Soviet Party. The letter was signed by Velko Chervenkov, and was principally composed of crude insults at the expense of Yugoslavia and her struggle in the war. At one point it said: "It appears that a few leading Yugoslav comrades have begun to deny the leading role of the Soviet Union in the struggle against imperialism, to deny some of the basic principles of Marxism-Leninism. The statement that Yugoslavia would have freed herself from German slavery is deeply untrue and harmful. Without the Soviet Union and the Soviet army there could have been no victory for people's democracy in any country." In his letter Chervenkov further declares that he will take every measure against the outbreak of similar manifestations in Bulgaria, and says: "In view of the close connections between Yugoslavia and Bulgaria, the Politburo of the Bulgarian Central Committee warns its members of the possible harmful influence of the anti-Marxist views of one part of the leading Yugoslav comrades upon the policy of the Bulgarian Party."

Since this letter had been adopted at the meeting of the Bulgarian Central Committee before Dimitrov had left for Prague, the Yugoslav Central Committee decided it was useless for any of its members to meet Dimitrov on his return. A telegram was sent to Dimitrov in Prague. This meant also a definite break of all negotiations for a federation of Yugoslavia and Bulgaria.

Those days were full of excitement in Yugoslavia. A wide discussion had developed in the Party in connection with the letters. It was clear that an overwhelming majority of the members was declaring itself in favor of the Central Committee's stand. May Day, which is celebrated in Yugoslavia with a big parade, had arrived. Žujović had orders from the Russians to make use of that day for a special kind of demonstration. On May Day he was not on the stand of honor, but in the procession, among the people, and thus he marched past the stand.

Four days later came the second reply of the Soviet Central Committee, even more venomous than the first. It included such statements as "the United States Ambassador in Belgrade behaves like the host in Yugoslavia," "The Yugoslav state and Party machinery are full of friends and relatives of the German Quisling and hangman General Nedić." Moreover it openly demanded for the Soviet Ambassador in Yugoslavia the right to obtain information from anybody he pleased, because he was also a Communist, "and had not only the right but the duty to talk to Communists in Yugoslavia occasionally on all questions that might interest them."

But the heaviest blow to the peoples of Yugoslavia were the attacks on the National Liberation Struggle and the sacrifices the Yugoslavs had made in the war. The letter alleged, for instance, that in May, 1944, after the German attack on Supreme Headquarters at Drvar, "the National Liberation Movement in Yugoslavia was in the throes of a severe crisis until the Soviet army came to the help of the Yugoslav people, routed the German forces of occupation, liberated Belgrade, and thus created the conditions indispensable to the coming to power of the Communist Party. Unfortunately, the Soviet army did not give and could not have given such help to the French and Italian Communist Parties. If Comrades Tito and Kardelj were to take these circumstances into consideration as an indisputable fact, they would shout less about their merits and would behave with more deference and modesty."

This passage, among others, deeply embittered all the Yugoslavs. How could Stalin and Molotov be so false as to state that after the attack on Drvar the National Liberation Movement in Yugoslavia had been in the throes of a severe crisis? On the contrary, the National Liberation Movement had then reached its peak. The German offensive was quickly broken and huge successes were achieved. The extent of Stalin's falsehood can be seen from the fact that *Pravda* for June 4, 1944, just at the time when according to Stalin the National Liberation Movement was in the throes of a severe crisis, wrote:

"Allied military operations have flared up successfully in Italy, special credit for which goes to the heroic struggle of the National Liberation Army of Yugoslavia against the Hitlerite invaders and their cowardly collaborationists Nedić, Pavelić and Mihailović. . . .

"The Germans are resorting to new adventures in order to achieve success. The German failure to capture Marshal Tito's headquarters is widely known. The German attack was broken by the resistance of Marshal Tito's heroic army. In Italy Kesselring requires the help of new troop reinforcements. But he can obtain them from nowhere, the more so as the eastern front urgently requires new reinforcements, and to withdraw German units from the west is hazardous. It is obvious that anticipating General Alexander's advance, the Germans wanted to free some of their divisions in Yugoslavia. Marshal Tito and his army wrecked and destroyed those plans. The front in Yugoslavia absorbs important German forces and makes it impossible for them to help Kesselring in his present heavy defeats. There lies the special significance of the stubborn attempts of the German-Fascist invaders to achieve some kind of success in Yugoslavia."

Stalin and Molotov attempted in their letter to disparage the successes of the Yugoslav Communist Party during the war:

"Comrades Tito and Kardelj speak in their letter of the merits and successes of the Yugoslav Communist Party; they say the Soviet Central Committee used to recognize these merits and successes, and is now silent about them. This, of course, is not true. No one can deny the merits and successes of the Yugoslav Communist Party. That is indisputable; but it must be said that the merits and successes of, let us say, the Communist Parties of Poland, Czechoslovakia, Hungary, Rumania, Bulgaria, Albania, are no less than those of the Yugoslav Party. Yet, the leaders of these Parties are modest and do not clamor about their successes, unlike the Yugoslav leaders who have split everyone's ears with their exaggerated boasting."

Here again Stalin and Molotov wish to distort history. Here, for instance, is what *War and the Working Class*, the organ of the Soviet Foreign Ministry, wrote on January 1, 1944:

"To be sure, in proportion to the scope and activity of the National Liberation uprising, Czechoslovakia lags behind other countries in occupied Europe, especially Yugoslavia, where there is a large-scale partisan army. Conditions for a partisan struggle exist in Czechoslovakia too. Her nonparticipation in this respect is explained by a number of reasons, such as the harmful influence of capitulationists of all hues, by the absence of a united central leadership in the uprising of the patriotic forces in the country. It must be said that the insistence upon passive resistance, denying the immense role of the people's forces in preparing their liberation, has been fomented by the policy of certain influential groups of Czechs in exile who have a negative attitude to the question of partisan struggle on a wide scale."

Here, according to the *Pravda* of April 7, 1944, is what Chervenkov said during the war about the Bulgarian army, which was fighting for Hitler:

"The speech of Velko Chervenkov was heard with the deepest attention. He spoke with indignation of the horrible crimes of the Hitlerites, the Bulgarian agents. With the Germans, and the gangs of Nedić and Mihailović, they are wreaking havoc, plundering and destroying Yugoslav towns and villages. Bulgarian army units are replacing the German divisions that Hitler is urgently sending to the Russian front.

"On behalf of the Bulgarian patriots the speaker addresses the Bulgarian people, the soldiers involved in a fratricidal war against the Slavs, calling them to wash away the shame they have brought upon themselves by fighting against their Yugoslav brothers.

"Stop the disgraceful military operations against the brotherly National Liberation Army! Join it in the struggle against the common enemy of all the Balkan peoples—against the German criminals. Follow the glorious example of the Bulgarian battalion 'Hristo Botev,' which has covered its banners with glory fighting side by side with the units of the Yugoslav National Liberation Army against the Hitlerite invaders."

By attacking the Yugoslavs at the point of their greatest pride— their devotion to their country and their willingness, so well demonstrated, to lay down their lives for it—Stalin's letter of May 4 deeply embittered even those Communists in the Yugoslav Party who were hesitant, who were asking themselves whether Tito was right.

Toward the close of their twenty-five-page letter of May 4, Stalin and Molotov rejected the request of the Yugoslav Central Committee that the Soviet Central Committee send a delegation to Yugoslavia to investigate on the spot charges in their first letter. The Russians asked for this question to be laid before the Cominform.

The Plenum of the Central Committee was called again for May 9 in Belgrade. The second Russian letter was read there, and a Yugoslav reply drawn up. It was extremely brief. It rejected the request that the question should be discussed at the Cominform meeting. The letter said:

"We do not avoid criticism on matters of principle, but we feel in such an unequal position that we find it impossible to consent to discuss this matter before the Cominform for the time being. Nine parties have already received your first letter without our previous knowledge and have taken a stand in their resolutions. The contents of your letter have not remained an internal matter for the two parties, but have gone outside the bounds of an admissible circle, and today not only our Party but our country is being insulted in some countries, such as Czechoslovakia and Hungary, as was our Parliamentary delegation in Prague. The consequences of all this are extremely painful for our country."

The meeting of May 9 also received the report of the commission on the case of Žujović and Hebrang. Its decision recommended their expulsion from the Central Committee and the Party, and was upheld unanimously. It was decided to acquaint the whole Party membership with this case and to explain what Žujović and Hebrang had intended. The government also decided that organs of the state authorities were to institute proceedings against them on a charge of treason. A few days later the public prosecutor ascertained that there were elements of a criminal offense against the security of the state and they were arrested. An extremely offensive telegram arrived from Moscow threatening the Central Committee in dire terms because of this arrest. In Moscow elaborate preparations were made to kidnap Žujović by plane from Yugoslavia to the Soviet Union. But it was too late. Žujović was in jail.

Thus Stalin lost the second round. The only two men in the Yugoslav Central Committee that he had prepared to split the Central Committee and the Yugoslav government, facilitating the ruin of the country and its subjugation by the Soviet Union, had now been publicly exposed and their intentions made known.

In Moscow they pressed ahead with plans for the meeting of the Cominform at which Yugoslavia was to be publicly anathematized. On May 19 a young man called Mossetov from the apparatus of the Soviet Central Committee arrived in Belgrade with a letter from the Central Committee signed by Secretary Souslov. The Russians asked the Yugoslavs to attend the Cominform meeting without fail, although they had already refused the Russian request once. It cannot be denied that heated discussions had taken place in Yugoslavia on whether to attend the Cominform meeting or not. The majority considered that the Yugoslav delegation should not attend, for it would have been the usual farce, in which the verdict was clearly predetermined. There would have been no discussion, because it was obvious that under Russian pressure all the Parties would have adopted attitudes toward the Yugoslavs without having seen any Yugoslav material. Relations were utterly unequal. To go to the Cominform meeting under such conditions meant to submit to injustice in advance.

Mossetov delivered the letter personally to Tito. Before seeing him he spread rumors in Belgrade that the Cominform meeting would take place in the Ukraine in the presence of Stalin personally, and that Tito would be doing the proper thing if he were present, too.

Although Mossetov was officially an employee in the Soviet Central Committee organization, the Yugoslavs had seen him during the early postwar years in the uniform of a lieutenant-colonel of the N.K.V.D. From talks with him it was evident that he had long been a specialist in Yugoslav affairs, for he had taken part in the investigations and liquidation of Yugoslavs in Moscow in 1937.

Tito received Mossetov, who delivered Souslov's letter.

Tito had had portraits of Lenin and Stalin in his study. It had so happened that morning that the nail fixing Stalin's portrait to the wall had become loose, and the portrait, instead of hanging on the wall, now stood leaning against it on the floor. This immediately attracted Mossetov's keen eye, and he stared at Stalin's portrait, probably thinking Tito had already given orders for the removal of Stalin's portrait all over Yugoslavia.*

---

* Actually, in Yugoslavia Stalin's portraits began to disappear of themselves as the conflict between the Soviet Union and Yugoslavia heightened. No orders were given by the authorities or by the Party to this effect. People on their own simply began to remove Stalin's portraits. The process lasted almost a year, and by the end of 1949 it was no longer possible to find a single portrait of him in the country. That year Stalin was seventy, and to mark the occasion trainloads of gifts were sent from all the countries of Eastern Europe to the Kremlin. Someone invented a joke in Yugoslavia that spread like wildfire, that a trainload of his portraits should be sent from Yugoslavia.

Tito accepted the letter and informed Mossetov that the Central Committee of Yugoslavia would reply to it. At the same time he told him he believed they would turn down the Russian request to take part in the Cominform meeting.

The next day, May 20, the Central Committee met and unanimously decided not to take part in the Cominform meeting.

It was realized that there was no guarantee that Tito would return alive from such a meeting. The Yugoslav Communists were familiar with the methods of invitations to "consultation" used by Stalin and Molotov for those who disagreed with them. In 1937 the whole Politburo of the Ukrainian Party was opposed to Stalin's Greater-Russian policy. Molotov arrived at Kiev on Stalin's orders and went to the Politburo meeting. He failed to persuade a single member that the Ukrainians were wrong. Then Molotov convened the Plenum of the Central Committee, but its majority also declared itself for the Politburo. Several days later an invitation arrived from Stalin asking the Ukrainian Politburo to consultations in the Kremlin. They responded and set out for Moscow. As they entered the Kremlin, the N.K.V.D. arrested them all and Stalin later had them shot.

Finally Tito informed Souslov of the Central Committee decision not to send a delegation to the Cominform meeting.

The Russians reacted on May 22. Their letter was extraordinarily typical of them. It clearly confirmed they had founded the Cominform not as a consultative body for the exchange of views between Communist Parties, but as a weapon with which to impose their will upon the other Parties, especially the Yugoslav.

Here are several passages from the letter:

"Comrades Tito and Kardelj write that they feel 'in such an unequal position that they find it impossible to consent to discuss this matter before the Informburo and moreover permit themselves to suggest that the Central Committee of the Soviet Communist Party has brought the Yugoslav leaders to such an unequal position.

"The Central Committee of the Soviet Communist Party considers that there is not a grain of truth in this assertion. There is no inequality nor can there be for the Yugoslav Communist Party in the Informburo of nine Communist Parties. Everyone knows that during the organization of the Informburo all the Communist Parties were guided by the indisputable view that each Party should submit reports to the Informburo just as every Party has the right to criticize other Parties. It was this principle that the conference of nine Communist Parties had in view, when it heard the reports of the Central Committees of all the Communist Parties in September, 1947, without exception. The conference of the nine Communist Parties was guided by the equal right of every Party to criticize every other Party when it subjected the work of the Italian and French Communist Parties to severe Bolshevik criticism.

"It is generally known that at that time the Italian and French comrades not only did not dispute the right of the other Parties to criticize their work but, on the contrary, bore themselves like real Bolsheviks and drew a lesson from it. Moreover, it is generally known that the Yugoslav comrades, with all the others, took at the conference the opportunity to criticize the errors of the Italian and French comrades, and that neither they nor any of the others considered that by doing this the other Parties were violating the principle of equality of the Italian and French Parties.

"But why do the Yugoslav comrades make such a radical change, demanding the abolition of established order in the Informburo? Because they think that the Yugoslav Party and its leadership should be in a privileged position, that the statute of the Informburo does not suit it, that they, while entitled to criticize the other Parties, need not themselves be subjected to criticism. But such morals, if we may say so, have nothing to do with equality. That is nothing but a demand by the Yugoslav leaders for privileges to be given the Communist Party of Yugoslavia which are not and cannot be enjoyed by any Party. We have always held the view, without which it is impossible for the Informburo to exist and work, that each Party is under the obligation to submit its report to the Informburo, where each Communist Party is entitled to criticize every other Communist Party. The refusal of the Yugoslavs to submit a report on their work before the Informburo and to hear the criticism of other Parties violates the principle of equality among the Parties."

At the end of his letter Stalin says:

"Regardless of whether the representatives of the Central Committee of the Communist Party of Yugoslavia report at the meeting of the Informburo or not, the Central Committee of the Soviet Communist Party insists upon discussing the state of affairs in the Yugoslav Communist Party at the coming meeting of the Informburo.

"The Central Committee of the Soviet Communist Party declares its agreement with the request of the Czechoslovak and Hungarian comrades to postpone the meeting of the Informburo until the second half of June."

Stalin wanted to gain time by postponing the session of the Cominform for a month, for he was firmly convinced that by a combination of external and internal pressures he would force Yugoslavia to submit.

During that period Gomulka interceded in a strange way. It appeared at the time to be completely in line with Soviet policy. Through one of his men Gomulka had sent a letter to the Yugoslav Central Committee appealing to the Yugoslavs to take part in the Cominform meeting, and suggested that he should come to Belgrade with Berman, one of the leaders of the Polish Party, to discuss the matter with the Yugoslavs.

Replying to Gomulka, Tito said that he was free to come to Yugoslavia, but informed him that the Yugoslavs "had decided not to attend the Cominform meeting, that they had given the idea deep thought, and that the decision had been taken by the Plenum of the Central Committee of the Communist Party of Yugoslavia."

The last of the leading figures from the countries of Eastern Europe to maintain friendly relations was Dimitrov. For May 25, Tito's birthday, which is celebrated in Yugoslavia, none of the leading figures from the Soviet Union or from the countries of Eastern Europe sent the customary congratulations except Dimitrov, who sent the following telegram: "Brotherly greetings and best wishes for your birthday."

Dimitrov also chose a Bulgarian boy to present a relay baton to Tito in the name of Bulgarian youth and sportsmen.

That same day the Yugoslav Central Committee countered with a bold move. It published in the press its earlier decision to convene the Party congress so as to enable the entire Party membership to give its view on the conflict between the Soviet Union and Yugoslavia. That was an unexpected blow for Stalin. It meant that Tito had decided on a referendum in Yugoslavia on the subject of the conflict with the Soviet Union. The congress was convened for July 21, 1948, in Belgrade. Tito was to give a report on the development and struggle of the Yugoslav Communist Party and on its role in the revolutionary transformation of Yugoslavia, and a report on the work of the Central Committee. A second report on Party organizational work was being prepared by Aleksandar Ranković, a report on propaganda by Milovan Djilas, on Yugoslavia's international and internal position and the struggle of the Yugoslav Communist Party to develop socialism by Edvard Kardelj, on the construction of socialist economy in Yugoslavia by Boris Kidrič.

It was also decided that one delegate was to be elected for the congress for every two hundred members of the Communist Party of Yugoslavia. One Party organization in Belgrade had even invited the correspondent of Tass to attend its conference in order to convince himself personally of the democratic method of electing the delegates. During this meeting the letters of the Soviet Party and the Yugoslav Central Committee were read, a discussion followed, after which the conference concluded by electing a delegate by secret ballot. What most embittered the ordinary people of Yugoslavia in these letters was the disparaging attitude toward the struggle and sacrifices the Yugoslavs had made during the war. Their reaction to the letters, as manifested at the meetings to elect the delegates, not only demonstrated steadfastness but resistance to injustice, one of the features of the Yugoslav character.

Meanwhile the Cominform had sent an official invitation to Yugoslavia to attend the meeting at Bucharest. A reply was sent on June 20 turning down the invitation. The reasons were stated concisely.

This meant throwing down the gauntlet. Stalin's last hope of the unconditional capitulation of the Yugoslavs had vanished. The Cominform met at Bucharest. The Soviet delegation was headed by Zhdanov, Malyenkov and Souslov. The Bulgarian delegation was headed by Kostov and Chervenkov. Rumania was represented by Dezh, Lucca and Anna Pauker. Hungary sent Rakosi, Farkash and Görö. From Poland there were Berman and Zavadsky. France was represented by Duclos and Fageon. Czechoslovakia sent Slansky, Shiroky, Geminder and Bares, the Italians Togliatti and Secchia. It is noticeable that the meeting was not attended by Gomulka or Dimitrov. Immediately before the meeting Dimitrov celebrated his birthday, and on June 17 Tito sent him the following message: "Accept my cordial congratulations and warmest wishes for your birthday." Dimitrov did not answer for eight days, but on June 26, when the

Cominform meeting had already begun in Bucharest and was considering what decision to take about Yugoslavia, he replied: "I thank you warmly for your greetings for my birthday."

Zhdanov, Malyenkov and Souslov had many difficulties during the meeting at Bucharest. According to information in Yugoslav possession, several participants opposed the adoption of a resolution against Yugoslavia in the form proposed by the Russians. Naturally, their names will not be mentioned here. The arguments advanced by Zhdanov, Malyenkov and Souslov having failed, Zhdanov finally said: "We possess information that Tito is an imperialist spy."

That was the chief argument of the Soviet representative against Yugoslavia. In the Cominform resolution published on the afternoon of June 28, Stalin did no less than force the representatives of six East European countries, among whom were several vice-presidents of government and foreign ministers, to join in the appeal to the citizens of Yugoslavia to force their government to submit to the Soviet Union. Should it refuse, the people were to repudiate it and set up in its stead a new government which would submit to the dictates of the Soviet Union.

In modern history no case can be recalled of such flagrant and open interference in the internal affairs of another state. Nor had the Soviet Union ever made such a gross open violation of international usage in her foreign affairs. But, on the other hand, there is no doubt that Stalin had never found himself in the situation where a country that he considered his natural hunting ground, his sphere of influence, ceded to him during the war as such, opposed him to such an extent. Hence his rage, his ruthlessness, his disregard for international rules and obligations.

It is quite clear that Stalin and the other Soviet leaders, as well as the leaders of some Communist Parties, believed that the publication of this resolution would immediately cause a rift in Yugoslavia, that the people would rebel against Tito's government because they had such faith in Stalin's authority. However, they lost sight of the fact that Stalin had the Communist Party of Yugoslavia, and Tito personally, to thank for his popularity in Yugoslavia.

The Russians and their puppets, who proved to know so little of Yugoslavia and of the events in this country, were firmly convinced that Tito would prohibit the publication of the Cominform resolution in Yugoslavia with all the means at his disposal. However, immediately after it was published, on the morning of June 29, the Plenum of the Yugoslav Central Committee met and adopted its answer to the Soviet charges. It was also decided that the Cominform resolution should be published in its entirety in the Yugoslav press and with it the Yugoslav reply; the people could decide for themselves who was right.

A traveler in Belgrade on the morning of June 30 would have seen people feverishly buying *Borba*, the organ of the Communist Party of Yugoslavia and the biggest daily in the country, and reading about the open conflict between Yugoslavia and the Soviet Union. Astonishment prevailed among the Soviet representatives in Belgrade when they saw *Borba* had published the Cominform resolution in an issue of five hundred thousand copies. Later it was learned that Lavrentyev and Yudin met that morning in the Soviet Embassy and exchanged only two words.

"Published?" said Lavrentyev.

"Published," said Yudin.

It was several minutes before they spoke again.

How firmly Cominform quarters were convinced that Tito would conceal the resolution from his people is indicated by the fact that as late as July 5 Duclos, writing in *L'Humanité*, accused Tito of not daring to publish the Cominform resolution for the people of Yugoslavia to read, hiding it from them by force. "The fact that the Yugoslav leaders have not published the Informburo resolution clearly indicates that they are not sure of their arguments and fear to put the truth before the people." Marko Ristić, the Yugoslav Ambassador in Paris, immediately sent Duclos a letter, drawing his attention to the falsity of his statement, and even enclosed a number of copies of *Borba*, but Duclos had nothing more to say. Neither had he any observation to make on the fact that the Yugoslav reply to the resolution had not been published in the Soviet Union, Czechoslovakia, Poland, Rumania, Bulgaria, Hungary, or in *Unita*. This example would indicate who relied on the people, and who on force and deceit.

How was the Cominform resolution received among the Yugoslavs at home and abroad? The great majority, which had not been conversant with the letters, simply could not believe their eyes. There were people who cried from despair in the streets that morning. But that was the first reaction. After the first pain came a wave of indignation, and pride. The whole country united as one man. Feelings rose high. Men of the street were proud of their country. The air was charged with feeling as it has been during the greatest events in the modern history of Yugoslavia. From many parts of Yugoslavia cables reported:

"People feel as they did on March 27th, when Yugoslavia broke down the Axis yoke and challenged Hitler."

The reaction of my own mother was very typical. She said to me, "We are very strange people. When Hitler was at the peak of his power, when the whole continental Europe was at his feet, we tore away the pact which we had with him. When Americans were at the summit of their power in 1946, when everybody in the world was afraid of their atom bomb which they had dropped on Japan a year before, we shot down their airplanes because they violated our national territory. And now when Stalin is bursting with strength, we reject his ultimatum. This reminds me of little Serbia rejecting the ultimatum of the Austro-Hungarian Empire in 1914. We are so strange a people, we know how to defend this land of ours."

On the other hand, among some Yugoslav Communists there was a firm belief that the whole mess with the Russians was initiated by Molotov, Zhdanov and Malyenkov, that Stalin was not behind them. They were led to this belief by long years of teaching that Stalin was the genius and the leader of the international proletariat. That is how these illusions are born. In Belgrade two telegrams had even been voted at a meeting, one to the Yugoslav Central Committee saying: "The charges against the Central Committee of the Party and people of our country will not in the least shake our faith in our Party leadership headed by Comrade Tito," and then the second to Stalin saying, "Comrade Stalin, we deeply believe in you, that you will do everything you can to remove this unjust accusation thrown at our whole country, our Party and our Central Committee."

When we consider how the Yugoslavs looked upon the Soviet Union during the days of the fiercest German terror in the war, and what the Yugoslav Party had done to popularize Stalin among the Yugoslav people, it is no wonder that the reaction in Yugoslavia was what it was at the outset. People simply could not understand that there could be any differences between Stalin's words and Stalin's deeds. But once they felt the blow on their own backs, their rage redoubled.

The reaction of many Yugoslavs abroad was similar. One Yugoslav diplomat had spent the whole of June 28 on an excursion with the editor of a Communist paper. On his return, the representative of a world news agency asked what comment he had to make in connection with the Cominform resolution adopted at Bucharest. The Yugoslav diplomat, who was uninformed of the letters, or any of the events, vigorously replied, "That is an impossibility. It is a pure imperialist fabrication."

The publication of the Cominform resolution found over four thousand Yugoslav athletes in Prague at a big Sokol rally. They had arrived in Prague on June 29, when the text of the resolution was published in all the papers in Prague. They lined up at the station and paraded through the streets of Prague with their streamers and with Yugoslav banners, singing songs to Tito. From the sidewalks, from the trams and from the balconies the people of Prague greeted the Yugoslavs warmly with cries: *"Tito nazdar!"* (Hello, Tito!) *"Zhivela Yugoslavia!"* (Long live Yugoslavia!)

That same afternoon the Yugoslavs performed before 280,000 spectators in a specially built stadium. There were particularly warm ovations to the Yugoslav sailors, seven hundred of them, who at the end of their exercise formed up so as to spell "Tito." The whole stadium rang with enthusiastic cheers and with chanting: "Ti-to! Ti-to!"

At the request of the organizers of the rally the Yugoslav sailors had to repeat their exercise on June 30, this time in the presence of 250,000 citizens of Prague. The manifestations for Yugoslavia and Tito were even more thunderous.

The Soviet Embassy took vigorous measures in Prague. Such manifestations for Tito two days after the publication of the resolution could not be tolerated. The Czech police were given orders to ransack the building where the Yugoslav athletes had been quartered, for they had hung a big portrait of Tito on the balcony. The Czech detectives arrived to remove the portrait and collect copies of the Yugoslav reply to the resolution which the athletes had mimeographed as soon as they had received the text and were distributing among the people of Prague. The Yugoslavs did not allow the detectives to carry out their orders. The Czechs then began to beg the Yugoslavs: "We personally do not want to. But we have orders from our Central Committee. You know, we are also Party members."

But the Yugoslavs did not admit them. One detective even tried to force his way in, but he was thrown out through the doorway, and the Yugoslav gymnasts laughed at him: "What kind of a Communist are you when you don't dare carry out the orders of your Central Committee? We were trained differently in Yugoslavia."

The N.K.V.D. then attempted to organize a counter-blow, trying to persuade some of the Yugoslav gymnasts to remain in Prague and declare themselves for the Cominform resolution. There were offers of money, and promises of high posts in Yugoslavia after Tito's overthrow, but all in vain. Of more than four thousand Yugoslavs, all returned to Yugoslavia. Had Stalin and the other Soviet leaders possessed a little sense, this might also have convinced them of the unity in Yugoslavia, of the Yugoslav reaction to the resolution.

There is no doubt that those days in Yugoslavia were extremely difficult. Yugoslavia was alone in the world. From the East came Stalin's anathema, from the West came misunderstanding and the old threats. Never in history had a small country been in a more desperate position. Those were fateful days. When Tito received the text of the Cominform resolution, he paced his room for fully three hours, pondering the disgraceful document. It was during those days that Tito had his first gall-bladder attack. He had suffered from it during the war, but the latest events had so affected his nerves that he had an exceptionally strong attack.

Yugoslav public opinion was especially embittered at that time by certain acts against Yugoslavia by Albania and Hungary. It was obvious that Stalin was trying to present the conflict as a clash not only between the Soviet Union and Yugoslavia but between Yugoslavia and the other people's democracies. As soon as the Cominform resolution was published, instructions arrived in Albania from Moscow that the Albanians should give vent to their anti-Yugoslav feelings. Not only were Tito's portraits publicly burned but Yugoslavs were assaulted, sick Yugoslavs were ejected from hospitals, and food was denied them and even to Yugoslav children.

In Hungary persecution of the Yugoslav minority began. One

Yugoslav, a Hungarian people's deputy, who refused to agree to the Cominform resolution was expelled from Parliament. On top of this, Rakosi, the Secretary of the Hungarian Party, touched the Yugoslavs in their tender spot. He, like Stalin, spoke with disparagement of Yugoslavia's part in the war. Rakosi said at a meeting in Budapest that even the Yugoslav uprising against Hitler in 1941 was "bourgeois nationalism."

To add to all this, Rakosi read a lecture on how they should have behaved during the war, to the Yugoslavs, who had in vain appealed to the Hungarians by radio to rise against Horthy and the Germans, because the Hungarian people had no one to lead them, because Rakosi was sitting in the Soviet Union, far behind the lines, instead of being with his people, sharing good and evil with them, as Tito was with his.

News began to arrive from Moscow. There were about 460 Yugoslav students at the universities of Moscow alone, besides several thousand in the military academies. Heavy pressure was brought to bear on them to declare themselves for the Cominform resolution. The Russians stopped at nothing in their efforts. The Yugoslavs were told that Tito had ordered the monument in honor of the Red Army in Yugoslavia to be torn down, that rebellion had broken out at home; some officers were offered promotion and high posts on their return to Yugoslavia after Tito was overthrown. An enormous number of Yugoslavs rejected these dazzling offers. Of the 461 students in Moscow, only one supported the Cominform resolution. The authorities prevented contact among the different groups of Yugoslavs in the Soviet Union so that many Yugoslavs outside Moscow, in Leningrad, Sverdlovsk, or Kiev, were unable to get Yugoslav papers.

There were also many false reports in the West about Yugoslavia. An official spokesman for the Italian Foreign Office announced in Rome that a state of siege had been proclaimed in Yugoslavia, saying that the Italian Foreign Office had this report from their Minister in Belgrade. Next morning this spokesman was obliged to deny this statement. A leading Yugoslav Royalist in the United States said: "Tito got what he deserved. The Iron Curtain is falling down more tightly and we, perhaps, will never hear again about Tito." A leading British morning newspaper in the editorial said that the Yugoslav government had already changed hands, that Marshal Tolbukhin was already in Belgrade. A very respectable news agency from the West announced that fighting was in progress in Yugoslavia and that a battalion of Yugoslav troops had crossed the border and asked for asylum in Greece.

Profound excitement also prevailed among Yugoslav exiles in the West. Božidar Kavran, the deputy of Ante Pavelić, the former Quisling President of Croatia, illegally crossed to Yugoslavia from Austria on July 3, and was immediately arrested. At the inquiry he declared he had come to Yugoslavia because he thought the time had come when Tito would fall. Before Kavran, nineteen Ustashi groups led by high officials had been arrested, after having infiltrated into Yugoslavia through underground channels. The first group, caught on July 20, 1947, and led by Ljubo Miloš, the commandant of the concentration camp at Jasenovac where over two hundred thousand people were killed during the war, admitted they had been sent to organize terrorist groups in Yugoslavia. They had brought arms and a radio transmitting station. The Yugoslav authorities took their transmitters and maintained radio connection with Pavelić abroad with particulars of the supposed successes. Pavelić sent this material on to various papers in the West, which wrote about rebellions and disorders in Yugoslavia. Pavelić even decorated some of the Ustashi officials whom he had sent to Yugoslavia through such channels, and promoted them. In prison the Yugoslav investigators even made a joke of it, organizing little functions at which they read Pavelić's decrees to the prisoners. Consequently when the Cominform resolution arrived, Pavelić thought the time was ripe for decisive action, and sent his deputy Božidar Kavran.

Such was the atmosphere in which the Fifth Congress of the Communist Party of Yugoslavia was prepared, when it was necessary to lay the question of the Cominform resolution before the Party rank and file.

On July 21 a total of 2,344 delegates gathered in the big hall of the old barracks of the king's guard in Topčider Park near Belgrade. These 2,344 delegates had been elected by 468,175 members of the Communist Party, which was the number of Party members in July, 1948.

Tito

Of the elected delegates, 979 were workers, 525 peasants, 102 soldiers, 499 intellectuals, 154 civil servants, 138 students, as well as members of various other professions.

There were 227 women delegates.

The length of Party membership averaged seven years and three months. Of the total of 2,344 delegates, 2,238 had fought in the war, 1,453 of them from the first day of the uprising in 1941. Among the 106 who had not fought, 17 had been in prison camps, during the war, and one in a concentration camp.

The hall was decorated with busts of Marx, Engels, Lenin and Stalin, and in the middle hung a painting of Tito. The whole Congress was broadcast over the Yugoslav radio network. During those six days all work virtually came to a standstill. Everyone sat by his wireless attentively following the events at the Congress.

It was opened by Tito. After the election of the Chairman, Tito began to deliver his report. He read for eight hours. He first of all gave the history of the roots of the workers' movement in Yugoslavia. He spoke of the Serbian socialist utopian Svetozar Marković, who in 1871 had published his paper *Radnik* in Belgrade, who had been with Marx at the First International. Tito also gave the history of the Communist Party of Yugoslavia, its factional struggles, its reorganization and so on to the war. There he gave a detailed account of the development of the Liberation War and our efforts in founding the National Liberation Army.

The Congress lasted six days. The reports were followed by discussions. One speaker followed another. So as to give every speaker a chance to take the floor the Congress continued its work at night. One after the other the speakers condemned the attacks on the Yugoslav Party. No one declared himself in favor of the Cominform resolution.

The Congress was attended by Barzenko, the correspondent of *Pravda,* and by Tass correspondents. They shook their heads doubtfully. The correspondent of Radio Prague, Olina Kreychova, was also there.

When they realized in Moscow that the Congress was firmly on Tito's side, they launched a series of attacks on it, saying that it was convened by terrorist methods, that the building where it was held was surrounded by cannons and machine guns. The 2,344 delegates were able to convince themselves with their own eyes of the false-hood of these allegations. *Pravda* announced that Swiss Trotskyists had sent their delegation to the Congress on July 24. This report was announced to all the delegates. The acting chairman at the Congress, Božidar Maslarić, read the following announcement: "As the Mos-cow radio reports, *Pravda* carried a report on July 24, from its cor-respondent in Bucharest, that some kind of Swiss Communist Party, generally known as a spy-terrorist group, has sent its delegation to the Fifth Congress of the Communist Party of Yugoslavia.

"The Chair of the Fifth Congress of the Communist Party of Yugoslavia declares that this report has been deliberately released so as to give the impression that the Communist Party of Yugoslavia is linked with Trotskyist spy groups, to justify before international opinion the unprincipled slander campaign that is being pursued against the Communist Party of Yugoslavia and new Yugoslavia.

"This slanderous report is all the more unhappy since the rep-resentatives of the Soviet press, led by the *Pravda* correspondent Barzenko, who are attending the Congress, were told yesterday, that is to say July 23, in answer to a question in this connection that it was nonsense and untrue, a fact they themselves were able to verify.

"The Chair calls on the Congress to condemn this latest falsehood and slander as a further attempt at lowering the reputation of our Party and of the Congress itself.

"Comrades, will those who are for this announcement raise their hands!"

Acting Chairman: "All." Then: "Is there anyone against? No. I announce that the Congress has unanimously condemned this latest slander." (Thunderous approval and applause.)

The *Pravda* correspondent never appeared at the Congress again, while Olina Kreychova, of Radio Prague, declared on the last day of the Congress that her Communist conscience did not allow such falsehoods to be used against Yugoslavia, and sent a letter of protest to the editor of Radio Prague for broadcasting falsehoods similar to those in *Pravda*.

The last day of the Congress approached, when a new Central Committee had to be elected. This was also the last chance for the champions of the Cominform resolution to declare themselves against the Central Committee and Tito, because voting was secret. Each delegate received the names of the candidates who had been submitted by the Committee for Candidature. They were all typed out on a sheet of paper, and each delegate at the Congress was empowered to cross out any name and to add new ones. Then the sheet of paper was folded and dropped into the ballot box. By ten o'clock all the delegates had voted.

The Electoral Committee opened the boxes in front of all the delegates and began to count the votes; 2,323 delegates voted. The results were reached by midnight. The Chairman of the Electoral Committee, Miloš Minić, stepped forward on the platform and began to read them. When he reached the name of candidate Josip Broz, he announced that he had received 2,318 votes, which means only five delegates were against him. Applause echoed through the hall, followed by cheers, which were drowned by a song invented on the spur of the moment:

"Comrade Tito, we pledge from our heart
That we shall not from your road depart."

The Chairman of the Electoral Committee tried to go on with the results, but the delegates would not let him be heard, for one song followed another, ending with the "International." Finally, five minutes later he continued to read the results.

The other leading members of the Central Committee received the following votes:

Milovan Djilas: 2,314, nine votes against;
Edvard Kardelj: 2,319, four votes against;
Aleksandar Ranković: 2,316, seven votes against;
Boris Kidrič: 2,317, six votes against;
Moša Pijade: 2,322, one vote against;
Svetozar Vukmanović: 2,318, five votes against.

The reading of the results was not over until well past one o'clock in the morning. Then Tito took the floor, and said:

"Comrades, on behalf of the newly elected central leadership of our Party, I thank you most cordially for the confidence you have vested in us. We thus take upon ourselves a serious responsibility. However, we shall be able to do our duty only with your full support.

"The unity demonstrated at our Congress, unity without parallel in the history of our Party, is the pledge that the Party will march forward with even stronger steps, both with respect to its own development and to the construction of our new socialist homeland.

"Comrades, we have summed up great experiences on the work of our Party at this Congress. Pass that experience on to our Party organizations, let them avail themselves of it, let them learn from these examples, both positive and negative. May the purity of the Party be preserved in our ranks, may the theoretical and political level of the members of our Party be raised still more, because that is the pledge for all our future victories.

"Comrades, I warn you we are in a difficult situation, in a trying period. Our Party is faced with a hard test and if only we preserve deep vigilance, unity and firmness in our Party, if only we do not lose our nerve, our victory will be certain."

And Tito ended his speech with the words:

"Long live the Soviet Union, long live Stalin!"

CHAPTER XXII

1948:

"We began to lose faith in Stalin, but not in socialism . . ."

ON THE fourth anniversary of the open break between the Soviet Union and Yugoslavia, I happened to be talking to Tito about those fateful days beginning in the summer of 1948. Tito was on his annual holiday on the Adriatic. He spent most of the day on a small rocky islet about five hundred yards long and not more than eighty wide. The islet is densely covered with laurel, rosemary and sage, with here and there a fig, lemon or orange tree. The southern shore is level and sandy and the deep blue water is clear as only the Adriatic can be. The day was sunny and cloudless, and there was perfect calm except for the first ripples of the mistral, that made such colorful shadows with the sun's rays on the sandy sea-bed. In the middle of the islet rose a stone wall and over it a tiled roof.

Koča Popović and I landed from a small boat and set out toward the wall where Tito was sitting. The sun was scorching, but the cool mistral tempered it, while from the thick vegetation of the island breathed the sweet intoxicating scent of the Mediterranean and the lazy song of the cricket floated on the air. Koča Popović stepped cautiously from stone to stone. He had left the hospital a few days before after a difficult spinal operation, and had come here to rest.

As we came closer to the stone wall, we were able to examine this strange shelter a little better. There were in fact three walls, one in the middle, the two others at right angles to it. They were covered by the roof, and provided perfect shade. In this shelter stood a long table with benches and a deck-chair. In the shade, by the table, we found Tito with a book in his hands. He was reading Upton Sinclair's

The Hundred Per Cent American. He motioned us to the bench next to him, and putting aside his book asked me:

"How do you pronounce the English word 'welcome'?"

Then he offered us each a glass of cold water from a big thermos flask. It must have been about ten o'clock. We went to the southern beach to bathe.

We were lying in the sun, staring into the blue distance where a big white merchantman suddenly appeared. It passed us, hurrying northward toward Trieste. Tito started.

"What the devil is that vessel!" he exclaimed. "She's going through our territorial waters!"

"She seems to be more than six miles out!" replied Koča Popović.

"You're quick to react!" I said to Tito.

"Yes, I'm quick. I have to be," answered Tito, "but I'm careful not to make decisions in a hurry."

Then we began to talk about Koča Popović's operation. Tito asked how many hours the operation itself had lasted, how many days he had had to lie in a cast, what pain he had suffered, whether any nerves had been injured.

I interrupted the conversation by suggesting that we should see who had the longer scar: Koča Popović on his spine, or Tito, who had been operated on for gall-bladder trouble in 1951.

We laughed at the proposal. And so we began to examine scars. Tito had the most. Looking at his strong body, I asked how he had got them. He first showed me a deep gash under his left shoulder blade, where the Cherkezi lance had pierced him in the Carpathians in 1915. Another scar recalled the Russian shell that had dropped in the middle of Tito's platoon on a night march.

"Thirteen of my men were killed there. The blast lifted me into the air and I got a contusion here in the neck."

Koča Popović said, "What about Milinklada in 1943?"

Tito showed his left arm muscle, which had been lacerated by a German bomb fragment when our troops were surrounded in the spring of 1943 on the border of Montenegro and Bosnia.

"It hit me nicely. I thought I was done for, dead."

Then Tito smiled a little, and went on:

"I dived for shelter behind a decayed beech tree lying on the ground, and the bomb fell quite near me. My dog 'Lux,' who had thrown himself across my head, lay in pieces. A little farther away lay the English Captain Stuart, with his feet sticking up. Still farther away Djuro. In all that havoc, my gaze fell on a shattered tree on which stood a small mountain bird, one of its legs shot away by the explosion. . . . The little creature stood on one leg and cried, 'peepee.' That was the first thing that burned into my brain after this calamity. Then Marko came up to me and, putting an arm around me, helped me to my feet. It is just about the anniversary of that battle now."

We were silent for ten minutes. Tito roused us from our memories:

"Then I have a scar on my right hand that I got while I was working in the Daimler factory at Wiener Neustadt in 1912. The piece of iron is still there."

Tito began to recall those days, when he was test driver on the newly completed cars.

"They could do about twenty-five miles an hour, a terrific speed in those days. Some cars even did thirty-five. How technique has developed!"

A hardly perceptible smile passed over Koča Popović's face. But it did not escape either Tito or me. We asked what was funny. The fleeting smile turned into hearty laughter.

"After the war, in 1919," said Koča, "my father bought a Daimler. It was white, and every Sunday afternoon the whole family, my father and mother, and the sons and daughters, would pile into the long, open car and drive proudly through the streets of Belgrade, our noses in the air. People would say, 'There goes Popović's bathtub.' "

We joked a little about Koča Popović's social origins, and the time the Soviet General Kornieyev, rather drunk, jeered at him as "Konstantin Popovič, general, millionaire, poet." Koča Popović gave the words a Russian pronunciation. He recalled the *Brüderschaft* he had drunk in 1946 with Stalin and Molotov. He got up from the sand and with lively movements began to describe the scene, imitating Stalin's words, "*Serb, preedyi soudah*" ("Serb, come here"), and then the same procedure with Molotov, and the unpleasant feeling of being kissed by Molotov's fleshy lips.

"Stalin's invitation, 'Serb, *preedyi soudah*,' was not exactly sincere; there was a touch of chauvinism in it," said Koča Popović.

The talk returned to Koča Popović's family. Tito remembered a cousin of Koča's, a painter called Žika Vlajnić, with whom Tito had stayed illegally when he came to Belgrade just before the war.

"I remember Vlajnić and his wife, Professor Adelina, well. How nicely those two people got on together. He used to call her Patsko, Patsko. And never after the war did they come to ask for anything; before the war they would have given us their last dinar. I saw them for the first time after the war on May 25. They came to congratulate me on my birthday. I had a talk with them, and they seem to be just as happy together. It's nice to see."

It was already nearly eleven o'clock and time to go into the water. Tito went first, we followed. The water was cool. Tito was showing us a trick he had learned as an apprentice at Sisak, standing on his hands in the water, with his legs held quite vertically.* Koča Popović did not dare try because of the injury to his spine; I tried, but failed, for whenever I ducked my head I lost all sense of direction under the surface.

Then we swam. I remembered a joke of Aneurin Bevan's, who had been to this islet with Tito last year, when it turned out he could not swim. We all laughed that an Englishman did not know how to swim, and he retorted, "I'm not English; I'm Welsh. And, anyway, why should I swim? We've got the British Navy!"

Koča Popović had left us and set out to catch some fish for lunch with his underwater harpoon. Half an hour later we left the shore. We had a small air-gun, and a special Colt pistol with a long barrel that took the same type of slugs as the air-gun. The pistol had a range of three hundred yards. Tito took the pistol and began to fire at a stone about ninety yards away. I was surprised to see what a steady hand Tito had; he overshot the target by half a yard with his first shot, he fell short of it by a yard with his second, but his third and fourth hit the stone. Tito was elated. He turned proudly to me:

"Whenever I'm tired, I shoot at a target. The main thing is, a man

---

* When the manuscript of this book was ready, I sent it to Tito to glance over it. When he read this page he wrote down a remark: "I did not learn this when I was a boy, but Koča Popović taught me this trick two years ago."

should always be doing something. It is awful to be inert. It has helped me a lot in life that I became interested in sports as an apprentice, wrestling and then fencing. That's what keeps a man going."

Tito continued to shoot. Suddenly his dog Tiger rushed toward the target. Tito lowered his pistol and called the dog: "Are you mad, do you want to get killed?" Tiger seemed to feel he was in the wrong and hung his head and began to whimper. Tito has Tiger with him the whole day long, talking to him, advising him; the dog is offended, ashamed, reconciled and finally ingratiating, but always at Tito's side. This has been going on for nine years, ever since the war, when Lux was killed and Tiger came to take his place.

It was noon. From somewhere along the shore a church bell echoed faintly. We went toward the shady shelter. Then came lunch: a fish Dentex caught that morning, grilled over hot coals. There was also the fish Koča Popović had with much trouble managed to catch with his harpoon. We had lettuce and beet-root salad, and drank wine diluted with water, called "bevanda."

The sun was burning with all its strength, but the heat was not oppressive. The mistral was still going strong. Koča Popović said that summer was the finest season of the year because the days are the longest; it always gave him a special joy when the days begin to lengthen, and a vague sorrow seized him as the days grew shorter.

"I am saddest when the birds begin to leave us in the autumn!" said Tito.

"I prefer the winter days, because they are the shortest. That's from the war, I suppose. During those days there were fewer planes," I added.

That started the subject of the war again, the physical effort: of what a man can endure far more than is imaginable if only his will is strong, if the goal he is fighting for is clear. On the other hand, how men can break down, how they suddenly become passive and apathetic, if they lose all prospects, if the goal they are fighting for disappears.

I recalled the June days of 1948.

"In that connection, I think the process we went through when it came to open conflict with the Russians is characteristic. First came shock but immediately afterwards incredible strength. This means that at least the overwhelming majority of our people never for a moment lost sight of our *goal* in those June days of 1948. . . ."

Tito was silent for a time, staring toward the open sea. I thought he had not heard my words properly. But he was thinking, for he said:

"In essence that is so. Only it was not such a simple process. There is no doubt that the whole conflict, especially the resolution, was a heavy blow for our people. We in Yugoslavia, in spite of many doubts, yet at heart had faith in the Soviet Union, in Stalin. Before my very eyes Partisans fell in the war with Stalin's name on their lips. It was not in vain that we had from year to year steadily spoken to our people about the Soviet Union as the country of socialism. We need not hide it, nor be ashamed now of having looked toward the Soviet Union openly and sincerely up to 1948. We are not ashamed of our illusions; on the contrary, we are proud of them. They were something positive, and reflected our deep faith in progress and socialism. And during those June days in 1948 when Stalin so ruthlessly, so brutally trampled them underfoot, it hurt us deeply, but we did not lose faith in socialism; we began to lose faith in Stalin, who had betrayed the cause of socialism.

"There was no question of disappointment or grief for breaking with the Russians. Those days were difficult because of other anxieties: the future of socialism, the future of this country, struggling to build socialism with its own resources in a way best suited to its own people. That was my greatest worry during June, 1948.

"It was clear to me that the conflict was not a passing affair, but that it marked a conclusive breakdown, a definitive conflict. The prospect was clear to me, but it was hard for me because I was then unable to see all the possibilities that presented themselves as a way out of the situation we found ourselves in. I did not know how the West would react, but I was ready to come to grips with every danger."

Tito was absorbed in his words, he had simply been carried away by them; and unconscious of doing so, he left the bench and began to walk up and down in front of the shelter, as he always does when he is deep in thought. That is how I saw him during the Fourth Offensive, when in the valley of the Rama he was considering which way to pierce the encircling enemy. That is how he was during the

Fifth Congress, when during recess he walked up and down in front of the building.

Tito now elaborated his idea: "There is no doubt those were difficult days, but great days as well. I had a similar experience in 1938, when I was in Moscow and we were discussing whether to dissolve the Communist Party or not. All the Yugoslav leaders at that time in the Soviet Union had been arrested; I was alone, the Party was weakened, without leadership; and I was there alone. Dimitrov asked me if I could succeed in carrying out my task—he said he had every confidence in me, but the N.K.V.D. was arresting men for whom, as he said, he would have thrust his hand into the fire.

"That is why, from one point of view, those days in 1938 were more difficult for me than in 1948. There was no Party in the real sense of the word. In 1948 there was a strong, united Party.

"In 1948 it was difficult not only because we had cut off relations with the Kremlin, but because they were basely attacking our young revolution. It was intervention in the true sense of the word such as the October Revolution had had to endure, only it was far easier for Lenin. He had the whole world proletariat on his side. Our revolution was being suffocated in the name of the Soviet Union. Our revolution was being suffocated by Stalin's pressure, which was compelling the whole workers' movement in the world to declare itself against us. I knew that one of our hardest tasks would be to overcome the slanders that Stalin was spreading.

"In this situation our fundamental task was to assure ourselves of the unhampered development of the people's knowledge of the causes of the conflict with the Soviet Union. The most important thing was that people should realize what the issue was, that they should free themselves of prejudice, of the long years of instruction, that they should understand the substance of the matter. That was not an easy job. The tremendous authority of the Soviet Union and Stalin was operating. It was with such authority, with his letters and with the Cominform resolution, that Stalin thought he would wreck the unity of our Central Committee at the first onslaught, that he would take the Party and government into his hands with the help of Žujović and Hebrang. This, however, did not happen. I think the decisive role was played by the internal democratic life in our Communist Party that we had established before the war. From the first day of the attack on us, with the arrival of the first letter in March, 1948, our men discussed them, point by point, expressing themselves where they did not agree, freely declaring what was not clear to them, or their failure to grasp certain things. I must admit the most difficult period in this respect during the first months of the struggle with Stalin was between the arrival of the letter of March 27 and the Central Committee session of April 13, when Stalin hoped Žujović would draw the majority of the Central Committee to his side. At that time there were some comrades who failed to perceive the chief causes of the conflict. Rather perplexed, they would come to me and ask questions. I explained and convinced them. I remember one of them telling me, 'To tell you the truth, I was downhearted; now I feel better. It's a good thing we have you, because when we feel bad we come to you, and you help us. But what you must feel, who can you turn to?'

"For me during those hours of trial I turned to the basic strength that the people of Yugoslavia had achieved during the war, and during the early years after it. They were a united people, fired with the consciousness of their own strength, of what they had done. There was a strong Party, too, full of experience. That is why it was easier in 1948 than in 1938.

"But one single thing required deep thought: how to get on and give Yugoslavia a chance to develop as she wants to, and in the way that suits her interests best. We are a small country and our only strength lay in our moral power, in our unity, in the degree of clarity with which we saw our prospects of development.

"During those days I realized that we should triumph only if, first, we made ourselves see clearly the cause of the conflict with the Soviet Union, and if that process was developed among the Yugoslav people in good time, and in the proper way. In so doing it was necessary to pay thorough attention to illusions about the Soviet Union that existed or left their traces among practically all our people. We dared not give free reign to indignation and reply to all the lies and slander coming from the Soviet Union, or in the name of the Soviet Union, merely with sharp rejoinders. It was necessary to allow Stalin time to do such things toward Yugoslavia as would move the people themselves to say: 'Down with Stalin,' instead of estranging ourselves from the masses by being first to raise such a cry in a moment of fury. Practice is life's best teacher. What Stalin did during the June days of 1948, what he had hinted at then, he soon confirmed with a number of his most brutal acts. From then on, at least as far as we in Yugoslavia were concerned, there was no great political problem in the struggle with the Soviet Union. The substance of the conflict was as clear as daylight to every honest man in our country. The people had freed themselves of illusions but not lost faith in socialism, because, in spite of the worst difficulties, their country was an object lesson to them how a small nation can build socialism."

Tito hesitated, lit a cigarette and stuck it into his patent cigarette holder, while I said, "Practice is the main thing. It is proved by the case of France and Italy today. Cominformism is still strong there. Its position can be said to be intact. The chief reason, among others, is that the people in those countries have not themselves gone through what we did in our relations with the Russians. The last thing I wish the French and Italian Communists, or in fact any of the Communist masses, is the arrival of Soviet troops in their country. How they would come to their senses overnight! The recent experiences of other countries have not been a sufficient lesson to them. The working class has a hard time of it in those countries. The shop windows are full, the bourgeoisie swims in plenty, but the hungry worker can only look on. On top of it all, thirty years and more of propaganda about the Soviet Union, about the land of Paradise."

Tito made no response and I went on, "In the world, not only among the workers, but in other sections of population, when the conflict between the Soviet Union and Yugoslavia is considered, the question is always asked how is it possible for Stalin to make a mistake: how could he, who cannot be said to be without wisdom and guile, make such a crude mistake as to estimate the situation so badly and to attack Yugoslavia without first taking all precautions so as to ensure the success of his attack?"

"Stalin's main weakness," Tito answered, "was that he had a superficial view of Yugoslavia. He did not realize, and did not want to, that something new was being created here. Because of this, he was unable to realize the essential character of our revolution, and particularly the fundamental things in it: the extent to which the consciousness of all the Yugoslav people was being fortified by the strength and beauty of the independence of their country, by the growing pride of our people, who had for so many centuries wrestled with difficult invaders, by the consciousness of creating something new.

"Back in 1944, Stalin had refused to believe that we had achieved all this in Yugoslavia during a terrible struggle. He was influenced by the number of failures suffered by workers' movements in the world between the two wars, and deep distrust toward everything outside the Soviet Union had taken root in him. And it is just he who is responsible for such a development in the workers' movements, which came about at least in part because the leaders in those countries followed his instructions blindly. That is the result of his inflexible view of things, his faulty estimation of the situation, and above all his methods of rigid leadership from one center.

"What a faulty appraisal of the situation in various countries was made in the Comintern alone! Take the Comintern resolutions between the wars, and let us see how far they corresponded to reality, how correct they were, how ridiculous they proved in life. Did not Manuilski say in 1939 that Germany was the country ripest for revolution? Yet, two years later, those same German workers and peasants, wearing Hitler's uniforms, rolled up to the very gates of Moscow.

"Stalin depreciated, still depreciates, the entire workers' movement outside the Soviet Union; he thought we in Yugoslavia would never triumph without his help; he was worried by our militancy even while we were fighting Hitler. Moreover, he put too much faith in his own authority. He thought no one could separate the Yugoslav people from him. He had serious illusions about the supposed traditional ties between the Russians and Yugoslavs.

"Because of his unrealistic assessment of the situation in Yugoslavia and his superficial view of the country, in the intoxication of victory in the war he estimated the situation in Yugoslavia badly and missed the mark when he attacked. He never for a moment tried to understand that something new was happening in Yugoslavia; he did not perceive the new spirit that had prevailed in our Communist Party since 1937, he refused to realize the fact that our people were accustomed to thorough discussions about everything, that our Communists do not accept matters simply by force of authority but because they first reach the conviction that black is black, and white is white. Many of our people went to the Soviet Union after the war, where they saw things that displeased them. Accustomed to think freely, they also gave free voice to their thoughts, without any malicious intentions, and Stalin took this to be a direct attack on him, on the Soviet Union. That made him still angrier.

"That Stalin miscalculated the situation in Yugoslavia was also greatly the fault of the N.K.V.D. These men did not dare tell him anything about Yugoslavia except what they thought would best please him. They tried to perceive what Stalin and those around him thought about Yugoslavia, and they accordingly burrowed everywhere in Yugoslavia hoping to find even the smallest crumb to confirm Stalin's mistaken view.

"I think Stalin did not make a mistake only in the case of Yugoslavia. He made many erroneous estimates of the situation after the war. These, in my opinion, are the cause of Stalin's faulty strategy in trying to overwhelm Yugoslavia. The appraisal of the situation was always wrong, and the means proposed for settling the situation in their favor were always late. And when finally in 1949 he had decided to resort to arms against Yugoslavia, the situation had already overtaken him. The Yugoslav question was no longer only a Yugoslav question but a world one."

A motorboat was approaching the islet. In it was Tito's secretary, Lieutenant Colonel Branko Vučinić, a Montenegrin from the Piperi, bringing him his post, telegrams and newspapers from home and abroad.

I said to Tito, "Stari, aren't you also perhaps one-sidedly informed of events at home and abroad, like Stalin?"

"What is most important for me," Tito laughed, "is what I hear directly in talks with the people. That is why I travel so much all over the country every year. I meet hundreds and hundreds of people, and when I am in Belgrade I receive many delegations. Besides this, as you yourself see, many people come to Yugoslavia from almost all parts of the world throughout the year, and some of them call on me. In talks with them I also learn many things that are happening in the world."

1948

Tito withdrew into a corner of the shelter, while Koča Popović and I went down to the shore. The sea around us was quite different. It had become a darker blue. We sat on the shore, for we had no desire to go into the water. We sat there discussing our conversation with Tito, the phases Yugoslavia had been passing through during the past four years, the collapse of Stalin's blitzkrieg against Yugoslavia in the summer of 1948, his stubborn efforts to force her to capitulate, his appeals to the Yugoslavs to rebel against their legal government by provoking internal disturbances, attempting to wreck the unity of the country, by isolating her from the whole world, by economic blockade, by incidents on the border, even threats with his armed force.

Yugoslavia had only one weapon: acquainting the masses with the causes of the conflict. That was the fundamental question. That solved, victory was certain. But that was no simple process, for there were people in Yugoslavia who did not see or refused to see the essence of the matter, people who were frightened by the armed might of the Soviet Union. It was such people that Stalin counted on when after the Fifth Congress he continued with all his strength to provoke internal strife in Yugoslavia, in the army, in the Party, so as to intervene when open disorder broke out in Yugoslavia.

A typical specimen of these people was Arso Jovanović. He was a captain in the Yugoslav Royal Army, and joined the Partisans after Yugoslavia capitulated in April, 1941. As an active officer Tito took him into his headquarters as Chief of Staff. It was necessary to attract former officers to the Partisans, and Arso Jovanović was to have been a kind of stimulus.

Jovanović remained Chief of the General Staff until 1946, when he went to Moscow and entered the Higher Military Academy "Voroshilov." While in the Soviet Union he was engaged by the N.K.V.D. A Russian girl, the daughter of a general, was sent to his company in order to demoralize him. Jovanović had a wife and children in Yugoslavia.

Jovanović, who had been trained as a typical officer in the Royal Military Academy before the war, had always lacked political vision. He always saw things in terms of numbers: whoever had the greater numerical strength on paper was the stronger. For instance, during the early years of the war he regarded with misgivings the Red

Army's chances of defeating the Germans. The same view led him after the Cominform resolution to doubt Yugoslavia's ability to withstand the far stronger force of the Soviet Union even for a short time. Like many other Soviet intelligence agents, he expected Yugoslavia to capitulate during the Fifth Congress. He had contacts with two other officers in Belgrade: Branko Petričević, the assistant chief of the political administration in the General Staff, and Vlado Dapčević, a colonel and commissioner in the Artillery Academy. The Fifth Congress disappointed all three of these officers. They expected that someone would get up and speak for Stalin. When this did not happen, they grew impatient and lost their heads.

It was at that time that the Danube Conference had begun in Belgrade with the participation of representatives of all the Danubian countries and of the United States, Great Britain and France. The Soviet government was represented by Andrei Vishinsky, the Rumanian government by Foreign Minister Anna Pauker. However, Anna Pauker was not only engaged on Danubian problems but on the task of conveying Jovanović and the other two officers to Rumania for the N.K.V.D.

Finally, during the night between August 12 and 13 Jovanović, Dapčević and Petričević left Belgrade by car for the Rumanian border, apparently on a hunting expedition. They stopped first at Bela Crkva, calling on a cousin of Jovanović's, a former noncommissioned officer, to ask him to enable them with the help of some officers to cross the Rumanian border in a tank. He was not at home. Then they decided to cross the border on their own. They found Svetolik Arabjac, the warden of the state farm "Sočice," and asked him to take them on a wild-boar hunt. He took them to a hunting preserve not far from the frontier. When darkness fell they ordered him to take them to Rumania. Nearing the frontier, they discovered a militia patrol lying in ambush for horse rustlers. Challenged by the patrol, Arso Jovanović fired his pistol, but missed. One of the militiamen in ambush fired twice, killing the warden with the first shot and Jovanović with the second. The militiaman fired three more shots, but Dapčević and Petričević had already vanished into the night. Petričević was caught the next morning in a neighboring village, Dapčević three weeks later. He had in the meantime got in touch with the Soviet Military Attaché in Belgrade, General Sidorovich.

Dapčević and Petričević were sentenced by a military tribunal to twenty years in prison.

On the morning the press published the communiqué on the case of Arso Jovanović, the Danubian Conference signed the new Danube Convention in the hall of the Kolarac Foundation in Belgrade. Anna Pauker signed on behalf of Rumania. In Yugoslavia she had also been engaged on such business as organizing a rebellion against Yugoslavia. That last day of her stay in Belgrade she made no more statements—like the one she made a few days ago—that "everything will be in order in Yugoslavia in a few days."

What were Stalin's intentions with Jovanović? Was he to have been the head of a new Yugoslav Government in Exile or commander of the troops that were to intervene in Yugoslavia? What the meaning was of Anna Pauker's statement, history will one day reveal. But it is obvious this whole case was a colossal failure for the Soviet intelligence service. Meanwhile, the whole gigantic Soviet machinery had gone into action to subjugate Yugoslavia. The foremost task was to disunite the country, overthrow her legal government, and thus bring her into a state of subserviency toward the Soviet Union. The attack on the spirit of the Yugoslavs began with all means and in every conceivable way. Yugoslavia became the central target for Soviet propaganda. The importance Moscow ascribed to this struggle to capture Yugoslavia is evident from the fact that Soviet and East European Soviet-controlled radio stations increased the number and length of their broadcasts to Yugoslavia immediately after the Cominform resolution, so that after a year there were fifty-six broadcasts a week in Yugoslav languages and only nine in English. The broadcasts for sixteen million Yugoslavs amounted to twenty-six hours and twenty minutes a day, while for the hundreds of millions of English-speaking people in the world there were only nine hours.

The Yugoslav government acted wisely in not jamming the Soviet propaganda. That had immense effect among the Yugoslavs, for it was obvious that Yugoslavia's only strength lay in the free decision of her citizens as to who was right and who wrong. On the other hand, toward the end of 1949 the Yugoslav radio stations began to broadcast in Russian. The Soviet government immediately organized jamming to prevent the words from Yugoslavia being heard in the Soviet Union. The Yugoslav cartoonists promptly took up this theme. It meant that Yugoslavia did not fear Soviet propaganda, for we did not prevent her citizens from listening in freely, while in the Soviet Union after thirty-four years of Socialism Stalin did not allow his socialist citizens to hear the words from Yugoslavia.

There is no doubt that radio propaganda is a mighty weapon, but Stalin did not stop at this instrument in his appeals to the Yugoslavs to overthrow their government. In the Soviet Union as well as the other East European countries, huge quantities of propaganda material were printed on thin paper in the Yugoslav languages for distribution in Yugoslavia. This material was sent to Yugoslavia either in diplomatic bags for distribution from the embassies and consular offices of the East European countries, or it was infiltrated into Yugoslavia through illegal channels. Special centers were set up for this purpose along the frontiers.

For instance, during the first weeks after the Cominform resolution there suddenly appeared in Yugoslavia copies of this resolution printed in the Soviet Union. As is known, the resolution called on the people of Yugoslavia to overthrow their government. Some people received the resolution by mail and also in an unusual way—it was sent along the rivers flowing from Hungary to Rumania into Yugoslavia. Bottles, small wooden boxes and similar floating receptacles were filled with copies. Bathers in the Danube and Theiss seized these bottles with the resolutions printed in Moscow and threw them away or used the contents for cigarette paper. These same pamphlets were also thrown into the water from Soviet vessels passing along the Danube through Yugoslavia. Later the Russians used special balloons to drop the pamphlets. When the wind was favorable the balloons were released over Yugoslavia: after a time they burst in the air and the pamphlets were scattered by the breeze.

But the Yugoslavs had already read the Cominform resolution when it was published, in their own newspapers, together with the Yugoslav answer. They were able to buy Stalin's letters together with the Yugoslav answers in every bookshop, at every newspaper stand in the country. But, ignorant of the situation in Yugoslavia, they were firmly convinced in Moscow that Tito would not dare publish either the resolution or Stalin's letters for his people. Their conviction went so far that they thought Tito would not allow the Central Committee to read Stalin's first letter. How stupefied Lavrentyev was when Žujović informed him that Stalin's letter had been read at the plenary meeting of the Central Committee on April 12, 1948! The Soviet bureaucratic machine was rigidly treading its well-worn path, and because of its poor estimation of the situation was making such foolish mistakes. The Yugoslavs had had occasion even earlier to convince themselves of the unwieldiness and obtuseness of the Soviet bureaucratic machine.

How extremely slow the Soviet bureaucratic machine is, and the experience the Yugoslavs have had of it, is best seen by the following instance. During the fighting in Yugoslavia in 1944 the Allied air force blew up the big railway and road bridge across the Danube that links the rest of Yugoslavia with the province of Vojvodina and with Rumania. Immediately after the liberation of Belgrade, the Yugoslav government asked the Soviet government to help Yugoslav engineers rebuild the bridge. Soviet engineers soon came, the bridge was completed in November, 1945, and traffic was running over it in full swing. A year later, the Soviet Foreign Ministry summoned Vladimir Popović, the Yugoslav Ambassador in Moscow, and a head of a department presented a note from the Soviet government informing the Yugoslav government that it was meeting its application sent toward the end of 1944 and that the Soviet government would help rebuild the bridge. Ambassador Popović explained to the official that the bridge had long since been open to traffic. The official was abashed, but insisted on Popović's taking the note, for he had orders to deliver it.

It was not long before Stalin lost the battle in Yugoslavia by such methods, especially since the substance of his propaganda was based exclusively on falsehood and half-truths, and therefore extremely contradictory. Almost every day the Yugoslavs were in a position to see this with their own eyes, to ascertain the inconsistencies between Stalin's words and deeds. Stalin's Machiavellianism was too transparent. On the one hand, he called on the Yugoslav Communists to be consistent internationalists and overthrow their government, while at the same time Soviet propaganda trumpeted the eternal friendship of Russia, including therefore the friendship of Tsarist Russia, toward Serbia, hoping this pan-Slav slogan would attract the Yugoslav petty-bourgeoisie to the Soviet Union's side against Tito. Or the Yugoslav Communists were called on in the name of internationalism, in the name of the "cradle of socialism, the country of the October Revolution, the Soviet Union," to overthrow their government; at the same time the White Guards, who had fled to Yugoslavia after the October Revolution, were appealed to by the Soviet intelligence service to help "Mother Russia."

Broadcasts were addressed to the poor peasants saying that Tito's government was working against them and protecting the kulaks, while other broadcasts to the rich peasants in Yugoslavia tried to rouse their indignation because "the government was taking their last grain of wheat." The purpose of Soviet propaganda was to make use of every vulnerable point in Yugoslavia, of every contradiction, regardless of the means. That is where it lost the battle, because it was not a battle of principle, and it could not be.

This inconsistency in Soviet propaganda was soon revealed in Yugoslavia. There were examples of it every day. In its broadcasts in Macedonian, the Moscow radio played upon the feelings of the Macedonians by alleging that Belgrade was oppressing them; that is, it played the old card in Yugoslavia: disunity among the people. On the other hand, in its broadcasts in Serbian, it said the Serbs were being oppressed in Yugoslavia.

And so Soviet propaganda continued to sink into ever deeper contradictions and ever more glaring falsehoods. For instance, the Moscow radio announced that people were not allowed to meet in the main streets, that military police patrolled the streets, that there were mile-long queues in front of the prisons, while the people in Belgrade saw that all this was untrue. Or the Polish radio reported that Milovan Djilas had fled from Tito and that he was in the Montenegrin woods, and a month later it turned out that he had gone to New York to the United Nations session as Yugoslavia's delegate. Or the Czech news agency, in order not to mention Yugoslavia, said that Hungary instead of Yugoslavia had defeated Norway at soccer by 3 to 1. Or a French Cominform paper, when enumerating the Danubian countries, would not admit that the Danube flows through Yugoslavia as well.

But what hurt the Yugoslavs most, what embittered them most, were the falsehoods about the National Liberation Struggle, about Yugoslavia's role in the war. Taking up the thesis of Stalin's second letter, of May 4, that the Red Army freed Yugoslavia, Soviet propaganda elaborated it in detail.

In all new editions of the Soviet textbooks, encyclopedias, dictionaries, and wherever anything was said about Yugoslavia, Tito and the war, all such material was rewritten after the Cominform resolution to show that the Red Army had freed Yugoslavia. These falsifications were made by the most responsible people in the Soviet Union, and even by Andrei Vishinsky himself in the capacity of the editor of the *Diplomatic Dictionary*. Here, for instance, is how Edvard Kardelj's biography appears in the two editions of the *Diplomatic Dictionary*, how even the question of Yugoslavia's liberation by the Red Army, among other things, is distorted in these biographical data:

"Edvard Kardelj (born in 1910), a Yugoslav statesman and diplomat. *During World War Two he was one of the leaders of the National Liberation Movement in Yugoslavia.* From 1943 Kardelj was the deputy President of the National Committee of Liberation of Yugoslavia, and then, *after the expulsion of the invader*, deputy President of the Ministerial Council, Minister for the Constituent Assembly and Chairman of the Constitutional Commission of the National Assembly. . . ."

The second edition of the biography reads:

"Edvard Kardelj (born in 1910), a Yugoslav statesman and diplomat.

"From 1943 Kardelj was deputy President of the National Committee of Liberation, and *after the liberation of Yugoslavia by the Red Army*, he was deputy President of the Ministerial Council, Minister for the Constituent Assembly and Chairman of the Constitutional Commission of the National Assembly. . . ."

Soviet propaganda trumpets to the Yugoslavs that the Soviet Union is the most steadfast fighter for equality in economic relations among all countries, quoting the statements made by Litvinoff in the League of Nations in 1931 "that to abandon aggression of an economic nature is a fundamental condition for peaceful co-operation among states in the economic field, regardless of their political systems," while in practice Stalin organized and enforced a savage economic blockade against Yugoslavia.

Tito

It was not by accident that Stalin resolved upon this. To start with, he timed his attack on Yugoslavia just when it was fighting the greatest economic difficulties. The first year of the Five-Year Plan ended early in 1948. Yugoslavia, a country that had passed through a terrible war and had been devastated to the extreme limits, even before she had recovered a little was called on by her government to tighten her belt, to sacrifice herself for industrialization. Stalin exploited the situation like a Machiavelli, counting on the further aggravation of the economic difficulties in Yugoslavia as a basis for provoking dissatisfaction among the Yugoslavs toward their government. He also took the following factor into consideration: for the bulk of her investments under the Five-Year Plan, one might say up to 95 per cent, Yugoslavia had concluded agreements either with the Soviet Union or with Soviet-controlled Czechoslovakia, Hungary, Poland, and Rumania. He calculated that by ceasing to send capital goods to Yugoslavia, by canceling foreign trade with her (over 50 per cent of Yugoslav export and import business was with the East European countries), he would prevent the accomplishment of the Five-Year Plan, and the construction of socialism, which the Yugoslavs intend as the reason for their whole struggle.

Gradually, step by step, Stalin enforced his economic blockade. As Yugoslav resistance mounted, the blockade was intensified. Thus, by the trade agreement with the Soviet Union of December 31, 1948, the volume of trade was reduced to an eighth, that is to six million dollars, of which lead exports were to absorb five million. The official communiqué of Tass stated that the Soviet government had reduced the volume of trade on account of the "hostile policy of Yugoslavia toward the Soviet Union." Thus the Soviet government publicly proclaimed economic discrimination toward Yugoslavia for political reasons.

Following the example of the Soviet Union, the other East European countries also canceled capital construction deliveries, and later foreign trade, so that all economic connections between Yugoslavia and these countries were severed.

The economic blockade did serious damage to our country with respect to capital goods. In many cases construction had already gone ahead, and in some important cases it was only necessary to mount the machinery. Although some of the machinery was in the process of manufacture or even completed and ready for dispatch (for instance, turbines for the water-power plants from Soviet enterprises in Austria), delivery was not made. It is impossible to estimate the volume of damage to our country's capital construction. It is sufficient to emphasize that we had agreements with those countries for the delivery of equipment worth three hundred and sixty million dollars.

However, the consequence of all this was also economic—and not only economic—damage to these countries too, above all to Czechoslovakia, and to some extent Poland (chiefly owing to the ensuing shortage of nonferrous metals), and in every respect to Albania. Yet, their governments agreed to lead these countries along such a path.

The economic blockade was calculated to isolate Yugoslavia and break her, in view of her lack of means for a rapid reorientation of her foreign trade.

In order to cause the greatest possible damage to our economy, and to increase pressure on our country, transport and other communications were unilaterally cut. Rumania stopped all railway and postal traffic; Hungary and Bulgaria reduced goods and passenger traffic, postal and telegraph communications to the minimum. Albania cut off all communications, barely maintaining the postal service.

Our navigation along the reaches of the Danube flowing through those countries was made difficult, while Rumania prevented the regulation of navigation through the Iron Gates in the Danube. Our vessels are prevented from entering the Black Sea. The Soviet government had violated the Danube Convention and is now trying to turn the Danube into a "Russian river."

There was one particularly dangerous example, when the Hungarians interfered with the flood control system. This international service, established under the convention of March, 1948, is indispensable for the functioning of the water system in the Yugoslav province of Vojvodina, and if recent years had not been dry, there would have been heavy floods on our territory in consequence of the Hungarian action.

These facts could not be concealed from the Yugoslav people, for they felt them in their everyday life. How hypocritical to Yugoslav ears sounded the words published in *Pravda* of June 30, 1951, that "the establishment of normal economic ties . . . is an obligatory condition for peaceful and fruitful international co-operation," or in *News*, a Soviet review in English published in Moscow, of June 30, 1951, that "the Soviet Union in its trade and economic policy has always pursued a course of developing trade relations and normal business connections with all other countries regardless of the difference of regimes and social and economic systems." How must all the tirades delivered during the economic conference held in Moscow during the summer of 1952 have sounded to the Yugoslavs! The difference between words and deeds in the Soviet Union is the cause of her defeat in Yugoslavia.

It had become obvious to the Soviet leaders during the first six months after the publication of the Cominform resolution that they would be unable to achieve their object in Yugoslavia with the methods and means they were employing. The Yugoslavs were stubborn. Stalin changed his tactics. To be sure, the bureaucratic machinery tirelessly repeated the old song, but new kinds of pressure were brought to bear on Yugoslavia. Frontier incidents began: Hungary, Bulgaria and Rumania, Yugoslavia's closest neighbors, were rapidly armed; troop movements toward Yugoslavia's borders began, and complete Soviet tank divisions appeared.

Immediately before the sword was brandished along Yugoslavia's frontier, in August, 1949, several Russian White Guards who had been working for the intelligence service of the Soviet Union were arrested in Yugoslavia. It must be understood that there were over three thousand White Guards in the Yugoslav state administration, of whom the majority had been engaged by the N.K.V.D. An end had to be put to this state of affairs, and several spies were caught. The Soviet government seized on this as a pretext to exercise further pressure and try to intimidate Yugoslavia. One morning, at about six o'clock, a representative of the Soviet Embassy went to the Ministry of Foreign Affairs, awoke the astonished porter and delivered a note to him from the Soviet government. This method of delivery was chosen so as to produce the greatest effect, to terrify Yugoslavia the more. Among other things, the note demanded an inquiry into the Yugoslav police and court organs that had arrested the Russian White Guards, and even the right of the Soviet government to control the manner of this inquiry. A similar demand was sent to the Serbian government by Austria-Hungary in 1914. Toward the close of its note the Soviet government threatened, word for word:

"The Soviet government considers it necessary to declare that it will not reconcile itself to such a state of affairs and that it will be compelled to resort to more efficient means."

The day that the note was delivered, the elements of a new Soviet tank division appeared on the Yugoslav-Rumanian frontier, forty-five miles from Belgrade as the crow flies. Yugoslavia replied calmly, rejected all the Soviet insults, and declared itself ready to hand over all the Russian White Guards, and other Soviet citizens, to the Soviet government. New Soviet notes followed. Moscow ignored the Yugoslav offer to return the White Guards and other Soviet citizens, for the Russians were not anxious for their citizens but were in fact demanding the right of their agents to work freely in Yugoslavia, the Soviet government always being able with a little pressure to get them released from prison. These and other notes contained a number of new threats and new insults, one of which was that the Yugoslav trials against the actions of Soviet subjects was like "a poodle barking at an elephant," typical Vishinsky humor.

In Moscow they thought it necessary to explain the conflict to world public opinion to find a pretext for the pressure on Yugoslavia. The Soviet government therefore staged a number of trials in the countries bordering on Yugoslavia, in order to present her as having aggressive intentions toward the Soviet Union and the countries of the Soviet bloc. Moreover, by these trials it was hoped to find justification before the people of the West European countries for greater and sharper aggression.

The greatest trial of this type was organized in Budapest in the autumn of 1949 against Laszlo Rajk, the Hungarian Minister of Foreign Affairs. Rajk allegedly confessed to his judges that he had been engaged in overthrowing the Hungarian government on orders from Belgrade, then "revealed" that Tito, Ranković and the other Yugoslav leaders were Gestapo agents.

The extent to which the whole Rajk trial was staged is seen from the following facts.

The indictment against Rajk states that Aleš Bebler, Yugoslavia's permanent representative to the United Nations, had had espionage connections with Rajk in a concentration camp in France in 1941. But in fact Bebler had been evacuated from Spain badly wounded in 1938 and transferred to Yugoslavia, where he was sentenced to prison the same year for subversive activity and from 1941 he was a Partisan unit commander. General Božidar Maslarić, the former Chairman of the All-Slav Committee, and now the Vice-President of the Croatian Government, was slandered in a similar manner. To increase the irony, from 1939 to the end of the war he was in the Soviet Union, in high political offices, and not in France as the indictment stated. It was the same in the case of Karlo Mrazović, Yugoslavia's Ambassador in Moscow at the time of the trial, and previously Envoy in Budapest. Mrazović was also in Moscow at the time the indictment claims he was in France. Colonel-Generals Ivan Gošnjak and Kosta Nadj of the Yugoslav army were accused of having been Gestapo agents from 1941, although from 1941 to 1945 they were commanders of strategic units of the National Liberation Army of Yugoslavia, and toward the end of the war commanders of corps that dealt heavy blows to the Germans by liberating considerable parts of Yugoslavia. (There has never in history been a case of agents being used to destroy dozens of huge units and thousands of troops of their masters, and to incite uprisings of whole nations against them.)

Svetozar Vukmanović-Tempo, at present a minister in the Yugoslav government, was accused, like Bebler, of having had espionage connections with Rajk in French camps before the war, although until 1948 he had never been abroad, and that year he only went to Bulgaria and to the Soviet Union.

Minister of the Interior Aleksandar Ranković was charged that he had been Rajk's superior in his work against the Hungarian state, and that in October, 1948—at a time when the Hungarian government was already on strained terms with Yugoslavia—he had gone to Hungary hunting in order to meet Rajk and give him "instructions."

Almost all our diplomats and diplomatic officials in the countries of Eastern Europe were slandered as Gestapo spies and agents in the service of the Western countries, in order to justify their expulsion and further hostile measures against Yugoslavia.

In short, all the leaders of the Liberation War of Yugoslavia, most of the federal and republican ministers, the prime ministers of the republican governments, all the leaders of the army, and the most prominent public figures were slandered by name as Gestapo agents. During and after 1943, this mass of men had, according to the indictment and the "testimony," gone over to American service, and still later had carried out deep political and social changes in their own country! It is clear what was intended by this foulness: to sully, to cancel out the contribution of the people of Yugoslavia in the war to the aims of the united nations; to deceive the nations who had fought together with them; to gain "moral" and "political" justification for the undemocratic and warlike acts against Yugoslavia.

The well-known Hungarian politician Mihaly Karolyi, the President of the Hungarian Republic during the Commune of 1919, who was Hungary's Envoy in Paris during the trial, sent a telegram to the Hungarian government on October 13, 1949, saying:

"Reading the 'Blue Book' on Rajk's trial, published in Budapest, I found a passage on page 61, first paragraph, where Rajk admits that he enabled Deputy Sulyok to flee abroad.

"However, I remember the conversation I had with Rakosi in the presence of Premier Dinyes early in August, 1947. Rakosi told me he intended to give Sulyok a passport so that he could leave the country.

"In his book published in German in 1948, Sulyok states precisely that despite Rakosi's promise, Rajk had refused to give him a passport, that he had only succeeded in escaping by outwitting the police.

"All this compels me to believe that Rajk's other confessions are also self-accusation, just as untrue as this part of his confession.

"I declare under oath that my meeting with Rakosi in Dinyes's presence took place as I have described.

"I solemnly beg the government to order a revision of the trial. I ask this with all the more vigor as I am convinced that if the judicial crime of executing the sentence is committed, it will certainly be exposed, causing untold damage to Hungarian democracy and constituting a serious threat to world peace."

Naturally, the Hungarian government did not respond to Karolyi's request, for the whole trial would have proved a clumsy frame-up whose purpose was not only to struggle against the people of Yugoslavia but to obtain subjection of Hungary herself.

CHAPTER XXIII

1949:

"Our revolution does not devour its children . . ."

IN STAGING fake trials in Budapest, Stalin committed a major blunder so far as Yugoslavia was concerned. Rajk's trial affected the Yugoslavs like oil on fire.

It was no longer an attack on the leadership, on individuals, but actually on the whole people, on the role Yugoslavia played in the Second World War. The Soviet fabrications at the trial had a disastrous effect even on those in Yugoslavia who had supported the Cominform resolution. When the trial ended in Budapest, a large number of books of the shorthand notes of the proceedings were smuggled into Yugoslavia from Hungary through various channels. One of these copies was given to Sreten Žujović, formerly Minister of Finance and a member of the Central Committee, who had sided with the Soviet Union from the outbreak of the conflict. As his activities threatened the security and independence of Yugoslavia he was arrested in May, 1948. Everywhere in the Soviet Union and in all the countries of Eastern Europe Soviet propaganda had extolled Žujović for a whole year, making a martyr and hero of him. Žujović read the book on Rajk's trial in jail, one might say in one gulp. When he had read it, a change came over him and he decided to support Stalin's policy no longer. Soon afterwards he was set free.

I had known Žujović for more than ten years. I knew him from the darkest days of the German offensive during the war, from the days of hunger. I considered him an exceptionally brave man. I was watching him in 1941 when the German Stukas dived and bombed us and he would fire back at them with his rifle. We became good friends. After the war he asked me to be his best man at his wedding.

But when the break with the Russians came, I could not agree with him.

After he left jail, I met him again. We worked together in the same office. I am director of *Borba*, the biggest newspaper in the country, and he is manager of it. We see each other every day. One day after work, I invited him to come to my home for dinner. He accepted my invitation. After the meal, we started to talk about 1948, about the Rajk trials, about Žujović's attitude toward the Soviet Union. This is what he said to me were his principal reasons for changing his mind in 1949 and leaving Stalin.

"I read the book on Rajk's trial. My first reaction was terrible. I think this or that attitude of our Party can be disputed, that this or that thing has been incorrectly worked out, that there is digression in this or that. Some people may say the whole Party policy is mistaken or incorrect. Some may go further and even consider that an ideological struggle should be pursued against our Party. But the sincere Communist convictions, the honor, uprightness and honesty either of individuals or of the Central Committee as a whole, or of our Party generally cannot be questioned or doubted.

"I know our people from the war, their efforts, their sacrifices and their dreams. I know of the death of so many fighters. From the granite pillars of the great edifice of our socialist homeland gaze their faces bright and pure, the features of people's fighters and heroes, who know the cause they fought and fell for. I know, too, those who came through. I know they are not resting on well-earned laurels but continuing to fight onward, untiring and steadfast.

"During Rajk's trial the leaders of the Soviet Party alleged not only that there were individual spies, but that the whole Party was Fascist. That is simply senseless, incomprehensible, immoral and monstrous.

"I know the members of our Party, I know who they are and what they are. I know they are the best working men, enthusiastic, proud of their Party membership, fighters for socialism, for everything lofty, pure and fine.

"This is how I thought things out as I read the shorthand notes of Rajk's trial. It was then that the heavy chain broke that had fettered my mind and soul. It became clear to me that I had only been a suitable pretext and a convenient blind tool, and that I was myself to have operated on behalf of a specific policy of dishonorable intentions and aims.

"I had not looked at it like that before. In the spring of 1948 these were my basic postulations:

"First, Yugoslavia would become a Soviet socialist republic and would join the structure of the Soviet Union; moreover, I considered it had to earn the right to be admitted to the brotherhood of the Soviet peoples.

"Second, our Party would merge with the Soviet Party and become a part of it.

"Third, the Soviet Union as the offspring of the October Revolution, a country of socialism, the homeland of the proletariat of the whole world, was a state with an administrative organization, with a leadership in the organization of economy and production that corresponded to the teachings of classic socialism and the postulates of Leninism, theoretically formulated and elaborated by Stalin. Therefore, there was and could be no comment or explanation—only silence.

"Fourth, the Soviet Party was the parent Party, the only complete and correct interpreter of Marxism-Leninism, the bearer of the ideological thoughts of Leninism, which it elaborated and deepened further, the only and final arbiter.

"Fifth, and above all: Stalin, the Leader, the Teacher.

"I am not a theorist, but a practicing Communist. Naturally, this does not mean that I never think or that I have never thought about theoretical problems. But my thoughts were the result of practice, about problems that practice presented and made one think about. When it was a matter of given postulates of Marxism-Leninism, I never went deeply into them. I only learned them so far as I was capable and simply accepted them as final truths. Least of all did I subject them to critical analysis, at least those postulates that derive from present practice in the Soviet Union and have acquired their conclusive form from the present leadership of the Soviet Party.

"On the other hand, during and after the war, our Party carried out and completed tremendous changes of historic significance, ensuring the victory of the revolution and the conditions for socialist construction.

"But one thing remained unchanged in me and in my mind: the

Soviet Party and the Soviet Union above all and the final arbiter.

"My apprehension was unable to emerge from this orbit, even when it was a question of obvious incorrectness or relationships detrimental to us. Even in these instances I considered that things should be as they enjoined and said, although I realized that we were suffering and making sacrifices. I held this to be correct and always found, or endeavored to find, reasons to justify those relations and acts that were detrimental to us.

"I was incapable of imagining that it was a question of incorrect, least of all of deliberately incorrect, relationships, nor could I imagine that Marxist-Leninists, men from the Soviet Union, could have fostered such relationships.

"Thus, this dogma and this fetish limited me, prevented me from further meditative development, turned me into an automaton and a suitable man to become their blind tool.

"I was fortified in this conviction by my meetings after the war with Soviet leaders and others, such as meetings with Molotov at San Francisco in 1945, during the sessions of the United Nations. Otherwise, these talks were without any special significance. Only one detail was interesting, to which I paid no attention, whose significance is clear to me only today. Molotov invited me to return to Yugoslavia by way of the Soviet Union. I accepted and on our return we spent the first night in the town of Fairbanks in Alaska. I shared a room with Kouznyetsov, the President of the Soviet Trade Unions. On the wall was a map of Alaska drawn on canvas with sketches showing what was manufactured at different places and in what quantity. Underneath it was written that Alaska had been bought in the year so and so, for so much and that it had been a complete wasteland. Kouznyetsov began to curse the Americans, and I remember he said: 'That is ours, it's Russian: they took it from us. We'll take it from them.'

"The talks I had in Moscow during my short stay in 1945 were of a general nature. My contacts with different representatives of the Soviet Embassy in Belgrade were of an official and business character conducted in the general and cordial spirit that prevailed up to the meeting of the Central Committee of March 1, 1948.

"My relations with the Russians, my talks with them derived from my earlier apprehension of the role and character of the Soviet Party and the Soviet Union. I really considered that there was nothing that should not be told to the Soviet Party or its Central Committee and nothing that it should not know, not only about our own but about every other Communist Party. And I thought they were in agreement and that they had no criticism to make of the work of our Party. It is true that during the postwar years I felt that something was not clear between ourselves and the Soviet Union. But I was convinced that all this was temporary and simply a matter of clarification between our leadership and the Soviet Central Committee. However, then came the session of March, 1948, when Kardelj and Djilas stated what had happened in Moscow, when there was open talk about the conflict with the Soviet Union. I was silent, I did not speak. I only felt that it was a question of something far more important, of great and fateful matters that went beyond the bounds of the Central Committee, and even of our Party, that it was no longer our affair alone. I called on Lavrentyev the next morning and told him what I had remembered of the session and of the matter discussed. Later I met him again. He advised me not to tell our Central Committee I had informed him of the session. I was taken aback.

" 'Why not?' I asked.

" 'Don't,' he answered curtly. 'At least, not now.'

"Thus I found myself in a false, a terribly false position. I was forced to hide from my comrades the fact that I had passed on things from the meeting to Lavrentyev.

"At one of our meetings Lavrentyev told me that the Soviet Central Committee thanked me for informing it of the session and hoped I would do so in the future.

"A session of the Yugoslav government took place early in April at which some important economic decrees were discussed. Later I met Lavrentyev and he asked me what the decree was about. He quickly dropped the subject and asked how some of the comrades looked. I didn't know what he wanted, and I said: 'Quite well.' Lavrentyev asked specifically, 'And how is Djilas?'

"I had actually noticed that Djilas was silent and worried. He is usually heard at the sessions, he always joins in the talk. I told Lavrentyev, and he nodded with satisfaction.

" 'Worried, you say?'

"I did not know at the time that Stalin's first letter to our Central

Committee had arrived. Lavrentyev had refused to tell me. He did so only on the eve of April 12, before the Plenum met. It was then that I hurriedly read the letter, and it was clear to me why he had asked his questions about Djilas and the others, because the letter had already been delivered to our Central Committee.

"I did not speak before the Plenum as I had planned and wished, being bound not to inform the Central Committee of my talks with Lavrentyev. On the other hand, I was unhappily aware of my position. But after the Plenum I remained convinced that talks would take place between our Central Committee and theirs, especially after our invitation to them to send their delegates to Yugoslavia. I imagined the dispute would really be cleared up and settled favorably.

"When I returned home, on the second day of the Plenum, Lavrentyev phoned me and told me he would send me the review *Novi Mir* he had promised earlier with the story of Polyevoy.

"That was only a pretext, because we had never spoken about it before.

"Shortly afterwards his secretary came to my home and in the review brought me the letter of the Central Committee of the Soviet Party. Lavrentyev was sure that Tito would not dare read the letter before the Plenum and had sent it to me.

"I informed the secretary that I had been expelled from the Central Committee and placed under Party inquiry and that I wished to see Lavrentyev. I had to be content with his counselor Armyaninov. I told him everything I could about the Plenum. I was deeply agitated and could not remember everything. For instance, I was totally incapable of relating the substance of the decision on my expulsion except that I had been called an anti-Party element and the basest of men. Nor was I able to relate the substance of the Central Committee's answer to the letter of the Soviet Central Committee, except that it expressed disagreement and considered it an insult.

"I told Armyaninov that the members had been greatly agitated and mentioned Djilas, who was evidently deeply pained and offended by the denial of our sincere relationships and love for the Soviet Union. Armyaninov waved his hands.

" 'We know that petty-bourgeois agitation,' he said.

"I could not restrain myself, and said, 'Listen, it was sincere.'

"He waved his hand again and retorted, "Oh, sincere. I wonder. . . .'

"After that things went on. May Day came, and the second letter, and then my arrest. I was no longer abreast of events, I no longer knew how things were developing, except that our Central Committee was unyielding. The days in jail passed one after the other. Then I received Rajk's book. My first reaction to it was one of rage. I asked myself how it was possible. Why, it was an attack on everything, on the country, on the cause of socialism.

"I came to my senses after that terrible book. I asked myself what the purpose was of the vilification during the hearing. There was no doubt that the basic purpose of the trial was to slander the leaders in Yugoslavia in order to justify the aggressive policy against our country. We had seen that in Yugoslavia the whole Party had supported the leadership. That is why at the Rajk trial the summary conclusion had been reached that the entire Yugoslav Communist Party was Fascist. We have seen that the entire people is for the Party. Therefore, make war on that people, destroy it!

"Such were my conclusions. I asked myself: Where have we got to? What is Marxism-Leninism, the most progressive teaching of the most progressive social class, of the proletariat? The answer: The extermination of a nation and its subjugation so that it may learn what socialism of the Soviet type is. Did it not mean that the leaders of the Soviet Party were reduced to forcing by war the peoples of Yugoslavia, who both in their consciousness and by deeds are building socialism, of forcing them by war to think and work differently because what they were thinking and doing 'was not socialism'?

"Then I asked to talk with Djilas, Ranković and the others. I asked for all the material, read all the papers. I was ever more convinced of the first feeling I had had when I realized the purpose of Rajk's trial. My name was to have been a cover for things that have nothing to do with socialism, a banner against my own country, against its right to build socialism. My conscience would not allow me to tolerate it any longer.

"Today I realize everything and the intentions of the Soviet leaders are clear to me. Those were tactics with a definite purpose, with just the purpose that Comrade Tito and the others had defined at the session of March, 1948. My views of things and events, insofar as they had led me to think that something was wrong, were what they were because I had measured them only by Russian values and they were not only unbalanced but hostile."

This is what Žujović said to me; much of what he said when he left jail. He wrote a letter to *Borba* explaining his stand. His statement produced stupefaction in the Soviet Union. Propagandists in the Eastern countries had claimed that Žujović was no longer among the living, but had been murdered in jail. Long articles were published to this effect by the Polish paper *Tribuna Ludy* and the Cominform organ in Vienna, *Volkstimme*. Radio Moscow announced on November 28, 1950, that Žujović was dead. Three days later Žujović called a press conference which was attended by more than forty foreign journalists, including the Tass correspondent.

But the *Volkstimme* of Vienna did not want to give up. It claimed that Žujović was killed and that Tito had sent to the press conference a double of Žujović. But this was too much even for Stalin, and Radio Moscow announced on December 11, 1950, that Žujović was alive and that Tito "held him in reserve in order to use him at an appropriate moment."

CHAPTER XXIV

1952:

"I was an ignorant young man and the Party took me, educated me, made me a man . . ."

ONE of the means whereby Stalin planned to bring about a split in the Communist Party of Yugoslavia was to create the suspicions that some of the members were Stalinists, to create a state of affairs in which nobody would trust anyone, in which everyone would be filled with suspicion and would begin a hysteria of quarrels, arrests and liquidations. Such had been the tactics on which his first letter was based. He first tried to cause a split between Kardelj and Tito by publishing a conversation which Kardelj was supposed to have had with the Soviet Ambassador in Belgrade with reference to Tito's speech of May, 1945, and later he tried to cause a split between Djilas and the rest. The following case will show some of the Cominform methods. The delegate from Montenegro, Veljko Mićunović, attacked the USSR very sharply in a speech he made at the 1948 Congress of the Communist Party of Yugoslavia, perhaps the most strongly worded speech of the meeting. Several days later, there appeared an article signed by V. Mićunović in the Cominform organ. The Soviet idea was for Tito and the others to think that Mićunović had made such a speech in order to hide his real feelings.

There were hundreds of similar cases of intrigues and false incriminations, but these tactics proved to be entirely without avail. Stalin showed once more in this case that he did not know the Communist Party of Yugoslavia, that he did not know the conditions under which it had developed and what had been its experiences. He did not know the base on which Tito had built the Party, especially after 1937, and the relationship he had created among its people, in which people believed in one another and had confidence in one another. During the prewar dictatorship one might remain confidently in one's apartment, while one's comrade was being tortured in prison to denounce his friends. Friendship was built on the knowledge that comrades did not break under torture. The war was an even harder school. Nowhere could one get to know someone as thoroughly as in the days of war. From moment to moment courage must be displayed; at any instance a friend might call for aid, and measure friendship by the response. The famine was very severe during the Partisan war in Yugoslavia, and this is a matter in which one could judge a person's character; whether he was greedy, whether he had respect for others, whether he was willing to share the last mouthful of food. Before the war, during the war and after the war, Tito continued indefatigably to develop this spirit of comradeship among people, this spirit of equality, the right for every man to have the opportunity to correct any mistakes he made, and not to have him answer with his life for the least mistake, as is the case in the Soviet Union.

And today, as the premier of a country as threatened by enemies as Yugoslavia, and which has so many internal and foreign problems, does Tito find time to take care of these problems, and do the affairs of state allow him to do so?

Tito is still living at 15 Rumunska Street in a medium-sized house, such as a fairly well-to-do doctor in Detroit might own. Two years ago, a wing was added to this house in which Tito's new office was placed. The rest of the house remained unchanged. Some space was also added to the part around the house and new trees were planted.

When large formal delegations come from abroad, Tito receives them in the former palace of the regent, Prince Paul Karageorgevich, who had been expelled from Yugoslavia on March 27, 1941, because of having collaborated with the Axis powers. The foreign press wrote occasionally about Tito dwelling in that palace. This is not true. When Lord Mountbatten, Commander in Chief of the British Mediterranean Fleet, visited Tito in the summer of 1952, this palace was mentioned among other things. Lord Mountbatten inquired about the palace and then started talking about his kinsmen and acquaintances, showing that he knew Prince Paul very well. Tito then told Lord Mountbatten why he did not want to live in Prince Paul's palace. There was one reason among others which he mentioned. Tito had given a big reception in that palace on New Year's Eve after the war and the following letter was sent to him on New Year's Day: "A happy New Year in another man's house." "Especially after such a greeting," Tito told Mountbatten, "I did not want to live in that palace."

Tito gets up very early in summer. He wakes up at 5:30 A.M. and in winter at 7 A.M. Every morning Tito performs his Swedish exercises for about half an hour. This is a childhood habit. Tito shaves himself. All this takes about one hour. He then has a walk in the park no matter what the weather, and whether there is snow, rain or sun. He walks alone, usually along the same paths. He has his breakfast around 8 A.M. Tito does not pay much attention to food. His cook is Dalmatian, a Partisan during the war who has worked for him since 1943. Tito has coffee for breakfast, bread, butter and sometimes an omelette. At his other meals he favors the usual Central European cooking, except for an occasional meal of Zagorje food in which his mother had been an expert: chicken čorba (a kind of thick soup with sour cream) and štruklje (homemade pie with cottage cheese). Tito drinks little during his meals, perhaps a glass of beer in summer, or Yugoslav wines. Guests may have plum brandy (šljivovica), vermouth or liqueurs. Occasionally in hot weather he enjoys a "spritzer"—wine mixed with soda—or water mixed with wine (bevanda).

He take his breakfast quickly and is in his office soon after eight. On his way there he visits his birds, most of them canaries, feeds them, sees to it that they have enough water, and then sits at his desk and studies the morning papers. He reads them very carefully, particularly articles and news about Yugoslavia. He is especially interested in letters to the editor, which often show the feelings of the people. For example, the draft Constitution that had been published in spring, 1952, was intended, among other things, to modify the Yugoslav electoral system. According to the draft, elections were to be held by indirect ballot, i.e., the District Assemblies were to elect the representatives for the Federal Assembly. Yugoslav papers received many letters from people who were against this indirect method of elections. Tito noticed this and suggested that the Legislative Committee open the discussion anew, concerning the methods of election. After long discussions it was finally decided to adopt the method of direct election of representatives in the draft for the Constitution.

Tito also goes through all the bulletins of the news agency Tanjug, which gives news from all the major world agencies, American, British, French, German and Russian. It is worth mentioning that his secretary does not underline the more important news or note it in any way, but that Tito goes through the bulletins by himself. The following papers and publications are also brought regularly to Tito: the London *Times*, the *Economist*, the *New Statesman and Nation*, Aneurin Bevan's *Tribune*, the European editions of the New York *Times* and the New York *Herald Tribune*, *Foreign Affairs*, *Neue Zürcher Zeitung* and the Moscow *Pravda*. Tito reads very quickly, grasping immediately the most important facts. Tito smokes when reading his papers. He used to be a heavy smoker, but now smokes only about twenty cigarettes a day. He always uses small cigarette holders, and has several of them. Tito wears spectacles when reading. He had difficulties with his eyes many years ago when a pin got into his eye, which caused an inflammation of both eyes. He had to be operated on and was requested by his physician to wear glasses for a certain time. He is now farsighted, and wears corresponding spectacles.

After having gone through the papers, Tito proceeds to his mail. Tito, naturally, receives a great many letters both from Yugoslavia and from abroad. Tito's secretary, a Montenegrin lawyer who was a Partisan during the war and is a lieutenant colonel today, opens all the mail. Every morning he and his assistants make a list of all the letters with a short résumé of their content. These résumés are typed on small pieces of papers which are clipped to the original letters. Tito goes through every letter, noting in a corner with a blue pencil what should be done about it. This is a big job and sometimes occupies a full hour. What are these letters, and what requests do they usually contain? Most of them are letters of complaint against some measures taken by authorities. All are forwarded to a special secretary of Tito's who verifies whether the complaints are warranted or not, and who requests additional data from government agencies or other institutions; a report is then made to Tito about the state of affairs and whether the petition is warranted or not. In most of the cases, perhaps 90 per cent, Tito gives a positive answer to the petition. There are all kinds of such petitions. It is the habit, for instance, in Yugoslavia, that families in which a ninth child is born invite Tito to be its godfather. There are also families of Partisans who lost their lives, complaining about the question of their pensions not being settled. Many of the letters complain about evictions. When people are evicted from their dwellings they usually write to Tito. It is interesting to mention that before his operation for a gall-bladder ailment, Tito received numerous letters, especially from villages, in which old women recommended all sorts of popular medications for such cases.* A special group of letters is written by workers, describing their inventions. These letters are especially carefully studied. In some cases the inventions are useful. There are also occasionally great illusions. Thus, for instance, a peasant who had during the war, in 1944, guided the Supreme HQ and Tito through a forest above Drvar, after the German attack, wrote to Tito in 1950 that he had discovered the perpetual motion. Tito immediately wrote him a long letter telling him that the perpetual motion was impossible and that the peasant had better employ his energy for the discovery of more useful things.

Tito also receives numerous letters from abroad. Most of these letters are from autograph collectors. Many people also write requesting materials concerning the conflict with the USSR. When fragments of Tito's story were published in *Life*, Tito received numerous letters from the United States. An American of Yugoslav descent sent him a picture of his house and a letter in which he said: "Tito, if you are ever in trouble, come to me. I will give you a room in my house."

After going through the papers and the mail, Tito studies state problems. He goes through the dispatches of representatives from

---

* Tito underwent a gall-bladder operation in April, 1951. This operation was performed very successfully by Yugoslav surgeons. On the day before the operation I visited Tito together with Kardelj, Djilas and some other comrades. We saw a film in the evening and then took leave of Tito, as the operation was to be performed early in the morning. Tito was very quiet all the time, but he was somewhat moved when he bade Kardelj and Djilas farewell. He took a rapid farewell without looking them in the eyes. When Tito woke up after the operation, according to his nurse, these were his first words: "How glad Stalin would have been had the operation failed. How easily he would have got rid of me."

abroad, and then studies various drafts of bills which are being prepared. In the morning he also usually interviews members of his cabinet and discusses some of the major matters they are working on. He receives visits from delegations or individuals from Yugoslavia, interviewing several thousand Yugoslavs throughout the year. These delegations usually represent various factories, co-operative farms, and mass organizations. If a congress is held in Belgrade, those who take part in it usually request to be granted an interview with Tito. At these meetings, which last between half an hour and one hour, the conversation is about the problems of the factory, institution or organization. Tito asks questions about the working conditions, and the people question him concerning foreign policy. A special category of visitors consists of Tito's old friends and kinsmen. Usually once a year Tito's chums from school and from villages around Bjelovar, in which Tito lived after World War I, and from factories in Zagreb, come to visit Tito, remain a day or so, receive some gifts and then take their leave.

Tito travels widely in the course of the year. He visits one of the six Yugoslav states every year, takes part in a celebration in the trade unions congress or the veterans' congress, or the anniversary of the uprising. He also visits great public works, co-operative farms, shipyards, and so forth. He usually comes unexpectedly, remains two or three hours and talks to numerous people. In the course of these conversations, Tito learns very much about the situation within the country and about the feelings of the people. I have often traveled with Tito throughout the country after the war. In October, 1951, I was with him in western Serbia, in the towns of Užice, Čačak and Kraljevo, where bloody battles had been fought with the Germans in 1941. We arrived by car and we were met before Užice by a group of more than 500 former Partisans who had assembled there to celebrate the tenth anniversary of the liberation of their native town from the Germans. Fires had been built on a hill before the town and lambs barbecued. The old Partisans took Tito there, sat around the fire, dined and then sang old Partisan songs. Hundreds of peasants came from neighboring villages. A conversation started after dinner. A veteran Partisan complained to Tito against the new bill regarding the categorization of civil servants:

"I joined the army during the war when I was but an eighteen-year-old boy. It was impossible for me to go to university during the war. After the war I had to work in the people's committee where we were so busy that I spent sixteen hours a day in my office and had no time to attend the university, and now I will get less pay than those who never fought the war but peacefully went to school."

Another veteran Partisan shared his opinion, requesting that this decree be reconsidered. The conversation lasted until late at night. Tito explained that those who were responsible for the decree had thought that each job should be performed by educated people and that this should stimulate people to improve their minds, but that it had been a mistake not to think of what would become of the Partisan veterans who had given up school to go to war. When Tito returned to Belgrade, he studied the draft of this bill and asked that it be improved in such a way as to render it possible for Partisan veterans to resume their studies.

Next morning Tito spoke at Užice. There was a huge number of peasants from that whole region who attended the Užice meeting. Tito spoke for about forty minutes. He did not prepare his speech in advance. He very seldom does, but on the eve of its delivery he usually paces for an hour or two thinking about the broad outline of what he will say and how to express his thoughts. He does this even when he prepares some particularly momentous speeches, such as the one he delivered in the Yugoslav Parliament on Trieste in April, 1952, and which inflamed the whole of Yugoslavia. In his speeches, Tito usually endeavors to establish contact with his listeners, watches their reaction, and according to it he sometimes speaks longer about his theme. That is why the speeches Tito makes directly to the people are far better than those that are broadcast. He may hesitate there and seem less convincing than when he speaks to the people. During the war, and especially after the war, Tito developed into a very good orator. At the beginning of the war his speeches were somewhat dry, he had difficulty in finding the right word, but the more he spoke, the more he improved. Today, Tito is considered to be, among the leading people in Yugoslavia, the best speaker at large meetings, although Yugoslavs are poor orators as a whole. During the war only Ivo-Lola Ribar, a member of the Supreme HQ, who was killed toward the end of 1943, was considered to be better than Tito in this kind of speech. In the West, where statesmen usually have special advisers and secretaries who compose the speeches, Tito's method of preparing speeches may seem unusual, but each country has its habits. As regards reports to Party congresses or to Parliament, Tito writes everything by himself. Various institutions give him the necessary data which he uses in his writing as he thinks best. This takes Tito considerable time. Tito, for instance, prepared his report to the Fifth Congress of the CPY in July, 1948, over a period of several weeks, working at it at least six or seven hours a day.

What are the security measures taken for Tito's protection when he travels in Yugoslavia, when he goes to conferences and meetings? The Kremlin would above all like to see Tito killed; one need only listen to Radio Moscow broadcasts speaking about Tito and inviting the population to kill him. In summer, 1952, they sent a terrorist trio from Bulgaria. This trio killed a lieutenant colonel who had the medal of the National Hero. The Russians have many means of smuggling terrorists over the Yugoslav border, which is more than 1,250 miles long on the satellite side. The Danube, too, flows through Yugoslavia and the Russian, Hungarian, and Rumanian steamships can easily carry in groups of terrorists. In spite of this constant danger, no extraordinary measures of security are taken for the protection of Tito when he goes to meetings. For instance, the measures that are taken are about the same as those taken to protect President Truman when he comes to New York to greet the United Nations. These measures cannot be compared to those taken in the USSR for the protection of Stalin. First of all, Stalin hardly travels in the USSR, except when going on vacations. Anyone can pass near Tito's home in Belgrade, but Stalin has a special street of his own, the so-called "Government Street," leading to his villa. Only very high Soviet functionaries are allowed to use it, if they are bearers of special permits.

Tito also grants interviews to numerous foreigners. These are in the first place foreign ambassadors, then representatives of socialist and workers' parties and trade unions, United Nations representatives, representatives from various religious organizations, Quakers, and, of course, journalists. Tito has done this since 1945, since the day the war was over. Some people in Yugoslavia were of the opinion that Tito should not grant interviews to so many foreigners, but he disagreed with this. In the first place he wanted to make no discrimination. Tito also considers that he hears many things during these interviews and learns the opinions of people coming from all over the world. The meetings between Tito and the British Labour members of Parliament, Morgan Phillips, Hartley Shawcross and later with Aneurin Bevan and his wife Jenny Lee, were particularly interesting. When the official delegation of the Labour Party was in Belgrade, it visited Tito one afternoon and remained three full hours. Problems of Yugoslavia were discussed, such as the problems of workers' councils and farm co-operatives, and then the experiences of laborites in England were discussed. When the discussion was over, the British guests were asked to dinner, and remained until midnight. Bevan visited Tito in Brioni, an island on the Adriatic where Tito usually spends two or three weeks in a villa. Bevan was particularly interested in the causes of the split between the USSR and Yugoslavia, in the forms the split took and in the Russian methods of pressure. He received detailed opinions on this matter from Tito and other Yugoslavs. At that time Soviet propaganda attacked Bevan with the same words it uses in attacking Tito. I was present at these conversations between Tito and Bevan and I drew their attention to these attacks. Tito laughed and said to Bevan:

"You see, Stalin hates every socialist movement in the world that objects to being subjected to him."

Tito gave Bevan detailed information on the extent of the military preparations of the USSR and the Soviet satellites against Yugoslavia, as well as on measures taken by Yugoslavia to protect its frontiers. Bevan agreed with Tito, but said that care should be taken that these measures caused no reduction in the standard of living in Yugoslavia, as this could also undermine the defensive power of Yugoslavia.

As regards his American guests, Tito was particularly impressed by Averell Harriman and Supreme Court Justice William Douglas.

Tito usually speaks to his English-speaking visitors with the help of an interpreter. Although he understands almost every word, he still has difficulties in speaking. He has started to take English lessons, and does so for a month or two, and then stops, resuming after six months. Tito has already made considerable progress in English, and the interpreters must be very careful when they translate for Tito, because should they shorten a thought or give it a different tone, Tito immediately interrupts and corrects. Apart from his mother tongue, Serbo-Croatian, Tito speaks several other Slavonic languages: Russian, Czech, Slovenian. He speaks German well (with a Viennese accent), understands and reads French and Italian. Tito also speaks Kirghiz, which he learned during World War I, when he was a prisoner of war in Russia.

At noon, when his guests take leave, Tito has his luncheon. According to the Yugoslav custom, luncheon is the main meal of the day, and Tito usually takes it with friends. His secretary is also present most of the time. After lunch, Tito returns to his room. He then usually reads books. The most important books which are published in Yugoslavia are placed every day on Tito's desk. He goes through them all and takes those he thinks are most interesting to his private library, to read after lunch. His favorite foreign authors are Balzac and Stendhal, Goethe, Dreiser, Mark Twain, Jack London, Upton Sinclair, Sinclair Lewis, Kipling and Brehm. I found numerous books on nature and animals in Tito's private library. Sometimes, Tito also plays chess after lunch. He is an average player, I should say even a little below the average. Last time I played eight games with him and I beat him 6 to 2, and I am considered a rather bad player. Tito's reputation as a chess player comes from a snapshot taken by John Phillips in 1944, in which Tito plays chess. Tito is usually very merry when he plays chess. He always comments on the moves of his opponent, but when he is in a strait he cogitates a long time before he makes his move.

Sometimes Tito goes horseback riding after lunch. This is one of his favorite sports. He usually rides in the wooded hills around Belgrade. In the afternoons, Tito spends most of the time alone in his room. If he does not read, he rests. Tito received an accordion from Slovenia for his sixtieth birthday. When I went to see him in the summer of 1952, I heard accordion playing in his room one afternoon. When he came down, I asked him who had played. At first he would not say, but later he owned that he liked to lock himself in his room and to play the accordion. Tito is quite musical. I asked him what is the music he liked best.

"Light Viennese music," answered Tito. "Of the classics, Beethoven and Tchaikovsky."

"What about jazz?"

"It is more like pandemonium than music."

"Maybe, but it is pandemonium that conquered the whole world, and even the USSR," I answered. "When I was in Kiev in 1947 with Kardelj, Manuilski took us to the Ukrainian National Theater. Jazz got the most enthusiastic applause from the public. Even in our country, youth is mad about jazz."

"True," answered Tito, "but I belong to the older generation."

Tito had many pictures and reproductions in his home. I asked him which was his favorite school of painting.

"Renaissance," he answered, "and of the later painters Delacroix and also early impressionists. I studied Gerassimov and the rest when I was in Moscow. This is not painting at all, although they call it socialist realism. It has nothing to do with the name they have given it. One has the impression that the paintings are done by people without a soul, as if they handled spades instead of brushes."

Tito began to laugh. He has a deep sense of humor. It is characteristic that during the war, in the most difficult moments, an optimistic atmosphere used to reign in Tito's entourage. It was particularly so in 1948, when the split with Stalin occurred. I remembered these days, when I told him:

"We have quarreled with the Russians, and now we are surrounded on all sides."

Tito answered:

"Was there ever a time when we were not surrounded? We were so before the war, during the war and even now. We shall break through."

We all laughed after that. Tito is of the opinion that only cheerful persons like jokes, but he is always careful that fun is not only poked at other people. If this should happen, Tito is the first to come to the rescue and tilt the balance to the other side. But he tolerates and even likes jokes on his account.

A few years ago, Tito used to go after lunch to watch games of soccer, which is the most popular sport in Yugoslavia. When big matches are played, there are as many as sixty thousand people watching the matches, out of Belgrade's four hundred thousand inhabitants. But Tito has stopped going to the matches lately although he keeps on following the results in the newspapers. I teased him that one of the reasons for this may be that Tito's favorite team, "Partisan," is in rather bad shape. Tito, however, does not want to show that he is their fan, because supporting various teams is the great passion of all Yugoslavs, and Tito would not like to hurt the feelings of the fans of other teams.

On Saturday Tito usually leaves the city and goes hunting. He hunts hare and game, according to the season. Tito is an excellent shot. But he does little actual shooting, preferring to walk in nature. Tito has a great respect for the hunting laws. He never hunts outside the season. After the war, he insisted on prohibiting the hunting of deer, as these animals had been decimated during the war. We had special difficulties with Russian officers, who had developed the custom of hunting hare at night with jeeps. The Russian hunters would drive their jeeps at night in the fields with all the lights on. If the hares found themselves in the rays of light they would be paralyzed with fear. The hunter would then approach with the jeep to within a few yards and shoot at the game.

Sometimes, but very seldom, Tito plays tennis in the afternoon. He is not outstandingly good at it, but plays it with a will. He runs after every ball, but his technique is bad and this prevents him from playing well. Tito likes to win, and makes great efforts to do so. He plays doubles, and very seldom singles.

In the afternoon Tito also sees his family. Tito's first wife, a Russian named Polka, died in 1938. Their son Žarko now has two children of his own, Franjo and Zlatica. Žarko Broz is a civil servant in Belgrade. Tito married in 1940 Berta Has, a Slovene, and they also have a son, Miško. After the war, Tito divorced her. He often sees Miško and his grandchildren. The son of his eldest brother, Martin, who lived in Hungary until 1948, also comes to visit him often. His other brothers and sisters live in Croatian villages or in Zagreb. His brother Slavko is the one of those he sees most often.

In the early summer of 1952 Tito married for the third time. His wife is Jovanka Budisavljevic, a tall, dark Serbian woman from Lika. She lost all of her family during the war in which she herself took part as a member of Partisans units.

Tito deals with affairs of state and military matters between 5 and 7 P.M. People come to see him, he discusses matters with them and decisions are taken. When talking to people, Tito listens very carefully to his interlocutor, always wants to grasp his thoughts, and if he disagrees he starts discussions and explains. He has won many people by his tactfulness, and through his wish to know other people's opinions. When he was younger, and also in some of the war days, Tito used to be unusually quick-tempered and nervous. But he became more sedate as the years went by. When any news used to come along, or we heard of heavy losses of some divisions or of the death of a comrade, Tito would immediately jump up and pace the room up and down, smoking cigarette after cigarette. Tito is aware of his quick temper, and has often told me:

"I am careful not to take decisions when I am angry. I am afraid to overdo things then. I therefore take decisions when I have calmed down."

The conflict with the USSR has had a deep influence on Tito. The gall-bladder attacks from which he suffered in 1948 were no doubt caused by the conflict with Stalin. Tito was especially angered by the unwarranted attacks and lies, although he knew Soviet methods better than anyone else in Yugoslavia.

What kind of man is Tito, what is his character, what is his opinion of himself and does he think of the impression he makes on his interlocutors? Tito has no doubt many unusually developed character traits, such as consistency and loyalty to his aim, the power to concentrate on the most important problem of the moment, the knowledge of how to create a good relationship with the people with whom he lives and works. He is, otherwise, a man with normal human wishes and passions. For instance, it has been his wish since childhood to have nice clothes; he wanted once to be a tailor and sew new clothes for his father, brothers and friends. As a young worker, he was always careful about his appearance and about being tidily clothed. He was careful about it even during the war, in the hardest days of the offensives. And even now, as Premier, he is careful about his clothes. Some Western observers reproach him with being fond of uniforms. But they seem to forget that Yugoslavia is particularly threatened, that the Yugoslavs like their army and are fond of uniforms, and that Tito, apart from being Premier of Yugoslavia, is also its Minister of Defense. How would it look if Yugoslavia's first soldier never wore a uniform?

Tito has also some minor weaknesses, like any other man. He is, for instance, somewhat ashamed of his handwriting. In the summer of 1952 he gave me the answer he had prepared to Stalin's first letter written to the CC of the CPY in March, 1948. Tito wrote an answer of over thirty pages, by hand. I took one of the pages of this manuscript in order to publish its facsimile in this book. Tito looked at the page and said:

"You did not have to choose this page, see how awful my handwriting is."

I answered, laughing: "It is not important at all what your handwriting is like. And anyway, every reader will see at the very beginning of the book that you always had the worst possible marks in handwriting when you went to school."

Tito has his secret wishes. He would like, for instance, to walk about the city like some ordinary man, to sit in a restaurant and drink a glass of beer. But this is impossible for many reasons. In the summer of 1952 Tito came unexpectedly with a group of friends to take his breakfast in a hotel in Opatija, a summer resort on the Adriatic. As soon as we had sat down hundreds of people gathered around him, cheering "Tito, Tito," so we had to finish our meal quickly.

What are the feelings of the Yugoslavs toward Tito? Is there a similar relationship to the one that reigns toward Stalin in the USSR? What is Tito's personal opinion on the part played by men in history? It should be known, in the first place, that the revolution in Yugoslavia took place under Tito's leadership, so that his name became the symbol of that very revolution, just as in other countries the names of the leaders of revolutions or the leaders of progressive wars have also become the symbols of a period, as, for instance, Washington in the United States, Cromwell in England, Robespierre and Marat in France, Gandhi in India.

But is there a kind of idolatry in Yugoslavia, as toward Stalin in the USSR? Is Tito compared to the sun, is Tito infallible, do people send him cables for his birthday telling him that they "bow to the earth before him," as was the case on the occasion of Stalin's seventieth birthday; is Tito "the leader of the people sent by God," as the Soviet patriarch named Stalin was a short time ago, using the same formula which had been used in Russia under the Tsars?

All this is nonexistent in Yugoslavia. This is a consequence of our entire development. This is also Tito's conception. The first time I heard Tito speaking of himself was at a public meeting during the war in the town of Bihać, at the convention of the AVNOJ. Old Ivan Ribar proposed a toast for Tito, telling of his merits in the war. It was the first time such a toast had been delivered. Tito was surprised. He got up and said:

"I owe to our Party every achievement I have made. I was an ignorant young man and the Party took me, educated me, made me a man. I owe it everything."

Ten years later, in summer, 1952, I again spoke with Tito about the part played by personalities in history. He told me on this occasion:

"An intelligent man cannot accept the theory that personalities create history. In my opinion, men make history and play a considerable part in it only if they understand the people's needs and wishes, and insofar as they become part of the people themselves. If a man separates himself from the people, if he tends to be set on a pedestal, then he will only inspire fear or hatred. I agree that the part of men is sometimes very great in history, because to say the contrary would be nonsensical and would negate reality. But the part of men in history is commensurate to the degree of consciousness possessed by the people at that time. The part of men is all the more important as it represents the wishes of the people, if they accomplish what the people want them to accomplish, but a man never is a motive power in history. The people are those who are the motive power, they are the ones who inspire their leaders and the leader is but the organizer and the formulator of the people's thoughts."

Although Tito is a very diligent worker, he tries to have a little rest during the day. His dinners are very light, yogurt, frankfurters and such. After dinner Tito sometimes watches moving pictures, preferring the relaxation of gay films, but sometimes enjoying historical and documentary films.

When he does not watch films, Tito has guests in the evening. His most frequent guests are Kardelj, Djilas and Ranković. Tito is a very sociable person. Being very hospitable, he always has guests. For New Year's Eve, for instance, he usually invites about forty of his friends. Hot doughnuts are served at midnight, there is dancing and Tito usually demonstrates the waltz he learned to dance in

Vienna in his early youth. Tito occasionally visits the theater and likes both plays and operas.

But discussions are what Tito likes best in the evenings. These evenings usually begin with a special game of billiards, "na špice," in which five small pins are placed in the middle of the table and must be hit only by white balls. If a red ball should hit them, some points are lost. One plays until one hundred points are won. Those who remain under fifty are teased.

Billiards are played for a short time. Then everybody sits down and discussions begin, usually on theoretical matters. I have attended several such discussions. I was struck by the unanimity between Tito, Kardelj, Djilas and Ranković. They have been working together for the last fifteen years, and common work has made them very close to each other, even as regards their way of thinking. Usually one of them lays down a thesis, for instance as regards the development of villages. This thesis is not usually accepted by all, and a discussion develops which sometimes lasts quite a long time. If an agreement cannot be reached that evening the discussion is resumed on the following. These are fair discussions, in which, of course, everybody reacts according to his temperament, but there is one thing which is particularly characteristic, and that is that all four of them endeavor to understand one another, and see eye to eye with one another, although they need not necessarily always reach the same conclusions.

These evenings with Tito, which usually end around midnight, when Tito goes to sleep, are very important for the solution of various questions. Discussions in general are very frequent among Yugoslavs. This is what is called "public opinion" in Yugoslavia. And Tito and the other leaders have to reckon with it to a considerable extent, because, without the deep conviction of an outstanding majority of Yugoslavs that the policy of their government is a sound one, the regime could not maintain itself for a single day, especially under the present conditions and when it is exposed to such a degree to Soviet pressure. There are no police forces and no arms which could prevent the Yugoslavs from expressing their opinion, were they to reach the conclusion that their government's policy was unsound. A lot of patient work had to be performed as well as numerous discussions held until the majority of the people became convinced that the USSR was leading an imperialist policy toward us. And even today great efforts are made and long discussions held with people concerning, for instance, the relations between Yugoslavia and the Western countries. These relations are not always quite clear to some well-intentioned people, who are sometimes afraid that Yugoslavia may be imposed upon and its independence threatened. That is why, in its relations with the Western countries, the Yugoslav government cannot go any further than public opinion wants it to. And this public opinion is best judged at lectures, meetings, in letters sent to the editors of various papers, and most of all in discussions which are held on an evening between ten or fifteen friends.

Tito started this practice in the CPY as far back as in 1937, and this was one of the big differences between our Party and the Bolshevik Party. Stalin did not have this in mind in 1948 when he attacked Yugoslavia. And this cost him a defeat. Some Western observers also seem to forget the existence of public opinion in Yugoslavia. They do not wish to make the effort to grasp the idiosyncrasies of each country, and this is one of the most serious mistakes that can be made in politics.

CHAPTER XXV

1952:

"Plenty of work is ahead of us still . . ."

AS I bring this book to a close, it might be worth while to discuss, however briefly, a few of the theories of the Yugoslav Communist Party which may also be of interest to the readers outside of Yugoslavia. I will deal particularly with the question of socialism and individual rights, the differences between the social order in the Soviet Union and that in Yugoslavia, "Titoism" and the possibility of the spread of "Titoist" movements.

I want to draw the reader's attention to one important matter. The theories I shall describe in this chapter are neither the official Yugoslav views nor the only Yugoslav views. In 1951 the Central Committee of the Communist Party of Yugoslavia stated, in a special resolution, the principle that the opinions of individual leaders of the CPY on theoretical questions are not obligatory for the Party membership. This resolution spurred in Yugoslavia the struggle of opinions without which there can be no development of thought.

If we ask ourselves today what Yugoslavia has gained since she came into open conflict with the Soviet Union, we can reply quite definitely that the Yugoslavs, by preventing the subjugation of their country, have defended their right to an unhampered, independent development. They have rejected the Moscow thesis that "imitation of the Russian icon is the only correct and possible road toward socialism."

Accordingly, the international significance of the Yugoslav resistance against Soviet expansion does not consist only in the fact that a small country maintained and successfully defended the principle of equality between states, and in particular equality among large and small countries. Beyond that, Yugoslavia's internal development, especially during the last four years, has shown clearly in practice all the absurdities of the Kremlin contention that their way must be the way of all other countries. Defending the right of each country to proceed freely in its own specific way, the Yugoslavs rose against a monopoly to socialism, even against a monopoly of their own.

The Yugoslavs do not consider their development to be the only development. It might be perhaps useful as an experience, but it is not the inevitable course others must follow. In Yugoslavia there is a belief that socialism in the world today is developing in various ways; that the elements of a new society are mingling with elements of the old society, that the elements of the socialist society emerge in a series of states, although they are not called by that name. In Yugoslavia there exists an opinion that a revolutionary way is not inevitable for all other countries, especially for the economically advanced countries. In principle, the view of the Yugoslav Communists is that no progressive movement should in advance renounce the philosophy of using the revolutionary way. But it is obvious that no one should make revolution for the sake of revolution. If the advancement of society, that is to say, the solution of economic, social and political problems, could be achieved without revolutionary means, so much the better.

It is clear to any serious student that classical capitalism has outlived its time, that the world marches in the direction of something new, in most different forms and on different roads. In the period of transition from feudalism to capitalism, there existed in the French Revolution a classical bourgeois-democratic revolution; nonetheless all other countries made their way to capitalism in their own particular way.

Yugoslavia is a small country; her experience, her internal development, are still not known to the world. The theoretical thought in Yugoslavia is only in the beginning of its development. It has not yet in a sufficient degree generalized the Yugoslav experience. No wonder then that the world looks at Yugoslavia in a one-sided and superficial manner. It looks, too, with a large body of prejudices, created by the knowledge of what has happened in the Soviet Union. No one in modern times has so much betrayed the noble ideas of socialism and communism, for the development of which all peoples of the world have contributed so much, as has the Soviet Union, a country which calls itself socialist.

One of the above-mentioned prejudices is that there is no difference between the Soviet and the Yugoslav development, that only since 1948 have the Yugoslavs sought to break away from Stalinism, that both countries entertain the same viewpoints on the development of society, on the problems of individual freedom and of socialism.

There is no doubt that the October Revolution in Russia in 1917 and the revolution in Yugoslavia in 1941 by their very character have much in common. In both countries, the working masses came into power through revolution. But, setting aside for the moment the differences in the development of these two revolutions, it is necessary to point out that the Yugoslav revolution was built on a far wider basis than that of the October Revolution in Russia.

The October Revolution rallied the people against the war, calling upon them to abandon the front lines; the Yugoslav resolution was carried out during the Second World War, calling people to the front to defend their fatherland. In the War for Liberation, patriotism and social discontent were allied, and as a direct result, the masses entered directly into the struggle. While, especially at the beginning, the Russian revolution embraced the working masses in but a few large centers, the Yugoslav revolution enlisted broad masses of peasantry, poor and even rich, under the leadership of the working class. Furthermore, the majority of the intelligentsia joined the ranks of the revolution, while in Russia they held back. In Yugoslavia, the revolution won the support of a part of the clergy, if only the lower clergymen of the Serbian-Orthodox and Moslem communities; the Russian clergy remained hostile.

By its national character also, the basis of the revolution was broader in Yugoslavia. While in the revolution in Yugoslavia (a multi-national state) all five Yugoslav peoples took part, the revolution in Russia (also a multi-national state) was carried out primarily in a few large proletarian centers, whose population consisted largely of Russian inhabitants.

Finally, the masses of Yugoslavia were further advanced, and enjoyed a higher cultural standard, than their equivalents in 1917 Russia.

Tito

In the spring of 1952, in one of his conversations with the Delegation of the Socialist Party of India, Tito pointed out that the Yugoslav revolution might have been almost bloodless had it not been carried out during the Second World War, and integrally associated with the war against the Germans, Italians and other enemies of Yugoslavia.

"Our revolution was not only a struggle for liberation from the occupier," Tito said, "but a revolt against an old social system. This gave our revolution its broad mass basis. If it had been only a proletarian revolution, it would not have had succeeded in Yugoslavia, or perhaps it could have been successful only with the aid of Soviet bayonets, in which case it would not have been a revolution at all.

"The broader the mass basis of a revolution, the more bloodless it becomes. We had the mass basis, but our war was a bloody one because our land was occupied. If there had not been occupiers, there would have been neither Quislings, Pavelić, Nedić nor other traitors, and the revolution would have been even more bloodless. Once the war ended, we had a huge mass basis of the revolution, and the class enemies did not dare resist; we nationalized their property and they did not move a finger or fire a shot. The problem of the nationalization of industry in Yugoslavia in 1945 was relatively an easy one. The owners of factories and enterprises could not resist as they did during the October Revolution, because the vast majority of the Yugoslav population were fully aware that the order that existed in Yugoslavia before the war would have been a hindrance to the future existence of the nation. In Yugoslavia, because of its belated development, the bourgeoisie could not play such an objectively progressive role as it had played in individual developed countries in the West; i.e., the class of owners of means of production had not developed the productive forces of the country but represented only an apparatus by aid of which the economically developed countries held Yugoslavia in a semi-colonial status, in a status of a half-developed country, as a raw-material source for the developed countries.

"During the war a substantial part of the nation's industry was nationalized because the owners had voluntarily consented to their factories contributing to the war potential of the occupiers. After the war, nationalization was fully carried out with the approval of the huge majority of the population. Not uncommonly in Yugoslavia, the former owner of a nationalized factory works today as a manager, engineer or clerk in his old firm or in another similar enterprise. In Yugoslavia, for all these reasons, there was no need for the physical liquidation of individual class groups, such as took place in Russia after the revolution. There were no mass deportations of hundreds of thousands of rich peasants into Siberia."

Subsequent development of these two revolutions had been different. The basic questions on which Stalin failed were the problem of socialism and of the individual freedoms.

In every revolution, at the outset, it is necessary to create a centralized state apparatus so that the aims of the revolution may be protected and successfully defended against attempts at counter revolution. This is, in fact, inevitable and at first progressive, but at the same time it forms the principal source of bureaucracy. Therefore the functions of the state should wither away from the moment the working masses take power. But in backward countries, as Russia was, there is always the danger that the state apparatus will begin as the servant of the community and end as its master. During the first Five-Year Plan, when huge industrial undertakings were begun, the power of the state apparatus began to increase rapidly. The rights of the workers shrank, the rights of the directors broadened steadily, so that this apparatus turned in the end into the master of the society. The development of the revolution in Soviet Russia came to a halt; the workers' rights were entirely destroyed; and the state went the way of state capitalism. Stalin has created the most centralized state in history. The entire country of two hundred millions of people possesses only one brain—that of the Kremlin.

In Yugoslavia the development has been otherwise. The achievements of the revolution are being protected in that there shall never be permitted a return to old conditions, no return to the defeated and discredited classes, there shall never be allowed the exploitation of man by man. The French Revolution has proclaimed: No freedom for the enemies of freedom. But the development, on the other hand, proceeds in the direction of socialist democracy, toward the withering away of the state, toward debureaucratization and decentralization, toward ever less interference with the work and life of individuals. In this respect the basic thing is the direct rights of the producers; namely, whether they may freely decide about their surplus labor, or whether this is done by state officials. In Yugoslavia the factories are turned over to the workers, they decide themselves where the surplus value of their labor will go, and thus has been created the fundamental basis for the future development of socialist democracy, of such a social order where socialism will, in the end, mean full economic and political freedom for each individual.

For that reason, the Yugoslav experience should be studied most carefully, and not routinely condemned. It is true, this development is in its first steps, but its foundation has been set.

Before Yugoslavia lies still another huge problem to be reckoned with—the problem of the village. It is clear that it would result in a sheer economic catastrophe if the village were permitted to sustain small producers with their primitive agricultural equipment. A terrific disproportion between industry and agriculture is already emerging. For that reason, in Yugoslavia immediately after the war, measures were gradually taken to bring the individual farm producers into co-operatives which could rapidly increase the agricultural production. In this field blind Stalinism was perhaps most damaging to Yugoslavia. Co-operatives were created after the pattern of the Soviet kolkhozes. Some Yugoslav leaders, in particular Edvard Kardelj, quickly sensed the error and insisted that co-operatives of a general type should first be created, and only later working co-operatives, but local officials, under the influence of Stalin's kolkhoz theories, raced into the creation of kolkhozes.

It should be pointed out, however, that the methods of organizing co-operatives were different from those in Russia. There was in Yugoslavia no physical liquidation of rich peasants as such. Neither was there the barbarism that took place in England at the beginning of the industrial revolution, when small village owners were wiped out overnight.

The problem of the village in socialism is the basic question with which the Yugoslavs now must reckon. They are fully aware that the solution lies in some form of co-operatives, but the proper form —one which would harmonize the interests of the peasant-producers with the interests of the community, which would stimulate the villages as the factories have been stimulated—such a form has not yet been found.

Here is how Tito enumerates the differences between the Yugoslav and Soviet social systems:

"The first difference, the principal one, is that we are building a genuine socialism, while in the Soviet Union the building up of socialism has degenerated into state capitalism under the leadership of a dictatorial bureaucratic caste.

"Second, socialist democracy in Yugoslavia is beginning to dominate the entire social life, and nothing impedes an even more rapid development except the lack of technology and a too-slow increase of tempo of socialist consciousness on the part of the citizens of our country. Yet, while in our country this democratic development is noticeable from day to day, in the Soviet Union there is no democracy at all. In the Soviet Union there is neither political nor cultural democracy, nor is there democracy in production; on the contrary, a real reign of terror dominates the scene. There, even after thirty-four years, the factories have not been given over to the workers. There is no freedom of thought and creative work in literature, science, music or anywhere else.

"Third, here in Yugoslavia the national question has been correctly solved, formally and in substance, and a federative state has been created out of six republics based on an equality in which the various peoples decide freely their lives and their futures. A national community has been created in which there is no leading nation to impose its will on the others, nor to suppress other peoples. In the Soviet Union, the national question has been solved on paper, but in substance nothing has been carried out except a formal creation of different republics governed by one nation—the Russian. By dictate of the bureaucratic leaders from Moscow, not only entire republics but whole nations are being forcibly moved and exposed to annihilation.

"In Yugoslavia the man means everything. Our aim is to create, as early as possible and in an utmost humane way, a better life for our people, for all individuals and for the whole community. We try, even under the hardest conditions, to take care of those people who labor for the materialization of socialism. In the USSR a man is a number, and the people a colorless mass which must docilely obey and fulfill all the orders of their leaders. There is in the Soviet Union no patient re-educating over to socialist consciousness, because there they do not build socialism but a superstate capitalism, which to the outside world shows all the qualities of imperialism and internally represents a strictly centralized bureaucratic absolutism. In Yugoslavia an ever-growing development toward decentralization of the economic, cultural and other life is noticeable, because only such a system is genuinely in accordance with the concept of power as resident in the people.

"In that consists the huge substantial difference between the Yugoslav system and that of the Soviet Union. There are many additional examples, many other differences springing out of either specific conditions in our country or out of the degeneration of further revolutionary development in Soviet Russia."

As we see, in Yugoslavia the state is withering away, and a socialist democracy is developing. But what of the Communist Party? What of the one-party system in Yugoslavia? For this I recur to a discussion held on this question between Tito, Kardelj, Djilas and Kidrič on one side and an outstanding socialist leader of Western Europe on the other. I attended this discussion. It is here described for the first time.

The Western socialist asked if the Communist Party in Yugoslavia were withering away.

"The Communist Party cannot continue to function in the same old way if at the same time the state is withering away," Tito replied. "If the state does not wither away, then the Party becomes, in a certain sense, an instrument of the state, a force outside of society. If the state really withers away, the Party necessarily withers away with it. Many of our own people do not realize this fact yet. We have to explain to them gradually of what this withering away consists, and we have begun to do so."

Visitor: "As far as we can see, the Yugoslav masses have very well understood two practical aspects of the withering away of the state: the decentralization and debureaucratization. They have well understood these specific steps, but have they truly understood the second theoretical part of the problem: the withering away of the Party?"

Tito: "This process will take a little longer."

Visitor: "In the West, where there exist labor, socialist and social-democratic movements and broad masses under their influence, they still may confuse the Yugoslav situation with that in Soviet Russia and its satellites. It may be they believe the state in Yugoslavia is an instrument of the Party, for you have a one-party system. It would be of great importance—not because of the bourgeoisie and the reactionaries, for they do not matter, but because of certain progressive people who do not see the difference—to clarify that.

"For these progressive people in the West it would be important if you could explain how you disassociate yourself from this Stalinist conception and how, to your mind, the one-party system and party dictatorship are a transitory means rather than an end."

Tito: "The fact is in that our socialist revolution and proletarian dictatorship are different from their Russian counterparts in all their aspects. Our revolution had a different basis from that of the Russian, and our Party had different partners, for our revolution developed under its own particular conditions in the course of the War of Liberation. Our basis has been much broader than that of the Russians, despite the fact that Russia is a huge country.

"I would like to point out the unsoundness of objections based on our so-called one-party system. We do have one revolutionary party which leads the country and provides its entire theoretical and practical line. But united in our People's Front we have all the citizens of our country who are in accord with the final aim and program of the Communist Party. These are not, necessarily, Communists; these are people who desire a change, who want a socialist society. This is not a one-party system. Rather, it is a means of uniting the citizens of a country in one Front, of which the purpose is the materialization of the program of the Communist Party. Aided by that Front we carry through this program. In Yugoslavia the Communist Party has organized the revolution, brought to a successful end its period of armed struggle and now is carrying out the complete social transformation.

"But you must also consider that in a revolutionary period it is absurd to speak about a multi-party system. What does such a system mean? Several parties mean several programs, and here in our land, there is only one program: to create a socialist society. Around this program is joined the vast majority of the citizenry of our country. Those opposed to this program cannot be permitted to impede its materialization. Out of sixteen million people we have eight million enrolled in the People's Front, all these people united around one program. That is something specific; what we have today in Yugoslavia is perhaps unique in the world. And this phenomenon can be easily explained and understood if one realizes that the basis of our revolution is huge and broad.

"For that reason I have always said that Yugoslavia's recent past cannot be applied without reservation as a pattern for other countries. Let us consider, for example, India, where there are many progressive parties, each with its own nuances. All these parties might maintain their separate programs, but they might also be able to unite around a final goal for which they could strive in common. And as they began to approach that goal, all these parties would tend to unite in the form of a Front.

"We wonder why the West wants a multi-party system, why the West wants us to go backwards, to throw away what we have achieved. This would mean only a retrogression, a return to capitalism, the conversion of our country into a satellite of this or that great power. The first business of a revolution is the liquidation of the multi-party system, whether the Communist or the Socialist Party is in power. We do not claim that those only who call themselves Communists can create socialism. We do not consider it to be a monopoly of the Communists. It can be achieved by a revolutionary socialist party. Therein lies the very difference between our view and that of the Soviets.

"It is not a question of form or name, but of the practical implementation of an idea.

"Finally, I would like to add this: such a development is not necessarily applicable everywhere. For example, the size of the party depends upon the degree of social consciousness of the proletariat. It could be larger, but we think that in our situation, in our undeveloped country, too large a party would only represent a great danger. Naturally, this is true only in a backward country. In developed countries it might be quite different."

Visitor: "Up to this point we are in full accord. We believe it would be an error at present to grant freedom to various bourgeois parties which might drag you backwards. Up to this point I fully agree. But we must also know this: what will be the role of the party when the management of the economy is entirely in the hands of the producers?"

Tito: "I shall answer that briefly. The role of the party is historically limited to a certain period. How the society will then arrange its affairs remains to be determined, but one party will not be necessary. The party withers away gradually. That does not mean that a one-party system will be superseded by a multi-party system. It merely means that the one-party system, having superseded a multi-party system, will in turn vanish."

Kardelj: "This phase is not so far away. I think we shall perhaps live to see it in our time."

Visitor: "It would be of great importance for us to be able to take with us such a statement, which, in my opinion, is the essential thing which distinguishes you from the Russian Cominform countries. To them the one-party system is an eternal matter and the state a timeless conception . . ."

Tito (interrupting): "Any movement in history which attempts to perpetuate itself becomes reactionary."

Visitor: ". . . and by the very fact that the state would seek to last eternally it would cease to serve the masses and would put itself into its own service."

Tito: "We do not consider that we have achieved the culmination, nor do we wish to become a new Roman Catholic Church with a pope at the head of it."

Kardelj: "Tito, ten days ago, gave an interview for the press in which the inevitability of this withering away was discussed. I mention this here to show that we have begun to discuss these problems in public. What is more, a series of concrete measures has already been taken. For instance, the secretaries of the Party committees no longer represent authority in the districts, and a Party member no longer has privileges merely by reason of being a Party member. But, still, plenty of work is ahead of us, still!"

In the West it is often believed that since 1948 Yugoslavia has been creating a new ideological line, a so-called "Titoism." Some people even have gone so far as to compare Tito to Luther, with Stalin cast as the pope.

I once brought this matter up with Tito. "Titoism as a separate ideological line does not exist," he answered at once. "To put it as an ideology would be stupid. I do not say that out of modesty. It is simply that we have added nothing to Marxist-Leninist doctrine. We have only applied that doctrine in consonance with our situation. Since there is nothing new, there is no new ideology. Should 'Tito-ism' become an ideological line, we would become revisionist; we would have renounced Marxism. We are Marxists, I am a Marxist and therefore I cannot be a 'Titoist.' Stalin is the revisionist: it is he who has wandered from the Marxist road. 'Titoism' as a doctrine does not exist. We try to find the most correct, the most humane and the most appropriate way to develop Marxism in practice. What exists in our country is socialism and cannot be called 'Titoism.'

"We, the Communists of Yugoslavia, do not consider Marxism-Leninism as something which must go on determined tracks, but as a means to be employed according to circumstances. It may often seem that we are by-passing. But Marxism-Leninism serves us as a means to lead us in the direction of the goal toward which we strive. Our way is not necessarily everybody's way (nor should it neces-sarily be applied everywhere). Neither Marx nor Engels could have foreseen everything for thousands of years in advance; they gave the analysis and the method of Marxism but they could not prescribe the road from one epoch to another."

This is Tito's opinion. But, if "Titoism" as an ideology of its own does not exist, it is not entirely meaningless if this term is used to reflect the desire of individual countries to resist the expansion of the great powers. This expression is in particular much applied in the case of Eastern European countries which are exposed to the oppres-sion of the Soviet Union. For the very fact that Yugoslavia exists as an independent socialist country after more than four years of open conflict with the USSR, that this Yugoslavia continues to find its own way to socialism—these facts are a nightmare to those in the Kremlin. Only this can explain the hysteria which overcomes the creators of the foreign policy of the Kremlin when relations with Yugoslavia are on their agenda. For four and one-half years, in her relations with Yugoslavia, the USSR has committed a series of gross mistakes, blunders and failures which can only be explained by Sta-lin's undisguised fury that this Yugoslavia continues to exist. There cannot be any doubt that Yugoslavia represents the hardest blow

Stalin has been struck since he assumed power. For that reason, the government of the USSR has rejected for four and one-half years all the attempts of the Yugoslav government to re-establish normal diplomatic relations between the two countries. Even during the session of the United Nations in Paris, in November, 1951, when the Yugoslav complaint against the pressure of the government of the USSR was discussed, the Soviet delegation refused to vote for that part of a resolution by which the General Assembly of the United Nations called on both countries "to conduct their relations and settle their disputes in accordance with the spirit of the United Nations Charter."

It is a unique phenomenon in the history of the United Nations that a member-country has voted against the principle that relations among countries should be based on the Charter of the United Nations.

What are the prospects that other East European countries under the domination of the USSR will move in the direction of Yugoslavia? The strengthening of the Soviet pressure in these countries, the ever-growing control, the unification of the armed forces of these countries, the enslavement of these countries in the economical and cultural field, lead some observers to the erroneous conclusion that this represents a *fait accompli* and that the Soviet Union will definitively subjugate these countries. There is nothing more incorrect than this conclusion. The constant purges, the strengthening of the police control—these are the best proof that resistance does exist and that it grows from day to day. We live in the middle of the twentieth century, when the right of self-determination of nations has become a reality for huge masses in Asia and Africa, when there is almost no corner in Asia and Africa where the people have failed to rise and demand this right. It is absurd to presume that the highly developed countries in the heart of Europe, such as Czechoslovakia, will long tolerate the oppression the Russians have brought to Central Europe, turning Czechoslovakia into their ordinary *guberniya*. And there is no doubt that in the resistance of all countries, the stand and fight of Yugoslavia plays a huge role. The fact that Yugoslavia remained an independent country, that she goes forward on her specific way—that is the very thing which helps the peoples of Eastern European countries in their resistance against Soviet expansion.

On the other hand, one should never forget that the USSR is strengthening her control of those countries, terrifying the working masses in those countries with the threat of a return to the old monarchies, the vast estates and all the evils that depressed them before the Second World War. They freed themselves of many of these troubles in 1945, but in place of one master another has come in the form of Soviet exploitation. But the fact remains that some of the achievements of 1945 have been preserved, as, for instance, agrarian reform and similar things.

These Soviet maneuvers are abundantly aided by shortsighted propaganda from some Western countries, in particular from the USA, which has almost no effect in these countries because it is directed by the most wayward emigrants, the most corrupted elements, of an era in those countries that has long since been buried by history. To be offered the alternative of Soviet domination or the return of these outlived social formations only aggravates the plight of the masses in these countries.

As for the situation in Asia, how are relations between the USSR and China, is Mao Tse-tung Stalin's satellite, what are the prospects of China going her own way? I have in many instances discussed these questions with Tito. Here are his words:

"Between the Soviet Union and China there exist divergencies of considerable character. But these conflicts are shelved for the moment because of the war in Korea. China is not completely under Russian influence. The facts show that the Russians have to reckon with the existing conditions in China, and in particular with the blunt fact that there are 450 million Chinese. If there were 50 million Yugoslavs, it is a great question whether Stalin would have moved so awkwardly to attack our independence. Furthermore, these 450 million Chinese have only emerged from their revolution. For that reason, the Russians have adjusted their relations to these facts, watching their steps and being careful not to go too far. The Russians have masterfully taken advantage of the Korean case to pull China to their side.

"Antagonistic attitudes of Western powers toward the Chinese revolution, since its very beginning, are pushing new China to subordinate itself to the Soviet foreign policy. It seems to me that a great mistake was made when the USA favored Chiang Kai-shek immediately after the war instead of seeking ways and means to come to terms with a majority of the Chinese people. A chance was missed, and such an error is very difficult to correct in a country which is in a state of revolution, in a revolutionary upsurge. At such moments people do not easily forget who has been a friend of their revolution, and who has been against it."

Having asked Tito what he thinks about the future relations between the Soviet Union and new China, he replied:

"The future development of the relations between them one could not predict. It is only possible to draw conclusions on the basis of the concrete facts of a given situation. But there is no doubt that the future development between the Soviet Union and new China will primarily depend upon the attitude of the Western world toward revolutionary China."

This is Tito's opinion on the relations between the USSR and new China. It was interesting to note how Stalin, having opportunity of making use of the Chinese revolution for the advancement of his foreign policy aims, used Mao Tse-tung and Ho Chi Minh in order to subjugate Yugoslavia. The Communist Party of China, on the basis of the Cominform resolution, did not even wait for an answer of the Central Committee of the Communist Party of Yugoslavia, but at once fully endorsed the above-mentioned resolution condemning the stand of Yugoslavia. Even more characteristic is the case of the government of Ho Chi Minh, whose movement was undoubtedly one of the most genuine and independent from Moscow. When the government of the Democratic Republic of Viet Nam was formed, in the beginning of 1950, Yugoslavia received a note from that government, on February 15, 1950, in which it was demanded that the Yugoslav government recognize the government of Viet Nam and establish with it diplomatic relations. At the same time on the Yugoslav government had been exerted a pressure from the West not to acknowledge Ho Chi Minh. Marshal Tito felt compelled to speak in public, on a meeting against such methods of pressure, and the Yugoslavs recognized Ho Chi Minh. An official release had been published on this recognition in the Yugoslav press, February 22 of the same year. Meanwhile, after only a few days, Yugoslavia had been furiously attacked—by use of the Moscow dictionary—over the facilities of the Viet Nam radio. In Yugoslavia people came to a conclusion that the government of Ho Chi Minh, probably on Moscow's orders, purportedly asked Yugoslavia for recognition in order to bring it in a difficult situation in its relations with France and the USA. And when Yugoslavia declared its readiness for establishing diplomatic relations with Viet Nam, the attacks against Yugoslavia commenced over the Viet Nam radio! This unprincipled attitude left a most negative effect on the Yugoslavs.

Thus, here we had one of the Yugoslav contentions on the prospects of the emergence of "Titoist" movements in countries under Soviet domination or in countries toward which the USSR has such intentions. In essence, "Titoism" is identical with the right of every nation to equality with others and to the right for independent development. That is, in reality, the basis of the foreign policy of Yugoslavia. It is based on the principles of the Charter of the United Nations.

For that reason Yugoslavia did not want to join any bloc or union, because it considers that the Charter and its system of collective security is the fundamental source of its international rights and obligations; that the sources of aggression are not different ideologies but desires of states for expansion.

This, in summary form, is the attitude of the Yugoslavs toward their main internal and international problems. It is the attitude of a people striving in its *own way* to build a society in which there will be no exploitation of man by man, in which an individual will be freed of the fetters of the state, in which he will fully enjoy all economic, social, and political freedoms. That is what Tito calls socialism.

Index

Index

Index

Index

441

Index

Index

ON THE *Moscow radio, Vladimir Dedijer—pronounced* Dediyer *—has been called an illegitimate son of an American and a relative of President Truman. In Yugoslavia, he has been described as Tito's Harry Hopkins. To Tito himself, he is one of his oldest party comrades and fellow-fighters in the Partisans' war against the Nazis and, since 1948, in the political warfare against Stalin. To his friends he is known as Vlado, a six-foot-three journalist, lawyer, translator, ping-pong champion, and now political personality in his own country. He is a member of the Yugoslav Parliament and secretary of its Foreign Affairs Commission, a member of the Yugoslav Delegation to the United Nations since 1945, and editor of* Borba, *the leading daily newspaper in Yugoslavia. He first came to the United States in 1931 at the age of seventeen as head of a Y.M.C.A. delegation. His brother, Stephen, a Princeton graduate and an American paratrooper in the war, is now working in Yugoslavia's Institute of Atomic Energy. He has been married twice, his first wife having been killed while serving as a major in the Partisan Army, and he has four children.*